P9-EFI-589

Among the Mansions of Eden

ALSO BY DAVID WEDDLE

"If They Move . . . Kill 'Em!":
The Life and Times of Sam Peckinpah

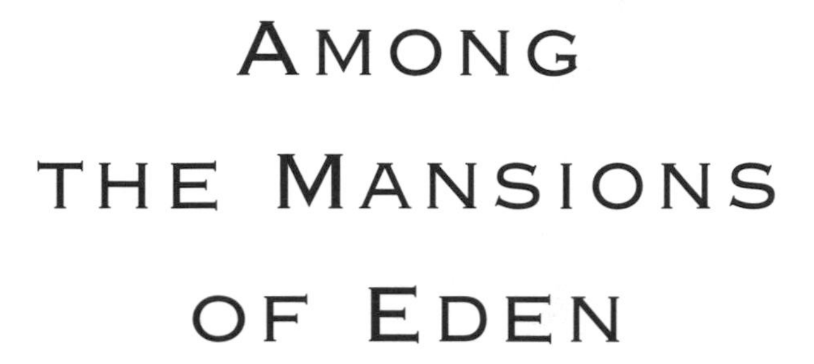

Among the Mansions of Eden

Tales of Love, Lust, and Land in Beverly Hills

DAVID WEDDLE

wm

WILLIAM MORROW
An Imprint of HarperCollins*Publishers*

Grateful acknowledgment is made to reprint the excerpt from *Death of a Salesman*. Reprinted by permission of International Creative Management, Inc.

HarperCollins books may be purchased for educational, business, or sales promotional use. For information please write: Special Markets Department, HarperCollins Publishers Inc., 10 East 53rd Street, New York, NY 10022.

FIRST EDITION

Designed by Mia Risberg

Printed on acid-free paper

Library of Congress Cataloging-in-Publication Data
Weddle, David.
Among the mansions of Eden / David Weddle.—1st ed.
p. cm.
ISBN 0-06-019817-6
1. Beverly Hills (Calif.)—History. 2. Beverly Hills (Calif.)—Social conditions. 3. Beverly Hills (Calif.)—Biography. 4. Rich people—California—Beverly Hills. 5. Celebrities—California—Beverly Hills. I. Title.
F869.B57 W43 2003
979.4'93—dc21 2002026421

03 04 05 06 07 JTC/QW 10 9 8 7 6 5 4 3 2 1

To Risa,
a beacon in the dark

★ CONTENTS ★

★ 1 ★

The Billionaires' Horseshoe

How did it happen? What transformed five and a half square miles of dusty bean fields and low arid Southern California mountains into America's Palatine Hill, the sacred high ground where its demigods—movie stars, industrialists, Wall Street Wizards, rock icons, media and fashion moguls—took up residence in some of the most lavish, phantasmagoric mansions the world has ever seen?

Certainly there was nothing particularly remarkable about this small patch of land on the western edge of the Los Angeles basin when Beverly Hills was conceived in the early years of the twentieth century. The hills themselves were part of the Santa Monica Mountains, a low coastal range that stretched from the center of the L.A. basin to Malibu at the northern tip of Los Angeles County. And the Santa Monicas were part of a network of coastal ranges—the Santa Margaritas, the Santa Anas, the Santa Ynez, and the Santa Lucia—that extended from the Mexican border to Monterey, just south of San Francisco. Four hundred and fifty miles of hill after hill, each one much like the next: their lower slopes carpeted with silver-white oats and blue lupine; their ridgelines—never higher than two-thousand feet—shaded by stands of sycamore, oak, and eucalyptus.

The key to the elusive charisma of Beverly Hills lies in real estate. Not in the land itself, but in the men and women who peddle it—the wily entrepreneurs who first managed to weave a little blue sky, sunlight, and parched earth into a dream that has captivated the American imagination for the better part of a century.

The Beverly Hills real estate hustler has always been a fascinating breed. On the one hand, they are manipulative cynics who prey upon their clients' overblown egos and illusions; and yet on the other, they are incurable romantics themselves who fervently believe the dream even as they exploit it to line their own pockets. They are, in short, snake oil salesmen and fever-eyed evangelists rolled into one.

John Bruce Nelson is one of the art form's premier practitioners. Nelson is not the largest broker in the city. The two corporate giants in Los Angeles, Fred Sands and Coldwell Banker, field more than 5,700 agents out of their sprawling office complexes and represent more than half of the properties on the west side. Nelson doesn't even operate out of an office but instead is headquartered in a 5,000-square-foot home in Bel Air, complete with a gated driveway and swimming pool. He employs two secretaries and a half dozen agents besides himself and his partner, Raymond Bekeris. Nelson sells an average of fifteen to twenty homes a year. But almost all of them are on the very high end of the market. Only thirty-five homes have sold for more than $10 million in the history of Beverly Hills, and Bruce Nelson brokered fifteen of them. When the world's richest men and women decide to shop for an edifice that will serve as a suitable shrine for their personal mythos, they often call upon Nelson. They come to him for his shrewd ability to appraise a property's true worth on the current market, for his extraordinary depth of understanding about architecture and interior design, and for his uncanny ability to match the personal panache of his clients with appropriately flamboyant estates.

It is a bright sunny afternoon in January 2000. Bruce Nelson is holding an open house for an $18.9 million estate at 1400 Tower Grove Drive. Most of the Beverly Hills real estate corps will attend. Tower Grove is a narrow street that makes a series of sharp switchbacks as it climbs to the top of Benedict Canyon. This region is known as "Beverly Hills post office"—though beyond the city limits and officially part of Los Angeles County, it still bears the coveted 90210 zip code and has always been considered part of the magic kingdom by the locals. As you near the top of the mountain, the land on the left drops away and the canyon yawns to reveal another ridgeline on Angelo Drive more than a half mile away. Huge homes line the lip of that far ridge, like a set of gleaming capped teeth. You round a final hairpin and a gigantic limestone structure looms into view like a giddy eruption from America's collective subconscious. Its proportions are preposterously huge, and the pseudo Beaux Arts château has all the authenticity of a Hollywood movie set, yet this clumsy grope for "European sophistication" and glamour is so spectacularly over the top that it provokes a weirdly exhilarating sense of vertigo. It's both hideous and awe inspiring, as breathtaking and coldly erotic as a Victoria's Secret cover girl. A plaque on one of the limestone pillars that guard the brick driveway bears the number 1400.

Bruce Nelson is sitting in the backyard beside a polished oval of turquoise water, as smooth and motionless as a gemstone, set in a slab of bleached concrete. At the far end of the pool a long buffet table has been assembled with a white linen tablecloth, and on it are a mass of fresh fruit, hors d'oeuvres, French pastries, and a sterling silver bowl filled with iced punch. Behind the table, a red-jacketed Hispanic man nervously tends to the placement of the refreshments. Bruce takes no notice. His hazel eyes stare from beneath leathery lids, past the house and the canyon to the spectacular 180-degree view of the L.A. basin. He doesn't look the part of a successful broker. A handsome but weathered man in his late sixties, he wears a green nylon windbreaker, navy blue sweatpants, and an expression of supreme boredom. From beneath the bottom of the windbreaker, the primary-colored tail of a Hawaiian shirt shifts slightly in the breeze.

Other Realtors who have come to look the place over emerge from the back of the house in immaculate Hugo Boss and Chanel ensembles. They make their way to the buffet table with studied casualness, select a few morsels, engage in idle chatter, then drift into the gravitational orbit of Nelson so they can solicit his advice about other properties currently on the market, or praise the makeover he'd done on this one. Nelson responds to their accolades with the apathetic gratitude of an overstuffed potentate, to whom obsequious fawning has become as common as the air he breathes. "Thanks," he says over and over again. "You should have seen the interior before I got hold of it. An absolute disaster."

"The thing I love about Bruce," Mike Steere, a writer for *Worth* magazine, observes, "is that he's achieved such a level of success in his field that he no longer needs to prove himself. You see these young brokers in their Armani suits and Rolex watches, like they've stepped out of an ad in *Vanity Fair*. They're wannabes. Bruce is the man. Everybody knows it, so he can dress like a pool man."

But Nelson's aspect undergoes a remarkable transformation when a woman in a gray suit, black stockings, black gloves, and a pair of oversize 1960s-style Doris Day sunglasses steps onto the pool deck. "Brucie, how aaarree you?" she calls out in a whiskey voice as she moves toward him on two thin legs and a pair of black pumps that echo on the concrete.

Bruce bolts to his feet. Her blinding white grin has shot a transfusion of energy into him. "Wonderful, now that you're here!" he calls out in a voice as bold and clear as a Broadway actor's. They embrace; she purses her thickly painted lips and kisses the air. Nelson introduces her to one of the Realtors. She presents a gloved hand and smiles, the flesh beneath her jaw unnaturally taut. "Hi," she announces, "I'm Suzanne Marx, development director for the Los Angeles County chapter of Boys Town. You know, Father Flanagan's Boys Town, like in the movie with Spencer Tracy. I used to work for the Reagans. I raised thirty million dollars for the Reagan Library."

"She's an institution!" Bruce chortles, positively bubbling over with mirth.

Suzanne waves a dismissive glove in his direction, then touches the curled lip of her white bouffant to make sure the breeze hasn't caused it to lose its shape. "Oh please." She laughs. "I'm not an institution." She pats Bruce's nylon-clad shoulder. "This man is the institution. He knows where all the bodies are buried." They erupt in conspiratorial laughter, implying those bodies, or the graves they lie in, must be very interesting.

Bruce slaps his hands together excitedly and says, "Well, come on, I'm dying to show you my new house!"

"And I'm just dying to see it."

Nelson leads the way down the thin cement path to the mansion, practically skipping with delight. The transformation is nothing short of remarkable. The tired old vaudevillian has been galvanized by the rising curtain and the blinding beam of the spotlight. *It's show time!*

Marx is not a Realtor, nor is she in the market to buy a house herself, but she is connected—hardwired into the old-money circuit, the WASP Republican money that gathers in the nooks and crannies of such top-dollar real estate as Bel Air, Pacific Palisades, and Pasadena. Her Rolodex is fat with the numbers of retired industrialists, financiers, venture capitalists, and their widows and former wives. Nelson lavishes more laughter and affection on her than on all of the Realtors combined because a word from Marx to the right person could put this place in escrow.

Nelson leads her through the enormous library, the two-bedroom two-bath guest apartment, the private gym, sauna, and dining room—"it comfortably seats fifty." His eyes glow with excitement, broad mouth grinning, hands waving about as if at any moment they might take flight from his wrists and flutter about the high arched ceilings as he points out such amenities as the polished parquet floors, the Venetian inlaid ceilings, and the fact that every room in the house has a balcony. He describes how he convinced the owner to tear out the mansion's original French whorehouse decor and redo the place from top to bottom. Under Bruce's supervision an army of interior designers ripped out the oriental carpets and refinished the floors, yanked off the dark wallpaper, painted the walls in bright cheerful tones, pulled the velvet curtains off the windows, and cut down the trees in front of the house to let that golden California sunlight come streaming through. "Every room has a view," he tells Suzanne. "Every single room."

Now it's easy to see why this man is the most successful independent real estate salesman in Beverly Hills. When he turns on the juice he manages to convey a genuine delight for the property he's showing, a feeling that this is the most amazing house in the most amazing location on the planet; a feeling that every detail is his own loving creation and that this edifice is more than a house, it's a work of art that he, the maestro, has decided to offer up to the one person in this world who has the taste and the class to appreciate it.

They walk into a blindingly white tiled kitchen. "It's like the kitchens in the château country in France," Bruce announces authoritatively. He points out the major features: yet more parquet floor, an enormous white tile counter with brass trim, heat lamps to keep serving dishes warm, warming ovens in the butler's pantry, gleaming stainless steel commercial ranges, and three monolithic Sub-Zero refrigerators. . . . This is no mere mortal kitchen; it looks like the galley of the starship *Enterprise*.

Overcome by the spectacle of it, Suzanne stops short and grabs the nylon sleeve of his windbreaker, crumpling it in her black glove. "Oh my God, Bruce, it's fantastic!"

"Isn't it?" Bruce giggles. "You can prepare a dinner party for two hundred fifty people in this kitchen, no problem."

"This is so much better than Iris's kitchen. I mean, this is a serious kitchen." The Iris that Suzanne's referring to is her close friend Iris Cantor, widow of B. "Bernie" Gerald Cantor, the Wall Street veteran who founded the securities firm of Cantor Fitzgerald. Iris owns a 34,000-square-foot home in Bel Air with six "bedroom suites," twenty-one bathrooms, a library, a wine cellar, and a ten-car garage. She recently put it on the market. "Can you believe it, Bruce," Suzanne's voice lowers to a catty whisper. "She's asking forty-five million dollars for it."

"It's overpriced," Bruce says with a condescending grin. "She'll never get it."

"I don't know what she's thinking." Suzanne shakes her head as she takes in the lustrous contours of Bruce's wonder kitchen. "Her kitchen doesn't even begin to compare to this."

"But, Suzanne." Bruce leans close to the serrated edge of her bouffant, his eyes narrowing to two wicked slits. "The woman doesn't know how to cook. She doesn't even know where the kitchen is!"

Suzanne erupts in raspy laughter, holding a clenched gloved hand to her shellacked lips. Bruce throws his thick head back and guffaws with her, exposing the gaps in his teeth left by his eroding gums.

They circle back to the home's thirty-five-foot-tall entryway. Bruce pauses so Suzanne can drink in the full grandeur of the slick black-and-white marble floor and the enormous T-shaped staircase. "This cost me four hundred thousand," he announces.

"You mean to redo the whole stairway?"

"The banister and trim."

"What's that banister made of?" Her eyes follow the glittering scrollwork as it makes its rococo journey up and around their heads to the two wings of the second floor. "Brass?"

"No, no," Bruce corrects her. "Bronze. Bronze is much more expensive than brass. And the carpet"—he gestures to the ocher and white fabric that ripples up the stairs—"was hand-loomed in France. We had the borders made in New Zealand. They're sewed in by hand. It took two guys three weeks to do it. We saw two thousand sample patterns, and this design was culled from everything we looked at."

"This is grand, grand, grand," Suzanne says in a hushed, reverent voice. "This will sell."

They start up the stairs into a shaft of bright light streaming through a pair of pediment-topped windows. At the landing they meet up with Bruce's business partner, Raymond Bekeris, who's just completing a tour with a married couple. The man has a fat leather satchel and a mischievous grin. "I'm ready to buy it right now," he says to Bruce. "I brought the cash with me."

Bruce throws back his head and laughs long and hard, then says, "Great, let's sit down and make a deal. By the way, have you met Suzanne Marx?"

Suzanne extends a gloved hand to them. "I'm development director for the Los Angeles County chapter of Boys Town. You know, Father Flanagan's Boys Town, like in the movie with Spencer Tracy. I used to work for the Reagans. I raised thirty million dollars for the Reagan Library."

"She's an institution!" Bruce chortles.

Suzanne waves a dismissive glove. "Oh please." She laughs. "I'm not an institution. This man is the institution. He knows where all the bodies are buried." They laugh again, as spontaneously as they did down at the pool.

Bruce slaps his hands together excitedly and says to Suzanne, "Well, come on, I'm dying to show you the upstairs!"

"And I'm just dying to see it."

They step into a convention center of a room, footsteps echoing on the omnipresent parquet. Bruce informs her that it's the master bedroom. Three thousand square feet of cuddling space. They move on to the his and her marble bath chambers—the glass shower stalls equipped with a half dozen high-pressure nozzles to pummel clean parts of your body that you've never seen—and then to walk-in closets the size of large studio apartments.

"What a house." Suzanne shakes her head in admiration. "And so much more tastefully appointed than Iris's."

Bruce narrows his eyes to wicked slits again. "Well, we all know that Iris's taste sucks."

Bruce throws his head back again and Suzanne holds a gloved fist to her mouth as their uproarious laughter echoes through the labyrinthine chambers.

"Step out on this balcony for a moment and look at the view."

Suzanne's palm nervously pats the rim of her bouffant to make sure it's holding its own against the breeze, but her worries melt away as she takes in the spectacular 180-degree panorama. The cool steady wind has swept the smog from the L.A. basin and left the air clear as polished glass. To the left, the glittering steel rectangles of the Century City high-rises push up from a carpet of one-story homes and businesses, winking diamond bright at their sharp edges. To the right, Santa Monica stretches out to meet the great rippling blue Pacific, a silver beam of sunlight hitting its dancing surface like a massive klieg light.

"You've got the whole city as your front yard," says Nelson. "People will pay anything for this, because there are only five homes like this in the entire town."

Suzanne shakes her head in wonder.

"This"—Bruce sweeps his hand in an arc that encompasses both the western and eastern rims of the canyon—"is what is known as the Billionaires' Horseshoe. See that home, right down there?" He points at an 18,000-square-foot Mediterranean villa to their lower left, clinging precariously to a thin wedge of land on the western rim. "That's the Manson murder house."

"You mean where Sharon Tate lived?"

Bruce nods. "Of course that's not the house. They tore it down; nobody would live in it. But it's the same lot. . . . Then right straight across from us"—he points again—"the one with the turret, that's Rupert Murdoch's house. His net worth is six point eight billion. And see that knoll to the right? Paul Allen, the cofounder of Microsoft—net worth forty billion. *Forbes* magazine just named him the third-richest man in America. He's building two fifty-thousand-square-foot homes, plus an amphitheater."

"What? For who? For himself?"

Bruce nods with a satisfied smile.

"Give me a break!"

"Two fifty-thousand-square-foot homes for about a hundred to a hundred twenty-five million dollars."

"Two homes," Suzanne repeats, trying to come to grips with such extravagance.

"And an amphitheater."

The 120-acre site where Allen is building is the former estate of Frances Marion— the highest-paid screenwriter in silent movies—and her husband, cowboy star Fred Thomson. Allen tore down their

10,000-square-foot Wallace Neff–designed mansion to make way for his megapalace complex.

"Now down here to the right"—Bruce points to the northwestern edge of the canyon—"that huge piece of land with the little cypress tree. That's one of the Marciano brothers, they founded Guess? jeans. He's spending about twenty-five million dollars to expand his house. Then right up here at the top of this street, that's Mark Hughes, the owner of Herbalife—net worth more than six hundred million. He's building a forty-five-thousand-square-foot Mediterranean villa on a hundred and fifty-seven acres that he bought from Merv Griffin. It's going to have a tennis pavilion and a million-gallon lake."

"A million-gallon lake!"

"And a tennis pavilion."

"So that's the horseshoe," Nelson concludes reverently, "and this house sits at the very end of it. Can you imagine?"

The tightly stretched skin of Suzanne's forehead engages in a fierce tug-of-war with itself, not quite able to achieve a furrowed brow. Despite all of her connections, it is indeed hard for her to imagine. Her friends and associates earned their fortunes in an earlier era—the Industrial Age. The new moguls of the Information Age have amassed megafortunes that were inconceivable when her dear friends, Ron and Nancy, took possession of the White House just two decades ago. Yet it was the Reagans who paved the way for this new epoch of unprecedented affluence.

It is in Beverly Hills that the true purpose of the "Reagan Revolution" became clear. Here in the canyons and slopes of these coastal mountains the "old-fashioned" values that he espoused were fully realized. Beverly Hills had crystallized as an epicenter for the West Coast elite during the previous golden era of Republican rule—the 1920s. It was during the decade of Harding, Coolidge, and Hoover that the first generation of movie stars, media moguls, and industrialists built opulent monuments to themselves on estates of 5, 10, 15, even as large as 410 acres. But the Great Depression redefined the political landscape, and for the next four decades the Democratic Party shaped the national agenda. The New Deal and the Great Society were financed by steep increases in taxes on income, property, and capital gains that turned the great estates of Beverly Hills into white elephants that few could afford to maintain anymore. One after another, the huge properties of the 1920s were subdivided, their oversize mansions torn down or remodeled beyond recognition.

Even the grandest estate of them all, E. L. Doheny's Greystone, fell victim to redevelopment. In 1955 all but 16 of its 410 acres were sold off to a speculator who converted Doheny's vast network of riding trails and citrus groves into the world's most expensive subdivision: Trousdale Estates. The Trousdale homes were only one story and modestly sized—an average of 5,000 square feet, with small yards that did not require an army of gardeners to maintain them. Conventional wisdom held that America would never again witness the fantastic preening displays by the superrich that had been common in the 1920s, because there would never again be a class of superrich who would be able to amass such stratospheric fortunes.

But conventional wisdom failed to anticipate Ronald Reagan's jihad against "big government" and "tax-and-spend liberals." Elected by a landslide in 1980, Reagan wasted no time ushering in massive rollbacks of income, property, and capital-gains taxes. This, combined with America's remarkable conversion from an industrial to a high-tech economy, helped create an economic boom that dwarfed even that of the 1920s. Silicon Valley, corporate mergers that spawned new media empires, and the booming stock market conspired to pump out new billionaires faster than a CD-ROM assembly line. The nouveaux riches of the Information Age embraced one of America's most cherished beliefs: *when you've got it, flaunt it!* In the early 1990s they came to Beverly Hills to enshrine their personal mythos on this hallowed ground that has come to embody all the crass, rapturous, and tragic facets of the American Dream.

The merger mania of Wall Street spread through the mountains and canyons north of Sunset Boulevard as young tycoons bought up one, two, three lots at a time and combined them into vast new estates that put those of the 1920s to shame. Media mogul David Geffen purchased the old Jack Warner estate, one of the few properties from the 1930s that was still intact, for a staggering $47 million. In addition to the 13,600-square-foot Neoclassical mansion, there were ten acres of gardens, fountains, pools, and tennis courts. But Geffen still felt a little hemmed in, so he bought up an additional nine acres from adjoining estates, giving him a total of nineteen, three more than Harold Lloyd's legendary Greenacres. Just over the eastern border of Beverly Hills, David Saperstein—founder of Metro Networks, the nation's number one provider of commuter traffic reports—bought three smaller estates that he merged into one six-acre property where he is currently erecting a 45,000-square-foot Beaux Arts manor, with a ballroom large enough to accommodate 250 dancing fools. Near the crest of the hills, developer Brian Adler has built Beverly Estates: fifty-five new limestone megamansions on two- to five-acre lots; more than half of them are worth more than $50 million.

"There is more money in this town today than ever before in its history," Bruce Nelson tells Suzanne Marx as they gaze across the mansion-studded contours of Benedict Canyon.

Suzanne's eyes drink in the Murdoch and Allen estates, tongue shifting around in her mouth as her salivary glands go into action. "They oughtta give me something for Boys Town. I have to raise eight million dollars for two shelters in downtown South Central. So these guys with all their money . . ." Her words trail off as her thoughts drift into a blizzard of imaginary pledge slips.

A week later, Bruce Nelson makes a lunch appointment with an acquaintance. "Where would you like to meet?" Bruce asks.

"How about the Polo Lounge at the Beverly Hills Hotel?"

"Oh God." Bruce's voice rises to an excited pitch. "I haven't been there in years. Sure, let's make it the Polo Lounge."

As he hangs up the phone, Bruce's pulse races with a mixture of excitement and dread.

The Polo Lounge. As significant in the Beverly Hills mythos as the Billionaires' Horseshoe. Designed by the legendary African American architect Paul R. Williams—who was not allowed to dine in his own creation—it was the red-hot center of the entertainment industry from the 1940s to the 1970s and the birthplace of the power lunch as well as such terms as "movers and shakers" and "heavy hitters." During those pinnacle decades you had to make reservations weeks in advance, unless of course you were one of the anointed regulars. Pass through its art deco portal and you would find yourself surrounded by the Hollywood pantheon: studio heads like Adolph Zukor, Harry Cohn; agents like Lew Wasserman, Swifty Lazar, Freddie Fields; and, of course, the stars—Clark Gable, Edward G. Robinson, Jack Benny, Marlene Dietrich, Judy Garland, Kirk Douglas, Frank Sinatra, Dean Martin, Johnny Carson, Warren Beatty, Liza Minnelli.

It was Hollywood's town square, *the* place to network, and more importantly, to be seen networking. "You wanted to be seen there, having lunch with a VIP," a man who was one of the most powerful figures in the industry during those years recalls. "You needed to establish and maintain the image that you were a player. If you had lunch there with Kirk Douglas, for example, who was an A-list star in those days, it showed that you were in on the action. It was also an important venue for making new connections because you could table-hop and build relationships with other important actors, writers, producers, studio executives, and agents. It was an integral part of the industry."

You will have no trouble getting a reservation at the Polo Lounge these days, almost any afternoon or evening of the week. It is no longer the red-hot center; in fact, there is no center anymore for an industry that has fragmented into hundreds of independent production companies, super stations, and cable television channels. The once tightly knit social fabric of Hollywood has subdivided into dozens of cliques, each favoring its own watering hole.

Perhaps a half dozen times a year, the Beverly Hills Hotel reclaims its old magic. During the Academy Awards or the Grammys, when banquet halls and luxury suites are in high demand, the city's oldest commercial establishment once again books big names. During the 1999 Academy Awards, *Vanity Fair* and Miramax rented cabanas at the pool and threw parties attended by Harvey Weinstein, Steven Spielberg, Jeffrey Katzenberg, David Geffen, Michael Caine, Quentin Tarantino, Mike Myers, John Irving, Gloria Estefan, Anthony Minghella—to name a few. That same year, Clive Davis's annual pre-Grammy party for Arista Records drew eight hundred artists and executives from the music industry. The stellar crowd was entertained with sets by Whitney Houston, Santana, and Natalie Cole. After the party broke up in the wee hours of the morning, the celebrities flooded into the Polo Lounge. Billy Joel sat down at the grand piano and pounded out a rendition of "Piano Man"; the others joined in, and the air was once again charged with the old magic.

But such moments are rare these days. Most lunch hours only a half dozen tables are occupied. White-coated waiters hover nervously around the few customers, eager for a request or a gesture that will give them something to do. This is the case when Bruce Nelson arrives there a few days after his telephone conversation. He looks much different this afternoon in a tan sport jacket and silk tie—a handkerchief deftly folded into his breast pocket, gray hair neatly brushed back along the thick contours of his head. He smiles politely and gives the tuxedo-clad maître d' his name, but his fingers betray his agitation, fiddling about the pockets of his jacket as the maître d' checks his name off on the largely empty reservation schedule and escorts him through the forest green lounge. They pass the sixteen-foot bar and a four-foot-by-ten-foot panoramic photo of a polo player swinging the long bamboo shaft of his rhino-skin-handled mallet. The lounge got its name because it became a favorite pit stop for such aficionados of the game as Will Rogers, Darryl Zanuck, Spencer Tracy, Walt Disney, and Tommy Hitchcock. The maître d' leads Bruce around the gleaming black enamel of the lounge's grand piano and into the back room, which overlooks a brick patio shaded by the thin leafy canopy of a Brazilian pepper tree.

Arriving at his table, Bruce warmly greets his companion and orders a cocktail. As soon as the waiter's out of earshot, his polite demeanor dissolves. Nelson shakes his head bitterly. "It's a shame, such a shame what they've done to this hotel," he mutters. The "they" he's referring to are the current owner, the sultan of Brunei, and his management team. Bruce and most longtime residents of Beverly Hills believe "they" bungled a recent restoration of the hotel and alienated its local customer base. "It used to be such a beautiful place. I grew up here. In the old days, this hotel *was* Beverly Hills. Everybody, and I mean everybody, came here."

He tries to shake off his bad mood and, when the waiter comes, orders a hamburger for old times' sake. "They used to make the best hamburgers in the world here, bar none," he says wistfully. As he talks over the next ninety minutes, the reasons for his emotional attachment to the hotel become obvious. For it was right here that it all began: not only Bruce's career in real estate but also the real estate business itself. It was here, a century earlier, that the region's first generation of land hucksters concocted a dream that would obsess a nation, and finally the world.

It began at the dawn of the twentieth century and California's second gold rush. The second wave of fortune seekers who invaded the state in the late 1890s weren't looking for shiny nuggets at the bottoms of creek beds. This time they were after the "black gold" that lay hundreds of feet below the grasslands of the L.A. basin. The invention of the internal combustion engine had created an insatiable demand for the stuff. When huge oil fields were discovered in Long Beach and Baldwin Hills more than 3,000 wells were drilled, and speculators began buying up large tracts of nearby real estate in the hope that they would strike another mother lode.

A small consortium of investors from the East Coast formed the Amalgamated Oil Company and joined the stampede. They purchased an old Spanish land grant known as Rancho Rodeo de las Aguas: 4,539 acres in the western portion of the L.A. basin at the southern edge of the Santa Monica Mountains. The acreage was equally divided between the flats at the base of the mountains—bean fields and grazing land, for the most part—and the hills themselves, which were covered with virgin forests of sycamore, oak, and eucalyptus trees. Hunters still stalked the ridgelines for deer and elk; fishermen teased their lures across the fast-flowing streams in Benedict and Coldwater canyons, filling their baskets with salmon and trout; and the nights rang out with the manic high-pitched cries of coyotes.

Amalgamated drilled for five years but came up empty-handed. The board of directors decided there was nothing left to do but sell the land back to a cattle rancher and write off the loss. One of their number, Burton Green, objected. Green was a shrewd operator. He had drilled the first successful oil well in Los Angeles at a site that would later become the Los Angeles Civic Center. He'd also opened oil fields in Bakersfield and Coalinga, California. Now he saw another way to get rich. Green pointed out to his partners that Los Angeles was growing rapidly, thanks to real estate promoters who had blanketed the eastern seaboard with fliers and newspaper ads extolling the wonders of the Southern California climate.

Thousands packed their belongings and boarded trains for California, clutching tightly to brochures that promised a paradise at the end of the line where clouds never tarnished the crystalline sky and the air was graced by the scent of orange blossoms and ocean spray. Between 1900 and 1910 the population of Los Angeles tripled, from 100,000 to more than 300,000.

Green argued that because it held such a huge parcel of land, Amalgamated Oil was in a unique position to exploit the demand for new housing. Why not plan and build an entire city? A city of the future, a city for the twentieth century.

The time was ripe for it. Since the end of the Civil War, Americans had pursued the Protestant work ethic with manic intensity and transformed the United States from a primitive backwater into the greatest industrial power in the world. The new century would belong to America, but this achievement had come at a stiff price. The rapid industrialization and massive influx of immigrants who were needed to man the machinery of the vast new factories and mills had caused most eastern cities to explosively expand with little or no planning. Filthy urban sprawl spread over the hills and river valleys of the East like bacterial cultures, creating vast labyrinths of congested streets and overcrowded slums shrouded by soot-choked skies. Scottish biologist Patrick Geddes came up with a new name for such hellscapes: Pandemonium City.

While urban planners fought an uphill battle to reform the blighted metropolises of the East, entrepreneurs like Green realized that California offered an opportunity to start over with a clean slate. In his landmark six-volume history of California, Kevin Starr has observed that at the beginning of the twentieth century, California offered "an alternative, the Mediterranean, semi-tropical paradise. Not the tropics, not the rainforests where nature burgeoned with chaotic abandon and threatened to overwhelm man and the civilization he struggled for thousands of years to erect. . . . But a mellow, manageable semi-tropical environment where nature could be sculpted to complement, soften and make urban life not just endurable but a truly balanced paradise."

A new kind of city for the new millennium, a planned community in which every street, house, commercial block, park, and fire hydrant would be laid out in advance. Other developers promised easterners a California Eden. Amalgamated Oil—Green insisted—could deliver it.

Green's vision triumphed. In 1906 Amalgamated Oil reorganized as the Rodeo Land and Water Company and set about building Southern California's first planned community. It was a concept uniquely suited to this region, where many other individuals and companies owned huge chunks of real estate that had once been Spanish land grants (enormous parcels of property, known as ranchos, that had been granted to the elite by the Spanish crown).

After the formation of Rodeo Land and Water, the first question Green needed to address was the name he would give his new city. Rancho Rodeo de las Aguas was too long, too unwieldy, and too Spanish.

He wanted something that would evoke the Greeks' metaphysical paradise, Elysian Fields, or the exalted realm of the Roman emperors on Palatine Hill. Then Green came across a newspaper article about President Taft's recent vacation in Beverly Farms, Massachusetts. "Beverly Farms . . . ," he said to his wife, Lillian. "What a wonderful name for our community."

Lillian thought about it for a moment and replied, "I think Beverly *Hills* would sound much better."

Beverly Hills it became.

Green hired a prominent New York landscape architect, Wilbur F. Cook Jr., to create the blueprint for his new community. It was a telling choice. Cook had worked with Frederick Law Olmsted—the famed designer of New York's Central Park—and on many other Southern California projects, such as Exposition Park, Palos Verdes Estates, the Los Angeles Civic Center, and portions of Griffith Park.

Cook laid out the first streets of the new city at the base of the hills, south of Sunset Boulevard, which at that time was a wide dirt road. Canon, Beverly, Rodeo, Rexford, Camden, and Crescent Drives were graded and paved. Instead of the dull grid pattern that characterized most eastern cities, Cook created wide curving boulevards and lined them with Mexican fan palms, elms, Canary Island palms, magnolias, Arizona ash, and Indian laurel figs. The land was divided into quarter and half-acre lots, which were hooked up for water, gas, and electricity, and put on the market for $300 or $400 apiece. Larger one-acre lots along Sunset Boulevard sold for $800 to $1,000.

But for the first few years sales were sluggish. Beverly Hills was only seven miles from downtown Los Angeles, but the roads that spanned that distance were little more than goat paths, and most prospective buyers considered the fledgling community to be too rural and remote. Besides, even with the freshly planted saplings lining the streets, the new lots looked stark: rectangles of raw earth with only power and telephone poles for landscaping. And beyond the barren lots, miles of dusty bean fields stretched off into the horizon. The easterners shook their heads in dismay. This didn't look like the Garden of

Eden that the ads had promised. They decided to play it safe and buy in the more established neighborhoods of West Adams and Hancock Park, which were close to downtown L.A.

Clearly something had to be done to upgrade Beverly Hills's image. Then Green hit upon it. Why not build a hotel? Not an ordinary hotel, but a world-class luxury resort that would draw visitors from as far away as Europe. This was hardly a stroke of genius—for resort hotels had been one of the primary tools of real estate development in Southern California during the latter half of the nineteenth century.

The first modern hotel in Los Angeles, the Pico House, opened in 1870. It quickly gained a reputation as the finest hotel in the entire Southwest and was a crucial conduit for the city's growth. The Arlington played a similar role for Santa Barbara, as did the Hotel Del Monte for Monterey, and the Raymond for Pasadena. But the most spectacular example of the genre was the Del Coronado at Coronado Beach in San Diego County. When it opened in 1889 it advertised itself as the largest tourist hotel in the world. The 399-room Queen Anne structure sprawled over seven and a half acres of the narrow peninsula that divided the Pacific Ocean from the Bay of San Diego. "As deliberate assertions of a romanticized Southern Californiaism, tourist hotels like the Del Coronado had utopian overtones," Kevin Starr has observed. "Like the agricultural colonies, they were statements of an ideal, in the hotels' case something about Eastern elegance being brought to Southern Californian shores."

But the example that Burton Green was most keenly aware of was the Hollywood Hotel, for he had watched how that resort sparked a building boom in a small rural town just three miles east of Beverly Hills. Built on the corner of Highland Avenue and Hollywood Boulevard—at the foot of the Hollywood Hills, which were the eastern edge of the Santa Monica Mountains—the hotel had been a modest institution of just 50 rooms when first erected at the turn of the century. By 1910 it had expanded to a 300-room resort that catered to wealthy vacationers from the Midwest and East. The tourists were so impressed by the Mediterranean weather that they began buying plots of land in the hills and building homes there. Real estate prices soared. In 1903 lots sold for anywhere from $150 to $400; now they were going for ten times that.

The key ingredient of the hotel's phenomenal success was its manager, Margaret Anderson. Anderson provided first-class service and was a relentless and highly skilled promoter. She built up her client base by procuring the mailing lists of other luxury hotels, then bombarding the prospects with flyers that featured hand-tinted photographs of the hotel's impressive Craftsman Spanish Mission Revival facade, and purple prose. "Midway between Los Angeles and the ocean . . . in the foothills, a garden spot of unparalleled charm . . . flowers in endless profusion, ripening . . . you'll find no hotel in Southern California more ideally suited than the Hollywood Hotel."

The problem for Green was how to find someone of Anderson's caliber to create and run his resort in Beverly Hills. People with her managerial skills, exquisite taste, and marketing savvy were difficult to come by. The solution was simple: hire Anderson. He lured her away from Hollywood by offering her ownership of the hotel in Beverly Hills, if she would design, build, and manage it. Anderson chose architects Myron Hunt and Elmer Grey—who had created such Southern Californian landmarks as the Huntington Gallery, the Pasadena Playhouse, and the Wentworth Hotel—to build her 300-room California Mission Revival hotel on a twelve-acre parcel of land at the base of the Santa Monica Mountains, adjacent to Sunset Boulevard.

Construction began in 1911. Rodeo Land and Water pumped more than $500,000 into Anderson's edifice, which expanded on the features that had made the Hollywood Hotel such a great success. The complex included a dining room capable of serving 500, a veranda that measured a seventh of a mile in length—offering strollers a panorama of the west L.A. basin—tea and billiard rooms, private baths and telephones in every room—then an unheard-of extravagance—and such modern innovations as a cold storage plant, electrical lighting, and a vacuuming system. On the grounds, walking paths wound through extensive gardens packed with orchids and tropical foliage, past fountains and fishponds. There were also tennis courts, a swimming pool, a stable with twenty-five gated Kentucky horses that guests could ride up into the still-wild hills, or along a bridle path that followed the winding length of Sunset Boulevard all the way to the foamy roar of the Pacific Ocean, some eight miles away.

As the great crescent shape of the hotel with its red-tiled roof, thick adobe walls, and central five-story rotunda rose skyward in the closing months of 1911, Green wanted to make sure that the first guests would not be put off by the dusty bean fields that surrounded it, so he employed an army of gardeners to lay two acres of emerald lawn before the hotel's massive front portico and adorn it with palm trees and lush tropical vegetation. They built an equally abundant park directly across from the Pacific Electric streetcar station where new arrivals disembarked. A large lily pond was strategically placed to be the first thing the easterners laid eyes on as they stepped off the car. They were then shepherded onto a smaller trolley (known as a "dinky") that whisked them through the newly minted Eden to the hotel's front door.

Green's brainchild was a fantastic success. The hotel opened in 1912 and within a few years usurped the Hollywood Hotel's position as *the* destination spot for affluent tourists. The visitors began buying second homes, and the first Beverly Hills real estate boom was born. The population grew from 500 in 1914 to 12,000 by 1926. In less than a decade it became famous the world over as the new playground of the superrich, the vacation spot for such members of the East Coast aristocracy as the Vanderbilts, Gillettes, and the Guggenheims, and permanent home of America's new demigods, the movie stars who began building palatial estates in the hills above Sunset.

Throughout the next five decades the Beverly Hills Hotel remained the hub of this rarefied community. For $250 a month, locals could join the Sand and Pool Club—so named because the hotel's pool featured a white sand beach beside its azure waters where patrons could sun themselves while sipping cocktails served by white-clad cabana boys. Of course the locals had pools of their own, but that wasn't the point. This was the place to see and be seen, to network and schmooze, to romp together in the garden and communally celebrate the California paradise.

And it was beside the lapping waters of that pool, among the baking oiled bodies of movie stars, as he inhaled the intoxicating mixture of chlorine, fresh squeezed citrus, and iced martinis, that Bruce Nelson found his life's calling—the vocation of Burton Green, the man who had spun this Valhalla out of thin air in the first place.

Bruce came to Beverly Hills in 1943. He was eleven years old and had grown up in Hinsdale, Illinois, an upper-middle-class suburb of Chicago. His father, John Nelson, was a successful architect who had designed many of the finest homes in Hinsdale. But World War II brought construction to a standstill and forced him into early retirement. Then a chronic sinus problem led John Nelson, like thousands of asthmatics and consumptives before him, to move west to California.

Bruce was nervous when he attended the first day of seventh grade at Beverly Hills's El Rodeo Elementary School. There he was, sitting smack in the middle of a sea of beautiful children, the offspring of the West Coast elite. To his left sat Virginia De Rochemont, daughter of Louis De Rochemont, a prominent producer at Fox; to his right, Jay Sandrich, son of Mark Sandrich, who had directed such classics as *Holiday Inn, Man About Town, Top Hat,* and *The Gay Divorcee*. (Jay later became a producer/director for such hit television series as *Get Smart, The Mary Tyler Moore Show,* and *The Bill Cosby Show*.)

Would the other kids ridicule Bruce's midwestern accent, or worse, simply ignore him? *What do I care, anyway?*—he thought as he wiped his damp palms on his corduroy pants. Then he noticed he was the only one in corduroys and a flannel shirt. The rest of the boys wore T-shirts and jeans, though they were expensive and neatly pressed.

A finger tapped his shoulder. He turned and a chubby dark-haired effervescent kid stuck his hand out. "Hi, I'm Jeff Selznick." Son of David O. Selznick—producer of *Gone With the Wind,* the most successful movie of all time—and Irene Mayer Selznick, daughter of Louis B. Mayer, head of Metro-Goldwyn-Mayer, the most powerful and prestigious movie studio in Hollywood, which employed 4,000 people and "more stars than there are in heaven" on its twenty-three soundstages in Culver City. Bruce couldn't believe he was actually talking to him. He answered Jeff's questions in a high nervous voice that seemed to belong to someone else—the words jumbled and stilted and incoherent to his ears, though Jeff seemed to understand them, for he nodded, laughed appreciatively, and finally asked, "Do you play tennis?"

Bruce nodded. He'd had his first lesson in Palm Springs on their trip west.

"Great." Jeff smiled. "Come over to my house after school and we'll play."

Just like that, he was in. And once you were in, you were in for keeps—Bruce discovered—a permanent member of a warm and supportive extended family. The next twenty years passed as one dizzying swirl of tennis matches, pool parties, outdoor barbecues, black-tie dinners, and screenings of the latest Hollywood films in private movie theaters on the estates of David O. Selznick; Jules Stein, the founder of MCA, the biggest talent agency in the world; comedian Harold Lloyd; Jack Warner, head of Warner Brothers Pictures, and on and on.

"It was a beautiful golden era," says Bruce, "a fabulous, gracious life that doesn't exist today anywhere. We were living this incredible fantasy." At most of the events the dinners were prepared by two or three chefs, and "the regular gang" included Jules Stein's daughters, Jean and Susan; Jack Warner's daughter, Barbara; Virginia Loew, granddaughter of theater magnate Marcus Loew; Jim Zukor, grandson of Adolph Zukor, head of Paramount Pictures; Joan Bennett's daughter, Melinda; Alan Ladd's daughter, Carol; and Joan Benny, daughter of Jack.

They were all members of the Sand and Pool Club and played on the tennis courts of the Beverly Hills Hotel alongside Charlie Chaplin—who cursed like a truck driver when he missed a shot—Errol Flynn, David Niven, Katharine Hepburn, Cary Grant, Randolph Scott, James Mason; the hotel's resident pro, Harvey Snodgrass, former National Clay Courts Champion; and Bill Tilden, winner of seven U.S. men's singles tennis championships and three Wimbledon tournaments.

After playing for hours, the gang pushed through a door in a wood partition that divided the courts from the pool and spread out among the tables of the Cabana Club Cafe to order hamburgers. Nothing he'd ever tasted before or would taste afterward compared with the juicy sirloin of those burgers melding with ketchup and cheese, thick tomato slices, and shards of red onion. Never again would he bask in such utter contentment and luxury as he gazed out across the expanse of oiled bodies stretched out on lounges in the sand, sipping cocktails garnished with slices of lemon, lime, orange, strawberries, and olive spears. The sapphire water lapped gently at the concrete rim of the pool and the air echoed with a *bong! bong!* and shudder of wood as Kate Hepburn sprang from the diving board to execute a perfect swan dive that raised a plume of chlorine-scented water toward the rustling fronds of the surrounding palm trees and the firmament beyond.

The pool manager, Svend Petersen—an Aryan Adonis who had competed on Denmark's Olympic swim team—commanded a squadron of cabana boys dressed in white tennis shorts and polo shirts. They hustled among the chaise longues, providing fresh drinks and fluffy terry cloth towels to the likes of Ingrid Bergman, Grace Kelly, Bette Davis, Tyrone Power, and Hedy Lamarr. Many stars lived within walking distance of the hotel and stopped by daily. Fred Astaire sauntered through the pool area every morning on his way to the lobby to pick up the trade papers; Lucille Ball liked to play backgammon at one of the tables; two former Tarzans—Buster Crabbe and Johnny Weissmuller—clocked laps in the pool, as did MGM's premier bathing beauty, Esther Williams.

A number of producers—game show magnate Mark Goodson and Joseph E. Levine, maker of such big-screen blockbusters as *Hercules Unchained, The Lion in Winter,* and *Carnal Knowledge*—set up shop in the pool's cabanas, complete with secretaries and multiple phone lines. Gossip columnist Walter Winchell filed stories from one of the cabanas, and Jacqueline Susann wrote potboiler novels in another.

There wasn't a better spot in L.A. to network. In 1956 a young garment industry salesman, Robert Evans, rented a cabana while he was in town setting up boutiques at Bullock's for Evan-Picone, a trendy line of women's pants that had won raves in *Harper's Bazaar, Vogue,* and *Mademoiselle.* One afternoon he was called over to the cabana of Norma Shearer, who had been one of the biggest female stars of the '30s and '40s. Shearer admired Evans's matinee-idol looks, and his charisma and authority—qualities that few young actors possessed. She asked if he'd be interested in playing her late husband, MGM wunderkind Irving Thalberg, in a new movie, *Man of a Thousand Faces,* starring her good friend Jimmy Cagney. Evans couldn't believe it at first. *This must be some kind of joke*. It wasn't. He got the part and soon found himself with an agent and another role in a star-studded production of *The Sun Also Rises*. This time he would play Ava Gardner's bullfighter lover. From there, Evans segued into producing. In the late '60s he became head of production at Paramount Pictures and green-lit such hits as *The Odd Couple, Rosemary's Baby, Love Story, The Godfather,* and *Chinatown*.

The most beautiful women in the world—Jane Russell, Simone Signoret, Ava Gardner, Cyd Charisse—made their way down the shimmering white steps to the pool, either for formal casting sessions or to advertise their talents to the producers and directors who gathered there. The ultimate babe-o-rama moment came on the summer afternoon when twenty-two-year-old Raquel Welch made her way to the pool deck. Svend Petersen—who'd honed a connoisseur's eye over the years—was struck speechless. "I swear to God," Petersen exclaimed after Raquel departed, leaving a trail of exquisite wet footprints on the stairs leading back to the hotel, "she has the most *incredible* body I've ever seen in my life. She had bad skin on her face, but her body was immaculate. It was *awesome*!"

But in Bruce Nelson's eyes the most glamorous star ever to step out on the pool deck was not a movie actor, producer, or director; not a politician, nor a Wall Street Wizard. It was the early 1960s when he first saw the man glide through the door from the tennis courts, racket slung over the shoulder of his white cable-knit sweater. The man's posture, his relaxed smile and swagger communicated that he was utterly at ease in this environment. His dark hair swept back from a broad forehead; thick black eyebrows framed a pair of Russian brown eyes that seemed to regard the pool as his personal playground. He moved liquidly from cabana to table to lounge chair, sharing warm handshakes, whispered intimacies, and devilish jokes that caused listeners to erupt with conspiratorial laughter. He seemed to know everyone and related to them as if they were all his close personal friends. Many people bragged about their skill at working a room; this man was the first Bruce had ever seen who had mastered the art of working a pool. "Who is he?" Bruce asked a friend as the stranger smiled, displaying a magnificent set of Burt Lancaster teeth.

"That's Mike Silverman," his companion responded. "You know, that new real estate agent everyone's talking about. They call him the Jewish Cary Grant."

Yes, of course, Bruce had heard of him. The silver-tongued New Yorker who'd arrived in town a few years ago with only a couple of bucks in his pocket and had taken the real estate business by storm. Before the advent of Silverman, Beverly Hills real estate was peddled out of drab little offices by gray-eyed, stoic-faced midwesterners who touted the great estates in the hills with about as much élan as a Kansas auctioneer might employ to sell off an underweight sow. Silverman went to work for one of these deadpan dirt dealers on a strictly commission basis and quickly established himself as a hotshot by displaying a flair for show business and hype that the citizens of Beverly Hills responded to.

Silverman's melodramatic ploys were already the stuff of legend. He had iced champagne waiting in the entryway of the homes that he showed—"presentation is everything"—and wrapped huge red ribbons around 10,000-square-foot mansions before handing the keys to his buyers at the close of escrow. He showed clients large multiacre estates via helicopter. When interviewed by television news shows (including *60 Minutes*), Mike stage-managed the taping at the Beverly Hills Hotel pool, arranging in advance for Svend Petersen to run up and effusively greet him—"Hello, Mr. Silverman!"—and escort him to a cabana, as if Silverman regularly worked there beside the big producers. He had Svend page him repeatedly throughout the interviews and feigned annoyance at the interruptions. "Svend, I told you to hold all my calls!" And then there was the afternoon that Silverman spotted a fabulously wealthy foreign businessman, who was rumored to be interested in buying a home, wading in the shallow end of the pool. Silverman stripped down to his tennis shorts, executed a perfect swan dive off the board, glided underwater across the length of the pool, surfaced beside his mark, and flashed that blinding Burt Lancaster grin. "Allow me to introduce myself"—and withdrew from his shorts a laminated, waterproof business card.

The old-fashioned Realtors sniffed derisively; Silverman was turning an honorable profession into an undignified circus act. But while they sniffed, Silverman stole their clients and quickly became known nationwide as the Realtor to the Stars. Only in a place as magical as Beverly Hills could a real estate agent himself become a celebrity.

As Bruce watched the man glad-handing his way across the crowded pool deck, it was as if an enzyme was released, flooding his cerebral cortex. Since graduating from high school, ten years earlier, Bruce had been drifting. He had majored in political science at Northwestern, done a two-year stint in the army, then came back to Beverly Hills, where he wandered from one dead-end job to another and tried to ignore his parents ever more insistent inquiries about what he intended to do with his life.

But now, suddenly, as he watched the approach of Silverman's blinding grin, he realized: *Hell, I could do that*. The more he thought about it the more sense it made. Growing up beside his dad's drafting table, watching him draw up plans for all those big homes in Hinsdale;

riding out with him to the construction sites to watch those drawings make the transition from ink and paper conceptions to timber and cement reality. Listening to his father critique the design flaws of neighbors' homes over the dinner table and absorbing osmotically Dad's consummate sense of style and interior design. And the last twenty years spent here among the Beverly Hills blue bloods—he knew them all intimately, their preferences, pet peeves, and idiosyncrasies. And he knew how to talk and act to put them at ease. Yes, it all seemed to point to this moment, this direction. He'd been waiting his whole life for this but hadn't known it till just now.

He got up off his chaise longue and approached Silverman—his mouth dry and tongue awkward. Mike shook his hand warmly and fixed his eyes upon Bruce as if he were the most important person on the star-studded pool deck. Bruce explained that he was interested in a career in real estate. Silverman didn't laugh or deride him, instead he nodded sagely and said, "Well, when you get your real estate license, come and see me."

So he did. And the rest, as they say, is history.

"And who had the hamburger?" the white-jacketed waiter inquires. Bruce turns away from his companion, away from his reverie of the past, and confronts the awkward imposition of the present. He raises his hand slightly, and the waiter sets the burger down before him.

"Can I get you gentlemen anything else?"

"No, thank you."

"Very good. Enjoy your meal."

As the waiter departs, Nelson glares at his meat patty with contempt. "They call that a burger?" It's a big fat juicy wedge of ground sirloin on a thick sesame seed bun with a generous slice of pulpy tomato and red onion to garnish it. But it isn't this burger Nelson's seeing, it's all those succulent burgers of the past that he ordered after running off the tennis courts with Jeff Selznick and the gang—burgers irretrievably lost to him now. They loom so large in his memory, no present-tense burger could ever hope to match them.

Bruce bites into his here-and-now burger, showing as much enthusiasm for it as he would for a mouthful of sawdust. "They ruined this hotel," he says, returning to his initial theme. "The local people couldn't wait for it to reopen, so the management had their goodwill. But then they did things to alienate us, like abolishing the Sand and Pool Club, relocating the tennis courts to the other side of the hotel so they no longer adjoin the pool, and automatically adding a fifteen percent gratuity onto the bills. And the Persian Room, the main dining room, is gone, so the Polo Lounge now serves as their dining room. It doesn't begin to compare to the dining rooms in the other hotels around town. Ah . . ." Bruce pushes his half-eaten burger away. "They ruined it, just ruined it. The only smart thing they did was keep Svend Petersen, the pool manager, who's been here for more than forty years. Have you met Svend? Oh, you have to meet him. He's the embodiment of what the hotel used to be. He knows where all the bodies are buried. Svend could tell you stories . . ." Bruce's expression suddenly brightens. "I bet he's working right now. Let's go see."

Bruce leads the way down a hallway past some luxury boutiques to a set of glass doors. He pauses to point out a glass case that features photos of the pool in its glory days. "That's the way it used to be." The photos are everything he described and more. A youthful Svend Petersen threads his way through a group of women in broad-brimmed straw hats—his thick blond hair swept back from a walnut forehead, polo shirt hugging the lean contours of his hard muscled torso.

"Come on, let's see if he's here," Bruce says.

Nelson descends a set of concrete stairs. As he approaches the pool deck, a barrel-chested man with a square jaw approaches, peering through a pair of tortoiseshell glasses. "Good afternoon, gentlemen," he says in a thick Danish accent. "Are you guests of the hotel?" The hair is white now, not blond, white as snow, but still thick, parted ruler straight and brushed neatly back along the strong contours of his head.

White polo shirt, tennis shorts, Nike-clad feet, the skin of his broad forehead freckled from more than thirteen thousand days under the California sun.

"It's me, Svend, Bruce Nelson." Bruce grins and holds out his hand.

Svend regards him warily for a fraction of a second, then his blue-gray eyes click with recognition and he grips Nelson's hand with both of his. "Oh yes, of course, I remember you, sir. How have you been?"

"Fine, just fine."

For the next few minutes their talk is filled with effusive remembrances of people who once frequented this place. Many have died, or don't get out much anymore, or have moved away.

Then the words trail off and Bruce takes in the expanse of the pool deck. The thirteen cabanas, their tables shaded by weathered white canvas, are empty, and so are the 160 lounge chairs. The sand is gone, filled in with concrete, and the sixty-six-foot deck is nine feet shorter than it used to be. The roar of passing cars on Sunset Boulevard reverberates off the concrete.

"You never used to hear that in the old days," Bruce says cryptically.

Svend's smile melts. He pushes his glasses up the bridge of his broad freckled nose; a melancholy invades his blue-gray eyes. "No," he allows quietly. "Well, you know, the street's wider now, and the traffic . . . A lot has changed."

"Yes, it has."

Bruce turns to the right, where a dozen tables sit before an outdoor bar. Only one is occupied, by a young European couple who were in the Polo Lounge earlier. They look deeply into each other's eyes and whisper intimacies—oblivious of Nelson and Petersen. Beyond them is a wood partition with a door in it. "That used to lead to the tennis courts," Bruce says. "Remember, Svend?"

"I certainly do."

Bruce laughs and shakes his head. "I'll never forget the way Kate Hepburn used to come bursting through there after a game. I can still hear her voice booming out, calling for the tennis pro, Harvey Snodgrass. *Haaarrrveeey!*"

Sven laughs softly. "Oh yes. And remember her doing cannonballs off the diving board with all her clothes on?"

They stare at the partition door for a moment that seems to stretch all the way back through the decades; stare as if they can't help hoping Kate will burst through it again. "Haaaarrrrvey!" But she doesn't. The door remains closed. The world it once led to is gone.

★ 2 ★

High Cotton

The great house is invisible from the corner of Hartford and Cove Way, but you can feel its presence looming somewhere beyond the dense tangle of shrubs, oak trees, and ranch-style homes that have grown up around it. The ornately patterned wrought-iron gate to the old estate is still easy to see. Seventy years ago it opened onto a long, curb-lined driveway that made a serpentine journey through three acres of immaculately manicured grounds to the pale green, crescent-shaped mansion at the top of the hill. The property was later subdivided, and today the driveway, now shrouded by a dusty canopy of oak leaves, travels a mere hundred yards before ending abruptly at the doorstep of a modest, two-story Spanish-tiled home that used to be one of the mansion's two guesthouses.

A year ago the remaining acre and a half of the estate and the mansion itself were put on the market by Portland Mason, daughter of James and Pamela Mason. Her Realtor, Steven Sherman of Hilton and Hyland Realty, used the property's obscurity as one of its major selling points. "It's only a few blocks from the Beverly Hills Hotel, and yet it's completely secluded," Sherman enthused. "In order to get this much privacy these days you generally have to go way up into the hills."

It wasn't always so obscure. When the 10,000-square-foot Mediterranean-style palazzo was first built in 1926, it was visible all the way from Sunset Boulevard, presiding over a vast slope of lawn and a fountain that cascaded down the hillside to a glittering Venetian-tiled pool. The souvenir shops on Rodeo and Beverly Drives sold postcards of it bearing the caption "Buster Keaton's Italian Villa," and tourists stopped on Hartford to snap pictures.

It's ironic that this is one of the last surviving silent-movie-star homes in Beverly Hills. Charlie Chaplin, Douglas Fairbanks, Mary Pickford, Rudolph Valentino, and Tom Mix were much bigger box office draws than Keaton and built larger and more luxurious palaces on the neighboring slopes. All have long since been torn down or remodeled beyond recognition.

Keaton was a midlevel movie star. His films were successful enough for him to command $3,000 a week by the mid-1920s—an astronomical figure at the time—but he never made the millions that the two most popular comedians of that era, Charlie Chaplin and Harold Lloyd, earned. The secret of Chaplin's and Lloyd's success was their screen characters—both managed to forge archetypes that had broad appeal. People the world over saw their own struggles to survive and find love in the cruel and dehumanizing landscape of the twentieth century dramatized by the misadventures of Chaplin's little tramp. And Americans saw their desperate desire to live out the Horatio Alger myth both mocked and fulfilled in Lloyd's thrill comedies, which often climaxed when his eager-beaver boy next door scaled one of the skyscrapers that had sprung up in every major city during the nation's first go-go era of unprecedented economic expansion.

Keaton's character—the stoic, unsmiling little man in the porkpie hat—was not nearly so accessible. One could never quite be sure what he was thinking or feeling behind those huge bottomless eyes. He never wept, as Chaplin and Lloyd did, but even his most riotous comedies were haunted by what critic James Agee called "a freezing whisper not of pathos but of melancholy." His movies had a weird disturbing edge that often left audiences more unsettled than amused. His greatest short comedy, *Cops,* was filled with Kafkaesque images of hundreds of blue uniformed police chasing the solitary figure of Buster down eerily empty streets. They caught him in the end, and the final shot featured Buster's distinctive porkpie hat draped over a gravestone—a shockingly stark visual to end a comedy on, especially in 1922.

A few critics—most notably Agee, Robert Sherwood, Carl Sandburg, and Luis Buñuel—recognized Keaton as a startling talent and praised him as Chaplin's equal, if not his superior. But most mainstream reviewers dismissed him as a plodding and unimaginative comedian. Mordaunt Hall, the lead film critic for the *New York Times,* greeted each new Keaton picture with condescension and, like most of his peers, regarded Buster as a minor comic talent unworthy of sharing the limelight with a true artist like Chaplin.

Chaplin and Lloyd remained wealthy until the end of their lives, but Keaton's career took a nosedive shortly after the coming of sound. By 1933 he had lost his wife, his two sons, his money, and the house on this hill. But in the end, Buster proved to have more staying power than his contemporaries. In the early 1960s, film festivals in London, Paris, Venice, and New York staged retrospectives of his silent movies, and Keaton's reputation began to soar. It has continued its ascent in the decades since his death in 1966. Today, revival screenings of his silent films draw capacity crowds in theaters around the world. His audience is larger now than it was during his heyday, more than seventy years ago. When two of Keaton's greatest movies, *The General* and *Our Hospitality,* were recently shown in Los Angeles, more than 2,000 people lined up around a full city block to see them.

Meanwhile, Harold Lloyd and Charlie Chaplin have not aged as well. There have been several attempts to launch a similar revival of Lloyd's films over the last forty years, with limited success. Lloyd created a character that was perfectly attuned to the zeitgeist of the '20s—thus he remains trapped there, like a fly in amber. His movies are quaint museum pieces that offer a glimpse of the past, but they will never again electrify audiences as they once did. Chaplin's tramp, a more universal and timeless archetype, still resonates with modern audiences, but his Victorian sensibility and simplistic cinematic technique make his films feel slightly dated—especially when compared with Keaton's cool underplaying, sharp sense of irony, and breathtaking virtuosity as a filmmaker. When today's critics speak of the cinema's two great comic geniuses, they refer to Keaton and Chaplin, in that order, for Keaton is now universally regarded as the greatest comedian, if not the greatest director of the silent era.

And like its master, the house at the top of this hill also outlasted most of its competitors. It played a pivotal role in both Keaton's fall from grace and his redemption. Without it, Buster might have remained a footnote in cinematic history.

To get to the house today, you have to drive up not Cove but Pamela Drive, which also adjoins Hartford Way. You pass three ranch-style homes on the right, which occupy what used to be part of the estate's great rolling lawn. The road narrows to a private drive and climbs steeply for fifty yards, then levels out into a large circle of asphalt before the villa's front door. The circle was once filled with a carefully cultivated flower garden, but the Masons blacktopped it over decades ago. Seventy years of rain and beating sun have battered the villa's once gleaming exterior, but the house, like the man who built it, is a survivor. It bears a striking resemblance to Keaton himself as he entered the seventh and final decade of his life: diminished in stature, its complexion weathered, its arteries hardening, but its weary frame still standing with a stoic determination to endure.

The villa had a succession of owners after Keaton vacated the premises in the early '30s, including Marlene Dietrich, Barbara Hutton and Cary Grant, and finally James and Pamela Mason, who bought it in 1949. The Masons subdivided the estate, sold off half of its acreage, and did some remodeling in the early '50s. When the couple divorced in 1964, Pamela kept the house but did virtually no maintenance on it during the next thirty-three years that she lived there. The roof leaked, paint blistered, wallpaper peeled, pipes rattled, patios buckled, and her menagerie of thirty-odd cats filled the mildewed halls with a pungent odor worthy of the Roman catacombs. It came to resemble the hoary old mansion of Norma Desmond, the reclusive silent movie star in Billy Wilder's *Sunset Boulevard,* in which Keaton himself made a cameo appearance.

After Pamela died in 1996, her daughter, Portland, put the villa up for sale. Many of the Realtors who came to look at the property felt the only marketable asset was the dirt. The villa itself was a white elephant—they told Portland; most potential buyers would want to tear it down and rebuild from scratch. But Portland had grown up in the house, knew its unique history, and was determined to hold out for a buyer who would restore the villa to its former glory. "It took several years to find the right person," says Marc Wanamaker, archivist of the Beverly Hills Historical Society and a friend of Portland's, "but she finally found John Bercsi, a young man who specializes in buying and restoring old estates, then selling them for a profit. He was very excited to have the opportunity to work on a house that had belonged to Buster Keaton and James Mason."

The facade of the villa has not changed since the day Keaton moved in. The same dragon head sconces guard either side of the ornate leaded-glass door, and the doorway itself is framed by an impressive arch of intricately molded concrete. Beyond the door is a sunken entryway. The great cool empty space smells of aged plaster, damp dust, mildew, and cat piss. A pair of white Roman columns frame a raised lobby that serves as an intersection for all of the wings of the house. To the left, the grand staircase and its intricate forged iron banister ascend through yet more Roman columns to the upper hall. Even in its present condition—lit only by gray light streaming in through the windows and covered by worn beige carpet—the staircase takes one's breath away.

Keaton built the villa in 1926, at the apex of his career. He owned his own movie studio, was making more than $150,000 a year, and had just finished principal photography of his masterpiece, *The General.* But this wasn't the house he first envisioned for himself. Buster longed to buy a ranch—with horse stables, a chicken house, a few head of cattle, and maybe a small orange grove—in the then rural San Fernando Valley. He'd been a child star in vaudeville and had grown up in an endless chain of passenger trains, theaters, and cheap boardinghouses. The only sense of permanence he had was during an idyllic four weeks that he spent on his uncle's farm in Oklahoma.

He wanted to re-create that atmosphere for himself and his two sons. But his wife, Natalie Talmadge—sister of Norma and Constance Talmadge, both major movie stars of the silent era—insisted that he build her an edifice that would rival her siblings' lavish homes and the great palaces that other stars were building all over Beverly Hills.

When Burton Green laid out the plans for his city of the future, he had no notion that such fantastic castles would be erected here. The first homes in the community were American Colonials—large, well constructed, and handsomely appointed, but undistinguished; the kind of houses that could be found in affluent suburbs throughout the East and Midwest. They were designed to appeal to Green's market niche: wealthy executives and professionals who were looking for second or retirement homes.

Green hadn't anticipated the advent of the film industry. Who could have? In one decade, from 1910 to 1920, the movie industry exploded and quickly overtook vaudeville as the most popular venue of mass entertainment. Almost all of the major production companies set up shop in Southern California because its dry sunny climate and wide variety of landscapes—everything from beaches to deserts to snowy mountain peaks—gave them the biggest bang for their buck. With the movies came movie stars. They loomed much larger—both figuratively and literally—than the stars of the stage. There was no television, and radio was in its infancy. To the public, movie stars existed only as twenty-foot-tall images on a silver screen, gliding through a fluid, silent, shimmering black-and-white world, communicating their inner life through dramatic gestures, facial expressions, and body language; their every emotional impulse elevated by a swell of sublime music from the orchestra pit. The stars quickly became icons through which ordinary Americans could romanticize their own unrealized dreams and passions, unspoken disappointments and heartaches.

"For the first time in history, mere entertainers possessed a power over the masses that eventually surpassed the strongest political identifications," Kevin Starr has observed. "On screen and off, their looks, their clothes, each detail of their personal histories (true or concocted) linked Hollywood stars directly to the deepest aspirations of their mass audience. This dynamic transformed Hollywood into an emotionally and imaginatively energized American place, touched by magic and myth."

The stars taught ordinary Americans the fine art of living. Audiences studied their every move to learn how to dress, enter a room, light and smoke a cigarette, mix a cocktail, dance the Charleston, woo a woman, or win a man. And no stars loomed larger in America's dream life than Mary Pickford—the precocious, golden-curled girl next door that exhibitors dubbed "America's Sweetheart"—and Douglas Fairbanks—the devil-may-care swashbuckler who embodied the idealized vision of Ivy League Anglo-American manhood. (In reality, he was Douglas Ulman, half-Jewish and the product of a broken home. Fairbanks's famous tan—which spawned America's love affair with sunbathing—was something he was born with. His mother, Ella, came from the South and harbored a lifelong fear that Douglas might have African American blood in him. After graduating from high school, Fairbanks applied to Harvard but didn't have enough credits to enroll as a freshman. He attended a few classes but did not become a full-time student and never earned a degree.)

When Fairbanks proposed to Mary Pickford in 1919, he decided to build a new home for his bride-to-be on fourteen acres of land in Benedict Canyon, at the site of an old hunting lodge. Doug had discovered the spot while horseback riding through the still-wild hills. He and Mary hired architect Max Parker to tear down the lodge and erect a twenty-two-room English country manor house in its place.

When it was finished, America's Sweetheart and her Prince Charming christened their new estate Pickfair. It became America's Buckingham Palace, more prestigious and magical in the public's imagination than the White House. The list of dignitaries who called upon its court included Albert Einstein, Amelia Earhart, F. Scott Fitzgerald, Henry Ford, Jack Dempsey, Babe Ruth, and H. G. Wells; as well as bona fide royalty—the queen of Siam, King Alfonso XIII of Spain, the duke and duchess of Alba, the duke and duchess of Sutherland, the earl and countess of Lanesborough, a honeymooning Lord and Lady Mountbatten, the duke of York; and Prince George of England, future king of the British Empire.

From the outside, Pickfair had a restrained grandeur, but inside the decor exhibited a schizophrenic aesthetic that would characterize most of the Beverly Hills mansions that followed in its wake. The first floor featured eighteenth-century furniture and frescoed ceilings. Mary's bedroom evoked the Italian Renaissance. On the third floor, the "Oriental room" was done in an East Asian theme that complemented a vast collection of rare artifacts Doug and Mary had acquired on their tour of the Far East. On the ground floor, Doug built an authentic replica of a Wild West saloon, with a twenty-foot polished oak bar taken from a cantina in New Mexico that Billy the Kid used to frequent.

Other stars quickly followed in Fairbanks and Pickford's footsteps. The rush to buy land propelled prices from $500 a lot in 1922 to $30,000 by 1925, making Beverly Hills real estate an even better investment than the skyrocketing stock market. The stars competed to outdo one another, pouring hundreds of thousands and even millions of dollars into their dream palaces. They were influenced not only by Pickfair but also by the fantastic sets they inhabited every day in their pictures; in fact many employed the very same architects, interior designers, and carpenters who worked on those sets so that fantasy and reality blended into a seamless continuum.

The construction of their new homes presented an opportunity to reinvent themselves, to shed their immigrant or small-town roots and become American icons who lived in phenomenal castles on high, like the Greek gods on Olympus. Thus a poor Italian immigrant named

Guglielmi became an Arab sheik called Valentino who resided in a cliff-top domain known as Falcon Lair. Greta Gustafsson, a barber's assistant, became Greta Garbo, a breathtaking international "Woman of Mystery" who transcended Protestant mores and dared to stroll naked through the cool spray of sprinklers on a vast lawn owned by her lover, John Gilbert. And Theodosia Goodman—a dark-eyed girl from Cincinnati, Ohio—became Theda Bara, an exotic and sultry vamp of "illegitimate Egyptian parentage" who ensnared weak-willed men in the sensual web of her Middle Eastern citadel.

Gloria Swanson bathed in a golden bathtub set in a room of black marble. John Barrymore sipped after-dinner drinks in his authentic recreation of an English taproom, shotgunned skeet on his private shooting range, and sought diversion in his zoo and aviary stocked with more than 300 rare birds. Douglas Fairbanks canoed along a network of streams that wound through the fourteen acres of Pickfair and afterward stretched out on a gleaming white sand beach beside the gently lapping waters of his Olympic-size swimming pool. Charlie Chaplin installed a massive pipe organ in his game room so the silent movies he screened there would have musical accompaniment. Harold Lloyd went one better by putting his pipe organ in a 110-seat home theater. Lloyd's fifteen-and-a-half-acre estate, which he dubbed Greenacres, was twice the size of Chaplin's and featured a thirty-two-room Italian Renaissance mansion, a 110-foot waterfall that was illuminated at night, an 800-foot lake, complete with canoes, and a nine-hole golf course.

Tom Mix, the most popular cowboy star of the '20s, didn't want his wife to feel fenced in, so instead of her own bedroom, he gave her an entire wing of their $450,000 home. She furnished it with an Aubusson rug and Louis Seize furniture. Tom had a wing of his own, decorated with mounted animal heads, Navajo rugs, and a vast collection of pearl- and bone-handled revolvers, each embossed with his initials. The walk-in closet in his bedroom stored more than 600 pairs of shoes, a purple tuxedo, and a diamond-studded platinum belt buckle, also embossed with his initials.

The public pored over magazines filled with glossy pictures of the rich and famous at play in these otherworldly pleasure palaces. Beverly Hills gift shops offered racks of postcards with color photos of the estates, and stands began to appear along Sunset Boulevard touting "Maps to the Stars' Homes!" Buses gave tours, and guides extolled the wonders of each mansion that they passed; cameras clicked and passengers murmured expressions of awe, craning their necks and straining their eyes in a vain effort to peer over walls and hedges and glimpse one of the Olympians sunbathing beside their glistening sky blue swimming pools.

It wasn't simply the opulence that captivated the American public. Opulent homes could be found in every city in America. But in no other city were there so many of them and such a dizzying concoction of wildly different styles. On any given street, tourists could see a Georgian mansion next to an English Tudor, next to a Swiss chalet, next to a Spanish hacienda, next to a Mediterranean villa, next to a house that brazenly incorporated all of these styles in one structure. Intellectuals deplored this eclecticism as a symptom of a hollow and derivative culture with no authentic aesthetic principles of its own. But the public instinctually understood it as an audacious celebration of assimilation, a tribute to the diverse influences that made their melting-pot nation the most vibrant society of the twentieth century.

It was a casting off of the nineteenth century's austere Protestant work ethic. Hollywood's elite ushered in the era of rampant consumerism by delivering the message that conspicuous excess was okay; more than okay, even, it was a virtue. And by no small coincidence, department stores, car dealerships, and a host of other retailers introduced monthly installment plans so the middle class could afford to buy modern luxuries that heretofore had been beyond their reach. The fabulous palaces of the stars had a profound impact on the way Americans lived. Following California's lead, families across the country sought to integrate the outdoors into their homes by adopting the patio, the barbecue, and the swimming pool as common features of their backyards. Game rooms also became popular. Billiard and Ping-

Pong tables, dartboards, and card tables were installed in converted garages and basements, mimicking in miniature the vast amusements found in the estates of Beverly Hills.

Not all of the stars were enthusiastic about their responsibilities. Some, like Buster Keaton, recoiled from the pretentiousness of the Beverly Hills lifestyle. But they were eventually made to understand that a home was more than a place to live, it was a valuable marketing tool that enhanced their popularity. Eventually even Keaton succumbed to the pressures from his wife, his producer, and the public, and bought three acres of land adjacent to Tom Mix's estate. As he and Natalie drew up plans to build the villa, Buster warmed to the idea and threw himself into the project with the same obsessiveness he put into his films. Keaton poured $300,000—a fortune in 1926—into the two-story Venetian country estate. When finished it would have more than twenty rooms, five bedrooms, six baths, plus quarters for a maid, a butler, and a gardener.

The floors were lined with oak and rare Italian marble; baronial fireplaces graced the living room, game room, and Natalie's bedroom. The light fixtures were crystal, the bathroom faucets gold plated, and a fountain stocked with goldfish bubbled in a foyer off the breakfast room. The grounds included three tennis courts, ornamental flower gardens, a running brook stocked with trout, and the grand fountain that splashed down the hill along a sixty-foot staircase that led to the Romanesque pool flanked by classical statues and an enormous cabana.

Keaton took great pride in his castle, but he never quite lost his ambivalence toward it. When escorting guests on a tour of the grounds, he would say, "It took a lot of pratfalls, my friends, to build this dump."

John Bercsi has set up his office in the villa's 500-square-foot dining room. He's filled it with a couple of overstuffed couches and a long foldout table piled with blueprints and photos of various portions of the house and grounds. There's a stack of books on architecture, landscaping, and interior design; scraps of paper protrude from their pages to mark key illustrations for quick reference. Bercsi's seated in a chair behind the table, studying a blueprint when a visitor arrives. He pops to his feet and strides swiftly forward to offer his hand. He's in his midthirties, wears a navy blue pinstripe jacket with matching trousers, a blue-striped button-down shirt, a gold-and-blue patterned tie, and black tasseled loafers. Three precise triangles of a folded white handkerchief protrude from his jacket's breast pocket. His dark hair is neatly parted, his face deeply tanned, the bridge of his strong Roman nose peeling slightly from too much sun, and his eyes are aflame with excitement.

"I don't know whether you noticed when you came in," he says, "we're redoing the entire roof. There were several bad leaks and there's been a lot of water damage." He sighs, rubbing the peeling skin on his nose with his index finger. "And that's just the beginning. We'll have to pull up all this cork flooring the Masons put in. There's hardwood underneath it, peg and groove. Actually, it's kind of a benefit in disguise because the cork's protected the oak; there's still three-quarters of an inch of meat on most of the floors. Then we have to rewire all of the electrical, put in new plumbing, a new kitchen, and"—a thin smile crosses his dry lips—"get rid of the smell of Portland's forty-five cats . . ."

His right foot begins nervously tapping the cork floor, as if keeping time to a swing band only he can hear. "I shouldn't complain, I guess. Those cats made it possible for me to get this place. Other people, the faint of heart, came to check it out, but they couldn't get past the cat piss and water damage." The San Fernando Valley twang recedes from his voice for a moment as it fills with genuine passion. "They couldn't envision what it will look like when it's restored, they just couldn't see it."

He leads the way out to the great flagstone patio that once looked down on the cascading fountain, the pool, and an acre of lawn. The stones have waffled and it now looks down upon ten feet of weedy hillside and then a chain-link fence that marks the boundary of the adjoining property. Beyond the fence, a chaotic tangle of shrubs, eucalyptus, and pine trees obscures the rest of the hill. All that remains of the fountain are crumbling chunks of concrete sinking into the leaf-strewn earth. Beside them a children's swing set stands mutely indifferent to the past.

Through the snarled greenery it's possible to catch a glimpse of violet water shimmering above glittering mosaic tiles at the very bottom of the hill. Keaton's pool now belongs to the backyard of one of the other houses. Behind it, the great cabana still stands, now overgrown by a mass of creeper vines that have swarmed over its roof and eaves. Seven decades ago, Keaton threw epic barbecues there on Sunday afternoons. Paul Whiteman's orchestra blared gold-plated jazz on the immense lawn while Buster grilled steaks, Chinese spareribs, and fat English mutton chops for Pickford and Fairbanks, Tom Mix (who snuck away from his wife through a secret passage in the hedge that separated their two houses), Louise Brooks, Irving Thalberg, Howard Hughes, William Randolph Hearst, Marion Davies, and scores of groupies who have faded into obscurity.

"Obviously, we've got to redo all of this. What's lacking is a backyard," Bercsi says, apparently unaware of the irony. "We're going to level the hill. It's about a sixty-foot-by-a-hundred-and-twenty-foot area, so we'll be able to put in a big rolling lawn. We'll redo the patio, using the same sorts of stones. It'll come out to a fountain centered where the old fountain was, but set farther back so your eye gets carried from the front door, through the entranceway, out here, and all the way to the fountain. And there will be some sort of hedge where the fence is to block out the view of the other houses. We're trimming the tops of these trees so your eyes will continue straight out to Century City and Westwood . . . Yeah . . ." He nods, staring at the crumbled ruins of the old fountain. "That's got to happen."

In the west wing of the villa, Keaton's old game room still looks largely as it did in the '20s. Here, Buster perfected trick pool shots and screened his movies for friends. There's a baronial fireplace in one corner, with its original andirons. High on the east wall a small slit of glass reveals a projection booth, which can be reached through a narrow stairway in the outside hall.

"Come take a look at what I found over here," Bercsi says, his voice high with excitement. He walks to the west end of the room, where a tall arched window is recessed into the wall. Above it, near the ceiling, hangs a blue metal cylinder that contains a movie screen. John points to it. "Mason put that screen in in the '50s. He also covered this window up and put a shelf here. I took the shelf out and uncovered the window to restore the room to the way it originally looked, and I found this." He reaches into a slot in the recessed wall and pulls out a towering walnut frame that slides on rollers and holds a tattered movie screen. It glides across the wall and covers it entirely. "This must have been Keaton's," Bercsi says proudly. "He must have watched all of his movies on it." A large flap of the smudged white screen has torn and fallen loose, hanging limply toward the ground. "Look at the dimensions of the frame," says Bercsi. "It's perfect for wide-screen movies. All we have to do is put a new screen on it and mask it."

After dinner and a movie, Keaton often sat down at a card table in this room to play bridge for two dollars a point with the most powerful men in Hollywood, producers Nicholas and Joseph Schenck, Irving Thalberg, Louis B. Mayer, and Samuel Goldwyn. The players won and lost as much $20,000 in a single evening, and tempers often flared. One night, Keaton played with Goldwyn as his partner. "My cards were bad and he [Goldwyn] became quite abusive," Keaton later recalled. Buster stared coolly at the balding mogul and said, "Do you want me to force the cards, or do you want me to break this bridge table over your head?"

"Oh, now you're a table thrower?" Goldwyn spat back. The producer's wife, Frances, quickly interceded and ushered her husband out to the car before the two came to blows.

"Bridge helped to undermine his life," one of Keaton's close friends, Buster Collier, later observed.

Bridge, and the villa itself. "It was a spectacular dream house that he built for himself," Pamela Mason said shortly before the end of her life. "He must have seen himself as the king and her [Natalie] as the queen. But—and this is so typical of everything out here—the minute they built it, they wrecked their lives and couldn't live in it."

Just one year after Keaton moved into the villa, he lost his independence as a filmmaker. His greatest features, *The General* and *Steamboat Bill Jr.*, failed at the box office. He lost his studio and was forced to sign a contract with Metro-Goldwyn-Mayer. It was in this game room, late one night after all the other guests had departed, that Charlie Chaplin solemnly advised Buster against going to MGM. "Don't do it. They'll ruin you helping you. They'll warp your judgment. You'll get tired of arguing for things you know are right."

Chaplin knew what he was talking about. Metro stripped Keaton of all creative control over his films and forced him to appear in a series of mediocre farces that reduced his charismatic screen persona to that of a bumbling imbecile. Buster hated working for the movie factory, but the enormous expense of maintaining the villa had trapped him. He couldn't afford to break his contract and seek independent financing elsewhere because he needed his $3,000-a-week salary just to keep his head above water.

Feeling powerless, he sought solace in the villa's bar, just down the hall from the game room. Because it was built during Prohibition, the bar is an enclosed room with a door on it that can be quickly locked to shield its contents from prying eyes. The bar itself is made up of gleaming black and white tiles, a copper-framed mirror, and a nickel sink, and the room still has its original wallpaper adorned with characters from the works of Charles Dickens. A mighty river of booze flowed out of here in the early '30s, and Keaton nearly drowned in it. By 1932, the Great Stone Face had grown puffy, his hair disheveled, and his speech slurred as he stumbled his way through pale imitations of his old silent pantomimes in his stilted MGM talkies.

He resented Natalie for forcing him to take on such a financial burden, and she couldn't stand his drinking. They began to fight often and bitterly. Their marriage finally unraveled directly above the bar on the second floor, where Natalie's bedroom takes up the entire west wing of the house. Three times the size of Buster's bedroom, down the hall, it has wide picture windows that once overlooked the vast lawn and pool. Today they look down on the backyards of other houses. The original floral wallpaper still clings to the walls, and the platform that once supported a bed Buster designed and built for his wife still pushes up from the floor.

Bercsi points to an odd bulge in the ceiling and some sloppy plaster work. "Water damage. The ceiling collapsed here a few years ago, and they did a rather hasty patch job. We're going to take it down and completely restore it as it was: a vaulted ceiling with four corners. It will be reengineered with steel reinforcement."

He leads the way to Natalie's walk-in closet and bathroom, which is the size of a large one-bedroom apartment. "We're going to gut this and convert it to a man's bathroom and closet," John explains, a note of apology stealing into his voice. "It's going to look like it's from the '20s, but it'll have a steam shower, a big bathtub, and modern plumbing. You have to have a modern bathroom to make the house marketable. Of course, we'll save all the gold-plated sink fixtures and tub spouts."

There are two tiers of clothing racks on either side of the closet. The upper racks pull down from the ceiling on straps, then spring back into place when released. It was here that Natalie stored her vast wardrobe of furs and evening gowns. She spent an average of $800 a week in the clothing shops on Rodeo and Beverly Drives, and owned more than 150 pairs of shoes.

One day, after a particularly vicious fight, Natalie fled the villa and refused to speak to Buster. In a fit of inebriated rage, Keaton picked up an extra at MGM, brought her back to the house, and led her upstairs to Natalie's bedroom. He opened this closet and began to yank clothes off of the racks and toss them at the bewildered girl. "Take whatever you want," he told her. "Do you like these?" He ripped more clothes from the rack and piled them onto the floor. "What about these?" He piled up more.

"Even through my alcoholic haze," Keaton later recalled, "I could see the girl, even as she accepted the clothes, was trying to humor me."

Afterward, Keaton took the extra to his yacht. In the early morning hours, Natalie and a team of detectives burst into the ship's stateroom, caught the two in bed together, and established grounds for a divorce.

MGM fired Buster a year later, and his days as a major star were finished. Natalie sold the villa, which she'd won in the divorce, and Keaton scrambled for bit parts and jobs as a gag writer for other comedians to pay his back taxes and alimony.

As Bercsi descends the grand staircase, his cell phone chirps. He pulls it out of his jacket pocket. "Yes? . . . Great." His eyes snap into sharp focus as he listens intently. "Half an hour . . . I'll be there. You have the address? . . . Excellent." He snaps the phone closed and pockets it. "I have to go meet some construction lenders at another house I'm restoring. They may give me the completion money. You want to come along and watch my dog and pony show?"

John majored in business at USC. He was quick with numbers and the classes in macro- and microeconomics interested him, but not as much as the crumbling Victorian mansions of the West Adams district that slumped on the periphery of the campus. They'd long been left behind by the elite's march westward; most served as rooming houses now or were boarded-up warrens for homeless squatters. He found their ruined grandeur mesmerizing, and his imagination conjured up what they must have looked like in their heyday before widening streets, gas stations, and liquor stores devoured their rolling lawns and carriage houses.

Soon he was spending his nights at the library, reading up on old houses and the architects who designed them. He fell in love with Wallace Neff's Spanish mission–style homes, Paul Williams's stately Colonials, and Rudolf Schindler's post-and-beam moderns. Hungry to know more, he began auditing architecture courses. "I'd sit in the back and listen. I never thought about the possibility of changing my major. I just did it for fun."

One summer he got a job parking cars for the beautiful people at the Beverly Hills Hotel, a half mile away from the Italian villa. He loved the rich leather scent of the Mercedeses, BMWs, and Porsches that he fetched for the guests, and the traces of expensive liquor and imported cigars that he caught on their breath as he opened the doors for them. Most of all he loved the feel of the crisp five-, ten-, and sometimes twenty-dollar bills the drivers slipped into his hand. One afternoon, Ted Turner came strolling out of the hotel with a stunning babe on his arm. He sent John to fetch his rented Camaro. John brought the car around, leaped out, and opened the door first for the babe and then for Turner. As Turner reached into his pocket for a tip, a lustrous Rolls-Royce Silver Shadow pulled up to the edge of the red carpet. Ted paused to admire it, then, as he handed John a ten, winked and said, "Son, where I come from we call that 'high cotton.' "

High cotton. John savored the words as the Camaro glided down the curved driveway toward Sunset Boulevard. He wanted to pick himself some of that.

After graduating from USC, he went to work as a bond trader, then as a mortgage banker for Metrociti Mortgage. But he never lost his fascination for old houses. In 1991 he bought a run-down nine-hundred-square-foot 1920s bungalow in West Hollywood for $280,000, fixed it up, lived in it for a couple of years, then sold it for a profit of almost $100,000. In 1993 he paid $380,000 for his first piece of Beverly Hills real estate: a small house on Tennis Court Row in Benedict Canyon. "My neighbors were Sylvester Stallone, Eddie Murphy, and Ann-Margret. I bought the smallest house on the street." He fixed it up and sold it two years later for $560,000.

The lightbulb went off. *Hey, I'm making more money at this than I am at my job!* So he ditched the job and went into business for himself. *Follow a few simple principles*—he told himself—*and you can't go wrong. Buy low, sell high, control your costs. The bigger the property, the bigger the profit margin.* Even in a booming market, it was possible to pick up underpriced houses from owners with a cash flow problem. "The basis for all real estate profits is someone else's misfortune," Bercsi sagely advises. "The Four *D*'s: Death, Divorce,

Destitution, or Disease—that's how good properties come on the market."

The key, as in any business, was volume. He had to buy more than one property at a time, and to do that he needed investors with deep pockets. No problem. The mortgage banking business had filled his Rolodex with them. So he began working the phone. The sales pitch was easy: "Beverly Hills is a brand name, like Coca-Cola. It's known everywhere in the world. There will always be a certain premium to a home in Beverly Hills, just 'cause of the name, and that zip code: 90210."

In the space of two and a half years he bought, restored, and resold eleven homes for $1 million to $2 million a pop, at an average of 50 percent net profit, and he has six more under construction at the present time.

Bercsi drives up what was once known as Mistress Canyon, because many married men used to buy their lovers small homes in this sparsely populated valley. Bercsi hangs a hard left onto a cul-de-sac called Monte Vista, then roars up a steep driveway and pulls to a stop behind several battered trucks and twenty-year-old American luxury sedans that belong to his Guatemalan construction crew. "Here it is," he says excitedly. John hops out and leads the way to a set of concrete steps at the end of the driveway. He points up the steep hill. "My Dracula house!" At the crest, a towering Transylvanian structure perches precariously on what appears to be a ninety-degree slope of raw earth. Most of its walls have been stripped away, revealing an intricate tangle of beams supporting four open floors and a gabled roof. From this distance it looks like mammoth toothpick sculpture.

"DA-DA-DA-DAAA!" Bercsi sings out the opening notes of Beethoven's Fifth Symphony, his eyes moist with emotion; an intoxicated smile nearly swallows his face. "Look at it! You expect to hear Wagner coming out of the windows and see ghosts running through the halls. It's so Gothic, so . . . over the top." He laughs. "You have to come back and see it when it's done. I think there's a lot of profit in this house. It's such a unique property, it's going to take the right kind of buyer, a bachelor who wants to go up there and—I'm not kidding—do drugs, pull up the drawbridge, have no one bother them, and throw wild parties."

How did Bercsi acquire such an eccentric structure? The Third *D*. It was in foreclosure, so he went to the bank and struck a deal. John gave them $40,000 in cash and promised to take over the former owner's loan of $430,000. That was a few months ago. Since then he's put $100,000 into it and now he's looking for a construction lender to kick in another $250,000 so he can complete the restoration. Construction lenders are usually private individuals—doctors, lawyers, and entrepreneurs—who are looking for short-term investments that will kick back a fat return of 14 percent, plus five to seven points.

And how does one convince a dermatologist from Denver to part with a quarter of a million of his hard-earned dollars? Bercsi smiles. "I've got to say a lot of it is smoke and mirrors. You've got to convince them of the worthiness of the project, first off. They've got to believe that it's a unique and special property that we'll be able to sell for at least as much as they have lent me, so they can get their money out of it. Secondarily, they look at—"

A white Jeep Cherokee pulls up the driveway and comes to a stop behind John's Range Rover. Bercsi squares his shoulders, the muscles of his face tensing. "Here are my lenders." Four men climb out of the Jeep. John tucks his nervousness away in a compartment of his mind and gives a confident and amused wink. "Now you get to watch the dog and pony show." And off he strides, down the driveway to effusively shake their hands.

Over the next hour, Bercsi takes them through every floor and room of the Dracula house, pointing out where fireplaces and Jacuzzis will be, describing the marble he'll put in the kitchen, the nozzles that'll be in the showers, and so on. The men follow, nodding, asking occasional questions, each pausing at various intervals to answer their chirping cell phones.

Finally, they're standing back on the driveway again, in front of the white Jeep the men came in. It's time to talk numbers. Bercsi tells them what he's invested so far and that with another $250,000 he'll be able to complete the house in four or five months. When it's finished, John projects he'll have invested a total of $680,000 in the property. "And what can you sell it for in a day?" one of the men asks.

"In a day, I can sell it for at least what I have in it."

"I would think so."

"I know a number of Realtors who would love to represent this property," Bercsi says authoritatively. "They're looking for product. I should be able to sell it for a million-seven, a million-eight."

The men shake his hand and promise to be in touch. As the Jeep backs cautiously down the driveway, John turns away with a delighted little-boy grin. "That's the dog and pony show." The oldest man in the group was the one with the money, Bercsi explains. No one told him that; they didn't have to. "He was the quiet one asking all the questions, looking around very carefully." Bercsi thinks it over for a moment, then shakes his head. "He's not going to buy. I just know it. I'll get a phone call tomorrow. He'll say, 'You know what . . . blah, blah, blah.' " Then he shrugs off his pessimism. "Hey, we'll see, maybe he'll go for it, maybe he won't."

On the way back to the villa, John indulges in his favorite pastime: window-shopping for houses that may one day come on the market. Normally it would be a ten-minute journey, but he makes so many detours up narrow winding canyon roads that it takes more than an hour. Bercsi's eyes burn with unbridled desire as he points out the features of house after house. Not that he loves every one of them; in fact there are many he detests, for he's a man who hates as passionately as he loves. And nothing enrages him more than to see an old house violated.

He pulls to a stop before Pickfair and shakes his head in disgust. Beverly Hills's first and most famous movie-star mansion is recognizable only by its name nestled in the frilly iron scrolls of the front gate.

Many movie stars have come to Beverly Hills, but few manage to stay here until the end of their lives. Tom Mix fell victim to the changing tastes of a fickle public. With the coming of sound, audiences gravitated to younger cowboys who were adept not only at riding and shooting but also at talking and singing. Mix, like most stars, proved to be a poor financial planner and was soon forced to sell his estate for a fraction of the money he sank into it. Charlie Chaplin was also forced out by shifting winds, but his were political. Hounded by the witch-hunting politicians and reporters of the McCarthy era, the little tramp was banned from reentering the United States when he left for a trip to England in 1952. Mary Pickford and Harold Lloyd were the only major stars of silent pictures to remain in Beverly Hills until their deaths in the 1970s. But this proved to be little consolation for them.

Pickford spent her last years wandering through the empty rooms of her Colonial mansion in an alcoholic haze. The dinner guests had departed long ago. Mary divorced Douglas Fairbanks in 1936, after she discovered he was having an affair with one of his costars. Fairbanks died in 1939 and Mary married Buddy Rodgers, an affable second-rate star, but she never stopped pining for her departed prince, and Pickfair would never again be the center of Beverly Hills social life. The parties grew fewer, the invitation lists shorter, and the guests more infirm and forgetful, until finally the parties stopped altogether.

Fairbanks's Wild West saloon on the first floor remained exactly as he had left it the day he walked out of Pickfair forever, some forty years before. Mary could never bring herself to dismantle it. Sometimes, during her nocturnal ramblings, she thought she heard his laughter emanating from there. She ventured in, eyes scanning the strange dark shapes of hats and branding irons hanging on the walls, and for an instant thought she spotted his Cheshire grin beaming from a shadow-filled corner. "Doug?" But the mischievous grin always retreated into the darkness beyond her grasp.

When Douglas Fairbanks Jr. visited Mary for the last time, he realized midway through their conversation that she thought she was talking to his father. "She was still in love with him, to the very end," he later explained.

Mary Pickford died in 1979. That same year an Iranian developer bulldozed Harold Lloyd's Greenacres. Lloyd had died of cancer in 1971, and his heirs couldn't afford to maintain the massive estate. The thirty-two-room mansion was spared, but the sixteen acres of grounds were subdivided. Harold's flower gardens, fountains, his Olympic-size swimming pool with its vast pavilion, the private lake, the golf course, and the waterfall fell before the plow. Nine years later, Pickfair was also bulldozed—or, in the parlance of Beverly Hills, "scraped"—by Pia Zadora and her husband, Meshulam Riklis, an Israeli industrialist. The couple then hired architect Peter Marino to erect their new home. Marino called the old Pickfair "a total, split-level ranch burger. Terrible and appalling," and praised Riklis as "my crazed, wonderful, mad billionaire." Marino promised to turn Pickfair into the "maximum 1930s Wallace Neff statement." Marino's "Neff statement" turned out to be a monstrous pink Frank Tashlin caricature of a Mediterranean villa that trampled over every aesthetic principle Neff stood for.

John Bercsi glares at the new Pickfair's mosquelike facade and lets loose with a tongue-trilling, Middle Eastern wail. "You can almost hear the grand mufti calling the faithful to prayer, can't you?" The smile fades from his face. "You know what really rankles me? They have the audacity to still call it Pickfair. It's like a sick joke. This is the most god-awful, gaudy exhibition of Liberace-meets-Louis-the-Fourteenth-Rosanne-Barr taste in the world."

He slips the Range Rover into gear and continues on. Heading down Beverly Drive, John passes the front gate of the Robert Evans estate. "We used to crash his parties in college," he reminisces. "We'd bring some pretty girls and they'd let us in. It was just wild! That's an absolutely beautiful home. It's a John Woolf. He's an architect that did French Regency stuff in the '30s, '40s, and '50s. Extremely tasteful. In terms of proportion and balance, that house is perfect. You walk in and it's got a fireplace in front of you in the living room. Instead of a blank wall, he has a window where the flue would be. You look through that window and you can see the lit fire in the screening room a hundred feet down on the property. So you're seeing from fireplace to fireplace. Just amazing."

Bercsi's eyes become dreamy. "One day that property is going to be an amazing redo. It's, I think, three acres. It goes street to street, from here over to Woodland. It's an amazing jewel box of a house—small, but you could actually build around the existing house. It's got a beautiful screening room/guesthouse. It's got a gorgeous north/south tennis court, a stunning pool—one of the most beautiful pools in Beverly Hills. . . . And you know, his health isn't good. . . . He's had a few heart attacks, a stroke . . ."

Bercsi drives in silence for a while, wistfully contemplating the likelihood of Robert Evans biting the First *D*.

He turns up Benedict Canyon and spots a bronzed figure up ahead on a glistening red-and-chrome Harley. "That's my friend John Levin," he says excitedly, accelerating to catch up with him. The man's leaning back on the long black leather seat. His tan muscular arms extend from a fluttering yellow body shirt to the splayed handlebars, and his longish brown hair rustles in the breeze beneath a sleekly tapered black helmet. "He's an emergency room doctor at Methodist Hospital in Pasadena," Bercsi explains, "but he's gotten into buying and selling homes, like me. He's done over twenty of them. We aren't really in competition because he doesn't do restorations—he's a scrape and rebuild guy."

Levin's Harley ambles leisurely up the canyon, hugging the double yellow line in the center of the road, which makes it easy for Bercsi to pull abreast of him. "Hey," John calls through his open window.

Levin glances over through a pair of aviator glasses, and his brown face parts into a sparkling white smile. He looks strikingly similar to Kevin Sorbo, the actor who plays Hercules on TV. "Pull over," Levin calls out. "I want to talk to you."

Bercsi pulls to the shoulder and Levin does also, a few feet ahead of the Range Rover. He swings off his bike and walks to the Rover, oblivious of the cars whooshing by up the canyon. Levin smiles, leaning his rippled right arm against the driver's side door. "I have something you might want in on."

"Talk to me."

Levin's broad left hand reaches under his shirt to caress the tawny hair on his awesome pectoral. "I just bought a house with three acres of land on Benedict for one million. I'm not interested in the house; I want two acres of the land because it abuts my property. You can have the house and the acre of land that surrounds it."

"For how much?"

"For what I paid for it. One million. . . . You interested?"

"I'm always interested. I'll come by and take a look at it."

"Excellent. Give me a call."

Levin tosses off an informal salute, strolls back to his Harley, and roars up the canyon into a corridor of golden light formed by the low-hanging sun. The moment hovers there, the sun like a giant ripe juicy orange, just begging to be picked; the air charged with possibilities, these canyons a giant game board from which millions can be made if you've got enough Monopoly money to afford a roll of the dice.

John turns over the engine and time begins again. "Levin's a hell of a guy," he says with genuine admiration as he waits for a break in the traffic to pull a U-turn. "Got himself a hell of a girlfriend too. You should see her: Victoria's Secret material, cover shot, and that's no lie. He's also an actor. He played an emergency room doctor in *Girl Interrupted*."

The sun falls behind the hills and blue-gray shadows swallow the canyon. The window-shopping's over. John heads back to the villa.

How long will Bercsi's golden moment last? The Italian villa was one of the crowning achievements of Keaton's career, and so it will be for Bercsi's, if everything goes according to plan. He and his financial partner, Christopher Bedrosian, laid down $5 million to buy the estate and will pump another three or four million into the restoration. That's five times more than John's invested in any previous property. "It's definitely a quantum leap forward for me," he admits. But Bercsi expects it to pay off big-time when he resells the villa for around $15 million. Like Keaton, he's unable to envision a sudden reversal of fortune. After all, property values have been climbing steadily for as long as he's been in the business of restoring homes.

But it hasn't always been so.

When Natalie Keaton put the villa on the market at the height of the Great Depression, she was distressed to discover the estate her husband had spent $300,000 on was now worth only $25,000. The same was true of other movie star mansions that were dumped onto the market at that time. Valentino's Falcon Lair sold for a paltry $18,000.

The cycle of booms and busts continued in Beverly Hills real estate throughout the next six decades. But Bercsi refuses to admit the possibility of history repeating itself, at least in his case. "I can't imagine buying property in Beverly Hills and getting less than what you paid for it. You can always make a profit in my business, if you know what you're doing, because in this town there's always somebody willing to pay for a finished house. And there will always be high-end buyers, even in a depression."

Bercsi bought the villa through Bruce Nelson, who says, "I don't know how John thinks he's going to get fifteen million dollars for that property. It isn't a very big parcel anymore, there are other houses all around it. There's nothing particularly distinguished about the architecture, and the house isn't even that big, by today's standards." Nelson sighs in exasperation. "Bercsi's living in a dream world."

Maybe, but in Beverly Hills that comes with the territory. And who can say where the market will be a year from now? For these hills and canyons are full of unpredictable twists and turns, and the earth here can yield hidden treasure when one least expects it—as Buster Keaton discovered twenty-three years after Natalie locked him out of the villa.

Bercsi roars up Pamela Drive and comes to a stop in front of the great house. The sun's still visible on this hilltop, but the shadows of the pine trees have lengthened, casting furry dark forms across the circle of asphalt. "Oh, I forgot to show you the gardener's shed," John says, leading the way. "It's over here."

He walks past the villa, a tennis court, and a three-car garage to a long shed with white concrete walls and a wood-shingled roof, or rather what remains of it, for the shingles have rotted away in places and left gaping holes. Light from the sinking sun streams through them, catching dust particles swirling lazily in the air. "It's over here," John says, walking to the north end of the shed.

In 1937 Keaton suffered yet another catastrophe. The refrigeration system in the vault that stored the negatives to all of his silent movies suddenly failed and the volatile nitrate film incinerated. For almost twenty years Buster believed his greatest work had been lost. He suffered countless humiliations during those two decades. When he was institutionalized for a nervous breakdown, *Vanity Fair* ran a photo of him sitting on his threadbare hospital bed, looking emaciated, pale, and hollow-eyed. Below it was the caption: "The man who was at one time considered one of the funniest comedians in the world." Newspapers across the country ran headlines about how the "ex-slapstick king" had been confined to a straitjacket on a psychopathic ward.

After he got out of the hospital and off the booze, Buster tried to write gags for the Marx Brothers. Groucho sneered at his efforts. "Do you think that's *funny*?"

And Samuel Goldwyn finally got revenge for that long-ago confrontation in the villa's game room by calling Buster in for an interview about a starring role in a big dramatic picture he was producing about the bare-knuckle boxer John L. Sullivan. When Keaton appeared before Goldwyn's desk, hat in hand, the producer pretended to be absorbed in paperwork. Finally, he looked up, stared at Buster for a long moment, and said, "I had this part in a picture that I thought you could do, but now that I see you I realize I was wrong. You'd never be able to do it."

Keaton didn't lose his temper this time, or beg for the job. He simply laughed and walked out.

Then one warm spring day in 1955, James Mason, the current owner of the villa, decided to clean out this gardener's shack, which was full of wheelbarrows, broken pots, and rusty lawn mowers. As he hauled out the accumulated junk of the five previous owners, he discovered a steel door with a safe lock on it embedded in a thick concrete wall at the far end of the shack. When he finally pried the door open, he found a cache of film cans: prints of all of Keaton's silent features and a good many of his short comedies, including the only known print of *The Boat* that would ever be found. Keaton had once used the shack as a cutting room and had forgotten about his private vault.

Mason called Buster, who was living in Culver City at the time, and Keaton came over in his station wagon with film archivist Raymond Rohauer to pick up the dusty cans. Rohauer transferred the movies to safety stock and began to show them at film festivals throughout the world. This led to the rediscovery of Keaton as one of the true geniuses of the American cinema.

When Buster appeared at the Venice Film Festival in October of 1965, he received a five-minute standing ovation. Fighting back tears, he said, "This is the first time I've been invited to a film festival, but I hope it won't be the last." It was. He died three months later of lung cancer.

The house he'd felt so ambivalent about building, which had often felt more like a velvet trap than a home, had remained loyal to him in the end.

Bercsi hunches slightly as he proceeds through the gloom of the shed. A shaft of light pierces a hole in the roof's rotted shingles, spotlighting the slab of concrete that forms the north wall. "There it is." John points to a tarnished steel door hanging half off its hinges. A tangle of spiderwebs trails from it to the concrete floor; the shadow of the removed combination lock is etched on the metal just above the handle. Inside the vault are a group of plain wooden shelves and an overhead lightbulb. Here the movies waited patiently for almost two decades.

"We're going to have to tear down the shed," Bercsi says reluctantly, "but we're going to preserve the vault, no question about it. It's a historic site."

John's cell phone chirps. He pulls it out of his jacket pocket. "Yes? . . . Uh-huh. . . . What year was it built? . . . How's the interior? . . . Right. Square footage? . . . How many baths? . . . Does it have a view? . . . Can we build one by taking down some trees? . . . I see. . . . All right, I'm on my way."

He pockets the phone, foot tapping the hard earth floor and eyes aflame. "That was one of my Realtors. She has a 1927 house she wants me to look at."

He crosses the driveway as the sun falls behind the western hills, the tasseled heads of the palm trees engulfed in reddish gold flames, climbs into his Range Rover, and takes off in search of another conquest, utterly certain of his invincibility. He is more than just a Valley boy who made good, more than just another slick real estate hustler looking to line his pockets with obscene wads of cash. He belongs to a great continuum of dreamers, those who came before and those who will follow after him—naive romantics all, possessed by the burning desire to grab hold of a piece of immortality, to leave their own unique footprints behind, whether it be on a roll of celluloid or a spool of recording tape, or in some freshly poured concrete.

★ 3 ★

Bachelor in Paradise

Seven o'clock on a Wednesday evening, in the cocktail lounge of the Four Seasons Hotel. Located on Doheny Drive, the Four Seasons is just a few yards east of Beverly Hills's city limits, but Beverlyites consider it to be an essential part of their community. Tonight, and every night, the lounge is packed with the entertainment industry's elite. The agents wear Hugo Boss and Armani suits, the talent the latest casual wear by Louis Vuitton, Gucci, and Charles Jourdan. The high visibility personality of the moment is Robert Duvall. He sits at a table near the rear of the room with a couple of other people, their distinguishing characteristics bleached away by the brilliance of his star power. *Behind your right shoulder. Who's he with? I don't know, a couple of guys. God, he looks old. He is old. Yeah, but he* looks *old, like Redford. Why doesn't he have some work done?*

Another demographic group glides among the elite. Their bodies are tanned and toned. Their sprayed-on ensembles cling to their voluptuous curves. Thin chains of gold and silver dangle provocatively around their hips, below bared expanses of sit-up-hardened bellies; lush tattoos adorn their ankles and shoulder blades. Their rich manes of hair glisten with supernatural highlights even in the subdued illumination of the lounge; exquisitely tapered locks dangle against slender throats and glowing cheeks that sparkle with body glitter. An equally impressive number of them can be found in the cocktail lounges of the Peninsula Hotel, the Beverly Wilshire, the Beverly Hills Hotel, the Beverly Hilton, and L'Ermitage. For Beverly Hills is, quite simply, the most powerful bimbo vortex on the planet.

They come here by the thousands from the San Fernando Valley, from the deserts of Arizona, the plains of Kansas, the big-sky country of Montana, the rust belts of Pennsylvania, and the aging boroughs of New York; from as far away as France, Germany, and Russia they make the pilgrimage here with dreams of winning fame and fortune, not through their own accomplishments or talents, but through those of the men they will attach themselves to.

Their role model is Darcy LaPier, a former Miss Hawaiian Tropics who successfully merged with one millionaire husband after another until she was able to retire—upon the death of her last conquest, Herbalife mogul Mark Hughes—as one of the wealthiest widows in the United States, at the ripe old age of thirty-five. For these women, the man becomes the career goal. The ultimate achievement is to stand at the altar with a rock or movie star, an A-list director, or a studio executive. For in that moment when his strong jaw parts to reveal a sparkling Colgate smile and he slips a Harry Winston twelve-carat diamond solitaire set platinum over her finger, all of his power, charm, fame, and wealth will be conferred upon her, and all of his achievements and attributes will be hers.

"Blame Cinderella," Mimi Avins, a journalist for the *Los Angeles Times* recently wrote. "Ever since that little minx snared Prince Charming, the slightly weird yet very rich foot fetishist, women's fantasies haven't been the same. . . . Millions of women have been influenced by the fairy tales rooted in our collective imagination . . . every success story lights the bonfires of hope." They have read about how Jessica Sklar met Jerry Seinfeld at the gym, Susan

Bridges met her husband, Jeff, while working as a maid at a dude ranch in Montana, Dylan McDermott introduced himself to Shiva Rose at a café and later married her—and see no reason why lightning shouldn't strike them too. After all, they were the homecoming queen at McKeesport High School, voted most popular, the star of every school play, the object of every wet dream of every boy in their town.

And so they come here, to the watering holes of the stars, and cast their feathered and painted lures, hoping for a strike. "The girls think it will lead to happily ever after," Dianne Bennett, who runs a Beverly Hills dating service, recently observed. "Hollywood sells itself very well in the 'burbs. The girls come here like lambs to the slaughter, without much information. And the men lie. They promise them very little. 'I really like you. Lie down.' "

Precious few manage to make it into a master bedroom suite of a Beverly Hills mansion for more than a night or two, for the field of millionaire bagging is as fiercely competitive as professional sports, acting, or popular music. After spending a year or two in cramped studio apartments, scrimping and saving every penny from their jobs as waitresses at Nic's Martini Lounge, or salesclerks at Fred Segal so they can afford a few hot outfits and the ten-dollar drinks at the Four Seasons, some begin to consider going after the short-end money until their Mark Hughes comes along. *Hey, if I'm going to lie down, why shouldn't I be well compensated for it? My time's worth something, isn't it?*

Thus the cocktail lounges of the Beverly Hills hotels are well stocked with women available at hourly rates, but like the bottles behind the bars, they're premium product and exorbitantly priced. Some find the short-end game to be incredibly lucrative and pursue it with single-minded intensity, joining the high-end escort and call girl services that thrive in Beverly Hills, or marketing themselves as independent operators. The Web pages of Internet sexual superstores such as L.A. Exotics are crammed with Victoria's Secret–proportioned women offering everything from vacation packages, to one- and two-hour sessions of "full-body" massage, to fantasy "role-playing" in amply equipped "playpens" that cater to every conceivable perversion and even a few inconceivable ones if the money's right.

Women who enjoy flaunting their sexual prowess in more public venues work in the strip joints, such as the Beverly Club—an upscale venue discreetly hidden behind a nondescript wooden door on Beverly Drive in the heart of the retail district—and the more down-and-dirty Star Strip, on La Cienega's restaurant row, just east of the city limits. Others try out for the skin magazines such as *Playboy* and *Hustler,* which have their corporate headquarters in Beverly Hills.

It's a slippery slope for a young girl from the 'burbs to navigate, and just how many slide all the way down it to S & M dungeons and massage parlors, rehab centers, AIDS clinics, and end up in a vacant lot with a bullet in the back of their head or an electrical cord wrapped around their throat, or on a scummy bathroom floor with a needle in their arm, no one can really say, for it's a population group the census takers and demographic wonks have little interest in. But for the men, particularly those who touch down in Beverly Hills with tens of millions of dollars, as Norm Zadeh did, the bimbo vortex can be a marvelous thing—a bona fide Garden of Eden, abundant with fruit ripe for the picking.

After striking the mother lode as a hedge fund manager in the go-go '90s, Zadeh came to the hills of Beverly to live out the Bachelor in Paradise dream—a fantasy every American male who's leafed through a *Playboy* and come upon the photo spreads of Hugh Hefner frolicking in the mists of the *Playboy* mansion grotto with bevies of bare-bummed bunnies has, however briefly, indulged in. Norm made the dream a reality for himself by founding *Perfect 10,* a skin magazine with a unique twist: all of its bounteous babes are 100 percent natural, no silicon implants. Zadeh makes sure of this by thoroughly inspecting the merchandise himself before it's slathered onto his glossy pages. And *Perfect 10* offers both quality and quantity. *Playboy* and *Penthouse* feature three or maybe four photo spreads per issue; *Perfect 10* features fifteen to eighteen—count 'em!—bare-naked ladies in each and every volume.

The venture hasn't made Zadeh rich—*Perfect 10* has only thousands of readers, compared with *Playboy*'s and *Penthouse*'s millions. But Zadeh was already rich; he isn't in it for the money, he's in it for the lifestyle. *Perfect 10* has turned this unassuming, short, thin, bald, self-described former "nerd" into a nationally recognized sex symbol. Norm has been featured in national magazines, newspapers, and on *The Howard Stern Show,* where he inevitably appears with scantily clad *Perfect 10* girls draped on his arms. Of course an essential element to the Bachelor in Paradise lifestyle is the mansion—a vast playpen within which the bachelor, like Hef, can frolic with his giggling harem. So Zadeh erected the *Perfect 10* Mansion at the top of San Ysidro Canyon. A regular feature of the magazine is "*Perfect 10* Behind the Scenes," which consists of shots of partially clad nymphets playing Frisbee inside the 16,000-square-foot pleasure palace or volleyball in the pool, or washing Norm's car and getting oh-so-sudsy-wet in the process. Always among the tittering, jiggling curvaceous throng is the gremlin grin of diminutive Norm Zadeh, the nerd-who-would-be-Hef, beaming a wouldn't-you-give-your-left-testicle-to-be-standing-where-I-am-right-now grin to his envious yet transfixed public.

Norm Zadeh's public relations woman, Eileen Koch, arrives in the Four Seasons cocktail lounge a little after seven. In her midfifties, she would still be very attractive if she weren't hanging on by her fingernails to whatever traces of youthful babedom she has left. Her bleached blond hair is long with bangs dangling over her lined forehead; her thin, aerobicized body has been shoehorned into a pair of expensive stone-washed jeans, and her white blouse is open at the neck to expose a pair of impressive breasts, but the skin has begun to crinkle, especially in her great freckled valley of cleavage. She's got large twinkling eyes, animated hands, and a coquettishness that must have once been quite bewitching but is now sadly out of sync with her weathered appearance.

She explains why Normie—who's running late but will be here any moment, she's sure—is her all-time favorite client. Normie is just the most fantastic, marvelous, warm, sensitive, caring, and generous client a girl could ever ask for.

All of a sudden, the fabled man is here, standing beside the table in the Four Seasons's cocktail lounge with the 1998 *Perfect 10* Model of the Year, Ashley Degenford, on his arm. He wears tight black pants and a short-sleeved black shirt and, on his long nose, a pair of large thick-lensed aviator-style glasses, the kind that used to be fashionable in the '70s. His eyes dance evasively about the lounge as Eileen makes the introductions, and then, with the barest suggestion of a smirk, he introduces Ashley. She has the face of a young Katharine Ross; her skin and hair are Polynesian brown, but it's her *Perfect 10* body that demands your immediate attention. Ashley's Venusian form explodes from a minuscule jumpsuit that looks like it was measured for a Barbie doll. She smiles as she exchanges greetings and draws an errant lock of hair away from her heaving mass of vertigo-inducing cleavage. "Shall we adjourn to the dining room?" Norm suggests. "It'll be easier to talk there."

He proceeds across the entire length of the lounge with Ashley on his arm, her hips swaying and the cheeks of her ass jutting, thrusting, and flexing out from under her Barbie doll shorts. A flabbergasted hush falls over the lounge as all eyes, even Robert Duvall's, focus on Ashley's audacious fanny. No one, not even Sir Anthony Hopkins himself, could command such attention from this jaded crowd.

Is Norm embarrassed at creating such a spectacle? Quite the contrary, he will later insist. "I kind of like it. Particularly when it's a big handsome movie star scratching his head and thinking: *Who the hell is this guy?* I'm *the star!*"

At the table, Norm continues to play the star by ordering vintage champagne for the entire party. As the wine steward departs, Jennifer Snow, another *Perfect 10* model, arrives. She has the bleached blond, hair-sprayed mane of a Las Vegas cocktail waitress—which she is, in the baccarat room of the Venetian Hotel, when she's not modeling in the nude. Jennifer wears a Vegas tan, designer jeans, and an aqua pullover blouse that also displays her ample cleavage. She has a high nasal voice that sounds remarkably similar to Judy Holliday's in her famous caricature of a dumb blonde. She apologizes for being late—the traffic at this hour is unbelievable. Norm smiles coolly and says he'll forgive her this time.

An array of appetizers arrives. The girls ravenously dig in as Norm launches into a series of disquisitions, one segueing seamlessly into the next, on a variety of topics that obsess him: Internet and insurance fraud, the federal deficit, stock market investment strategies, the drug war, and the weaknesses and strengths of the American economy. One of the reasons he founded *Perfect 10,* he explains, was to create a forum for expounding his views on important issues of the day. And expound he does, through the appetizers, the salad, the soup, and halfway through the main course. Norm doesn't make eye contact with his audience as his words flow on and on, he is completely engaged with himself, fascinated by every nuance of his brilliant insights. The women's faces go slack, their eyes glassy, but Norm doesn't seem to mind that his elaborate philosophical constructs form an unbreachable barrier between him and his guests; in fact, you sense that's the point—he'd rather keep people at a safe distance. But that doesn't mean he wants them to drift away altogether. After consuming pounds of incredibly rich gourmet food, Ashley Degenford settles back against her chair's burgundy striped satin upholstery, her eyelids drooping like those of a sated lioness as Norm's words flow over her. ". . . I also predict, and I think that's in my next article, that because the Japanese have done such a great job in the past. . . ."

Without warning, Norm's eyes slash through his aviator glasses at Ashley. "If you're bored you can sleep." Ashley bolts upright, her eyes brightening as she pumps fresh fascination into them. Norm smiles in an attempt to dismiss his anger—"I'm just kidding"—and resumes his monologue. ". . . because the Japanese have done such a great job in the past at beating us on copiers, TVs, cameras, and everything else, they're gonna beat us in computers eventually. . . ."

Norm's wisecrack was a warning shot, and Ashley, Jennifer, and Eileen heard it loud and clear. Like a team trotting out after half-time, they redouble their efforts to lean forward with expressions of spellbound enthusiasm. Whenever Norm pauses briefly, they leap in with excited affirmations. *That's soo true, Normie! I never looked at it that way before. What a provocative insight. I hope you write about it in your next column. Oh, you should, Normie, you definitely should!*

After dessert, Zadeh pursues another favorite theme that generates more interaction with his guests. "There's a funny thing about women," Norm muses as he stirs his coffee. "Fortunately for us not-so-good-looking guys, they don't care that much about looks. In fact, some *Perfect 10* models only feel comfortable with really ugly men. You have to be really ugly to go out with one of these girls, because they are insecure or whatever and they don't like good-looking men. Now let me ask Jennifer Snow a question, although she's been known to be with internationally renowned models. Is a man's appearance incredibly important?"

The tawny skin of Jennifer's high cheekbones tightens as she attempts an honest response. "Norman, you're gonna make me sound shallow. When I first meet a man, yes, appearance is very important to me. I look at him, and he has to be handsome. I think: big, handsome, tall."

Ashley and Eileen exchange apprehensive glances. It's clear from the rigid-as-tempered-steel smile on Norm's mouth this wasn't the answer he was looking for. "But the guy could be unattractive," he gently persists, "but have a sense of confidence or something. It's not really a physical thing. He doesn't have to be like six three."

Jennifer laughs. "Well, he does."

Norm sets his coffee down and sits back, the smile still fixed there, his eyes like two hot diodes behind his thick glasses. Jennifer catches Ashley's warning gaze, at last realizes she's committed a grave faux pas, and clumsily attempts to backpedal. "No, but wait, I have to say this: I, once I get to know the person, once I develop a friendship with him, and I believe that that's what I was trying to say about you, Norm, is that you're so sweet and you're so kind and you are so giving, but you are self-confident and self-assured and you don't expect anything and I think that's where a woman feels comfort with you, and so as far as that's concerned then she starts falling in love with you because she's so comfortable and then she starts to see who you really are. So it doesn't matter what they look like at that point, but you have to get past that point, I think."

Norm decides to accept this rambling apology. He shrugs and picks up his coffee again. "Well anyway, I still believe—and I don't think she contradicted me—I still believe that the looks side of it is not particularly significant at all. I have seen many *Perfect 10* models with guys that are very average-looking and sometimes not particularly appealing at all. They tend to go a little older. I think young girls go for the power and the age and the security."

Eileen nods enthusiastically. "They go for the intelligence."

Oh yes, and there's one other thing they go for—Zadeh suddenly remembers. Money. Lots and lots of money. It wasn't until Norm became a multimillionaire that his sex life turned around. "First I had to get the money to get the girls. Sorry to put it so bluntly."

Ashley smiles and nods over this bit of cosmic wisdom. "That's the bottom line, guys."

It took Norm Zadeh a long time to learn this simple lesson. Forty hellacious years of celibate nerd-dom, wondering why he was such a failure with women—a four-decade-long dry spell before he finally realized: it's the money, stupid.

The waiter pours more coffee and Ashley plucks at a false eyelash, trying to fight off the cellular ache of fatigue as Norm strolls down a circuitous memory lane, recalling his epic journey to this table. . . .

★

His father was Lofti Zadeh, a world-famous mathematician and computer scientist who wrote a landmark research paper on fuzzy sets, which provided a basis for programming computers with linguistic instead of numerical variables to create artificial intelligence systems that would more closely approximate the workings of the human mind. Lofti was a certifiable scientific genius but a reluctant and remote father—if his son is to be believed.

"He didn't ever want to have kids," Norm explains. "My sister was a mistake, and I was a planned accident by my mom because she didn't want my sister to be alone." A recent issue of *Perfect 10* featured a photo of Lofti paying a visit to the *Perfect 10* mansion. Father and son stand side by side in the picture, and clearly they sprang from the same gene puddle: identical in height, both bald with huge frontal lobes and thin chests. Lofti drapes a paternal hand around his boy's narrow shoulders, presenting the image of a proud and nurturing dad. But this is not the man Norm remembers from childhood—his descriptions of his father seethe with venomous resentments. Norm likes to imitate Lofti's voice; his rendition sounds like methane gas whining out of a puckered anus. And when Norm impersonates his father talking to his mother about their son, Lofti refers to his boy not as Normie or Norm or even Norman, but as "the idiot"—the appellation Jerry Lewis gave to the spastic, emotionally regressed nerd he played in movies Norm saw while he was growing up. *Look at the idiot*—Norm imitates his father saying in a typical anecdote—*watching TV again. Can't you talk to the idiot? See if you can get the idiot to go outside. Why doesn't the idiot try reading a book for a change?* Yet when asked if his father really called him an idiot, Norm drops his eyes and admits softly, "No, but I knew that's what he was thinking."

He may not be far off the mark. Norm's mother, Fay Zadeh, told a reporter from *Barron's:* "My husband meant well, but he couldn't give his son the affection that a child expected. Therefore Norman has insecurities."

Norm craved his father's approval and went to great lengths to win it. At three he tried to count to a million. He graduated from high school at sixteen and entered U.C. Berkeley, where his father was chairman of the department of electrical engineering. He must have won some measure of respect from the old man, for at seventeen his father allowed Norm to review the papers that Lofti was writing for academic journals.

Yet what Norm remembers most keenly are the stinging moments of disapproval. "Dad didn't like me watching television, so he'd hide the tubes. I used to find them and put 'em back in. He'd walk in on me watching TV and say, 'You're gonna be a garbage collector when you grow up. You stink!' "

School, in the early years, provided an escape. He remembers grammar school as a kind of paradise lost. He hadn't yet fallen behind the size of the other boys and was one of the finest athletes on the playground—an ace at kickball, dodgeball, and relay races. He had a full head of rich brown hair, and girlfriends? Ah, the memories to this day fill him with delicious longing. The sensation of their full round wet lips pressing against his face, planting kisses on his cheeks, his eyelids, the tip of his nose, and at last his mouth; their warm moist breath fogging the lenses of his glasses, the adrenaline-roaring thrill of their lean prepubescent bodies arching against his, provoking a bewildering but not at all unpleasant swelling in his trousers. "I used to brag that there were forty-two girls in fourth grade and I had forty-two girlfriends," he says wistfully. "Their moms used to drive station wagons with all of these girls in them by my house, just so they could see where I lived. I have some love letters even now from Mary Alice Newman and some other girls . . . Marti something. . . ." Norm's eyes drift away, lost in a mist of half-remembered faces, barely recalled voices, and now faint smells and textures.

Ashley Degenford leaps into the momentary silence with a supporting observation. "He was the most beautiful little boy you've ever seen, if you see his fifth-grade pictures."

Norm's eyes snap back into focus at the abrupt recollection of the cataclysm that drove him from that prepubescent Eden. "Dad had a semisabbatical at MIT. I had to leave my incredibly popular situation." He was yanked out of school in California and dropped into the center of hell when his parents enrolled him in a rough-and-tumble public school in Cambridge, Massachusetts. "The kids weren't as smart or educated, and there were some who were held back a couple of years and *they did not like me*. I was afraid . . . for the first time I was scared for my life. Then, fortunately," he says with a heavy dose of irony, "I got this break. My sister didn't like the private school that my parents had sent her to, and they said, 'What are we going to do to salvage our investment?' And my dad said, 'Well, there's the idiot over there. Maybe he can go there.' " Norm emits a high tight laugh. There is no mirth in it; it sounds like an amphetamined whinny of rage.

Norm had to skip from seventh to eighth grade to gain admittance to the school. He passed the necessary tests, then threw himself into his studies with a fury, earning straight A's. And how did his father reward him for this outstanding performance? "I was just reaching puberty and it was pretty serious and my dad said, 'You know, the Idiot is actually not doing that bad. Let's leave him here.' "

Lofti had to attend to some duties at Berkeley and wanted Fay to come with him. But he didn't want to take Norm out of school yet again—or so he said—so Lofti arranged for his son to stay with an MIT professor and his family and finish the school year. Norm felt he'd been abandoned, left to fend for himself in a hostile environment. "After the first three days I could sense this family didn't want me around," he explains. "So I'm sitting there and I have to stay with them for four months, so I went from being an extrovert to an introvert right during puberty." He laughs.

Norm took refuge in math. His calculus book became his most cherished possession. The other kids ridiculed him as a Poindexter, a brain . . . a nerd.

Four months later, he returned to California but was stuck into high school classes where everyone was a year older than him. No matter how hard he tried, he was never able to get back in sync with his peers. "I was a complete outcast. I did not go to any high school dance. I remember I asked Mary Snugg out. I got drunk on whiskey to get my confidence and called her up and was turned down. That was the first time I ever asked a girl out on a date. So although I was very popular when I was really young, during puberty and the very horny years I was just masturbating away. I got nowhere. It was brutal."

The next summer, his parents took a vacation in Europe and his sister went away too. Thirteen-year-old Norm was left alone in their large house. The maid came in twice a week to clean and buy him groceries, but he felt abandoned once again. Before each of these anecdotes, Norm says, "I'll tell you another cute story." But they are never cute; they always turn out to be another installment in his adolescent parade of horrors.

"I'll tell you another cute story. I did sleep with a girl when I was sixteen, but I didn't perform well. I'm just about to enter her and I say, 'When was your period?' She said it was about fifteen days ago. I realized I needed to put a rubber on, so I ran and got a rubber, frantically tried to put it on. By the time I got it on I lost my erection, so I couldn't enter her. Then I got the erection back and she had stopped lubricating. I went into her without the rubber and I hurt her 'cause she wasn't lubricated and she felt . . ." He removes his glasses and presses two fingers to the bridge of his nose. "It was a complete fiasco. And she married somebody else the next week." The very next week? Sounds a little far-fetched, but it's clear that in Norm's mind that's exactly what happened.

Coupled with the almost daily sexual humiliations were the anti-Semitic barbs. "Kids would come into a room and say, 'I smell a dirty Jew!' " The words reverberated with his father's accusations. "You stink!" And the sense of his Quasimodo-like repugnance, his slimy, smelly, flaky, oozing, pimple-pus-popping physical wretchedness overwhelmed him. "Believe me, it was brutal."

Beneath the self-loathing, a lava pool of rage boiled and frothed. A hatred built for all of the blond, blue-eyed beautiful ones who had grown taller and stronger and more sexually potent than he could ever hope to be; for his father who he felt had abandoned him from the first day they dragged him out of the warm, wet womb into the blinding horrors of this world; for the world itself that never made a place for him. And so he began to wreak vengeance in crafty, covert ways. "I'll tell you another cute story. I used to masturbate on my parents' bed three times a day. I don't think they ever knew!" He laughs. And then there was poker. He had his father's facility with figures and easily outplayed most of his contemporaries. With a deck of cards, he lured them onto his turf. Now he was stronger, faster, and as merciless to them as they were to him in the schoolyard. *Why don't we make it interesting? Wanna play for money? How much you got on ya?* He stripped them of their allowance in one sitting, and when that was gone he took their *Playboys*.

Playboy! Later, on his parents' bed, with those glossy pages spread out before him, all of his longing, his pent-up desires, his hurts and shames and anger and loneliness coalesced into one grand obsession. It would become a quest, as monomaniacal as Ahab's lust to harpoon the Great White Whale: to escape this weary unbright cinder, to find the exit, a way out, the long-forgotten lane to paradise. There was such a place, and others had managed to get there, he discovered as he leafed through the lushly colored images of centerfold goddesses draped over bearskins before blazing fireplaces, on chaise longues beside glistening azure pools, or on the satin sheets of vast round beds. And at last, his very favorite favorite favorite part! The parties at the *Playboy* mansion. *Yes! Yes! Yes!* Robert Culp, Tony Curtis, Clint Eastwood, Sammy Davis Jr., Bill Cosby, and Peter Lawford sauntering in pajamas through supple tangles of long-legged Bunnies, shaking it up on the dance floor, prancing through the gardens, and always by the end of the evening plunging into the grotto, a delicious mass of wet bodies writhing in the froth. And hovering above them in the mist was Hef, in a silk bathrobe with pipe in hand, an airbrushed Dionysian demigod, smiling beatifically at what he had created.

★

Hugh Hefner perfected the Bachelor in Paradise lifestyle, but he certainly didn't originate it. Many single men who came to Beverly

Hills before him with enormous amounts of money at their disposal were hit by an epiphany: *I now have the resources to sleep with an unlimited number of fantastically attractive women.* And after a moment or two of struggling with the moral implications of this, concluded: *Why not?*

A long procession of starlets and star-fuckers made the pilgrimage to Charlie Chaplin's boudoir, and John Gilbert and John Barrymore threw orgiastic parties in their hilltop retreats. But it was Howard Hughes who perfected the assembly line approach when he bought RKO Pictures in 1948. The dashing multimillionaire-aviator had already dated virtually every major female star in Hollywood and bedded many of them, but with RKO he had the machinery of an entire movie studio at his disposal to funnel a steady stream of ambitious lovelies to his bungalow at the Beverly Hills Hotel. Hughes spent hours poring over magazines, circling fashion models and beauty queens, and scanning movies for hot-looking extras. A legion of private eyes spread out across the United States tracking the women down in their hometowns and taking more photographs for Howard to examine. The finalists were brought to L.A. and given screen tests that narrowed the field still further. Finally, a chosen few were ushered into Hughes's bungalow. All he had to do was dangle a contract in front of their fame-hungry eyes and they'd strip down to their panties before he had a chance to undo his collar button. *Like the man says: "Movies are your best entertainment."*

Once under contract to RKO, the girls were made to adhere to a strict schedule of acting lessons, photo sessions, and reconstructive dental work. Howard personally drew up customized hygiene and diet programs for each of his starlets. He considered them his property and was determined to protect his investment. Their phones were tapped; private detectives kept them under surveillance twenty-four hours a day, and whenever the starlets went out in public they were escorted by Hughes's operatives to make sure they did not fraternize with other men.

If a psychologist had been able to strap Hughes to a couch, he might have concluded that Howard had some control issues, and that this once introverted boy, who constantly changed schools as he moved around the country during his childhood, who never had a grounded home life, did not now know how to form deep and lasting relationships. *Maybe so, Doc*—one can imagine Hughes responding with a taunting grin—*but if you don't mind me asking, exactly how often are you getting laid?*

Hugh Hefner could not hope to match the scale of Hughes's Bachelor in Paradise operation, but Hefner refined the conceit into a complete way of life. He showed millions of American men that it's possible to build a self-enclosed pleasure dome, a realm of pure sensual delights, intoxicating tastes and textures, charismatic friends and endless frivolity, with a harem of fun-loving chicks on twenty-four-hour call.

Hefner created *Playboy* magazine on a kitchen table, in a tiny apartment on the South Side of Chicago, in 1953. It was the era of "the organization man"—an entire generation of American males had been molded into crew-cut briefcase-toting I-Like-Ike zombies by the conformist forces of the cold war. They lived in suburban tract homes that were barely distinguishable from those of their neighbors, ate the casserole recipes their wives had gleaned from morning cooking shows, and settled down in their living/death rooms after dinner with a scotch and water to watch *Leave It to Beaver, Mister Ed,* and *The Wonderful World of Disney* on their twelve-inch Zeniths. As they lay in bed at night beneath their electric blankets, staring up at the acoustic ceiling, their pulses raced, their lungs burned, and their chests ached for *something* . . . another war maybe, a catastrophe, something wild and out of control, something that would make them feel alive again.

Hefner gave it to them. He walked the tightrope with an uncanny sense of balance—creating photo spreads just racy enough to make men's blood roar as they furtively snagged an issue from a newsstand, but classy and tasteful enough to keep the authorities from cracking down. *Playboy* was an instant sensation. The first issue, featuring a centerfold of Marilyn Monroe, sold 50,000 copies. By 1971 circulation had skyrocketed to more than seven million. After divorcing his first wife in 1959, Hefner set about weaving his own myth as "Hef," the pajama-clad superplayboy who had turned his life into a never-ending Dionysian romp. He began throwing weekly parties at his Chicago office. He invited whatever celebrities happened to be in town and ran photos of the festivities in the magazine. He hosted his own TV talk show, *Playboy's Penthouse,* set in his ultrasleek bachelor pad equipped with a seven-and-a-half-foot round rotating bed and an Ampex video system to record the action that took place there. Each episode featured hip and happening guests like Lenny Bruce, Ella Fitzgerald, Nat King Cole, and, of course, hot and cold running chicks.

Playboy became one of many tributaries to the counterculture flash flood of the '60s. Most of the teenagers who flocked to San Francisco for the Summer of Love in 1967 had first been awakened to Dionysian possibilities when they happened upon Dad's *Playboys*, stashed under the cushions of the living room couch or in the bottom drawer of his bedside table. California became the epicenter of the sexual revolution, and Hef, always highly attuned to minute shifts in the zeitgeist, moved his command post west. *Playboy*'s corporate headquarters moved into a skyscraper in West Hollywood, and then into an elegant state-of-the-art complex in Beverly Hills. Hef bought a thirty-room quarry-stone Tudor country manor house with six acres of grounds in Holmby Hills and christened it the *Playboy* mansion. Although it lay just beyond the western border of Beverly Hills, the *Playboy* mansion became an integral part of the city's male culture and profoundly influenced dozens of wealthy bachelors who moved to Beverly Hills in the years that followed.

At the mansion in the 1970s, the Bachelor in Paradise life reached its apogee, walled off from the prying eyes, judgmental attitudes, and conventional concerns of the outside world. Time seemed to stand still there; the divisions between days melted and the afternoons and evenings stretched into one glorious unending holiday. There were parties every day now—all-male turkey dinners on Monday, cards on Wednesday, old movies on Friday, and first-run movies on Sunday, celebrity tennis tournaments on weekend afternoons, and then the superparties on New Year's Eve, Valentine's Day, Halloween, Super Bowl Sunday, and the theme parties like the Midsummer's Night Dream Party, for which the dress code was pajamas for the men and lingerie for the women. The mansion had a game room that surpassed the finest amusement park arcades, a movie theater appointed with plush leather seats and the latest projection and sound systems, lush gardens where one could wander off with a Playmate or two, a private zoo with more than 130 species of exotic birds—parrots, toucans, flamingos, and peacocks—wandering about the grounds, the largest redwood grove in Southern California, and of course, the silver-white mists of the grotto, where naked sirens waited with open arms. Jack Nicholson, Warren Beatty, Mort Sahl, and Rod Stewart bathed in those baptismal waters. James Caan saw no reason to return to the outside world. He actually lived in the mansion for a time during the '70s and slept with seventeen consecutive Playmates—a feat surpassed only by Hef himself. The Rolling Stones partied there for a week straight, and so on and so on and so on.

By the century's end, *Playboy* had acquired the respectability of a public institution, thanks to a rash of raunchy imitators like *Hustler, Swank, Jugs,* and *Screw,* and the hard-core pornography pumped into every American home via cable and satellite, which made Hef's fare look staid by comparison. The *Playboy* corporation had become a much-valued source of tax revenue for the city of Beverly Hills and a prominent civic booster that sponsored jazz concerts, cultural events, and made sizeable contributions to local charities.

Hef deftly repositioned himself not as a crass exploiter of women but as a patron of the arts and champion of feminist causes by sponsoring a series of television documentaries on landmark women, such as Frances Marion, a film pioneer and the most prominent screenwriter in silent movies. To assure that he did not become too respectable, Hef showed up at the documentary's premiere—held at the Writers Guild Theater in Beverly Hills and attended by many of the top writers, producers, and directors in movies and television—with a pair of twenty-two-year-old bleached-blond twins, Sandy and Mandy Bentley. Hef told reporters that Sandy and Mandy had allowed him to "see life afresh through youthful eyes."

If two pairs of youthful eyes can do that for you, imagine the possibilities of seven! By the time he attended a Friars Club roast a few months later, as the guest of honor, Hef had expanded his stable of blondes to a half-dozen plus one. Some found the spectacle of a seventy-five-year-old man having sex with women who were old enough to be his granddaughters embarrassing. Others thought it was grotesque, while others saw it as a victory of the human spirit, but no one could deny that Hugh Hefner was living the Bachelor in Paradise fantasy right out to the end.

"Bernie Cornfeld's great ambition was to live the life of Hugh," says Marc Wanamaker, a close acquaintance of the former mutual fund king. But Cornfeld discovered that it was much harder than it looked to re-create Hef's Eden.

In the 1960s, Cornfeld was known as the King of Europe's Cash. His Investors Overseas Services mutual fund had more than $2 billion in assets, and Bernie was personally worth more than $150 million. His empire collapsed like a house of cards in the early '70s amid charges of fraud. Cornfeld spent six months in a Swiss jail and while there he had plenty of time to think. *What am I busting my balls for? Lost most of my money, yeah, but I've still got $15 million. At forty-three, that should be plenty to live out the rest of my life in style.*

And he knew exactly the style he wanted. Cornfeld had partied at the *Playboy* mansion a number of times and was intimately familiar with all of the elements one needed to create *the life.* When he was set free, Bernie headed to Beverly Hills and moved into Grayhall, a 16,000-square-foot English country manor on an acre of land north of Sunset that looked like a scaled-down version of the *Playboy* mansion. Cornfeld immediately set about remodeling it. He moved a large four-poster bed with a sturdy mattress and heavy-duty springs into the master suite, covered the walls in red velvet, and installed a large mirror on the ceiling. He added a pool and a two-story cabana with a wet bar, then invited Hef over to advise him on the subtleties of grotto placement. (A powerful filtration system was a must.) Then he added a wing adjacent to the master bedroom suite into which he moved a half-dozen hard-bodied and hard-partying nymphets. His deal with the girls was simple: *You have the run of the house and can help yourself to anything in the kitchen and the bars. All I ask is that you be available to me, 24/7, capisce?* Bernie began dressing in pajamas and a silk bathrobe, took up pipe smoking, and held wild parties, movie screenings, and orgies.

And yet . . . it had the quality of a road show version of a Broadway hit—all the same songs and dances, but something was missing, the spectacle seemed stale. Marc Wanamaker served as a movie projectionist at many of the parties and recalls a disturbing undercurrent in them. "Nobody was there to see Bernie—Tony Curtis, George Hamilton, the producers and directors, these people who were supposedly his friends. They were there to meet other people and make connections of some kind. The girls were there to either land a rich man or—if they were actresses or musicians—to meet someone who could further their career. Even I was looking for something, I'm not sure what . . . an opportunity of some kind, like everybody else. Who are you going to meet? Maybe I would meet a producer and get involved in a film, or maybe I'd meet some great rich woman or something. But that never happened and after a while it got to be boring. And there was Bernie, alone. Alone with all these people around him. It wasn't sad, it was pathetic."

Fifteen million did not turn out to be enough to carry Cornfeld to the end of his days. He forgot one important element of the Hugh life: a media empire that generates fresh millions to support it. Bernie's Hugh Life evaporated in the late '80s when he ran out of money. He sold Grayhall and moved to England, where he died a few years later, a forgotten man.

Others who attempted to live out the Bachelor in Paradise fantasy found that it could lead beyond mere dissipation to degradation and even disgrace. When he took over Paramount Pictures in 1966, Robert Evans was a Hollywood wunderkind—Valentino handsome, erudite, and hipper than Our Man Flint. For the next six years he seemed to be bulletproof, pulling Paramount back from the brink of insolvency with hit after hit—*Rosemary's Baby, The Odd Couple, Love Story, The Godfather, Chinatown*—and turning it into the most successful studio in Hollywood. Evans bought an aging French Regency mansion on two acres of land just off Benedict Canyon in Beverly Hills and spent hundreds of thousands of dollars to remodel it into an *Architectural Digest* estate that reflected his new status as the ultimate player. When finished, it had a pool, tennis courts built by Gene Mako—then the premier designer of hard-surface courts—and a garden with more than two thousand rosebushes. Paramount installed a state-of-the-art movie theater with a sixteen-foot-wide screen and furnished the entire house in French antiques.

When Evans married Ali MacGraw, the ravishing star of *Love Story*, in 1969, his happy-ever-after life seemed complete. But almost as soon as he put the pieces together, it all began to fall apart. When MacGraw left for Texas to film *The Getaway* with Steve McQueen in 1972, she stopped taking Bob's phone calls. Evans flew down to the location and learned from director Sam Peckinpah that his worst fear had come true. Ali and Steve had embarked on a torrid affair. When she returned to L.A., MacGraw filed for divorce and claimed custody of their son, Joshua.

Ah, fuck it—Evans concluded. He had money, power, charisma, and the greatest bachelor pad in the Western Hemisphere—not as big as Hef's maybe, but far classier. Why not enjoy it? He embraced the bachelor life with a vengeance, filling his French Regency with gorgeous wild things and bowls of grass, ludes, and more white powder than they had in Aspen. Jack Nicholson—a vigorous exponent of *the life*—often stopped by to party.

Evans ordered takeout from Elizabeth "Alex" Adams, the infamous "Beverly Hills Madam," L.A.'s premiere flesh peddler from 1971 to the late 1980s. Adams lived in the hills above Sunset, on Doheny Drive, in a house full of paintings by Salvador Dali and Picasso. She could afford fine art because she ran a stable of 250 zipper-popping lovelies who commanded $1,000 to $1,500 per session from rock stars, record and studio executives, and visiting Saudi Arabians (including members of the royal family).

In the late '80s, Evans and many other Hollywood heavyweights shifted their business to Heidi Fleiss, the daughter of an L.A. pediatrician who had dropped out of high school and into one of Bernie Cornfeld's parties at Grayhall. As documentary filmmaker Nick Broomfield observed, "Heidi fell hopelessly in love with his [Bernie's] lifestyle." She became Cornfeld's main squeeze, and on Heidi's twenty-first birthday Bernie gave her a Rolls-Royce Corniche and $1 million in cash. But when Bernie's money dwindled, so apparently did Heidi's love. She'd gotten used to the high life and decided to finance it by going into competition with Adams. Since Bernie had been a steady customer it was fairly easy to poach some of Adams's top producers. Adams was old, fat, and uncouth, Heidi young, hot, and hip, so the male clientele quickly gravitated to the challenger. By the late '80s Heidi had stolen Adams's crown as the premier madam for the rich and famous. She bought a $1.5 million house off Benedict Canyon in Beverly Hills from Michael Douglas and raked in about $1 million in cash annually.

But while Fleiss got rich off of Bachelors in Paradise—and many duplicitous husbands—Evans's fortunes took a nosedive. *Prudent fi-*

nancial manager would not be the first words one would use to describe him. Fred Clapp, an LAPD vice squad officer who focused on high-class call girl rackets, preferred to call Evans "the biggest whoremonger in Hollywood." Whoremongering's expensive, so is cocaine, and by the '80s Bob didn't have the cash flow for either. He had given up his job as head of production at Paramount, thinking he would make more money as an independent producer with a piece of the profits of the movies he made. But his Midas touch failed him and he made a string of flops like *Marathon Man, Black Sunday, Players,* and *Popeye*.

In 1982 he staked everything on *The Cotton Club,* which would be shot by *The Godfather*'s director, Francis Ford Coppola. Evans put the movie together with independent financing, which meant he had to scramble to find chunks of cash from a patchwork of wealthy individuals. One person he turned to was Roy Radin, a coke dealer acquaintance of Bob's current girlfriend, Laynie Jacobs-Greenberger, who was a dealer herself. Radin never came up with any cash and Evans forgot about him, until Greenberger was later accused of murdering Radin, whose body had been found in a desert canyon. Radin was shot a number of times in the head and, as an added flourish, a stick of dynamite had been ignited in his mouth. Prosecutors hauled Evans in for questioning. He claimed to know nothing about Radin's death and was never charged with a crime. But his former mistress apparently knew plenty; she and three accomplices were convicted of murdering Radin.

Of course it all came out in the press, and if that wasn't bad enough, a few years later a bunch of former Hollywood hookers published a tell-all book, *You'll Never Make Love in This Town Again,* in which a former prostitute, Liza Greer, recalled visiting Evans's home when she was just sixteen. Another hooker, Alexandra Datig (called "Tiffany" in the book), came with her. Greer wrote that the two girls joined Evans in his famous screening room for drinks, Quaaludes, and cocaine. Then he led them into the bedroom for a three-way, in which Bob directed the action. "Tiffany, you touch Liza there . . . Liza, you lick Tiffany there." At the climactic moment, Evans said, "Tiffany, would you please piss on me?" She promptly complied.*

The destruction of his reputation was complete. The press ridiculed him, and frankly, he seemed to beg for it. Like a living portrait of Dorian Gray, Bob's Latin lover features had transmogrified during the years of abuse into those of a microwaved toad; he projected an aura not of glamour but of sleaze. Evans tried to keep up appearances, but with his dated hipster lingo, Robert Goulet hair, '70s sunglasses and wardrobe, he came off like a Terry Southern caricature of a two-faced Hollywood dealmaker. Even Bob wasn't buying the act anymore; he finally committed himself to a hospital because he feared he might commit suicide. He later rebounded from his depression, but Hollywood never again considered him to be a serious player.

But such cautionary tales did not discourage Norm Zadeh, perhaps because he had spent too many years wandering through a babeless wasteland, eking out a living as an untenured college professor and part-time backgammon hustler. Norm had thrust himself into every venue he could think of to meet women: bars, discos, singles groups, personal ads, even folk dancing classes. He managed to go out with a few girls, but they always broke it off after a couple of dates, telling him he was too needy, too self-sufficient, too emotional, too cerebral. *Christ!*

Then, on a visit to Beverly Hills, he received a divine revelation. He was hovering on the edge of the dance floor in the Beverly Hills Pips Discotheque and Backgammon Club, which was owned by real estate broker Stan Herman and none other than Hugh Hefner him-

*Evans threatened to sue the book's publisher, Dove. But the two parties apparently reconciled when Evans later struck a deal with Dove to publish an audiotape version of his autobiography.

self. Writhing about on the floor were the most amazinglicious women—right out of the pages of *Playboy*. And all of them—*every fricking one, look at that!*—dancing with guys twenty, thirty, even forty years older than them. *What are they doing with them?*—he wondered. Then it hit him. The answer was so simple he couldn't believe it had taken him so long to come upon it. Women love movies where the heroine falls in love with a penniless painter or writer because in real life it's a choice they rarely feel free to make. No, what women really wanted—Norm concluded—what they were really after was not sensitivity, romance, a hard body or huge dick; no, they were after one thing, and one thing only: moolah. They wanted the men who drove up in the Rolls-Royces, Jaguars, Ferraris, and Mercedeses, the men with stock portfolios thicker than the Los Angeles telephone directory. This revelation did not disgust or disillusion Norm; it came as a relief. Now he understood the rules; now he knew what he needed to do.

It took a while, but he finally discovered a lucrative use for his prodigious mathematical skills. In 1990, Norm registered as a broker and investment adviser and began raising money for hedge funds. His superb grasp of numbers allowed him to take full advantage of the biggest economic boom in American history. By 1994 he was managing more than $159 million, earning average annual returns of 29 percent and a personal income of more than $9 million a year.

He bought a house on Shadow Hill Way in Coldwater Canyon, above Sunset, for $1.7 million, and finally, at long last, the great sex drought came to an end. "After I started to go to strip clubs, my whole relationship with women changed," Norm says, his voice ringing with excitement. The strip club. What a fantastic innovation! There, the Summer of Love lives on and on and on. None of the game playing you have to endure in a singles bar; none of the false-faced, verbal Chinese water torture of a first date; not even the tired seduction rituals of the Pips club. Just straightforward, honest communication. Each party asking for exactly what they want and getting it. "There is no better way to meet good girls than to go to a strip club," Zadeh enthuses. "You can look at every girl and you can talk to them." His voice cracks, as if unable to quite believe the miracle of it. "I'm actually pretty good with women in the sense that I don't push them. I respect them and I'm very generous to them. I developed, if you don't mind me being a little immodest, a very good approach. I would hand these girls a thousand or fifteen hundred dollars, and that got their attention. They would say, 'You know, this guy's not bad!'

"You can pretty much go out with whoever you want. They're accustomed to rubbing their bodies against all kinds of different men, and looks are not all that important to them, so if a guy comes in and he's nice and respectful and clean and not in completely terrible shape, he's got an excellent chance, if he's generous, of going out with these girls, which to me is wonderful. It's like I'm in a candy store and I've got all the cash and I'm saying to myself, 'Well, let's see. I'm gonna be real nice to you. I'm gonna be so nice!' "

It was a stripper who inspired him to start *Perfect 10*. He was dining at the Four Seasons with a ravishing stripper friend who had tried out for *Playboy* and been turned down. She was heartbroken, her dream shattered. Norm smoldered. "She was a great-looking, all-natural girl, a very sweet girl," he explains. Yet she'd been rejected, and Zadeh knew damn well why: implants. They'd taken America by storm in the late 1980s. Now any woman could have huge firm Jayne Mansfield knockers; the things thrust skyward like the Grand Tetons even when a gal lay on her back, which made them ideal for photo spreads. *Playboy* and *Penthouse* began using more and more silicon-enhanced models, young men got used to jacking off to them until finally they began to prefer artificial breasts to real ones, even large, well-formed real ones, and all-natural full-figure girls were pushed off of the pages of the skin magazines almost altogether. Norm considered it an outrage, pressuring young women to deform themselves and put their health at risk for a fashion fad. His admiration for Hefner, a man who had done so much to shape his values and aspirations, curdled into disdain. "*Playboy* has damaged many, many women," he says bitterly, "by foisting upon them this vision of ideal beauty."

Then he decided to turn his anger in a positive direction. *What can I do? How can one man make a difference?* Thus the concept of *Perfect 10* was born. He hired photographers, editors, made deals with printers and distributors, and recruited young women from top modeling agencies. How much did it cost him? That depends on what day you talk to Norm. He told a *Los Angeles Magazine* reporter that he sunk $1.8 million in the first issue, then a few days later told a journalist from *U.S. News & World Report* he invested $2.8 million. Today, he claims to have invested more than $20 million in *Perfect 10* since its inception. (Zadeh's claim that the magazine has a circulation of 100,000 seems suspect, considering it's difficult to find it on many newsstands.) Whatever he's spending, it's a sweet little write-off for a man of his income, and one that provides many ancillary benefits.

Such as having a former *Playboy* Playmate of the Month show up at his door to audition for a photo spread. Norm couldn't fucking believe it; just a few short years ago he'd never even seen a Playmate in the flesh, and now here was one of his major fantasy throbs begging him, Norm Zadeh, the idiot, the nerd, for a job! Before he knew it her blouse was off. They jiggled slightly before him, goose bumps rising across her tan lines. *So what do you say, Norm, do I get the job?* He ran his tongue over the dry edge of his upper lip. "Your breasts look pretty good. . . . But are they real?" She stared steadily into his eyes as she sauntered over to him. *You want to feel them?*

"They were real all right," Zadeh says with a self-satisfied grin. "That's not the whole story, but that's all I'm going to tell you, because the rest of the story is a lot better!" He erupts in a high-pitched cackle.

To keep a constant stream of naked young things flowing over his threshold, Zadeh employs dozens of photographers and talent scouts whom he pays $1,000 a head for finding new girls in places as far away as Russia. It's an intelligence network that surpasses even that of Howard Hughes. Does Norm, like Hughes, develop an intense personal interest in his models? "Sure," he admits. "But I don't even like sleeping with some of them. It's just if I don't, they get upset." *The Bachelor's burden.*

Of course the final capstone to *the life* was the *Perfect 10* mansion, which he built in 1997 on seven acres of land in Beverly Park, one of the world's most exclusive subdivisions, at the top of San Ysidro Drive. His neighbors included Vanna White, Magic Johnson, Roseanne Barr, Rod Stewart, and Sylvester Stallone. The other homes were traditional European in style—Tuscan villas and French country manors. But Norm chose to build something radically different: a 16,000-square-foot postmodern, bone white modular mansion with twenty-five-foot ceilings and glass walls in many rooms that look out on neat rectangular lawns, a pool, tennis courts, a heated waterfall, and the surrounding hills.

It's the antithesis of Hef's moldy old English castle and the kind of house you would expect to encounter in a Jacques Tati movie entitled *Mr. Hulot Goes to Beverly Hills,* or *Mon Bachelor.* The gaping airplane hangar rooms with their blinding white walls and blond wood floors look like the halls of a postmodern museum, except no art hangs on the walls and almost no furniture takes up the floor space. There are very few personal items of any kind. A rectangle of black leather couch sits before a TV set flush into the blond-wood-paneled wall, and that's it, no surrounding bric-a-brac, no personal mementos or pictures. The bedrooms consist of little more than a square bed and a side table.

To enter the house, you must drive through a stainless steel gate that looks like the pod bay door of an intergalactic starship, then walk across a slab of cement to a monolith of beveled glass that serves as the front door. As you approach, the door swings open automatically. Norm greets you with a *Perfect 10* girl at his side. She wears long brown hair, khaki combat pants, and a sweatshirt. Norm's in his usual uniform of a black buttoned-down shirt and black pants, with one special flourish: a pair of peach loafers. He leads the way into the hollow rooms, his footsteps echoing through the adjoining chambers, and comes to a stop just outside a glass-walled transom that leads to another wing where a camera crew is busy with a *Perfect 10* shoot. Crew members wander past with pieces of equipment and the vexed expressions of those under a deadline. Through the glass walls a naked model is visible—a stunning brunette, her Cyd Charisse legs encased in black silk stockings and a wicked garter belt.

A photographer approaches Norm with some Polaroids of the girl. Zadeh studies the snapshots, which serve as a rough sketch of the portrait. "Yeah. I like the look. I like. I like."

"Tighter?" the photographer asks.

"Yeah, well, you should probably get a little closer."

"I am. I am."

"I like the outfit and I like the look. I like the makeup."

Relieved, the photographer hustles off.

Blond, olive-skinned Nickie Yager passes through. She wears jeans and a simple pullover. "So I'm seeing you tonight, okay?" Norm calls out to her.

"Yeah." She flashes a moist white smile. "Seven."

"It might be about seven-fifteen. Just call me."

Later, Amber Rangel wanders in, carrying several postal packages. She has dark brown hair and wears tight slacks and a T-shirt, but no shoes. Norm's eyes fasten on her painted toes. "Look at my little Amber's feet."

"I don't like my feet." She wiggles the toes.

Norm's eyes dilate. "You have the most beautiful feet in the world."

She giggles. "Thank you."

Without taking his eyes off them: "I mean, anybody that has feet that cute has to be a nice person. No, seriously, there is not a mean molecule in that body."

Giggle. "Thank you."

"Monika Zsibrita had these feet that were all kind of shmushed together and I never liked her feet at all and sure enough—"

This is a more in-depth exploration of her pedal extremities than Amber feels comfortable with. She picks up the packages. "Have to go mail these suckers."

"Okay, babe." Norm smiles as she hurries off. "Have a good

weekend." He sighs dreamily, then reflects on his newfound ease with *les femmes.* "I have a confidence now. I'm confident that I'm gonna do okay sexually, even if I'm not a major stud. I can massage them and make them feel good, and I'm confident that they will appreciate my understanding and compassion for them. I think I have a much better understanding of what turns women on and what worries them. I'm in a position now where they're at my mercy. They're calling me; I'm not calling them. It's not that I'm playing hard to get. I'm just too busy to almost care, and that's attractive to girls. It's very attractive to girls."

So is the fact that Norm offers them financial aid. How many is he actually supporting? "Probably about seven . . . actually eight that I'm supporting right now. Some are *Perfect 10* models, some are not. I give them enough money to live because they are not making it with whatever they are doing—whether it's modeling or whatever."

Norm Zadeh has achieved what so many men have wished for, if only for one fleeting orgasmic moment; he has penetrated the centerfold world, moved in, and set up house there. And yet . . . a worm wriggles in the apple. Despite all he's achieved he's still bedeviled by the world beyond these bleached white walls, a world that refuses to recognize his accomplishments, to finally accept and approve of him. People continue to betray and ridicule and say mean things about Norm, and it cuts him to the quick. The latest article in *Forbes,* for instance. The *Forbes* reporter called him a porn peddler. A porn peddler! When he doesn't even do full-frontal beaver shots like *Playboy,* let alone the hard-core cocksuckingcumonmyface sleaze that *Penthouse* and *Hustler* smear all over their pages these days. "I'll show them pornography," he bitterly vows, "if they want to go on some of these Web sites and look at five penises in these girls' butts and vaginas. That's pornography!"

And then one of his models had the audacity to threaten him with accusations that he committed certain, well . . . improprieties. Norm attempts to set the record straight. "I was supporting this girl for years," he explains. "I didn't even kiss her. After taking care of her for a couple of years, I finally wanted a hug and we negotiated a fair price for the hug because she's got a real problem with men. I was lying on the bed on my back, breathless, waiting for this—I've got clothes on. She comes and gives me a crisscross hug. Her boobs are not even on my body. You know, you understand what's going on here?"

A cooler mind might realize at this juncture that a full explanation of the facts might not be in his best interests, but Norm can't contain himself, his words race on. "Very clever for her to come up with this. So we go through a couple more months of new negotiations. Finally, I meet her price. She agrees to a hug. She says, 'Look, this is gonna be very hard for me to do. Lie on your stomach.' So I'm lying on my stomach. She gets on me like she's riding a horse. She gets on the small of my back 'cause she has horses, she likes horses, so I guess she's pretending I'm a horse. Then after she was sitting on my back like I'm a horse for a while, then she laid and rested her breasts on my back. Then after she did that for a while she felt comfortable enough to hug me. This is not sexual harassment if you support a girl for three years until you finally get hugged."

Satisfied he's cleared the air on that score, he returns to the subject of journalists. What really galls him is the way a *Barron's* writer played amateur psychologist, trying to imply, hell, damn near coming out and saying that something in Norm's childhood, some childhood trauma, has warped his relationships with women! *Outrageous!*

Norm seems sincerely unaware of how he circles back to childhood traumas again and again in his nonstop stream-of-consciousness monologues, all but drawing giant yellow arrows for journalists to follow. The other subject that Norm circles back to as often as he does his childhood—so often you can't help but wonder if there's a secret connection between the two—is Hef. And he circles back now, launching into a wrathful denunciation of his former idol that seems a little out of proportion with his alleged crimes. It is an outrage, an abomination and a disgrace the way Hef encourages young women to get implants, the way *Playboy* uses lighting tricks to hide the fat asses of some Playmates, the way Hef locks Playmates into exclusive contracts that hardly pay them a living wage. Then Norm's attack becomes personal. He points out that Hefner has recently admitted to experimenting with bisexuality in the context of group sex in the '60s and '70s. "That's a long time to experiment with guys if you're surrounded by beautiful girls," Norm says with bitter glee. "I personally think that *Playboy* is a scam, it's a facade; he doesn't really like women, he actually likes men. The reason I say that is because he has done many things to degrade women. . . ."

Norm leans forward slightly, voice dropping to a more confidential tone. "I saw a recent shot of Hefner's dick in a girl's mouth. You can see from the picture that he shot it himself. They're putting that up on these Web sites. His dick is not very big either. That's pretty funny." He whinnies. "I thought: *Yes! Great! I thought I was small, but not as small as Hef!"* He laughs again, long and hard, very hard. The free association continues: "Of course, I've seen some of those guys in those porn pictures that are huge. When you look at some of these Web sites you get, really, some of these guys are sickening, but you can be too big too, you know?" This thought reassures him. "You can be too big too."

Then he leads you into an adjoining room filled with desks and computer screens, past a *Perfect 10* girl in a formfitting T-shirt and pants, working at a console, to his own desk, which has a total of five computer screens. This is where Norm manages his hedge fund business. He searches through some files and produces a photo of Hef—or someone who looks like him, or a body with Hef's head grafted onto it—sticking his penis into a woman's mouth. "The coup de grâce," Norm says. "Look at his hand. He's pressing the button, he's pressing the flasher. Look at her, she's wide open. This is a staged shot. And his dick is not amazing."

As you walk back through the airplane hangar of a house toward the front door, he falls quiet. "I did not intend to build the house this big," he says at last. "I wanted like eight to ten thousand square feet, but they [the homeowners' association] wouldn't let me because they were afraid it would diminish the look of Beverly Park. It just kept growing and growing. I live here all alone. I feel lonely a lot. . . ." He sighs and shrugs. "Still, it's nice to have money so you can enjoy life. . . ." And then in a confidential tone: "I just built it for my dad. Just to piss him off."

His angry laughter echoes through the great chamber.

★ 4 ★

The East Side Kids

April 1, 2002. April Fools' Day. Couldn't pick a better date for the Last Roast, no sir. It's a small house—only about 300 people. Was a time when the roasts were held at the Beverly Hilton and drew audiences of more than a thousand. And the dais has thinned—just a half-dozen arthritic survivors from the old days. Not even the real old days when it all began on the Lower East Side, but from the recent old days of early television: a barely ambulatory Sid Caesar, a brittle Red Buttons, Jayne Meadows hidden behind a three-inch mask of makeup, Buddy Hackett, Norm Crosby, Rose Marie, and Larry Gelbart, a former writer for Caesar who went on to create hit Broadway shows (*A Funny Thing Happened on the Way to the Forum*), movies (*Tootsie*), and television series (*M*A*S*H*).

Milton Berle has presided over hundreds of roasts over the last fifty years, and been roasted himself at least a half-dozen times. An incorrigible scene stealer, driven by an uncontrollable compulsion to hog the limelight, in the past he has constantly interrupted the other comics with ad-libs and one-liners. More than one comedian has lost his cool, whirled, and shouted, "Shut up, Milton!" But there will be no such outbursts today because Milton Berle lies in a coffin at the foot of the stage. The long gray raincoat and fedora that became his signature costume in later years have been draped over the casket's highly polished wood. "The Thief of Bad Gags," "Mr. Television," "Uncle Miltie" has been silenced at last.

Don Rickles, who rose to prominence in the 1960s by adopting Berle's razor-sharp insult humor, steps up to the podium. He glances at the coffin, then fixes a pointed gaze on Berle's wife, Lorna. "I would like to be paid for this."

Red Buttons follows, noting that Rickles is "the greatest argument against human cloning."

Next up, Larry Gelbart, who observes that Berle "had a propensity for giving other people's material a new home."

The audience laughs warmly but without true enthusiasm. Despite a valiant effort to marshal forth the irreverent high spirits of the once great roasts, a malaise hangs over the crowd. They are burying not only a friend but also a way of life that started on the Lower East Side of Manhattan at the beginning of the twentieth century and finally died here, with this man, on the opposite end of the continent, at the dawn of the twenty-first century. In the back of the old comics' eyes, terrible doubts writhe. *The Friars Club. My god, what's going to happen to the Friars?*

The day of reckoning, so long feared and anticipated, has arrived at last.

"The big problem is getting younger people in show business to join," says the current abbot of the Friars Club, Larry King.

It's the summer of 2000. Milton Berle will not die for another twenty-one months. Berle is the abbot emeritus of the California Friars, and for the past fifty years he has been the driving force behind the club—organizing most of the roasts, special events, and charity fund drives, and presiding over the marathon bridge and gin rummy games in the card room. But Berle is not the drawing card he used to be, and the club's in trouble. Membership has plummeted from 1,300 people fifteen years ago to fewer than 500 today. So the board of directors pressed Larry King into accepting the position of abbot, in the hope that the popular talk show host has enough star power to draw new blood into the club.

Was a time when the Friars didn't have to worry about that. Was a time when they had to beat new applicants off with a stick. A person had to be sponsored by a Friar before he could apply to become a member, and a committee scrutinized each application to ascertain if the candidate was Friar material. In those days the Friars was the hottest private club in Beverly Hills, where the greatest wits of a generation—Groucho Marx, Jack Benny, Milton Berle, and George Burns—gathered to exchange legendary barbs over epic games of bridge; where the world's biggest movie stars—Bob Hope, Mickey Rooney, James Cagney, Jimmy Stewart, Gene Kelly, Gary Cooper, Humphrey Bogart—clambered for a chance to be insulted with rapier-sharp one-liners at the infamous roasts; where the members of the Rat Pack—Frank Sinatra, Dean Martin, Sammy Davis Jr., Joey Bishop, and Peter Lawford—drank, smoked, bragged about the broads they banged, and busted each other's balls in the silver-blue smoky aura of the Camelot years.

But those days are long gone. Now the Friars will take anybody with a pulse and the $1,000 initiation fee—well, the fee anyway, the pulse is negotiable.

Larry King felt honored when the Friars asked him to serve as abbot. His idols—Alan King, Steve Allen, and Frank Sinatra—had all held the position; he didn't see how he could refuse. But reviving interest in the club has been an uphill battle . . . maybe, King reluctantly admits, even a losing one. "For some reason, the younger people, they look at the club as . . . They're not as much interested in the heritage of the business as the previous generation was. There's no camaraderie anymore."

But Friars keep trying. For instance—Frank More, director of membership, explains—the club's putting on an exciting event for new members next week. "You gotta come," More insists. "We're going to have live music—a tribute to Motown that'll be utterly fantastic." Knockoff bands will perform the hits of The Temptations and The Supremes, and More promises a star-studded crowd that will include Drew Carey, Matthew Broderick, Daryl Hannah, Gary Busey, Anthony Michael Hall, and Dan Aykroyd. "It's going to be an unbelievable evening!"

The Friars Club is located on the corner of Charleville and Little Santa Monica Boulevard, just a stone's throw away from the Peninsula Hotel. Designed to resemble an eighteenth-century French country villa, the drastically chic Peninsula has usurped the Beverly Hills Hotel's position as the most prestigious social venue in the city. All night and every night, the horseshoe-shaped stone-tiled driveway of the Peninsula is crammed with caravans of BMWs, Rolls-Royces, Bentleys, Ferraris, Lamborghinis, stretch limo Mercedeses, and the most coveted new set of status wheels—stretch Humvees. They roll up to the hotel's awninged entrance where white-uniformed doormen part great monoliths of glass to admit the biggest stars and power brokers in the entertainment industry.

Despite a new coat of cream-colored paint, the Friars' neo–art deco facade pales by comparison. Its aerodynamic superstructure was as svelte and ultramodern as a Boeing 707 when the building first rose toward the palm-fringed sky back in 1961. But that was almost half a century ago. Today, the 25,000-square-foot building is about as cutting edge as an *Our Man Flint* movie.

On Motown Night, a red carpet stretches along the sidewalk to the club's glass doors. Before the doors stands a trio of security men with black suits, dark moussed hair, and walkie-talkies. They hover watchfully, eyes keenly surveying the landscape, as if they expect the Peninsula's crush of limousines and attending paparazzi to execute a sharp U-turn and head their way any moment. At present, the only people in front of the club are four middle-aged overweight autograph seekers who hover at the edge of the velvet ropes that guard the sanctity of the red carpet, arms tightly gripping their autograph portfolios as they eagerly await the arrival of the promised celebrities.

Inside, things aren't much livelier. The decor of the ballroom is strangely schizophrenic, a delirious pastiche of early 1960s Morris-Lapidus-Fontainebleau-Hotel-ultramodern and an Elks Club in Des Moines. The bar is the epitome of *Ocean's Eleven* chic: long and curved, its rim padded with a succulent lip of tan leather. Beyond it is an elevated stage like you'd find in a high school assembly hall, with an oversize microphone on a stand. A blue banner dangles haphazardly from the far wall with gold letters spelling out the Friars' motto: "*Prae Omnia Fraternitas,*" which means "Before all things—brotherhood."

About twenty people meander through the huge room—older Jewish couples for the most part, veterans of the garment and jewelry industries, doctors, and lawyers who bought memberships decades ago for the status and glamour value. But there are also a few young single men—entry-level members of the entertainment industry who thought this would be a good place to network and now wander about with perplexed expressions and the slow-dawning realization that they've made a dreadful mistake. As the evening progresses the place fills up with more elderly people and a few perplexed young ones. But the advertised celebrities never materialize, with the exception of an enfeebled Steve Allen (who will also be dead in a few months). The tables that bear reservation cards for Paramount Pictures, Warner Brothers, Fox Studios, and "The Media" remain empty.

"To be honest," Larry King sighs wearily, "the future is questionable. We're doing our best . . . I don't want to be the last abbot, but we can't continue to have more members dying than joining. . . . When Milton Berle goes, a big part of the club will go with him. It's gonna be a tough day."

But in the summer of 2000 that day is almost two years in the future, and every afternoon in the Friars' ballroom an ember of the way it used to be still glows.

Now ninety-two, Berle is not too steady on his feet and fragile as a dry twig. But he can still be found in the ballroom every afternoon holding court before an entourage of elderly showbiz veterans—all of them men. Many of them, like Buddy Arnold, Hal Kanter, and Irving Brecher, once wrote for Berle. Their hair is white, or bears the unnatural hues of artificial dyes, or is store bought; their teeth are either long and yellowed, the roots exposed by eroding gums, or brilliant white, ruler-straight dentures. All of them are immaculately dressed in suits and ties, or polo shirts and slacks; their nails manicured and lacquered, the air surrounding them rich with the scent of cologne.

Milton's been sitting in the same spot for four decades: to the left of the bar, under a painting of the great Al Jolson, in a big overstuffed horseshoe chair, next to a multiline telephone. For years he booked sports bets on the phone, but he doesn't follow sports much anymore. *The players these days. A new set of faces every year. Who can keep track of them? Sammy Sosa. What kind of name is that? Sounds like a fag hairdresser. DiMaggio, Mantle, Yogi Berra—now those were ballplayers.*

These days the phone is used to settle arguments with his entourage over a past that's slipping away from them. "What the hell was the name of that play?" Berle raises a trembling hand to push the tortoiseshell glasses back up his nose. They once fit him well but now have grown huge, covering his cheekbones. "It opened at the Booth Theater and starred Anne Bancroft and Henry Fonda."

"*On Golden Pond*?" one of the entourage ventures.

"No," Milton growls with annoyance, more at his own failing memory than at his friend, "that was a movie with Katharine Hepburn."

"It was a play first."

"I know, but that's not what I'm . . . ah!" Milton waves off further explanation. A strand of snow-white hair droops over his pallid forehead. Once the hair was jet-black and paved immaculately to the contours of his skull by gleaming layers of pomade. Now it's thin and as finely spun as cotton candy. His eyes suddenly brighten behind their huge panes of glass. "Abe will know." Berle tugs at the beige sweater beneath his tan cashmere sport jacket and reaches for the phone.

Punches the numbers unsteadily. Listens for a moment, then emits an irritated sigh and growls into the receiver. "Abe, you putz, where are you? Call me back when you get in, it's important."

The afternoon game in the third-floor card room has broken up. A dozen elderly men exit the elevator in the foyer and file into the ballroom. Some wander over to the tables for an early dinner; others—including Dick Van Patten, former star of the hit television series *Eight Is Enough*—join the ranks of Berle's entourage, where the talk has turned to a favorite subject: Uncle Miltie's schlong. The dimensions of Berle's penis have long been a cherished Hollywood legend, but cherished nowhere more than here at the Friars. The jokes and anecdotes begin to flow, one after another after another.

"This is a true story," says Dick Van Patten. "You remember Forrest Tucker, the actor from *F Troop*? Well, he was very well hung also. And people were always speculating on who was bigger, Forrest or Milton. Finally, they said, 'We're going to settle a bet, right here at the Friars Club.' They got Milton and Forrest—everybody was there, Don Rickles and George Burns, and all the rest—and Forrest pulls his out first. Then Milton lets his out, and it gets longer and longer, much longer than Forrest's by far, and he's still letting it out! Finally Buddy Hackett says, 'Milton, hold it, just pull out enough to win the bet!' " The punch line, which most of them have heard before, is greeted with a healthy round of laughter. "That's the honest-to-god truth. And it happened right here at the Friars Club."

They continue—comparing Milton's member to the Washington Monument, the Empire State Building, and speculating that the Holland Tunnel might be a tight fit. The men greet each new punch line with a roar of unhinged frivolity. The first couple of anecdotes are amusing, but by the fourth or fifth Johnson joke queasiness sets in as you realize they're strangely obsessed with the subject. It's almost as if the fixation on Milton's massive member has grown in direct proportion to the club's declining potency as a social institution.

Finally, the peter preoccupation exhausts itself, and the talk segues to the fabulous broads the men banged, or didn't but desperately wanted to. The cataracted eyes brighten with memories of a time when the juices flowed fast and furious.

"Hey Milton, tell them about Pola Negri."

"Pola Negri, sounds like a bottled water."

"She was the original vamp, in silent movies, ya moron! Milton nailed her. Didn't ya, Milton?"

Milton smiles. "We toured on the Keith circuit together, in 1932. I was twenty-six, good-looking; she was thirty-five, still a knockout. It was a long tour, one thing led to another, and we ended up sharing the same toothbrush. You might say I became intimately familiar with her back molars." The group erupts in laughter. "At the end of the tour we went our separate ways. Six months later I pick up the paper and what do I see? A picture of Pola Negri with Hitler. How do you like that? She dumped me for the Führer."

"And he only had one nut!"

The men roar. The laughter has triggered Berle's adrenals. He's sitting taller in the overstuffed chair now, the wisps of his white hair tickling the chin of Jolson on the painting behind him. He launches into another anecdote about the time Al Capone asked him to headline at the opening of a new club in Chicago.

"Al Capone requested you *personally*?" one member of the entourage who has not heard this tale before exclaims in disbelief.

"Sure." Berle's eyes burn intensely, the overhead lights illuminating flecks of dandruff and faint blue-gray fingerprints on the lenses of his oversize glasses. "Remember, back then I was Milton Berle. . . ."

The phrase does something to him. As the others continue, interrupting one another, eager to grab the spotlight with stories of their own, his gaze grows introspective and melancholy. At each new outburst of hilarity, his mouth arches up to simulate a smile, but the eyes show no sign of comprehension. They have drifted away. To the old old days. When he was Milton Berle. When this club was the domain of giants like Benny, Burns, Groucho and Harpo, Georgie Jessel, Eddie Cantor, Danny Kaye, the Ritz Brothers. . . . Oh, if these walls could talk, what memories they'd give voice to. The one-liners, the comebacks and toppers, like bullets ricocheting off rocks in a Hollywood western. Biiing! Banggg! Bazzziiing!

He remembers it more clearly than what he had for breakfast this morning. The tension in the air when they sat down together, like fighters entering a ring, sizing one another up. Jessel was the fastest ad-libber; Groucho the nastiest; Kaye the freshest; Burns the driest wit; Benny the subtlest. . . . A few tentative probes, a jab or two, then someone would connect and unleash a breathtaking combination. Anything could set it off. The most mundane subject. Like cigars. Groucho smoked only the finest; Burns preferred cheap El Productos and enjoyed exhaling in Groucho's direction to get a reaction.

Groucho grimaced. "Don't you ever inhale?"

"Not while I'm sitting next to you, Groucho."

"That must be a Lawrence Welk cigar."

"What is a Lawrence Welk cigar, Groucho?"

"A lot of shit with a band around it."

Milton urged Burns to try one of his expensive hand-wrapped Cubans. George asked how much they cost. When Milton told him, Burns grimaced. "Before I smoked it, I'd have to fuck it first."

Oh, it was a beautiful thing. Like watching the 1927 Yankees grind the Pittsburgh Pirates into sawdust.

The boys of the round table. They were more than colleagues; they were blood brothers, bound together by a common background and dream. All of them the sons of European Jews who had fled the poverty and virulent anti-Semitism of the Old World for the promise of the new one. These sons of rabbis, tailors, and haberdashers rode the magic carpet of American show business out of the cold-water tenements of the Lower East Side, Harlem, Brooklyn, and the Bronx all the way to the enchanted Hills of Beverly. No more shtetls, no more ghettos or pogroms, no more living in fear as second-class citizens. Here they resided in plush homes with broad green lawns and sky blue swimming pools, and actually became the ruling elite. How did it happen? they silently wondered as they sat together at the Friars, blowing cigar smoke and cracking wise. It had all seemed to unfold like a fantastic dream.

Groucho's real name was Julius. His father, Simon Marrix, emigrated from Germany to become a barely successful tailor on New York City's Lower East Side. Eddie Cantor was born Isidore Iskowitz. His mother died when he was not quite two and his father abandoned him, so he was raised by his grandmother, Esther Kantrowitz, a Russian Orthodox Jew. She eked out a living as a street peddler, hawking candles, spools of thread, and other sundries.

George Burns began life as Nathan Birnbaum. He shared a one-room apartment with his parents and nine brothers and sisters at 95 Pitt Street in Manhattan. Nathan's father—a helper in a kosher butcher shop—died of influenza when Nathan was six. George Jessel was born in the Bronx. His father fell ill when George was nine; the boy was forced to quit school and find a job to help support his family. Jack Benny was the only one who didn't come from New York, but otherwise his background was the same. He was born Benjamin Kubelsky, the son of Polish immigrants who settled in a lower-class section of Waukegan, Illinois, where his father owned a haberdashery store.

They slept in stifling, windowless rooms, two, three, or four to a mattress; crept down drafty hallways in the middle of the night in hole-riddled socks to reeking toilets that every tenant on their floor shared; bathed in tin washtubs, in the same cold brown water their siblings had used before them; played stickball in the teeming streets, in air thick with the scent of sweat, drying laundry, and raw sewage.

They sought deliverance from this hellscape through the mystical portal of American showbiz. And the biz in those days was vaudeville—the nation's first form of mass entertainment. But unlike the assembly line product cranked out by the Hollywood studios today, vaudeville bristled with vitality, unpredictability, and an eye-popping diversity that reflected the great melting-pot society at the dawn of the twentieth century.

The most prestigious vaudeville theaters in the country were in

New York: Hammerstein's Victoria, the Hippodrome, and the Palace. For just one thin dime the children of the East Side could step through towering bronze doors and be transported to an enchanted realm of vaulted gold-leaf ceilings, massive crystal chandeliers, gold-braided curtains, and bubbling fountains. They lived like sultans for two whole hours, enthroned on velvet seats as the greatest entertainers the world had ever assembled performed for them. There were the dramatic actors—Lillie Langtry, Alla Nazimova, John Barrymore, Sarah Bernhardt; the singers and dancers—Lillian Russell, George M. Cohan, Pat Rooney; the magicians like Harry Houdini, "the handcuff king," who could make a live elephant disappear before your very eyes. And then there were the comics: the Three Keatons, Leon Errol, Marie Dressler, W. C. Fields, Ed Wynn; and Fred Karno's ensemble of English comedians, which included Charlie Chaplin and Stan Laurel.

Julius, Nathan, and Isidore sat in the peanut galleries of those New York palaces drinking in the exalted realm beyond the footlights through wide excited eyes. They knew almost immediately that they wanted to be part of that incandescent world. But how could a threadbare Jewish kid, reeking of the mold and urine stench of the tenements, leap the great chasm that stretched between the gallery and the stage? Impossible. Couldn't be done. *You're dreaming, pal.*

But then they saw *Him*. Al Jolson. The Great Jolie—King of American Showbiz. He was billed as "The World's Greatest Drawing Card." No brag, just fact. Jolson danced, did dialects and imitations, performed comedy and drama with equal facility. He mesmerized audiences with his unlimited energy and boundless versatility. "There is no other performer who holds such an absolute dictatorship over his audience," Alexander Woollcott wrote.

"Al Jolson wasn't just a musical comedy star," Eddie Cantor later said. "The Great Al was an American institution."

And yet this dynamo, this *American* institution, had the same humble beginnings as Cantor and the other East Side Kids who hung on his every gesture. He had been born in Russia in 1886 as Asa Yoelson. His father, Rabbi Moshe Reuben Yoelson, brought the family to America when Asa was a young child.

"Jolson's success on stage, screen, radio and phonograph was a triumph unimaginable for the son of an Orthodox clergyman," Sean Levy has astutely observed in his book, *King of Comedy*. "Asa Yoelson had won over the goyim, and so long as he could caper up and down that magical riser, he could be a celebrant of his own acceptance into American society. The applause of American audiences scoured the Old World from his skin, and he emerged as a new kind of performer. . . .

"Jolson dazzled audiences of all ethnic compositions, but his act was especially appealing to Jews. They knew that the immigrant story—a primal upheaval early in life followed by a long quest for acceptance by a large, suspicious public—was at the core of Jolson's hunger for applause. Jolson's career became a kind of hallmark of the American Jewish experience, especially in the eyes of those who followed him to the stage."

And follow him they did. But success did not come easily to any of the East Side Kids. They struggled for years, living out of steamer trunks, on dusty trains and in cheap rooming houses, working the small time, the Gus Sun circuit, in all the backwater towns of the Midwest, South, East, and West. They changed their stage names, changed their partners, honed their routines, and slowly, through a painful, monotonous process of trial and error, formed personas that audiences responded to. Gradually they worked their way up to the medium time, the Pantages and Orpheum circuits, then the big time, the Keith-Albee circuit, and finally they reached the pinnacle of American showbiz, the Palace Theater on Broadway and Forty-seventh Street.

Milton Berle was ten to fifteen years younger than the others. The last one in the water, just in time to catch the tail end of the wave. Momma had the dream first, then force-fed it to him—without her he would never have set eyes on Beverly Hills.

Halloween night, 1914. Six years old, living in a railroad apartment at 957 Tiffany Street in the Bronx. His parents couldn't afford a store-bought costume for him, so he got hold of a pair of his father's pants and some shoes, which he put on the wrong feet. A derby, a cane, a little shoe polish below the nose, and—*voilà!*—he became Charlie Chaplin. A perfect scale model of the little tramp—that's what a neighbor said. He told Milton's mother about a Charlie Chaplin look-alike contest that was going to be held at a movie theater in Mount Vernon. First prize was a silver loving cup. "You should enter Milton. I bet he could win."

Genuine silver. That had to be worth a nice hunk of change. So Momma hustled him onto a streetcar the next day and they rode out to Mount Vernon and—what do you know?—he won! It had cost a whopping forty cents in streetcar fares to get there. Momma was cleaned out, so they walked home. It took all night and half the next day, but Sarah Berlinger didn't mind. When they finally got to the apartment, she proudly placed the cup in the center of the kitchen table. It turned out to be tin, painted over to look silver, and was worth only a few cents, but to Sarah it was far more valuable than money. She saw it as proof that someone in the family had talent. "When I took the contest she saw a door opening," says Berle, "and she was determined to get her whole family through it to where it was safe and warm."

For as long as Milton could remember, their life had been precarious and cold. His father, Moses, was a sharp dresser, charming and affectionate to his wife and five children—but a good provider he was not. He kept a little notebook filled with get-rich-quick schemes, but none of them ever materialized. Moses drifted from one job to another—painter, traveling salesman, night watchman—and his family hustled from one cold-water railroad flat to another, always one step ahead of their creditors. Four times they were evicted and found themselves standing in the street with all of their worldly possessions—a couple of banged-up chairs, the scuffed kitchen table, a dresser that held all of their frayed clothes, and a cracked vanity mirror—all of it vomited onto the sidewalk. "An eviction is something that stays with you all of your life," Berle says. "I still grow cold and sick thinking about it. To suddenly find your whole life piled up in the street. . . .

You're torn between protecting what's yours and wanting to run away and hide in shame."

Sarah Berlinger was determined that the fourth eviction would be their last. If Moses couldn't provide for them, then her talented son would. She enrolled Milton in dance classes and got him a job as a song plugger in a music store. Then she found him a pretty young girl to perform with and booked their song-and-dance act at the many fraternal halls that thrived in those years: the Beaver Club, the Elks, Masons, Knights of Pythias—he played them all for anywhere from three to five dollars a performance. A talent scout spotted him, and he landed a part in a juvenile musical review that played a small-time circuit in Philadelphia.

His big break came in 1920. The Shuberts decided to revive *Floradora,* a musical review that had been a hit twenty years earlier. Twelve-year-old Milton was recruited to be part of the "Baby Sextette," six boys and girls who reprised the hit song "Tell Me Pretty Maiden." They previewed in Atlantic City, Philadelphia, and Washington, D.C., then opened on Broadway. He had made the big time before his bar mitzvah!

Opening night on the Great White Way. The audience was packed with Gotham's glitterati: critics, vaudeville stars, even opera singers. Backstage, Milton's pale tuxedo was drenched in perspiration. For the rest of his life the flop sweat would never leave him. He took off his top hat, wiped the dampness from the band, then noticed it smudged his white gloves, sighed, and replaced the hat. Suddenly, Momma appeared at his side and drew him away from the others. Her long chin pressed close as she whispered, "When you start the number, what foot do you step out on?"

"My right one." It was an odd question. He'd been performing the routine flawlessly for weeks now. Did she think he might suddenly forget?

She placed her two mannish hands on his shoulders and looked him straight in the eye. "Tonight, start on the other foot."

Milton didn't know why she wanted him to do that. It sounded like lunacy. He'd ruin the number and his career. But Momma was adamant. "Do I ever give you bad advice?" He looked into her unyielding gaze and realized he had no choice.

And so he stepped onto the stage on his left foot, completely out of sync with the other boys, and for the first time heard it: that terrifying, awe-inspiring sound of two thousand people roaring with laughter. Like a single great beast out there in the dark beyond the footlights, the reverberation of it rippling through his blood. They kept right on laughing all through the number, and soon he found himself playing to it, accenting his awkwardness, pretending that he was trying but unable to match his actions to the others. He exited to wild applause and found a livid J. J. Shubert waiting for him backstage. Shubert unleashed a torrent of invective, called Milton a "little monster," and accused him of ruining "a Shubert opening night"! Milton burst into tears and, as Momma had coached him, claimed he'd been nervous and confused. "Never mind excuses!" Shubert thundered. "Through the whole number they laughed." Then the great producer slyly lowered his voice and asked, "Can you do it again tomorrow night?"

Momma had taught him the value of laughter—like money in the bank—and how to steal a scene. Forget being a good trouper, a team player—only the audacious ones rise to the top.

And Momma's audacity knew no bounds. Now that she had a son in a Broadway show, a Shubert production no less, Sarah wasted no time building relationships throughout the theatrical district, relationships she didn't hesitate to exploit. Which is how they ended up backstage at the Palace, where Momma barged into Eddie Cantor's dressing room and forced Milton to do his imitation of the great comedian. "Go ahead, Milton, show Mr. Cantor how terrific you do him." It wasn't all that terrific really. He hopped around a lot, singing "Yes, We Have No Bananas," patting his hands together and rolling his eyes like an epileptic. Cantor stared at them as if they were a couple of straitjacket cases. When Milton finished, Cantor shooed them back out the door. "That's very nice, kid. Thank you for coming."

Undeterred, Sarah Berlinger next stormed the Winter Garden, where the great Jolson himself was doing a concert. She was on excellent terms with the doorman, so when Sarah explained that little Milton desperately wanted to see his idol and was so disappointed to discover the show was sold out, the doorman waved them through so they could watch from the wings. Momma led him through the darkness of the left wing, stepping around curtains and ropes, ducking under sandbags, until finally they had a clear view of the brilliantly lit stage where the Great Al was finishing a rendition of "I'm Just Wild About Harry."

Milton's thighs trembled; he couldn't believe it, here he was, not ten feet away from him, close enough to see the rivulets of sweat rolling down the burnt cork makeup of Jolson's black face. His mind flashed to an incident a couple of weeks ago. He and Poppa boarded an elevated train to go into Manhattan. They were just settling into their seats when a group of men in black suits and hats got on. They had bushy beards as dark as their suits and long curls that spilled down over their ears. The lines on Poppa's forehead cut deeper and his lips curled in around his teeth as he got to his feet. "Come on." He led the way to another car. As they settled into their new seats, Poppa emitted a sigh of relief and explained that they weren't "that kind" of Jew.

Milton watched Jolson crank the song to a feverish finale: "And he's just wild about, cannot do without, he's just wild aboooout meeeeee!" The audience bolted to its feet, the applause like a herd of buffalo stampeding through the theater; and the shouts, the ecstatic cries, like a band of wild Injuns pursuing them. Jolson thrust his arms out to accept the accolade and Milton thought: *This. This is who I want to be.*

Jolson waved to the crowd for quiet, then finally silenced them with his famous two-finger whistle. "You ain't seen nothing yet!" he said, and then launched into "Swanee," which he had introduced a year before in the hit show *Sinbad.* The hairs on the back of Milton's neck rose, and he completely forgot why they had come here, until Jolson finished the song on one knee with his arms thrust out to the ecstatic crowd. Momma's hand gripped the base of Milton's neck, her voice cutting through the applause like a knife. "Now!"

She shoved him hard. He stumbled forward, regained his footing, and found himself standing on an immense plain of blinding bright stage, the dizzying chasm of the audience before him. The clapping stopped and an eerie silence fell over the theater. Jolson turned to see what had caused it, and Milton nearly wet himself. Audiences adored the Great Al, but his fellow performers lived in fear of his Old Testament–size temper. Jolie's clown-white lips spread into a Cheshire grin, but his white-rimmed eyes weren't smiling as they focused on Milton, the irises smoked like dry-ice pellets. Milton wanted to turn and run for it, but he felt the stern unyielding immensity of Momma behind him and dared not retreat.

"Well, well," Jolson said jovially, playing to the crowd. "Looks like we have a visitor tonight. How about that, folks?" The audience laughed appreciatively. "What brings you here, sonny? Tell Jolie."

Milton stammered that he did an imitation of him. Jolson blinked—checkmated by a twelve-year-old. He didn't dare crush this kid in front of thousands of fans, though Milton could see by the flare of his nostrils that he wanted to. Instead he turned toward the orchestra pit and graciously called for the conductor to play "April Showers." Milton threw himself into it, trying to ignore the quiver in his throat as he sank to one knee and belted out a nasal approximation of that famous voice. The audience applauded, more for his chutzpah than for his talent. Jolson, still grinning, put a fatherly hand on his shoulder—"Well, that was just great, sonny, just great"—and shoved him back into the wing.

Momma blustered her way past the irate theater manager and they escaped to Seventh Avenue before Al could finish his set and bring the Wrath of Jolie down upon them. As they made their way down the sidewalk, disappearing into the river of pedestrians, Momma said, "You were good, Milton, but I've heard you do him better."

No Broadway producers offered starring roles to Milton after his unauthorized appearance at the Winter Garden, but the invasion of Eddie Cantor's dressing room paid off. The older comedian invited the boy to lunch at the New York Friars Club. The Friars Club! Milton could hardly believe it was happening as Cantor walked him through the awninged entrance of "the Monastery" on Forty-eighth Street. It did indeed resemble a church, one of those great cathedrals in Europe: marble walls and Corinthian columns rising to a high arched ceiling, an ornately carved oak doorway ahead of them. He was standing in the Pantheon of American showbiz!—treading over the same polished ground that Victor Herbert, Raymond Hitchcock, Will Rogers, Sam Harris, Sophie Tucker, David Belasco, Pat Rooney, Joe Frisco, and Lew Dockstader walked upon.

The Friars was established by the Press Agents Association in the autumn of 1904 and quickly expanded its membership to include theater owners, actors, and producers. Jewish performers flocked to it because few other private clubs in Manhattan would accept them. But unlike today, when the club will take any warm body that has a $1,000 initiation fee, the Friars only admitted performers who had achieved a high level of success—small-timers need not apply.

Milton felt especially honored when he and Cantor stepped out of the elevator and into the hushed quiet of the oak-paneled dining room. A group of men sat at a white-clothed table at the far end of the room, half obscured by a cloud of blue-gray tobacco smoke. Cries of welcome greeted Cantor, and as Milton followed him into the acrid mist he began to recognize the faces . . . George M. Cohan, Fred Allen, Gentleman Jim Corbett, and Enrico Caruso. Cantor took hold of Milton's shoulder and drew him close to the faces, looming large as the sculptures of Easter Island, and said, "Fellas, I'd like you to meet a friend of mine, Milton Berlinger. He just opened in his first Broadway show."

The rest of it passed in a smoky blur, big hands jutting toward him, a flurry of congratulations, his own tremoring voice, high as a girl's as he answered their questions. A chair slid toward him. "Here, Milton, have a seat." He never moved from it for the rest of the meal. Sat there in stunned silence as the men traded barbs, puns, and shoptalk.

"Enrico," Cantor baited the famous opera singer, "you speak English like your boat won't dock until Thursday."

"That's my joke!" Fred Allen snapped.

"No," someone else interjected, "it's Willie Howard's joke."

The words were witty and graceful; the men slipped in and out of dialects as they traded stories about their life in the theater and the fantastical acts they played with. He sat there drinking in the raucous laughter, pulse racing, wanting desperately to be a part of it, to sit at this table not as a guest but as a full-fledged member, trading jokes, stories, and mock insults. Vowed silently to himself that very afternoon that he would one day.

But to do that, he would have to make his mark in vaudeville as something much more substantial than a member of a chorus in a musical review. And so, like Cantor had, and Benny, Burns, Jessel, and the Marx Brothers, he threw himself into it. Years of touring the small- and medium-time circuits, teaming up with partners, then trying to make a go of it as a single.

"I floundered around for years," Berle explains. "I began doing a monologue when I was fifteen. I played all of the small theaters, weeding out all the jokes that didn't get a laugh and trying to find a character for myself." Audiences were tough and unforgiving. If they didn't like you they held their noses, booed and hissed and, if you were especially inept, threw fruit and vegetables at you.

But if you could stand the heat, there was no better arena for learning your craft. "It was a great training ground," Berle says, his voice softening with nostalgia, "because you played in front of audiences in different cities and towns all across America. You learned how different audiences in different regions reacted; you learned what to do, what not to do. They gave you a mass response, instantly. Because there were hundreds of theaters to play in, you had the opportunity to hone your act. That was the great advantage to being in vaudeville. When you flopped, you knew you had to make changes before you got to the next town and replace the material that didn't work."

He learned to mirror the audience's hostility by specializing in put-down humor. He'd look at a man in the front row and say, "Oh, I see it's novelty night—you're here with your wife." Or if a woman was slow in taking her seat, Milton would snap, "Sit down, lady. We all saw the dress." The crowd howled, like pack animals, eager to pounce on the smell of drawn blood. They may not have liked him, but they respected him and waited eagerly for his next glib one-liner. Theater managers liked the way he commanded the stage and began giving him work as a master of ceremonies who introduced the other acts. It was perfect for him. He became Milton Berle, the smart-aleck ringmaster, a sly conjurer who called forth the delirious wonder world that was vaudeville. He not only introduced the acts but also joined them, doing duets with the singers; appearing in a blond wig, a dress, and stockings among a chorus of dancers as they step-kicked out of the wings; or leaping into the middle of a Hungarian acrobat troupe to help them form a human pyramid. Of course he bollixed it up and caused the troupe to collapse in a chaotic tangle of twisted limbs and knotted torsos. Audiences couldn't get enough of him. By the late '20s Berle's salary climbed to $450 a week.

Then came the sea change. Jolson himself ushered it in with the first talking picture, *The Jazz Singer,* in 1927. Vaudeville's audiences had been steadily declining for more than a decade as movies gradually usurped its position as the most popular form of mass entertainment. The advent of talkies and radio delivered the deathblow. The great vaudeville circuits withered and merged and withered some more. In 1932 even the mighty Palace threw in the towel, changing from a vaudeville to a "presentation house," which mixed a small number of live acts with movies.

One by one the East Side Kids made the move to the West Coast to begin new careers in movies and radio. Almost all of them settled in Beverly Hills, but they did not build megapalaces like Pickfair and Greenacres. The Great Depression had struck. With millions of Americans out of work or coping with drastic salary cuts, the public's fascination with the fortunes that Douglas Fairbanks, Tom Mix, and Harold Lloyd lavished on their fairyland estates faded—in fact, people began to resent such ostentatious preening displays. The era of conspicuous consumption was over; Americans gravitated instead to images of the suburban ideal: a stable, sober, placid community in which citizens supported one another through good times and bad. The stars of the

'30s took note and built luxurious, but considerably less pretentious, homes.

George Burns and Gracie Allen erected a simple two-story Colonial house on 720 North Maple Drive. It had six bedrooms—two of them suites with sitting rooms and dressing quarters—an open dining area instead of a formal dining room, servants' quarters, and a medium-sized swimming pool. It was large and handsomely appointed, but not palatial—the kind of house one could find in the wealthy suburbs of any American city. Jack Benny had the most popular radio program in the country and was earning $55,000 a week—an astronomical figure at the time. Yet when he moved to Beverly Hills he built a white brick Georgian house on a one-acre lot at 1002 North Roxbury Drive that was only slightly larger than Burns's. There were a few concessions to Benny's status as the highest-paid entertainer in show business—a five-car garage, a thirty- by sixty-foot swimming pool with a mosaic-tiled octopus on the bottom, a library, a pool house with dressing rooms for men and women—but it was a far cry from Valentino's Falcon Lair.

The Marx Brothers were now getting $250,000 a picture, but Groucho's house on Hillcrest didn't even have a swimming pool because he feared it would attract "freeloaders" who would run up his grocery and liquor bills. Harpo Marx and Eddie Cantor moved into similarly modest homes just a few blocks away from the others. Together they created the aesthetic that would dominate Beverly Hills for the next forty years. It would remain the wealthiest city in the country, the embodiment of the American Dream, but in an era of economic retrenchment and rising income and property taxes the dream had become less grandiose and more in line with middle-class values. When NBC produced a television special on Beverly Hills's fiftieth anniversary in the late '50s it transmitted images of such movie stars as Jimmy Stewart and Bob Cummings on their front lawns with their wives and kids after returning from church just down the street. The message was clear: *we're just like you and your family, only we're a little more rich and glamorous.*

Milton Berle had entered showbiz later than the others, and the big breakthrough came later for him as well. In 1937 RKO signed him to a two-year contract at $3,000 a week. But despite his best efforts, his two features, *New Faces of 1937* and *Radio City Revels,* failed at the box office and he returned to the stage, acting as an MC in presentation houses, playing nightclubs, and headlining in Broadway shows. Finally, more than thirty years after Momma dragged him to that Charlie Chaplin contest in Mount Vernon, lightning struck in 1948. He was doing a radio program, *The Milton Berle Show,* out of New York. The show's sponsor, Texaco, came to him and said they wanted to create a program for a brand-new medium: television. Did Berle have any ideas? He thought about it for a few days, then decided: *Hey, why try to reinvent the wheel? Why don't I do the act that I've spent the last twenty-five years perfecting?* So he pitched it to them: "Let's do a combination vaudeville-nightclub show—a non sequitur review. We'll have all kinds of acts, singers, dancers, jugglers, and acrobats, and I'll be the master of ceremonies." The Texas oilmen loved the idea. They decided to call the show *Texaco Star Theater.*

It was like the first days of silent movies all over again. Because the moneymen and power brokers had no idea what to do with the new medium, they gave writers, directors, and stars free rein to develop shows as they saw fit. Berle had complete creative autonomy—as Keaton had when he owned his own studio in the 1920s—and he used it well by single-handedly creating one of the new medium's most popular and durable genres: the variety show. Jay Leno, David Letterman, and Conan O'Brien still follow the *Star Theater* template: the opening monologue, the kibitzing with the band leader, the wisecracks exchanged with celebrity guests, the forays into the studio audience to tease and embarrass and play practical jokes, and the ad-libs when a joke dies. "Today, jokes that die are put in purposely by Leno and Letterman and others, because dying is just as funny, if you know how to do it," says Berle.

At the opening of every show he appeared in an outlandish costume—as a king, an aviator, a caveman, Lady Godiva—but he never really *became* a character in a sketch the way Sid Caesar, Jackie Gleason, or Red Skelton did. For him the sketch was merely a framework for riffing one-liners, his character merely a clownish costume and a set of false teeth. He called attention to the false reality of the sketches as often as possible by taunting his fellow actors. "You don't remember your line, do you?" And when they cracked up, he chastised them. "Let the audience do the laughing!" He remained, first, last, and always, himself, Uncle Miltie, Mr. Television, the greatest showman of all time, greater even than Jolson!

No brag, just fact.

Texaco Star Theater pulled a rating of 80.7 in its first season—80.7! Today a show's considered a hit it if gets a 12. When the program aired on Tuesday nights, restaurants, theaters, and nightclubs all across America sat empty. The show was credited with selling millions of television sets and creating a nationwide audience that helped the new medium overtake movies and radio in just a few short years. Letters poured into the studio at Rockefeller Center by the thousands, addressed to "Uncle Miltie, U.S.A." NBC paid him $11,500 a week and he made hundreds of thousands more licensing Uncle Miltie comic books, Uncle Miltie chewing gum, T-shirts, wind-up cars, *everything but Uncle Miltie jock straps, for chrissake!* On May 16, 1949, he became the first show business figure to be featured *on the same day* on the covers of *Time* and *Newsweek*. You want to talk cutting edge—baby, he was it!

He moved to Beverly Hills in 1955 in triumph: he had signed to star in the first nationally broadcast color show, and it would be produced in L.A. Berle was bigger than George Burns now, bigger than Groucho, Benny, any of the men who gathered at the round table at the California Friars. He bought a Rolls-Royce Silver Shadow and moved into a house above Sunset with his wife, Ruth, and daughter Vickie. It was what they called a "ranch-style" house—a new type of home born out of the postwar suburban building boom. It spread out horizontally instead of vertically—one low-slung story sprawled over the crest of a grassy hill. Inside there were knotty pine and wormwood walls, a plethora of overstuffed chairs, ottomans, and low rectangular couches covered with vibrant fabrics; an upright piano, a black lacquered coffee table as big as a coffin, ceramic ashtrays the size of Doughboy pools, and an immense set of oak bookshelves, which held two of his Emmy Awards, the leather-bound scripts of his shows, and a hi-fi system for his ever expanding collection of stereophonic recordings.

He was living out the American Dream, a dream, hard as it was to believe, now available even to Jews. In Beverly Hills they no longer huddled in shtetls or tenements in fear of the next pogrom. More than 20,000 of them had settled here—almost 60 percent of the city's population. Many, of course, were in show business—movie and television writers and directors, producers and actors—but not all of them. Just as many had made their fortunes in Los Angeles's burgeoning garment and jewelry industries, or as lawyers or doctors. They had followed the East Side Kids' lead and moved into houses on Canon and Crescent, Roxbury and Hillcrest Drives. They joined the Friars and Hillcrest Country Club, founded in the 1920 just south of Beverly Hills by prominent Jews who had been banned from the lily-white Los Angeles and Wilshire Country Clubs. They attended services at Temple Emanuel on Clark Drive, or Beth Jacob on Olympic Boulevard, and dined at Nate and Al's delicatessen on Rodeo Drive. They ran for city council and the school board, and became the ruling elite in the most elite city in America.

But no sooner did Berle grasp the dream than it slipped away, like water through his fingers. The new show failed to rekindle the magic of *Texaco Star Theater*. Suddenly, it was much tougher to make audiences laugh. A crazy costume or outlandish sight gag wasn't enough anymore. The field had gotten crowded. His success unleashed a stampede of comedians—Sid Caesar, Martin and Lewis, Jackie Gleason, Red Skelton, Lucille Ball, and Phil Silvers—onto prime-time television. The public, you couldn't blame them really, chased after the newest sensation, and the tube, that glowing voracious tube, devoured material faster than a Tasmanian devil. Routines he'd polished for years in nightclubs and vaudeville were exposed to millions and used up in just a few short seasons. He continued to break new ground, only now it was as the first television star to flame out from overexposure. The critics turned on him and attacked the very qualities they'd once raved about. Instead of "audacious" he was now "overbearing." Once he'd been "zany" and "irreverent," now he was "frantic" and "tasteless."

The series got canceled. He tried another, *Kraft Music Hall*, which lasted a season, and another *Jackpot Bowling*—from Mr. Television to a bowling announcer in just a few short years—and then there were no more series. He did a few specials, some movies—*It's a Mad Mad Mad Mad World* and *The Loved One*—headlined in a Broadway play that closed after a few performances, played Vegas, dinner theaters, even tried another series in 1966, but it lasted only seventeen weeks. The years passed, one after another after another, and the gigs grew fewer and further between. He was forced to scale back. He had traded the super-ranch-style home for a seventeen-room Mediterranean villa on North Crescent Drive with an Olympic-size pool, but the nut was too big now, so Mike Silverman sold it for him. "To this day, Milton thinks we could have gotten more money for it," Silverman says with a laugh. "Every time he sees the buyer he gives him a dirty look."

Berle moved into a smaller house on Alpine, in the flats south of Sunset. It only had ten rooms, but it was still impressive: 5,000 square feet that included a grand foyer with hand-painted wood ceilings, a sixty-foot living room, a library . . . and a modest pool with a cabana.

And he still had the Friars Club, thank god for the Friars. When he stepped through the door he was *the man* once again. "Hello, Mr. Berle. How are you today?" *Fine, fine, thank you, Rosario*. "Your usual, Mr. Berle?" In those hallowed halls vaudeville, burlesque, the Catskills, and the old nightclub circuit never died. It lived on every afternoon in the corner by the bar beneath the portrait of Jolson. *You remember that cocktail waitress, the redhead at the Rio Cabana? Do I remember her? I still have her teeth marks on my schwantzinhickle. What an overbite that girl had. So I walk on and this audience, talk about cold, they were frostbit. I look at them and I say, "We have a wonderful show prepared for you. But it won't be ready until next week." You should have heard 'em. Did they laugh? Laugh? They screamed like a bunch of hyenas with the clap. Say that reminds me of the time I was playing the 500 Club on the same bill as Jack Randall, you remember the singer Jack Randall? . . .*

And of course there were the roasts. Oh, the Friars roasts, what a beautiful thing they once were. The biggest names in showbiz—Mae West, Orson Welles, Burt Lancaster, Liberace—fought like alley cats for a chance to be roasted by the Friars. And they were roasted by the greatest collection of comic minds ever assembled: Bob Hope, Phil Silvers, Buddy Hackett, Morey Amsterdam, Cary Grant, Neil Simon, Joe E. Lewis. The one-liners were simple yet as elegant as a haiku. The time he got up and said, "I don't want to stand here and tell a lot of old jokes, but I'd like to introduce a guy who will: Henny Youngman." The laugh that got! Like they were tearing their arms off and beating each other over the heads with them. Or the Sinatra roast, when he looked over at Frank and said, "We are all here for one reason and one reason only. You can sum it up in one word . . . fear!" Like a trainful of epileptics in heat, they howled.

But then even the Friars started to change. One by one, the boys began dying on him. Cantor in 1964, Benny in '74, Groucho in '77. *The ranks are thinning, boys.* They left gaping holes on the dais at the roasts. Someone had to fill them so it fell upon the second bananas—Jan Murray, Jack Carter, Marty Allen—Catskill and nightclub comics who almost but never quite made the big time. With work in the outside world drying up, they became like fish trapped in an evaporating pool, fighting over the few flies that were left. The roasts grew less witty and by degrees more desperate, angry, and, finally, ugly. One-liners like "What can you say about Rickles that hasn't been said about hemorrhoids?" ruled the day.

Then the lawsuits. Like waves on the beach, once they started coming they never seemed to stop. That schmuck David Peters accused the club of raking the pots at the card games and diverting money raised at charity events into the general operating fund to keep the Friars solvent; and Berle personally of not paying dues and pilfering all kinds of freebies from the bar and kitchen. And who the hell was Peters? He owned a goddamned travel agency, for chrissakes, never stepped in front of the footlights in his life, and he had the audacity to accuse Milton, who had practically founded the California Friars and kept it alive all these years. . . . Ah, what's the use of getting aggravated? The whole thing blew over and they moved on . . . to more lawsuits.

Gloria Allred, an attorney, claimed they were a discriminatory organization because they didn't allow women to join. She sued and won, so they have women members now. They're even going to put the first portrait of a woman on the wall: Phyllis Diller. But that didn't satisfy the culture police—like hounds who smelled blood, they wouldn't leave the Friars alone.

There was the Whoopi Goldberg roast in 1993. It happened at the New York club, but the shock waves rippled all the way to the Pacific. Ted Danson came out in blackface, told a lot of off-color jokes about blacks, and ate a watermelon. The shit storm that unleashed. *In poor taste, reinforced cultural stereotypes, demeaning to blacks.* My God, Danson was shacking up with Goldberg at the time, and she wrote the material for him! Besides, the roasts had always been off-color and full of insult humor. *That's why they call it a roast, folks.* There was a time when the world wasn't afraid to kid itself, when blackface was an accepted and cherished showbiz tradition, worn proudly not only by Jolie, but even by great Negro performers like Bert Williams and Bill "Bojangles" Robinson. That's right, they used to black up with burnt cork, just like the white performers. But the legions of the politically correct didn't want to hear it. They complained about the Danson incident and another roast of Roseanne Arnold, in which a couple of the guys made jokes about Sandra Bernhard being a dike. "This is not good clean fun, saying these kinds of things," Gloria Allred told the press. "These are the old boys sitting around chuckling about their prejudices. It's not just offensive but harmful to the rights of people they're attacking." *If you don't like it, lady, why the hell did you join the club in the first place?* But it generated a lot of bad press. People got scared, what with the declining membership and all, that it was off-putting to the younger generation. So they don't have roasts anymore. After almost a hundred years, they gave them up. Now they have "tributes," so no one will be offended.

"The blue roasts are outdated; it's hackneyed," the current abbot, Larry King, explains. "It's getting old because you can see somebody say 'fuck' on TV. Seeing someone say 'fuck' is nothing now, but when I was thirty years old and went to my first Friars roast in New York and I heard Maurice Chevalier say 'fuck,' I thought I'd die. Now, of course, it's on cable. So we're doing tributes now where we honor people. It's mostly just a lot of fun."

Yet membership continues to shrink. Why? Because—Berle believes—when you change a thing, when you muddy its purity, you begin to kill it. Can't these young people see that? Ah, why get worked up over it? He can't change it, any more than he can change the fact that Ruth died. Thirty-six years of marriage over in that instant when she lacked the strength to draw another breath. What do you do when the woman you shared three and a half decades of life with ceases to be? . . .

Move on.

So he married Lorna. Sold the ten-room house with the modest-size pool and moved into a two-bedroom condo with no pool at all. He had to auction off most of the things he'd stuffed into those big houses: the antique walnut Friedrehrbar grand piano, the French marquetry bombé two-drawer commode, the Louis Quinze Vernis Martin curio cabinet, the five-piece French Empire bedroom set, the antique Venetian painted bed, the antique oriental altar tables and Ning Po carved cabinet; the thirty fine oil paintings and watercolors by Émile Bernard, Charles Pettitt, William Dommersen, E. Garren, J. Holland, F. Calvert; the Dresden porcelains, the antique French Louis Quinze boulle bracket clock, the jewelry, the furs, the books. . . .

It's a hell of a thing. You spend your whole life acquiring stuff, like it's some kind of contest, like it's going to prove something to somebody, but in the end you give it all up again and it doesn't much matter because all of the people you were trying to impress are dead. In the end, you're no better or worse off than you were eighty years ago back in the Bronx, when the landlord stacked those banged-up chairs, the scuffed kitchen table, and the cracked vanity mirror on the sidewalk.

George Burns would appreciate the irony. Can see that wily smile now, through a haze of blue-green cigar smoke. *You're right, Milton, it's a hell of a thing.*

George died four years ago. Not quite seven weeks after his hundredth birthday. *Bastard. Leaving me alone with these lightweights.* Milton used to say he wanted to live to be one hundred. Only eight years to go, but he's not so sure anymore. The world he worked so hard to assimilate into has played a dirty trick on him. It's vanished into thin air, like a magician's silk handkerchief. The business he gave his life to no longer has a place for him. They call his style of comedy corny, old-fashioned, but when he sees these comics today he thinks maybe the public could use a little of his old-fashioned humor. Don't these young comics have any pride, any sense of integrity? Where's the craftsmanship, the technique that he spent decades perfecting? "Technique requires discipline," he explains. "It takes years to learn what to do and what not to do—how to approach an audience, how to reach an audience, how to make them like you before you make them laugh at you. You have to make love to an audience. Theatrical success is a matter of consistency of style. That's what these young comics lack today. Consistency. Their routines have no opening, no middle, no end. They're nothing but a bunch of scattershot one-liners." He shifts irritably in his seat, the loose spotted skin of his forehead drawing taut with anger. "You cannot do, should not do, non sequiturs. Because it just looks like you have no faith or honesty in your monologue."

But nobody cares about craftsmanship anymore, or tradition, or history. When Milton signed to do *Texaco Star Theater* back in 1948, he negotiated a fifty-fifty split of the profits with NBC and an agreement that the network would preserve kinescopes of all the episodes. But when he contacted NBC a few months ago and said he wanted to release the shows on home video the way Jerry Lewis and Sid Caesar are now doing with their old programs, the network told him they'd lost the kinescopes. Unlike Buster Keaton, he had no secret vault in a villa with back-up copies to show the world who Milton Berle used to be. These young Turks at NBC in their Armani suits, who looked to be all of twelve years old, had the nerve to stare him in the eye and say he didn't own a stake in the shows anyway. They figured he was a feeble old man who'd limp away, crawl under a rock, and die. But they figured wrong. Berle hired a team of lawyers, sued them for $30 million in damages, and—what do you know?—they found the missing shows. Now they claim to be eager to help him release the kinescopes on the home video market. Sure, it's a great relief, but the fact that he had to go through all that. . . . He built that network, single-handedly. Go back and read your history. There wouldn't even be an NBC, if it wasn't for him.

And then the RuPaul incident. MTV asked Milton to make an appearance on their music awards show. They wanted to pair him up with this RuPaul character because he or she—take your pick—is a female impersonator and Milton was famous for dressing up like dames on the *Texaco Star Theater*. So Milton shows up for the blocking right on time because "I am one that respects what I'm doing, and the word is rehearse, practice, know your lines." RuPaul arrives late and tells the director he doesn't want to rehearse. "Don't worry about me," he says. "I know exactly what I'm doing." I mean, who is this character? What training has he had? How many years did he spend on the stage honing his craft? Does he even know the meaning of the word?

So the first time Milton meets him is onstage in front of thousands of people and cameras broadcasting live to homes all across America. RuPaul swishes up to him and Milton feeds him the set-up line from the script: "I used to wear dresses, but I don't anymore."

And RuPaul's supposed to say, "Why don't you?" So Milton can deliver the punch line: "Because it's a drag."

But instead this queen looks at him and says, "What do you wear, diapers?" Insinuating that Milton's so old he can't help pissing his pants.

Oh, he wanted to hit him, not with his fist, but with a razor-sharp topper that would send them rolling in the aisles. His mind rifled through his 10,000-joke memory bank and found the perfect comeback. *Hey, listen, I may be eighty-six, but I feel like a twenty-year-old. Unfortunately, there's never one around. . . .* Beautiful. An absolutely perfect gut-buster. But something went wrong in the wiring—a short. He could see the words but couldn't transmit them to his mouth. As with an old fighter, the instincts were still there but not the wherewithal. Stared into the camera with a deer-in-the-headlights expression as the audience laughed at the idea of him shitting his pants.

While doing a concert for his ninetieth birthday, he slipped on the stage and fell on his back. The doctors said he had had a stroke. He talked about performing again when he felt better, but he didn't feel better and the talk gradually faded.

The only place he appears these days is right here, below the portrait of Jolson. He's glad there are no windows in the ballroom, for the streets of Beverly Hills that he so enjoyed strolling along when he was the king of television have become unrecognizable to him. The shops have foreign names now—Jimmy Choo, Bon Choix, Frette, Bottega Veneta, Votre Nom, il Pastaio, XOXO—and the old landmarks have vanished. The Brown Derby, Romanoff's, both gone. Chasen's, even Chasen's, for chrissake. What's it been, four years now? Five? Closed down after fifty-eight years.

He gets little sympathy from the kids who run these new places. Just the other morning in the *Los AngelesTimes,* Jerry Prendergast, general manager of Café Morpheus, told a reporter: "You have to live with the realization that this town changes a lot. Everyone comes here to get away from tradition."

Berle slumps wearily in the horseshoe chair, sinking so deep into his clothes it looks as if he may melt away altogether. They used to call him a show business giant; now he's a dinosaur, a fucking fossil, about as at home in this world as an unthawed Neanderthal.

The entourage chatters on around him, oblivious to the stillness that has fallen over his face. "If you believe that one, you believe there's going to be a Richard Simmons Jr." They croak with mucus-filled hilarity, stomp their feet into the thinning carpet adorned with the Friars' emblem. Berle reaches a blue-veined hand into his coat pocket for a cigar, then hesitates. *That's right. No smoking. A new city ordinance.*

"How about it, Milton?" one of the entourage asks. "Did you ever bang her?"

With a mighty effort, Berle pushes his atrophied cheek muscles upward in an exhausted approximation of a knowing smile. The entourage erupts with laughter again. "What I tell you? He had them all, even Marilyn Monroe. If only his zipper could talk."

★

Twenty-one months later, three hundred mourners file out of the chapel and onto the sidewalk, under an overcast April sky. The TV reporters swoop in, thrusting microphones, cameras, and blazing lights at the celebrities. "Mr. Caesar, can you say a few words about Milton Berle? What impact did he have on the American entertainment scene?"

Sid Caesar's wizened face crunches in concentration. How can you put it into a sound bite—the life of a man and the larger story he was a part of, the experience of an entire generation now fading like those muddy kinescopes of Berle's old shows that they've been running on all the stations? Blurry images and muffled sound, fragmentary shots of a man dressed as an outlandish Viking, as Lady Godiva, a mad maestro playing a Salvador Dali piano that explodes to smithereens the moment he touches the keys. How do you explain it to your grandkids, born into an era of three-dimensional surround-sound computer games, how can you make them understand? They squint at the distorted kinescopes, shake their heads, and say, "This was funny to you?"

You try to get through to them, try to make them grasp the importance. "He was the first, the one that proved to the networks who were skeptical that the same man could do a different show every week.

They did it on radio, but that was easy. TV was an altogether different business. You had to have a stage, lights, costumes. Most of all you've got to have talent. He made it easier for everybody. . . . We all owe him something."

That wasn't what Caesar meant to say, it doesn't begin to convey the man's significance, but it's too late. The reporter's eyes glaze over, she's lost interest. She turns to her cameraman: "I think we've got enough. Thanks so much, Mr. Caesar, that was great." He would like to tell her more. *You had to be there. You had to live through it to understand.* But they are already packing up their equipment and moving on.

★ 5 ★

The Persian Frank Sinatra

It's well past midnight. The fifty white linen–covered tables that have been set up in the huge backyard are illuminated by a chiaroscuro pattern of moonlight sifting through the leafy canopy of three enormous eighty-year-old Chinese elm trees. The men's blue-black Armani and Bijan suits glisten, and the women's diamonds twinkle like lightning bugs. Most have finished dessert and all turn toward the south end of the lawn where the musicians return to a bandstand bathed in rippling light from the nearby swimming pool. A singer steps up to the microphone. He's tall and handsome, with moussed hair, a white jacket, and a turquoise shirt that looks phosphorescent under the moon. The sextet kicks into a traditional Persian ballad. The melody ripples and curls around itself like thick twirling strands of esfand smoke, and yet it sounds oddly off-kilter, distorted and harsh around the edges because the musicians are using western instruments. It's a weird hybrid of techno West and esoteric East, yet perfectly appropriate for these people without a country, who now inhabit a strange world composed of equal parts past, present, and fantasy.

The singer raises the microphone to his mouth, manicured nails gleaming as his lips part and the Farsi lyrics issue forth. His warbling voice is plaintive, torn by unendurable heartache and delicious rapture. The wedding guests fall silent and lean forward, listening intently. One of them, a man in his late fifties, taps the shoulder of the only Caucasian in attendance. The older man's mouth opens to expose a gleaming crescent of teeth. A grimace or a grin? It's impossible to tell. He gestures to the singer and says, "They call him the Persian Frank Sinatra. He sings much better than your Sinatra, I think."

His words are both a challenge and a plea for affirmation. And his grimace/grin expresses an odd mixture of belligerence, ambivalence, and insecurity common to many of the Persian men in their late fifties and early sixties who find themselves marooned in this city on the edge of the Pacific. They, like all of the members of this wedding, are part of Beverly Hills's burgeoning Persian community, now 7,000 strong—the most powerful social force to invade the town since the European Jews arrived in the 1930s. Over the last twenty-five years the Persians have transformed Beverly Hills and been changed by it for the better or worse, depending on your point of view.

For many, the American experience began more than thirty years ago when they came to the United States to attend college. In the 1960s, Iran—then ruled by Shah Mohammad Reza Pahlavi—was one of the most westernized countries in the Middle East. Wealthy families considered it a status symbol to have a son in an American university. (Few Iranian women were allowed to pursue a college education in those days.) The University of Tehran established an exchange program with UCLA, and USC was another popular choice because it had a strong international business program. By the late '60s there were approximately 1,000 Iranian immigrants living in the United States, the vast majority of whom were students. At USC the number of Iranian students grew from 88 in 1970, to 469 in 1976, to 998 in 1978. Growth also skyrocketed at UCLA, which had 44 Iranian students in 1964 and 266 by 1975. But to some Iranians an American university was more than an educational opportunity; it was a life raft, held in reserve in case a flash flood should strike.

A small Jewish population had lived peacefully in Iran for more than 2,500 years, ever since Cyrus the Great, the founder of the Persian Empire, conquered Babylonia and freed its Hebrew slaves. Cyrus invited the Jews to live in Persia, where they flourished as merchants and traders. They continued to prosper under the Shah; many Jewish families—such as the Nahais, the Levys, the Rads, the Elghanians, the Mooradis, and the Simtoubs—amassed huge fortunes by selling real estate or insurance, running hotels, importing antique rugs, marble, or manufacturing and selling anything from jewelry, to textiles and chewing gum. Yet even after two and a half centuries, the Iranian Jews never felt entirely at ease in a country that was 98 percent Muslim. In the fifteenth century they absorbed a flood of Sephardic refugees from Spain who had fled the anti-Semitic attacks of the Spanish Inquisition. And the lessons of the Russian pogroms and the Third Reich's Final Solution had not escaped them. "They always felt insecure," Baroukh Beroukhim, former president of the Ettefak, a Jewish academy in Tehran, has observed. "They . . . sent their children abroad to go to school as a means of having a little branch out there somewhere that would become the only hope if things got bad."

One of the first Persian Jews to arrive in Beverly Hills, Daryoush "Dar" Mahboubi, would have an enormous impact on the city. The son of Mirza-Agha Mahboubi, who ran a hugely successful chewing gum company in Iran, Dar attended UC Berkeley in the 1960s. Instead of returning to Iran after he obtained his degree, Dar moved to Southern California and began funneling the family fortune into real estate. First he bought some commercial property in Anaheim, near Disneyland. Next he purchased a house in Beverly Hills, the former residence of television producer Quinn Martin on North Crescent Drive. Then he snatched up another Beverly Hills parcel—a medical building on the corner of Wilshire and Linden.

Dar's brother, Behrouz, graduated from the London School of Economics in 1966 and joined Dar in Beverly Hills. Over the next ten years the Mahboubi brothers divided their time between their business interests in Iran and Los Angeles. Their father died in 1969, and as the 1970s drew to a close and the rumbles of revolution began to teeter the Shah's regime, their mother and sister joined them in Beverly Hills, which now became their permanent home.

Saeed Nourmand, another key figure in Beverly Hills's Iranian Jewish community, arrived in Southern California shortly after the Mahboubis. Saeed's father ran a thriving import-export firm in Iran, and in 1965 he sent Saeed to America to attend NYU. Later, Nourmand transferred to the State University of New York at Buffalo, where he obtained a degree in engineering and met a striking young blond sociology major named Myra Krul. Saeed soon fell in love with Myra. "She was my soul mate," he explains. "She understood me. She shared my values in family and the need for members of a family to support each other. She was not prejudiced. I was a foreigner yet she looked at me as an equal." He also fell in love with America. "It was the land of opportunity. One of the things I always admired about my dad was he was a self-made man and I wanted to be able to do the same. I wouldn't have a chance in hell if I went back to Iran that I would ever be able to do what Dad did. I thought that in this country I could accomplish that."

So instead of returning to Iran, Saeed married Myra and in 1970 drove west. He was looking for engineering work, and California, with its thriving aerospace industry, had plenty of it. Saeed and Myra bought a house in Van Nuys, but it was only a stopover. Nourmand—a product of Iran's upper class—had left his country behind, but not its values. He was determined that he would one day occupy one of the great hilltop manors that L.A.'s elite resided in on the city's west side. An unforeseen career change seven years later would get him there. In 1977 he bought a huge home with the coveted Beverly Hills zip code.

Jews weren't the only Iranians to settle in Beverly Hills before the fall of the shah; a few Muslims came as well. These were not the fundamentalists who eventually fueled the revolution, but secular Muslims from wealthy westernized families who displayed only a token commitment to their faith, or no commitment at all. However, they were deeply committed to making money, and a few had figured out angles for making a great deal of it in the United States.

One of them was Rahim Soltani. Soltani was in the business of buying and selling antique Persian rugs, and in the course of his travels he discovered that many wealthy Americans had passed through Iran on tours of the Holy Land during the 1910s and '20s. These tycoons of the Industrial Era—bankers; railroad, oil, iron, and steel barons; industrialists and stock market high rollers—bought up every authentic-looking artifact of "high culture" that they could get their hands on, including hundreds upon hundreds of fine Persian rugs. Many of those rugs, still in mint condition, could be picked up for a song from estate sales in the crumbling Victorian mansions of America's swiftly decomposing rust belt. So Rahim came to America in the late 1960s and began doing just that: buying up old rugs cheap and selling them back to the oil-rich elite of Iran for a fat profit. (Soltani's customers included the Shah, who bought so many antique rugs that he decided to build a museum to display them.)

Soltani amassed a small fortune and a great affection for America. He saw the storm clouds gathering over his country and so brought his wife, Zahra, and son, Ali, to the United States in 1971. Zahra was pregnant with his second son, and Rahim wanted the boy to be born in the United States so that he would be a citizen. They moved into a house in Anaheim, where a number of Muslim Iranian immigrants were settling, and divided their time between America and Iran. Business continued to boom, so in 1975 Soltani moved uptown to Beverly Hills and bought a house in Trousdale Estates.

There were only a handful of Iranian families living in Beverly Hills by the mid-'70s, but the seeds had been planted, and from them the Persian community would eventually burgeon.

In 1978 the terrible *mosibat* that the Persian Jews so long feared suddenly materialized. On the surface, the Shah's "White Revolution" had worked wonders, ushering Iran into an era of unprecedented economic prosperity. But behind the sunny facade of modern Iran a great sea of discontent boiled. Women may have had the right to vote, but the parliament they voted for, the Majlis, was a paper tiger. The Shah exercised absolute control over the government and used his secret police, the Savak, to brutally silence dissidents. The quickly expanding economy benefited only a small class of wealthy elite; there was no middle class, and as the economy continued to grow, the gap and the resentments between rich and poor grew with it.

In the late 1970s the Shah's many enemies—civil libertarians, the poor, and Muslim fundamentalists who bitterly opposed the western values he promoted—united behind a Muslim religious leader, the Ayatollah Ruholla Khomeini. Khomeini's venomous denunciations of the Shah catalyzed the masses; thousands of angry protesters filled the streets demanding that the Shah step down, and the leader's military machine began to lose control of events on the ground.

Many wealthy Iranians—both Jews and Muslims—kept hoping the Shah would be able to tough it out and reassert control, but others saw the writing on the wall and began packing. Gina Nahai was one of the lucky ones. The daughter of a wealthy clothing retailer, Gina had been attending a Swiss boarding school since she was thirteen. She returned to Iran for a few weeks in the summer of 1977, then left again with her mother for Los Angeles, where she had enrolled in UCLA. She had no inkling she would never return. "As far as I know, my clothes are still hanging in the closet," she says with an ironic laugh, almost a quarter of a century later.

"Before the revolution, a lot of Iranians had money abroad," she explains, "not necessarily in the States, but in Switzerland and Europe. They were the families with fabulous wealth, who could store money away and didn't need it. When the noise started, people got nervous about whether the Shah was going to last or not, and a lot of them sent money out of the country. Some sent their families to America, thinking it was a temporary thing." Gina's father was one of the fortunate ones—he managed to get most of his money and himself out before the Shah fell. Her mother's five sisters and their families joined Gina and her parents in Beverly Hills, where they followed Rahim Soltani's example and settled in Trousdale Estates.

In June 1978, bloody riots swept through Iran's major cities. The Shah declared martial law. His troops opened fire on protesters, killing and wounding 2,000 of them. It only added fuel to the fire as thousands more rushed to the streets to oppose the monarch, and oil workers went on strike, choking off the lifeblood of the economy. In the now lawless streets, anti-Semites rose to the top of the froth; the windows of Jewish merchants were smashed, offices trashed, merchants roughed up, children and women taunted and threatened. The pattern was all too familiar. "It was terrible," Guity Nemani later observed. Nemani abandoned a successful family rug business, her home, and most of her belongings when she fled the country with her husband and three children. "There was so much hatred on the streets. . . . Anyone who had a little money, anything, was not safe."

Those who had already laid the groundwork for a new life in the United States, like the Mahboubis, found the transition easier. By 1978 the Mahboubi brothers had moved most of their assets to America. But they felt far from smug as their country went up in smoke. "The last few times I went to Iran there were fires in the streets," Behrouz Mahboubi says in a low, hesitant voice. "They were setting fire to the banks and financial institutions. . . . It was terribly sad, but I got out of there just in time. I found out later [when Khomeini came to power] I was on the enemies list. My chauffeur called me soon after I left and said some people had come to the door of my house, just like you see in the movies where the Germans come to the door and say, 'Mr. Mahboubi? Please come with us.' "

Rahim Soltani was also well prepared. He moved his rug business to the United States, where thousands of loyal customers were arriving every day. More than 600,000 Iranians flooded into Southern California. The Muslims settled in Orange County and Palos Verdes; the ethnic Armenians in Glendale, which already had a sizeable Armenian community. Approximately 30,000 Persian Jews moved into Encino, Westwood, and Beverly Hills. More than 7,000 Iranians immigrated to Burton Green's utopia—a huge influx for a city with a population of just over 32,000. A few hundred of the Persians were Muslims and Baha'i (another religious minority), but the vast majority were Jews.

Why Beverly Hills? Well, for one thing such prominent Iranians as Dar Mahboubi, Saeed Nourmand, and Rahim Soltani already lived there and, like immigrant groups who came before them, the Iranians wanted to live close to others of their kind. "They thought that away from home they should at least be among friends," Nourmand explains. Especially rich friends—money translates into power no matter what country you're living in. And they had heard that Beverly Hills was a city where Jews lived not as a minority, but as the ruling elite. "Beverly Hills is a Jewish city," Behrouz Mahboubi told the new arrivals. "Everything is run by Jewish people, including the city council."

"When you come from a place where they've thrown you out after two thousand seven hundred years, you're obviously scared and you want to go somewhere safe," says Dariush Fakheri, publisher of the *Judea Chronicle,* a political-sociological journal for Iranian Jews. Fakheri was a student at Eastern New Mexico University when "the noise" started. He moved to L.A. shortly after the fall of the Shah. "Beverly Hills was perceived as safe, both in the sense of having very little crime and from the standpoint of the Jewish community."

And that Jewish community welcomed the Persian refugees with open arms . . . at first. Dariush Fakheri cofounded an organization called SIAMAK—the Persian acronym for the Iranian Jewish Association of California—to help Persian Jews overcome culture shock and acclimate to their new environment. He asked for and received enormous help from the American Jewish Federation of Greater Los Angeles, and a number of temples that threw open their doors and welcomed Persian Jews to their services. It was the first step on the long road to assimilation.

"Most of the Jews in Beverly Hills originated in Europe," says Behrouz Mahboubi. "They had sympathy for the Iranian Jews who were in the same situation that they had once been in."

And the Persians were drawn to Beverly Hills by another major asset: the prestige factor. The first Persian immigrants were incredibly wealthy, and they wanted to live in the kind of plush surroundings that they'd grown accustomed to. "Beverly Hills is known all over the world," says Fakheri. "Every rich family in the Philippines and Saudi Arabia wants to have a house in Beverly Hills. It's where the stars are, and everybody wants to be next to the stars."

The arrival of thousands of wealthy Persians looking to buy property sparked the biggest Beverly Hills real estate boom since the 1920s. The market had been in the doldrums throughout most of the recession-ridden '70s, but that changed almost overnight and Saeed Nourmand was uniquely positioned to capitalize on the new land rush. A few years earlier, the recession and drastic cutbacks in the space program and defense spending decimated the aerospace industry. Nourmand found himself standing in long unemployment lines with hundreds of other engineers and began to wonder about another career path. So he went to real estate school, got his license, and opened Nourmand and Associates on Canon Drive.

Mike Silverman had become the premier real estate agent of the 1960s because his sensibilities were perfectly attuned to the needs of his client base: the European Jews. Now Nourmand's star rose by performing a similar service for the Persians. He knew their tastes, what they were looking for in a home, their concerns, and how to cater to them. And, like Silverman, he put on a first-class dog and pony show. Nourmand's slick theatrics would have won a nod of approval from Burton Green himself. "He would sell the Iranians an entire package," says Gina Nahai. "They could afford the best California had to offer, so Nourmand would rent a limo to pick them up at their hotel. He not only showed them houses, but he also gave them a tour of the entire town. That was the package: Beverly Hills itself."

As the clients sipped chilled Perrier, Nourmand pointed out palatial homes and extolled the wonders of the Southern California climate. *There's no humidity here. It's a dry desert heat. Have you ever been in New York in the summer? Believe me, you don't want to go.*

And see how grown-in the landscaping is? Shades the house, keeps it cool. You don't even need air-conditioning here. I'm serious. . . . Crime? What crime? There's no crime here. You know what the average police response time is to an emergency call? . . . Two-point-eight minutes. How about that? The crooks and the robbers and the drug dealers, they drive around Beverly Hills. They don't want any part of this place because the cops here make the Savak look like a bunch of schoolgirls. Speaking of schools, why don't we take a spin by the high school. . . .

The Iranians were the first wave of immigrants in history who could afford to buy the American Dream outright. No tedious toiling for one, two, or even three generations, working their way up from dreary assembly line jobs to foreman, then floor manager and finally mill superintendent to pay for it on the installment plan, no sir, they wanted it right now, cash on the barrelhead, and Nourmand gave it to them—for a slight commission, of course.

"The buying power of the Persians was a heck of a lot stronger than any other force in Beverly Hills," says Nourmand. "They were coming here with lots of cash, very substantial sums of money—as in hundreds of millions of dollars in many cases."

Most of the Iranians gravitated to Trousdale Estates, where the first Persian immigrants had already bought large hilltop homes. The Trousdale houses averaged about 5,000 square feet and usually sold for between $120,000 and $400,000. Most Iranians did not haggle over the price as they normally would because they couldn't believe the prices. The exchange rate for their rials had been very favorable, and property values in Iran had been much higher, so the Trousdale homes seemed incredibly inexpensive. "I had a client who was baffled by how cheap these properties were," says Nourmand. "He wanted to know if I had an explanation as to why such an affluent neighborhood in such an affluent country was selling properties for so little." *Simple,* Nourmand replied, *America has the highest standard of living in the world.* The client nodded thoughtfully and decided to buy not one house but four—one for himself and his wife, and one for each of his three children. The experience was not unique. Many of the Iranians bought two and three homes, either for relatives, or as investment properties.

Thus Nourmand became one of the most successful independent brokers in Beverly Hills. "At one point I was selling twenty to thirty percent of the homes in Trousdale," he says. "It was a no-brainer. I had the support of a lot of friends and relatives in the beginning, but once we became a force other clients besides Iranians came to us. Today we do business with the who's who of Beverly Hills." Like the brokers who came before him, Nourmand realized the American Dream by selling it to others.

But not all of the Persians who came to Beverly Hills were filthy rich. In fact many had little more than the clothes on their back when they first arrived. Many had stayed in Iran, hoping the revolution would peter out, that the Shah would return to reclaim his throne and the good times would roll once more. By the time they realized this was a pipe dream it was too late; the Islamic government had seized their assets, or worse.

Parviz Danielpour belonged to one of the wealthiest Jewish families in Iran. Like most of the elite, he lived on the north end of Tehran in a marble-lined mansion with hot and cold running servants. He showered his lovely wife, Ziba, with expensive presents: a white Cadillac convertible; diamonds, rubies, and sapphires of every conceivable shape and configuration, and a twelve-karat gold wedding ring. Parviz didn't flee when the Ayatollah overthrew the Shah. He believed his family's spotless reputation and high social status would protect him. He was wrong. When Parviz looked at the paper one morning the blood drained from his face. A headline accused him of being a spy for Israel, even though he had never been to that country.

Parviz ran a textile company with his brother, Albert, and on the way to work he called the office. His brother got on the phone with a strange stilted voice. "No, don't come here." Parviz asked what was wrong, but Albert only repeated the same strained words. "Don't come here." Parviz made a U-turn, went home, and told Ziba to round up the kids and "get your stuff together. You have to get out of here."

Ziba, her daughter, Shirin, and son, Payman, left at once for America, to which some of their relatives had already immigrated. Parviz promised to join them as soon as he managed to liquidate some of his assets and move the money overseas. But before he could do so he was arrested. Parviz languished in jail for three years before he was able to bribe his way out, buy some false identity papers, and ride a camel across the Makran Mountains and the Great Indian Desert to Pakistan. From there he bought a plane ticket to Israel and then America. It was a terrible ordeal, but better than what happened to Albert. He was one of the first Jews assassinated by Khomeini's death squads.

"When I saw my father again I was four years old," says Parviz's daughter, Shirin. "He had this mustache. He didn't have a mustache the last time I saw him—he'd grown it to conceal his identity—and he frightened me. I didn't believe he was my father. . . . It was very hard."

Like thousands of other Iranians who'd lost their fortunes or never had them to begin with, the Danielpours moved into an apartment south of Wilshire Boulevard, in an area that the elite disdainfully refer to as "South Central Beverly Hills." When Wilbur Cook laid out his original blueprint for Beverly Hills in the early years of the twentieth century, he conceived of it as a kind of north-to-south grid that would chart the economic strata of the new community. The superrich would live in the great estates in the hills above Sunset Boulevard; the merely wealthy would reside in "the flats" between Sunset and Santa Monica; then came the commercial district, which stretched from Santa Monica to Wilshire; the blocks south of Wilshire, all the way to Olympic Boulevard and the city's southern border would be filled with modest-size apartments. Here the servant class would live.

The affluence grid still exists nearly a hundred years later, but the population of "South Central," or "Baja Beverly Hills," has changed over the decades. Eventually the apartments became too expensive for the servant class, and most of them moved east, farther south, or out to the San Fernando Valley. They were replaced by retirees; single working mothers who wanted to get their children into the excellent

Beverly Hills schools; lower-level entertainment industry workers such as script supervisors, assistant directors, and character actors; and upper-middle-class twentysomethings who talked Mom and Dad into financing their dreams of becoming big-time film directors and movie stars so they could one day move north along the well-delineated ladder of success.

In the early '80s, the Iranians who escaped with little more than the shirts on their backs joined the ranks of these great unwashed. They crammed two and three families into one apartment and started over from scratch, working cash registers in convenience stores, or pumping gas. And like other immigrant groups before them they scrimped and saved until they could buy those gas stations and convenience stores and move from the apartments to condominiums and homes of their own. Parviz Danielpour went to work for a jewelry wholesaler in downtown Los Angeles, and Ziba—who had never worked before—became a secretary for her father and brother, both doctors who had set up practice in Beverly Hills. "My mom had to ride the bus to work, buy her own groceries, and take them home on the bus," says Shirin. "I don't know how she did it." Slowly, as the years passed, things got better. Parviz started a new textile company and managed to put both his kids through college. "Twenty years later they've made it," says Shirin. "They live in the Wilshire corridor in a nice big condo. My mother drives a Jaguar and she's happy because her children went to the best schools—one's a journalist and the other's in medical school. That's the great thing about America: it gives you an opportunity, and my parents grasped that opportunity."

The Iranians who lived south of Wilshire had to overcome formidable obstacles, but those who had hundreds of millions of dollars in the bank also found it difficult to adjust to life in America. All right, so they had the big house north of Sunset with the swimming pool and the gardens and more marble and statuary than in all of Ancient Babylon. But now what? "You take someone who was very successful and was self-sufficient in Iran and now you bring him here," says Saeed Nourmand. "What the heck is he going to do here? He wakes up in the morning, puts on his suit and tie, shaves . . . and then what? Where the heck is he going to go? What the heck is he going to do? Who the heck would hire this man?" Even the wealthy Persians realized they would have to create opportunities for themselves.

Rahim Soltani continued selling rugs, only now he sold them to the 600,000 Iranians living in Southern California. As time went on he diversified into antiques. Business was good enough to enable him to send his oldest son, Ali, to law school at Loyola Marymount. In 1987 David Orgell, owner of one of the oldest businesses in the Beverly Hills retail district, died suddenly while on vacation in Italy. His wife and two sons attempted to run his high-end antique store on Rodeo Drive and four other outlets in the Los Angeles area. But they were ill equipped for the cutthroat world of retail sales and soon had to file for bankruptcy. Ali Soltani used his legal expertise to help his father buy the Orgell operation for a sweet price, and thus the Soltanis became one of the premier purveyors of antiques, glitzy knickknacks, and fine jewelry in the Rodeo Drive district.

Dar Mahboubi decided to become a major player in commercial real estate. He bought two parcels on Rodeo Drive, including the Luau Restaurant, a venerable but somewhat frayed-at-the-cuffs Polynesian eatery. Then he took on limited partners and spent approximately $30 million on two-thirds of a block that fronted on both Beverly and Canon Drives. It included eleven shops, a food market, and a large parking lot. He also snatched up the Barclay's Bank building at Brighton Way and Camden, Hunter's Bookstore on the corner of Rodeo and Little Santa Monica, key corners on Dayton and Bedford Drives, and a nine-acre parcel in the city's largely unused industrial zone, just east of the city hall, where he planned to build 144 luxury condominiums priced at $750,000 each.

To veteran real estate players, Mahboubi's $500 million buying binge looked foolhardy. California had one of the highest property taxes in the nation; his tax nut alone would probably soon drain even his enormous cash reserves. But then the California voters passed Proposition 13, which instituted approximately a 50 percent cut in property taxes and limited future increases to no more than 2 percent a year. Suddenly Mahboubi looked crazy like a fox. He now owned many of the key properties on the Monopoly board and had the capital to put hotels on them.

One might have expected the old-time citizens of Beverly Hills to be grateful for the Persians' economic contributions to their community—for they were considerable. Between 1975 and 1980 the number of banks grew from four to thirty-four, and bank deposits shot up by $710 million. Building permit revenue rose from $18.4 million to $31 million during that same period. More important to long-time residents, property values skyrocketed as the Iranians bought thousands of homes at top-dollar prices. Houses in Trousdale shot up to anywhere from $1 million to $4 million by the late '90s—ten times what their value had been before the Iranians arrived. By the millennium real estate prices were rising at approximately 20 percent annually. The city's assessed valuation (the total assessed value of its land) grew from $454 million in 1976 to $9.8 billion by the century's end.

But the Beverly Hills veterans were not grateful for the Persians' contributions; in fact, they bitterly resented them. To them, the Iranians were carpetbaggers preying on Americans who had been battered by a decade of soaring inflation, gasoline shortages, a faltering dollar, and a weak economy. They were exploitive foreigners, driving hard bargains with families that were losing their homes, and snatching family businesses from the hands of grieving widows and distraught children. They drove real estate prices through the roof, assuring that the children of long-time residents had no hope of buying a home of their own in Beverly Hills.

The houses many Persians built seemed to purposely rub salt into the wounds of older residents. Some Iranians, like Saeed Nourmand, loved the traditional Beverly Hills homes. Nourmand bought a Mediterranean-style house on Whittier Drive and painstakingly restored it. But the Caucasians didn't notice the houses that were carefully restored or those that were tastefully remodeled. They fixated on the gaudy, over-the-top preening displays that so many Persians seemed to favor: the white wedding-cake mansions the size of the Taj Mahal, plastered with marble from roof to driveway and surrounded by teeming entourages of poorly reproduced Greek statuary; the huge curving staircases covered with leopard skin carpet and bordered by stainless steel banisters. Oh, it was just too hideous to think about—these barbarian hordes, savaging Camelot—but how could one not think about it when every time you turned around there was another white monstrosity looming on a hillside like an extended middle finger waved in the faces of old-time residents.

So it's little wonder that when the Persian heavyweights—Dar Mahboubi, David Yadegar, and Jim Damavondi—began to implement their plans to convert the Rodeo Drive district into a retail center that would rival Paris, London, or New York, the locals mounted a grassroots resistance movement called the Committee to Save Beverly Hills. The League of Women Voters, and senior citizens and local merchants who were being forced out of their apartments and stores by skyrocketing rents, piled into city council meetings to vociferously oppose the Iranians' plans. They filed a blizzard of lawsuits and convinced a U.S. attorney to investigate city councilman Richard Stone's cozy relationship with Iranian developers. (Stone—who denied any impropriety—worked for the Iranians as a consultant while serving on the city council, where he voted to approve many of their development projects.) In Trousdale Estates, Caucasian homeowners mounted a campaign to stop Iranians from adding oversize swimming pools, sundecks, and tennis courts to their hillside properties.

The Persians believed the European Jews who led this backlash were motivated by more than simple antigrowth sentiments. They detected a whiff of an old and familiar bigotry: the contempt that an immigrant group feels, after it has successfully integrated, for the next bunch that clambers off the boat. "You know, it's funny," says Shirin Danielpour, "we have this older generation of Americans here in Beverly Hills who say they don't want the blacks or Hispanics living here—they only want affluent people. They call in to the *Beverly Hills*

Weekly, where I'm the managing editor, and complain all the time. But then the Iranians moved here and they say, 'We've got to get rid of them because they have too much money!' "

To try to bridge the barrier between the European and Persian Jews, Nanaz Pirnia, a psychologist and president of the Iranian American Parents Association, spoke before audiences of parents and students at Beverly Hills High School. "I would tell them about what we'd been through before we came to this country and at the end I would get a standing ovation," says Pirnia. "They would be very touched. Then I would get the first question, 'When are you [people] going back to Iran?' The teachers would ask this. And I always said, 'We're not going back. There is nothing to go back to.' "

The Persians had no intention of backing off from their plans to remake the city. The Committee to Save Beverly Hills didn't. That is, they didn't manage to save their concept of Beverly Hills. Oh, they won a few battles. The city council passed an ordinance that limited the expansion and remodeling of homes in Trousdale, but that didn't stop the Persians from obliterating the subdivision's Greek-Goddess-All-Electric-Gold-Medallion aesthetic that had so powerfully evoked the postwar sensibility of the 1950s. The Iranians went right ahead slapping marble and polished granite paneling over the houses' stucco walls and adding huge facades on the front entrances—gaping porticos framed by a proliferation of arabesque waves, curves, and arches, mammoth Doric, Ionic, and Corinthian columns, Greek statuary, and baroque white wrought-iron fences.

Mahboubi eventually gave up on his condominium project, but he sold the property to another developer who put in an equally dense office complex. Elsewhere in the retail district, the Iranians buried the protesters with a lava flow of cash. Local politicians simply couldn't resist the potential tax revenues. Project after project followed the same pattern: a storm of outcry from old-time residents and volatile public hearings, followed by some token concessions from the developer and approval by the city council. In 1982 Mahboubi tore down the Luau Restaurant and in its place erected an exclusive upscale shopping mall called the Rodeo Collection that set the new tone for the retail district. Its three-level outdoor complex was an avant-garde amalgamation of traditional European and postmodern architecture that housed such chichi tenants as Gianni Versace, Louis Vuitton, and Fendi. On the opposite side of Rodeo, Mahboubi bought a parking lot and pumped more than $2.2 million into the construction of the Bijan Boutique—an ultra upscale clothier.

Meanwhile, Hamid Gabbay—who had run one of the largest architectural firms in Iran before immigrating to Beverly Hills—became one of the first Persians to get directly involved in city politics. He used his architectural expertise to gain a position on the planning commission. "It was a very influential commission," he explains, "and we did a lot during the ten years that I served—writing new codes, shaping and allying various interest groups to change the shape of the commercial district."

"Before Gabbay got on the planning commission, there was no outdoor dining in Beverly Hills," says Nourmand. "It was a law that you could not serve food outside, even though it is one of the most ideal places in the world to have outdoor dining. It was a completely alien concept that people could sit out on the sidewalk and eat." But not to Gabbay, who had studied in Italy and grown to love the great outdoor cafés of Rome, Florence, and Venice where patrons lingered for hours over cappuccini and caffè lattes, chatting with each other and passersby. Outdoor cafés brought people together, stimulated political debate and artistic discussions, and enriched the cultural life of a community. Why shouldn't Beverly Hills—one of the wealthiest municipalities in the world—embrace the sophisticated lifestyle of the great cities of Europe? Gabbay mounted a passionate argument to the commission, got them to rewrite the code, and sidewalk cafés sprung up all over Rodeo, Beverly, and Canon Drives.

Iranians made their presence felt in the public schools as well, where 25 percent of the students were now Persian. The Iranian American Parents Association raised more than $600,000 for the Beverly Hills School District between 1994 and 2000. School announcements were now printed in Farsi. The district hired a full-time

Farsi-speaking language specialist and a home-school coordinator to help Iranian children assimilate and to sensitize administrators and teachers to the Persian students' needs. Every March the Iranian American Parents Association celebrated Nowruz, the Persian New Year, by throwing a fund-raiser for the school district. When the association threw the first one in a private home in 1994 it drew only a small group of people and a couple of low-level city officials; six years later the affair was held in the grand ballroom of the Beverly Wilshire Hotel, and drew more than 1,500 people, including all the major players in city government—a tacit admission that Iranians had become a political force to be reckoned with.

The Iranians, it would seem, have arrived. The second generation has graduated from Beverly Hills High and gone on to UCLA and USC. Most entered professions that typify second-generation immigrants: law, medicine, engineering. A few have even begun to pursue more esoteric fields that become an option only after an immigrant group feels materially and socially secure; there are now Iranian journalists, artists, actors, film and television producers and directors, even a bestselling novelist, Gina Nahai.

They seized the American Dream faster than any immigrant group that came before them, and improved upon it. And yet . . . in the older men that you talk to you can see, in the back of their eyes, a lurking shadow, a doubt, a slow festering anxiety that something's terribly wrong here.

You begin to sense where the problem lies when they wax nostalgically about the old country—Iran before the revolution. A wistful look comes over them as they talk about it, because for all its shortcomings—the vicious caprices of the Shah, the corruption, the social inequities—it was a rich man's paradise, a patriarchal utopia that will never be again.

"In Iran the center of the family was one person who made decisions," Behrouz Mahboubi explains. "The father made decisions and everybody else followed, whether it was money, business, education, anything. Nobody questioned."

"In Iran when you get older you gain respect," says Saeed Nourmand. "In this country when you get older, you are discarded. In Iran, although a younger person had become the breadwinner and the decision maker, that person still went to his father and grandfather to seek advice as to what he should do and as to what he should not do. They went and got permission or the blessing of the elder. When I was growing up in Iran, we ate breakfast when my dad ate breakfast. We had lunch when my dad had lunch. We had dinner when my dad had dinner. It didn't matter when my dad came home. My dad may have come home at seven o'clock, he may have come home at nine o'clock, he may have come home at eleven o'clock. We waited. That was the way it was. Now I'm not saying we didn't eat anything until he came home. We munched on something, a snack. But dinner was served when Dad came home."

Nourmand says this not with resentment but with the same nostalgia that Behrouz Mahboubi exhibits when he says: "I did not dare smoke in front of my father until I was thirty-two. If my father saw me smoke a cigarette, he would beat me up, because he said, 'You're not supposed to smoke,' and that's it. I was educated in England in the 1960s. When I went back to Iran I was twenty-two and dating some Muslim girls. My father found out and he was critical about this. He called me and said, 'I want you to get married.' I got married when I was twenty-three. I've been married for thirty years. I don't know if that was right or wrong, but it worked. I've had a fairly happy married life. We have three children and two grandchildren. We've never been separated and it worked."

Ali Soltani has become the driving force, the marketing strategist and manager of day-to-day operations at David Orgell. His father, Rahim, is happy to take a backseat and concentrate on his rug business but proud that his son has enough respect for tradition to consult him on every decision, big and small. "He comes in and asks me, 'Can I go home?' That's out of respect. Ali runs this business ninety-nine percent, but he comes to me ten times a day to ask, 'Can we do this?' I never say no. I always say, 'Yes, good.' "

But the Soltanis are an exception. Most of the older men felt the sand begin to shift beneath their feet the moment they stepped onto American soil. It all began, and ended, with the television set. So many channels here, hundreds of them. They all got big-screen TVs because you had to have the biggest and best of everything—that was the name of the game in Beverly Hills. Some even had sets that rose out of the floor on miniature elevators. But the older men, they could never quite figure out how to work the damn remotes here—they had thousands of buttons, line one, line two, antenna A and B, then the controls for the surround sound, the VCR, and the DVD. You'd be watching a show and try to turn up the volume and suddenly you've switched to a Korean soap opera a thousand channels away from the station you were on. You'd throw the thing down and stalk out of the room cursing. Who had the time for TV, anyway?

The kids did. It didn't matter how old they were, before they could even talk they knew how to work those damn remotes. Every time you came home they were watching the thing, eyes big and wide as an owl's drinking in a never-ending cascade of lush color images of beautifully toned young people, always young, always beautiful and smart, full of grace and decked out in the latest Banana Republic–Gap wear, cavorting through fantastic wonderlands, their every movement and emotion scored with music that told you how to feel and when to feel it. The kids voraciously devoured everything that screen fed them. They didn't even react when you called out their name. Finally you had to shout to get them to turn, and when they did, it was with these alien eyes. American eyes. They had American eyes now. The images from that box had gotten inside their heads and changed them. You tried to get them to hold on to the old ways. You spoke Farsi to them, told them the old folk tales about Mullah Nasredin and his wily mule, or Rostam and his magical horse, Raksh; or read them the poems of Molavi and Molonan; or told them about how you had to escape from Iran after the revolution by riding a camel across the Great Indian Desert. But their eyes were no longer wide as they listened to you; they sagged and glazed over, and you realized that your life experiences, fantastic as they seemed to you, paled in comparison to those of Indiana Jones and Luke Skywalker on that TV screen.

Then one morning when you drive them to school they ask you to let them off a block before you get there. You say that's silly and their voice rises, shrill with panic. "No, let me off now! I don't want the others to see!" And you look in their American eyes and realize it's you they don't want the others to see. They're embarrassed by you . . . ashamed.

And one day you try to discipline them and they scream defiantly, "I'll report you! I'll report you to the school, and they'll send you to jail. You have no right to hit me!" *Right?* In the old country only the father had rights. Here, all of a sudden, it seemed he had none.

"In this country, if you tell your children to do their homework, they threaten to call 911 and have you arrested," Behrouz Mahboubi bitterly complains. "If you raise your voice they accuse you of some kind of abusing. *Abusing.*" He says the word with a mixture of bewilderment and contempt. "I don't know what that is. But they say it. 'You are abusing me.' 'You are harassing me.' 'You are torturing me.' I don't know all these words—they find them in the dictionary. . . . For twenty-five hundred years in Iran things were a certain way, then all of a sudden we land in a place called California and it changes. All of a sudden there is no more respect. They say to the parents, 'You have no right to talk to me like this.' 'You have no right to do this.' " He emits a strangled laugh of incredulity and shrugs his thick shoulders. "How can parents bring up their kids if they have no rights?"

And as they grow older it only gets worse. In Iran, the parents arranged marriages. A daughter was married off by the time she was eighteen years old, usually to a man of thirty, sometimes older, a successful businessman or professional, a good provider for her and her children. "In Iran there were very few divorces, even though ninety-five percent of the marriages were arranged," says Mahboubi.

But in this country the daughters balk. "He's too old for me." Age used to be a good thing, a sign of wisdom and stability. But the television has taught them to hate it. They want one of those young pretty boys they see on the screen.

You try, patiently, to explain the virtues of the man you have chosen for her. She cuts you off, wailing, "But I'm not in love with him!" *Love?* They learned that from the TV also, and the movies, the songs, the advertisements, everywhere you look in America they're always talking about love—*Love Before Breakfast, Love in the Afternoon, Love Me Tonight, Love in the City, Love at the Top, Love on a Pillow, Love on the Ground, Love on the Run, Love Me Forever . . . Love! Love! Love! Love! Love!*

There's no escaping love in America, and now your children chase after those shadows on the screen of people running hand in hand along beaches, kissing on mountaintops, embracing as the music swells to a crescendo and the camera pulls back back back and fades slowly out. But what happens after the fadeout? You try to explain to them that that kind of love never lasts, that no one will be there to play romantic music while you're doing the laundry or cleaning the toilet or arguing over the bills, or packing up your things to flee to another country again. "A marriage based on passionate love, after a year or two it ends in divorce," says Mahboubi. "This would never happen in Iran, in the community I used to know." Marriage isn't about lollipops and love, it's an arrangement, an alliance between two people against a hostile and dangerous world that doesn't give a damn about you. And who better to pick a strong ally for you than your father, who's better equipped to do that? But you try to tell them this and they laugh at you. *They laugh!* Not the slightest bit afraid, because if you dare to raise a hand, to abuse or harass, there's 911 and the police all too ready to haul you away. They dye their hair blond now, some of these girls, and go out with Americans even, and *marry them*!

"Here, the situation has changed," Rahim Soltani laments. "Here, the kids marry who they want, then they say to you, 'Oh yeah, this is my wife.' Or they don't even marry. I know a lot of Iranians who have babies and never marry. The new generation doesn't believe it's a bad thing."

In Iran you could turn to your wife for support. But since coming here she's been watching the TV too. *Oprah Winfrey. The View.* "Shhh! Not now, honey, *The View*'s on!"

And they've learned new words too. Community property. Those were the first words they learned. "In Beverly Hills there are a lot of divorces." Mahboubi sighs with great weariness. "Obviously, a lot of wives have learned how the system favors them, especially in California. They take advantage of an opportunity they didn't have before. That is why we have a lot of divorces. Primarily, it's a money situation, because they know that either way they get half the money. In Iran, according to Iranian law, the woman didn't get anything, and there were very few divorces. I've seen a lot of people in the last few years in very bitter fights in court with millions going to lawyers. None of this would happen in Iran."

It's evident in the tension in their eyebrows, the tautness of the lips pulled flat against their teeth as these men talk: the stinging realization that they've been cheated. *You play by one set of rules your whole life, you follow the system they gave you, you go without food until your father comes home, humbly solicit his advice when you don't need or want it, submit to his choice of a wife, a stranger who he tells you to bind your life to, and then, when your hair has grayed, your face withered and bones grown brittle, when it finally comes time for you to reap the benefits that you've keenly anticipated for decades, when it's your turn, they change all the rules on you!*

But Gina Nahai does not mourn with these men, or long to return to the patriarchal paradise of prerevolutionary Iran. She has learned to love the freedom of America, despite all of the uncertainties, anxieties, and responsibilities that come with it. America has allowed her to blossom, to pursue a career as a professional writer. She has written two bestselling novels—*Moonlight on the Avenue of Faith* and *Cry of the Peacock*—an achievement that would have been unthinkable in the old country.

Yes, divorce was rare in Iran—Nahai explains—because women had no civil rights. Those who dared to leave their husbands lost everything because all of the material assets belonged to the husband by law. Even if a woman remained a faithful companion, she had no guaran-

Coldwater Canyon in 1910, shortly after the Rodeo Land and Water Company decided to transform a nondescript 4,539-acre parcel of property into Beverly Hills. *Photograph courtesy of Marc Wanamaker/Bison Archives*

The Beverly Hills Hotel after its completion in 1912. The hotel was a world-class resort and a cunning marketing tool. It seduced wealthy easterners into buying vacation homes and sparked Beverly Hills's first building boom. *Photograph courtesy of Marc Wanamaker/Bison Archives*

Gregory Peck and Lauren Bacall at the Beverly Hills Hotel pool during the filming of *Designing Woman* (1957). *Photograph courtesy of Marc Wanamaker/Bison Archives*

John Bruce Nelson shows off one of his listings. Nelson is the premier independent Realtor in Beverly Hills. He spent his youth hanging around the pool of the Beverly Hills Hotel and found his calling there. *Photograph by Bradley Thompson*

Svend Petersen, the pool manager of the Beverly Hills Hotel, holds Faye Dunaway's Oscar for *Network*. Dunaway's husband at the time, Terry O'Neill, stands on the left. For almost fifty years, Petersen hustled drinks and towels to the stars. *Photograph courtesy of the Beverly Hills Hotel*

Mary Pickford and Douglas Fairbanks at Pickfair. They built the first movie-star mansion in Beverly Hills in 1919. Other stars quickly followed in their footsteps. *Photograph courtesy of Marc Wanamaker/Bison Archives*

Buster Keaton in his bedroom at the Italian villa. Keaton's wife pressured him into building a movie-star palace in Beverly Hills in 1926. *Photograph courtesy of the Academy of Motion Picture Arts and Sciences*

John Bercsi reflected in Buster Keaton's mirror at the Italian villa. By the late 1990s the Italian villa was one of the last silent-movie-star palaces still standing in Beverly Hills. Bercsi saved it from the wrecking ball and restored it to grace. *Photograph by Bradley Thompson*

The exterior of Keaton's long-lost film vault at the villa. In 1932 Buster moved out of the house in an alcoholic haze and forgot about the vault at the back of the gardener's shed that contained prints of most of his silent films.
Photograph by Dennis Kightley

The interior of the film vault at the villa. In 1955 the home's new owner, James Mason, stumbled upon the vault and discovered the cache of Keaton's silent masterpieces.
Photograph by Dennis Kightley

Grayhall mansion, shortly after it was built by Harry D. Lombard in the early teens. A 4,000-square-foot great hall would be added by Silsby Spalding in 1919. In the decades that followed, Grayhall's "high-class" aura attracted owners who hoped that, like a Brooks Brothers suit, the mansion would cloak them in respectability. *Photograph courtesy of Marc Wanamaker/Bison Archives*

Living inside the centerfold—Norm Zadeh and friends. After he made millions as a hedge-fund manager in the 1990s, Zadeh built a postmodern mansion in Beverly Hills, filled it with young wild things, and started *Perfect 10* magazine. *Photograph courtesy of Norm Zadeh*

Bernie Cornfeld (*left*) hangs out with Raquel Welch and director John Milius. Cornfeld's greatest ambition was to emulate Hugh Hefner's Bachelor in Paradise lifestyle. He partied his way through a $15 million fortune and died a forgotten man. *Photograph courtesy of Marc Wanamaker/Bison Archives*

Milton Berle; his wife, Ruth; and daughter, Vickie, enjoy the good life, December 22, 1955. Berle was the youngest member of a generation of American entertainers who grew up in the urban ghettos of the East. They saw show business as a vehicle for upward mobility. *Photograph courtesy of the University of Southern California Cinema/Television Library, Special Collections*

Left to right: Milton Berle, George Jessel, and Edward G. Robinson at a Friars Club event on December 28, 1960. The Friars Club became the favorite Beverly Hills watering hole of Jewish American entertainers in the 1950s and '60s. Its celebrity roasts were legendary. *Photograph courtesy of the University of Southern California Cinema/Television Library, Special Collections*

Left to right: George Burns, Muhammad Ali, Milton Berle, and Phil Silvers at a Friars Club event in the 1960s. *Photograph courtesy of Marc Wanamaker/Bison Archives*

Left to right: The East Side kids—Eddie Cantor, Sammy Davis, Jr., unidentified man, Jack Benny, and George Burns—trade one-liners with future president Ronald Reagan at the Friars Club. *Photograph courtesy of Marc Wanamaker/Bison Archives*

Saeed Nourmand, the premier Persian Realtor in Beverly Hills. Seven thousand Iranians immigrated to the city after the fall of the shah in 1979. *Photograph by Bradley Thompson*

This house is typical of the original homes built in Trousdale Estates. In 1955, 410 acres of the E. L. Doheny estate were sold off to a speculator who created the world's most expensive subdivision. Because of the era's high income and property taxes, the Trousdale homes were only one story tall and of modest size. *Photograph by Bradley Thompson*

When the Persians arrived, many bought homes in Trousdale and remodeled them to suit their ostentatious tastes. This house typifies the result. Veteran residents were outraged and formed the Committee to Save Beverly Hills to lobby for building code restrictions. *Photograph by Bradley Thompson*

Prince Michael Dimitri Alexandrovich Obolenski-Romanoff, a flamboyant con man who opened a restaurant in Beverly Hills. The city of self-mythologized people welcomed him with open arms and made his establishment the premier eatery in Los Angeles. *Photograph courtesy of Marc Wanamaker/Bison Archives*

Left to right: Michael Romanoff (*standing*), Sophia Loren, Jayne Mansfield, and Clifton Webb at a party at Romanoff's. *Photograph courtesy of Marc Wanamaker/Bison Archives*

Bijan Pakzad's clothing boutique on Rodeo Drive. The statue of Louis XIV (*on the right*) sets the tone for a store that caters to some of the wealthiest despots on the planet. *Photograph courtesy of Bijan Pakzad*

Bijan Pakzad, laughing all the way to the bank. He clothes the world's wealthiest men—movie stars, corporate titans, presidents, and kings. A complete ensemble can run as much as a million dollars. *Photograph courtesy of Bijan Pakzad*

Fred Hayman gives Y. A. M. Tengku Puteri Datin Seri Paduka Zahariah, the princess of Malaysia, billiard instructions during her visit to his Rodeo Drive clothing store on December 23, 1992. In the 1960s Hayman founded the legendary Giorgio boutique with his wife, Gale. *Photograph courtesy of Marc Wanamaker/Bison Archives*

Lana Turner, Johnny Stompanato, and Cheryl Turner at Los Angeles International Airport, March 3, 1958. Stompanato was a Mafia foot soldier with ambitions to marry Lana, and to produce and star in his own movies. *Photograph courtesy of Marc Wanamaker/Bison Archives*

Private investigator John Lane, behind his desk at the Omega Group, one of several security firms with James Bondian titles that profit from the paranoia of movie stars and media moguls. *Photograph by Bradley Thompson*

Beverly Hills High School in 1936. The school looms almost as large as Monument Valley in the American zeitgeist. The front steps became the domain of the slackers in the 1980s and '90s. *Photograph courtesy of Marc Wanamaker/Bison Archives*

A match made in hell: Darcy LaPier and Mark Hughes. When Darcy saw Mark's Rolls-Royce, his $6,000 suit, Cartier watch, gold rings, and cuff links, it was love at first sight. She was the fourth beauty queen that he married; he was her third millionaire. *Photograph by Henry Miller, courtesy of NewsCom*

tee of financial security because upon her husband's death his assets automatically went to his oldest son. "So these women who were with their husband for fifty years would be at the mercy of their son and daughter-in-law," says Nahai. "And if their son didn't support them, they literally starved in the street. The men lament because their wives have become so uppity since they've moved to Beverly Hills. Why have the wives become so uppity? Because they were so miserable in Iran, but they couldn't do anything about it."

And the patriarchs who opine about the rock-solid family values that existed in Iran often fail to mention those values included a double standard about sexual behavior. If a husband caught his wife in an act of adultery, he could commit an "honor killing" without fear of punishment from the authorities. "A crime of passion committed by a male toward a female was considered understandable," Nahai explains. "He got off scot-free." If a man was of a more lenient nature and decided to merely beat his wife black and blue, well, that was acceptable too, of course. Or if he decided a little public humiliation might help her see the error of her ways, he could remove her veil, shave her head, mount her backward on a mule, and ride her around the neighborhood. "If a man only suspected his wife of adultery but didn't catch her in the act, he could still kill her and get off without spending a day in jail," says Nahai.

And men? Well, men had different needs of course, that went without saying. A man had to have some outlet, some means of relief from the stress and responsibilities of being an absolute dictator. It was a given that most men had a mistress, maybe two or three. But their wives had better not complain about it, if they knew what was good for them.

"Our lives are a thousand times better in America than they ever would have been in Iran," says Shirin Danielpour. Like Nahai, Shirin has thrived in the free society of the United States. She obtained a degree in journalism and became the managing editor of the *Beverly Hills Weekly*, a scrappy little newspaper that has stolen the limelight from the ancient and moribund *Beverly Hills Courier*. Thanks to

Shirin, the *Weekly* became the first local publication to offer in-depth reporting on the city's Persian community. "Thank god for America—I mean, really," she exclaims. "In Iran we had wealth and we lived like royalty, but my mother wouldn't in her wildest dreams envision her daughter as the managing editor of a newspaper. In Iran I'd be married off and raising kids by now. You talk to any of the first-generation Persian women in Beverly Hills—their daughters are getting their master's degrees or going to law and med school. We've assimilated. We've learned that it's good to move forward, get an education and become something."

Shirin has even dared to publicly criticize the rampant materialism of Iranian-Americans, and to proclaim that it's time for them to "put their money aside and start looking to each other for love." Her stance has provoked a volatile reaction. At social gatherings, men have cursed her and called her a disgrace to her people. But Shirin's far from shaken by such vitriolic outbursts; in fact they only solidify her determination to bring down the barriers that have entrapped Iranian women for centuries. There's a quiet confidence in her steady, big-pupiled gaze, a calm certainty that she will prevail that's altogether absent in the ever-shifting eyes of the older men who attack her. As their dark irises dart right and left, from object to object, unable to find safe harbor anywhere in their surroundings, they reveal glints of rage, uncertainty, and most of all, fear. The sand beneath their feet continues to shift ever faster, and try as they might, they can't seem to get a foothold.

★ 6 ★

"Beverly Hills Is My Country"

Bijan Pakzad was born in Tehran, Iran, on April 4, 1944. His lineage, he proudly notes, "was privileged." Though he attended the finest private schools in Switzerland and Italy, he could muster little enthusiasm for such mundane subjects as math, science, or history. Form, not function, captivated his imagination. For as long as he can remember, he was obsessed with colors and textures. He reveled in a world not of ideas but of style.

The epiphany came at age ten. "The details was," he says in his heavy Persian-Italian-Swiss accent, "I had been with my father at my aunt's home and they wanted to take a picture." Bijan set the camera up on a tripod, with a timer so that he could both be in the photo and take it. "But before we say 'cheese' and take a picture, I stopped to fix everybody collars and jackets to be straight. I wanted everybody be organized, very well dressed and very nice to put in the picture. I was very much for clothes. I really wanted to be different and be very expert and be number one in my field if I grow up." The field, he realized, would be fashion. Like Oscar Wilde, he would devote his life to aestheticism, to "the search after signs of the beautiful." Though he couldn't have articulated it then, he instinctively understood, as Wilde had, that a concern for moral lessons or weighty ideas was sheer folly—form, not content, was what mattered. It was the capacity to render, to create something of beauty, and not the capacity to feel, which brought true art into being and brought one closer to the divine. "I wanted to be famous," he explains. "I wanted to be rich. I wanted to do a statement for the men in the world."

After finishing school, he returned to Tehran in 1966, at the age of twenty-two. He did not have to earn his first million because, as he says proudly, "My father gave it to me." Amply capitalized, he opened a women's clothing boutique called The Pink Panther in an exclusive suburb of Tehran. Times were good for Iranians at the top of the food chain. Booming oil exports pumped billions of dollars into the economy, and those who were hardwired into Shah Mohammad Reza Pahlavi's patronage network had plenty of money to burn on extravagant luxuries. The Pink Panther was a huge success. Bijan soon opened a second boutique for men. He traveled extensively to Florence, Naples, and Paris, importing the latest designs in menswear. Then he began to create his own. Word spread through Tehran's upper echelons that this young designer was extraordinary. Bijan filled the armoires of the most powerful men in Iran, including the Shah.

But as the Shah's regime began to crumble in the mid-'70s, Bijan joined the ranks of many talented and wealthy Persians who were relocating to America, and followed his close friend Dar Mahboubi to Beverly Hills. For Bijan, it was love at first sight. The city had almost everything: sunshine, palm-lined boulevards, and most important, thousands of potential customers with unlimited bank accounts.

And there was one other element, crucial to every great love affair: the city needed him. For though they knew how to build beautiful cities, these filthy rich Americans dressed worse than gypsies. "A European man get dressed in suit and tie every day," he explains. "Not in America. People are absolutely so bad dressed, especially men. This country, compared to any other country in this world, is number one in service, in everything but fashion. Regarding men's fashion is very, very poor. Is unfortunate, that's in the people's blood to not be very well dressed. I realize this country need my help."

He had found his calling. He would lift these wealthy Americans out of the fashion gutter and lead them to stylish salvation. Mahboubi gave him $2.2 million to build a boutique on Rodeo Drive filled with the finest textiles the world had to offer. Now all Bijan had to do was entice the ill-dressed Americans through the front door. A formidable challenge. The other menswear stores on Rodeo—Theodore Man, Carroll & Company—were well entrenched, and Bijan was a complete unknown. How could he possibly hope to win over the showbiz elite? Then, as if by divine revelation, the answer came to him: through the lure of exclusivity. *Make it difficult, and they will come.*

He locked the front door and painted in tasteful script across the front window: "By appointment only." Beverly Hills residents, window-shopping along the boulevard, stopped before those words with perturbed brows. Unable to believe them, they reached out and attempted to push open the door. A dead bolt held it fast. *Son of a bitch. Whoever heard of a merchant who doesn't want to let you in his store? What the hell's he got in there anyway?*

They began to call and make appointments. Once they gained admittance they were not disappointed. Never in their wildest fantasies had they envisioned such merchandise! Mink-lined denim jackets for $7,500, $15,000 vicuña coats, $100,000 alligator coats lined with chinchilla, $19,000 silk-lined ostrich-skinned vests, $4,000 jackets made out of the finest Irish wools, and $1,500 shirts of Egyptian cotton, woven in Britain and sewn in Italy. Limited-edition silk ties, personally designed and numbered by Bijan because, he explained as he deftly slipped them around their collars, "You would hate to go to a coronation and see someone wearing the same tie."

And it wasn't just a matter of picking out a couple of shirts, a jacket, and a pair of trousers—Bijan could design an entire wardrobe for you, an ensemble for a season at Monte Carlo, and another for your board meetings and another for formal dinner parties. He not only created a wide variety of clothes that could be mixed and matched, but he also assembled a personal manual of style, filled with photos of your textile repertoire and instructions on what combinations could be put together from it. A full wardrobe could run more than $1 million. Bijan deftly assuaged whatever guilt his customers might feel about spending all that cash on clothes when they could be feeding the starving millions of Africa, or educating the illiterates of Appalachia, or blah-blah-blah. *Don't trouble yourself with such thoughts, my friend. They are beneath you. You are a man of distinction, a man who towers above the crowd. A man with special needs, extraordinary requirements. We both know that.*

As Bijan explained to a reporter from *Talk* magazine: "I am absolutely not shocked if someone comes into my store, as someone from Northern California did last week, and spends $250,000. A smart man. If he was not so smart, he wouldn't be so powerful or wealthy." Bijan understood that these men did not spend fantastic amounts of money on clothing out of narcissism or an immature need to compensate for inner feelings of insecurity or self-loathing. No, Bijan understood—as only a man of rarefied intelligence and taste could—that his clients had the guts, the chutzpah, the power, panache, and insight to make a bold lifestyle statement, to define themselves as unique individuals, as dynamic shepherds in a world of sheep.

And when he took their shoulders and gently guided them into a cubicle of mirrors that reflected their image over and over to create endless corridors of duplicate selves clad in the finest Russian cashmere, English wool, Egyptian cotton, and African ostrich the world had to offer, the garment master would whisper, *Behold, the Bijan man! What defines him, my friend? Contemporary and discerning characterize two incisive qualities of the forever-compelling Bijan man. Wise, but bewitching, he is undeniably individual and possesses a voracious charm. A devoted gentleman and occasional rogue, the Bijan man adores attention. He always maintains his elegant presence with daring originality and is confident in making decisions, especially in matters of aesthetics. A man of many moods and minds, he is mysterious and pleasantly perplexing. This is the Bijan man.*

Yes! They saw in the infinite corridors of selves so many possibilities, so many facets, so many admirable qualities! They emerged from Bijan's cloistered realm with a beatific born-again glow. Word quickly spread, not only through the canyons of Beverly but across continents and oceans, a whispering campaign among the world's most wealthy and powerful men: *You must see Bijan. He changed my life!*

And so they came. The stars: Jay Leno, Sir Ian McKellen, Siegfried and Roy, Anthony Quinn, Jack Lemmon, Al Pacino, Robert De Niro, Larry King, Sir Elton John, Paul Newman, Pierce Brosnan, Tony Bennett, Ed Bradley, Sidney Poitier, Stevie Wonder, Warren Beatty, Harrison Ford, Arnold Schwarzenegger, Sean Connery. The media moguls: Michael Eisner, David Geffen, Kirk Kerkorian, Aaron Spelling, Walter H. Annenberg, William Randolph Hearst III, Michael Bloomberg, Rupert Murdoch, Barry Diller, Ted Turner. The captains of capitalism: Steve Wynn, Bill Gates, William Barron Hilton. The artistes: David Hockney, Martin Scorsese, Steven Spielberg, Francis Ford Coppola, Stephen King, John Irving. The royalty: Prince Charles, Prince Rainier, King Mohammed VI of Morocco. The politicos: Vernon Jordan, Senator Christopher Dodd, Kofi Annan, Vice President Al Gore, Nelson Mandela, Prime Minister Tony Blair, and Presidents Reagan, Bush senior, Clinton, and Bush junior.

"One one-tenth of one percent of the world's population can afford to shop in such splendor," Steve Stalder, a member of Bijan's sales force, told a reporter. "When these men walk into the room, people tremble."

All except Bijan. "Because I *dictate* to powerful men," the maestro explains. "They give me their money, I give them my style! . . . I don't want to sound like a monster, but I love power, I love women, I love my ego."

Some of his most loyal customers are despots, men of privileged lineage—such as the Saudi Arabian princes and the sultan of Brunei—who received their first billions from their fathers; who live in unrestrained luxury because they have monopolized most of their countries' natural resources and utilize "proactive" police forces to arrest, torture, and terrorize any have-nots with the audacity to question the natural order of things. It is for these very special men that Bijan placed outside the front door of his shop a $250,000 bronze statue of Louis XIV, the French monarch who proclaimed "I am the state"—who built Versailles and lived there in fantastic luxury while the people of France slowly starved to death. "He was one of the most well dressed men in history!" Bijan enthuses. And it was for the men of Louis that Bijan designed his limited-edition Colt .38 Detective Special with an eighteen-karat gold barrel, inlaid diamonds, and a napa leather handgrip signed by Bijan—a must for trend-setting tyrants the world over.

But in the 1980s Bijan felt a sudden urge to do something for the little people. Why shouldn't the masses be given an opportunity to buy a little piece of luxury? He was undoubtedly inspired by a fellow retailer a few doors down Rodeo. Fred Hayman, owner of the Giorgio boutique, had bottled the Beverly Hills mystique by creating Giorgio perfume, and distributed it to retailers across America. Moved by the same egalitarian impulse, the wardrobe maestro produced Bijan Fragrance for Men and Perfume for Women and launched a publicity blitzkrieg to spread the word to the multitudes that they too could share the good life. Thus billboards appeared, and ads in glossy magazines, featuring Bijan laughing exultantly with supermodels and celebrities such as Bo Derek and Michael Jordan. Now even an insurance adjuster in Des Moines, a tool and die manufacturer in Milwaukee, could become a Bijan man, and their wives, Bijan women.

His press releases wove a carefully crafted Bijan mystique, and glossy magazines that gobbled up the millions he spent on full-page ads were more than happy to regurgitate the copy he fed them in the guise of profile pieces. In one particularly penetrating treatise, entitled *Bijan—The Man, The Mystery, The Legend,* the sultan of the stitch defined himself thusly: "Perceived throughout the world of fashion and fragrance as the most enigmatic and mysterious designer, Bijan carefully and meticulously orchestrates the manner in which every element of his companies and image are highlighted. Although some may consider his hands-on nature somewhat controlling, Bijan insists he is a mere *perfectionist*! A compelling, intuitive and compassionate man, Bijan is quite often misunderstood. He's driven, he's unpredictable, he's untamed yet sophisticated."

Every detail of his life was a carefully calculated expression of the Louis XIV aesthetic. He bought a two-acre French country manor in the hills above Sunset with a panoramic view of L.A. and filled it with works by Picasso, Renoir, and Warhol; and purchased a half-dozen luxury cars, including a $400,000 custom-made yellow Bentley, a black Bentley for more somber occasions, a Rolls-Royce, and a custom-made Mercedes-Benz SL-600; sixty-five jewel-encrusted watches; and his own jet. In 1997 Bijan claimed to have spent $10 million (or in some interviews $12 million) to renovate his boutique, which he packed with such Versailles-like extravagances as a $200,000 two-story glass and mahogany front door, a $1 million Botero painting of a well-dressed corpulent couple, entitled *The Rich,* a $1 million chandelier composed of 1,000 dangling Baccarat crystals filled with Bijan perfume, and a $750,000 collection of Napoleonic swords.

He had 200 employees now—sales reps, marketing executives, copywriters, accountants, secretaries, and gofers—and he enlisted them in his never-ending quest to refine his own myth. "He had this little black journal and he asked certain people to write about him in it because he was going to include their quotes in his autobiography," says a former employee. "The president of his perfume company wrote in it, his personal accountant wrote in it, his personal assistant, his sales manager, his vice president—almost everybody was asked to write in it." No fools, they laid the superlatives on thick. Afterward, Bijan would pore over their words, nodding his head in agreement.

A former employee recalls: "Someone was getting him coffee once and they asked him how he wanted it. He said, 'Beige.' That was Bijan. If a receptionist arrived at the showroom a half hour late because her car broke down, that was not acceptable. But if she cruised in and said 'I'm late because I was trying on a new lipstick,' that was acceptable. All of his female employees had to be attractive, and if a receptionist didn't wear nylons or her makeup wasn't perfect, he would fly off the handle. He'd say, 'She has to go. This one has to go!'

"You see, with Bijan, it's all about presentation."

The same could be said about every retailer on Rodeo Drive. The street surely would have won the admiration of P. T. Barnum, for it is a phantasmagoric midway packed with the world's most skilled carnival barkers who expertly manipulate the egos of the ultrarich, making them feel enlightened and sophisticated for buying outrageously priced merchandise—much of it as gaudy as the baubles you'd win at a dart booth, except these are made of Lalique crystal, platinum, and adorned with diamonds instead of rhinestones. The exteriors of the stores are a wild mélange of European architecture with a proliferation of copper roofs, bronze doors, marble and limestone colonnades and Corinthian columns, neo-Renaissance and postmodern sculptures. There is even a stretch of cobblestone street that approximates Paris's Latin Quarter. It all has the antiseptic, derivative quality of a theme park, which may not be inappropriate, for it has become the fourth most popular tourist spot in Southern California. Each year, twelve million Americans, Europeans, and Far Easterners wander up and down the boulevard to gape at the retail palaces.

Inside, the stores are just as grand. Many feature sweeping U-shaped staircases straight out of Hollywood costume dramas and are packed with galaxy-shaped chandeliers, grand gold-framed oil paintings, Renaissance-style sculptures, and antique furniture worth hundreds of thousands of dollars. The merchandise is often indistinguishable from the art pieces. At Hermès a $20,000 purse is displayed on a pedestal, encased in a glass cube and lit by a number of spotlights, as if it were the Hope Diamond. In many stores individual dresses hang on chrome racks like Warhol sculptures—and they might as well be; in the Versace store, for instance, a custom-made gown can run $100,000.

The street wasn't always so theatrical. When Wilbur Cook laid out the blueprint for Burton Green's utopia in the early 1900s, he established a twenty-block commercial district smack in the middle of Beverly Hills. It was bounded on the north by Santa Monica Boulevard, on the east by Rexford Drive, and on the west and south by Wilshire Boulevard. In time it would become known as the Golden Triangle—the most fashionable and expensive retail district in the world. But its beginnings were humble. When Green first broke ground on his City of Tomorrow there was one retail outlet in all of Beverly Hills: a grocery store run by George Brusso and his wife. It was typical of family-owned general stores found in small farm towns throughout the South and Midwest—an institution that belonged to the city's past, but not to its future.

In 1907 the Rodeo Land and Water Company erected the first structure of the new commercial district: the Peck Building, on the southwest corner of Beverly Drive and Santa Monica Boulevard. It was followed by a new grocery store in 1914, a drugstore (Homer's) in 1920, and a furniture store in 1921. By 1923 there was a grand total of eight retailers in the district. As the decade progressed, the rate of growth rapidly accelerated. By 1933 there were 291 commercial buildings.

For many members of the movie colony, maintaining a glamorous appearance was an essential business expense. So the new stores—Helena Rubinstein, Saks Fifth Avenue, I. Magnin & Co., W & J Sloane, and Robinson's—catered to customers like Gloria Swanson, whose annual clothing bills averaged $25,000 for fur coats, $50,000 for gowns, $9,000 for stockings, $5,000 for shoes, $10,000 for lingerie, $5,000 for purses, $5,000 for headdresses, and $6,000 for perfume. Yet the retailers remained essentially provincial. They imported a relatively small number of gowns, shoes, and hats from the major designers in New York and Paris—much like the better stores in prosperous cities across America did. But no great designers lived in Beverly Hills or even had showrooms there.

The restaurants also served Hollywood's aristocracy, and a few became legendary. The original Brown Derby opened in Los Angeles in

1926. A second Derby opened in Hollywood in 1929, and finally a third in Beverly Hills in 1931, on the corner of Wilshire and Rodeo Drive. Nick Volpe's charcoal sketches of the celebrity customers—Eddie Cantor, Al Jolson, Jack Benny, Fred Allen, James Cagney, Clark Gable, the Marx Brothers, Fanny Brice, Jean Harlow, Bette Davis, Joan Crawford, and many more—adorned the walls. The Derby originated the Cobb salad—avocado, hard-boiled eggs, bacon, lettuce, tomato, and turkey with blue cheese dressing—and its cuisine compared favorably with the fare of upscale restaurants in most American cities, but it was hardly world-class.

How, then, did things begin to change? The transformation was brought about by an idiosyncratic genius who transformed a prosaic public institution into a dream machine for the superrich. His name: Prince Michael Dimitri Alexandrovich Obolenski-Romanoff, once heir to the Russian throne, a man who had killed Rasputin, served in both the British Army and the Cossacks, been educated at Oxford and Harvard, and had a torrid love affair with a Hapsburg princess. Unlike most princes, Romanoff was a self-made man. He started out in life not as royalty, but as a working-class Lithuanian Jew and made his way through a number of identities before finally settling on the Russian prince. He was an English gentleman named Willoughby de Burke, artist Rockwell Kent, Professor John William Adams from Yale, Mr. R. A. Adams of New York, Arthur Wellesley, William A. Wellington, Count Gladstone, Captain Chitterin of the British Army, and a dozen other personas before he assumed the title of Romanoff and came to Beverly Hills, a community largely populated by self-mythologized people who were uniquely equipped to appreciate a man with his creative talents.

He was born in 1889 as Hershel Geguzin, in Vilna, Lithuania. When his father, Emmanuel, was killed in a street brawl, his mother, Hinde, had to take over the family dry goods business. She had little time to lavish on the youngest of her six children. Perhaps out of desire for attention, Hershel soon developed a rebellious streak. He refused to work in the store, played hooky from school, and, when his mother lectured him to straighten out, ran away from home for days at a time. When Hershel turned ten, Hinde decided her son might stand a better chance in the freewheeling land of America where stubborn individualism was regarded as a virtue. So she sent him off with her cousin Joseph Bloomberg, who, like hundreds of thousands of European Jews, was heading across the Atlantic for New York.

Hinde had the store to look after, so instead of taking her son to the train station herself, she assigned the task to Hershel's older sister, Olga. As the train pulled into the station, Hershel fell into his sister's arms and wept—the abandonment he felt at that moment must have been cataclysmic. In the decades that followed he would grant interviews to newspapers across America, each time assuming a different persona and back story and reshuffling real incidents from his past with imagined ones. Every once in a while a trace of authentic emotion would bleed through the performance. One time he told a reporter that he had been born in New York and that his father had died when he was six. Then he added pointedly, "I do not remember my mother."

After passing through Ellis Island, Hershel found himself living with his cousins in a crowded cold-water tenement on Manhattan's Lower East Side. He hated school even more in America than he had in Lithuania, and detested synagogue. Like Milton Berle, George Burns, George Jessel, and the Marx Brothers, he was determined to evade the dreary life of manual labor that almost everyone else in the neighborhood had resigned themselves to. And like those other East Side Kids who would one day join him in Beverly Hills, Hershel was drawn to a world of fantasy. He found his never-never land not in a vaudeville theater but within his own prodigious imagination. In time, he would draw the rest of the world into his romantic epic. He wrote the scenes as he went along and cast the people he encountered in roles as his leading ladies, villains, and comic sidekicks.

Hershel soon ran away from the tenement and survived by selling newspapers on street corners, and sleeping in pool halls and doorways. A concerned citizen reported the ragged street urchin to the Manhattan Hebrew Orphanage, which handed Hershel over to the New York

Juvenile Asylum. For the next five years, authorities tried to place him in foster homes, but the boy kept running away. Social workers coached him to be deferential to wealthy visitors—if he managed to charm them they might adopt him. His guardians schooled Hershel in the social graces and behaviors of the rich. He absorbed their lessons but did not put them into practice until later in life, and then it would be in ways that would surely have shocked his earnest instructors.

By the time he was nineteen years old, Hershel was on his own again. He took a job on a cattle ship, crossed the Atlantic to England, and wound up working in a tailor shop near Oxford. This somehow led to a position as a valet to upper-class boys attending the university. Hershel studied their refined manners carefully and soaked up a wealth of trivia about Eton, Cambridge, and Oxford—everything from the best bars to the sexual peccadilloes and academic quirks of various teachers. For the rest of his life, if he met a man from any of these schools he could converse with him as if he too were an alumnus.

At some moment now lost to history, he crossed over to a world of his own devising. He began appearing in London's best private clubs as Willoughby de Burke, an Oxford man, and for a time was accepted as an equal. Then someone who had lent him money and never been repaid reported Willoughby to Scotland Yard. Detectives launched an investigation, but by that time the changeling had crossed the channel.

In 1922 Paris was awash with American expatriates and refugees from the Russian Revolution. Former Russian army officers and members of the aristocracy were forced to take menial jobs to survive. So when a short man in his early thirties, who now called himself Harry Gerguson, took a job as a book stacker in the American Library in Paris, it was not surprising that he found himself sorting volumes with a pair of deposed Russian princes. He studied the men's mannerisms carefully with his penetrating brown eyes and peppered them with questions. There was plenty of time to talk, and the princes didn't mind sharing their dramatic back stories.

Soon the cafés on the Left Bank where the Americans hung out were graced by an exciting new personality: a bona fide Russian prince!

The progeny of a stark utilitarian culture, these Americans harbored a fetish for the trappings of European royalty. They couldn't get enough of his anecdotes about grand balls, romances with Hapsburg princesses, and duels of honor. He appropriated anecdotes from Hollywood costume dramas, but it didn't seem to matter. The more outrageous the tale, the more they loved it.

So he ventured into the Ritz bar, the watering hole of the truly wealthy Americans. The gilded furniture and crystal chandeliers reminded him of his opulent past, and he could not help but recount to the other patrons how he had once lived a life of pampered luxury. How cruel, how absurd that he should now be forced to scramble for his next meal! Of course, he would be back in the chips soon enough, when his trainload of family heirlooms and jewelry arrived from the Baltic. For you see, he was no longer just another garden-variety prince, he was now none other than Michael Dimitri Alexandrovich Obolenski-Romanoff, heir to the crown. The Americans bought him drink after drink and were only too happy to advance him temporary funds so he could live in the style he was accustomed to.

It proved so lucrative he took the act on the road in the years that followed, adding flourishes such as a top hat, a monocle, a walking stick, and the Legion of Honor medal, which he wore proudly on his lapel. Romanoff toured on transatlantic ocean liners, always dining at the captain's table, and stayed at the finest hotels and estates in New York, St. Paul, St. Louis, Tulsa, and Cambridge. Even the cream of Boston society accepted him with open arms when they read the glowing letters of introduction written by the crowned heads of Europe. Mike attended Harvard for a time, lectured on Russian history in salons and public venues, summered in Newport, Rhode Island, where he was invited to parties thrown by the Vanderbilts, and gave interviews to newspaper reporters who were eager to write about the charismatic prince who had become the latest high-society sensation.

His popularity often led to his downfall; he was exposed as a fraud dozens of times and thrown in jail for bouncing checks, failing to repay loans, and running minor confidence schemes on his admirers. But the strange thing was this never seemed to do long-term damage to his popularity, probably because he never took people for large sums of money—just enough to buy a few rounds of drinks, to pay a hotel bill or buy a new wardrobe. Romanoff was in it not for the money but for the theater, the persona, the life. In time, New York society came to view him as a loveable rogue, a celebrated phony who lent a little Erich Von Stroheim panache to an otherwise routine social affair.

Whenever he was arrested, police officers, judges, even prosecutors inevitably fell under the spell of Michael Romanoff's charisma. He was acquitted, given suspended sentences, put on probation, but did very little hard time. Once, when Mike was facing deportation because immigration officials refused to believe his claim that he'd been born in America, Romanoff's probation officer, Edmund Collins, arranged a meeting in a stark interrogation room. He too had taken a liking to the prince. "Why not tell me the truth so I can help you?" Collins implored. "If you were indeed born in New York, as you claim, then why in heaven's name do you pretend to be a dead prince from Russia?"

"Let me explain," Romanoff replied in a strangely candid moment. "Have you ever been in a bare room in a new house with a view overlooking a park? You look at the park and it is marvelous. You look at the bare walls, and you find them absolutely repulsive. They cry for adornment. That is I. I don't lie because I desire to be a crook and a thief, but because I wish to associate with persons whose lives I believe to be frankly adorned. Frankly, I will lie to you as long as you know me. If I told the truth, I would feel like a bare wall." A few nights later, expecting the worst in his trial, Romanoff lay down on his cot and slit his wrists. He was saved by an attentive guard, and later in court a sympathetic judge gave him a suspended sentence.

When Romanoff was finally deported in 1932 for a long list of crimes, New York society mourned the loss of its favorite scalawag, and Alva Johnston wrote a five-part piece on him in *The New Yorker* that became a template for the modern magazine profile. When Mike snuck back into the United States a year later, he discovered he had entered the realm of myth. Attending the Beaux Arts Ball at the Waldorf-Astoria, he stepped into the ballroom to thunderous applause.

Authorities soon became aware of his presence and a federal grand jury indicted Romanoff again for perjury and entering the country illegally. He faced up to fifty-five years in prison, but Judge John C. Knox heard his plea of guilty and placed him on probation.

In 1936 Romanoff arrived in Los Angeles as a national celebrity. When he started going to the Clover Club, a gambling casino on Sunset Boulevard frequented by Hollywood's elite, his presence drew huge crowds. Management offered him a sweet deal: if he would show up every night, they'd arrange for him to win at the tables, as Claude Rains would later do in *Casablanca* (a bit no doubt inspired by Romanoff).

With a steady cash flow for the first time in his life, Mike moved into an apartment in Baja Beverly Hills, at 209 South El Camino Drive, bought a Cadillac Coupe, and courted a bevy of Hollywood starlets. Then he decided to throw a party for himself and sent invitations to the film capital's A-list, engraving each invite with an imperial *R.* The card began: "To Discharge His Social Obligations, Past and Future, We Have Received Commands From His Imperial Highness, Prince Michael Romanoff . . ." and went on to invite the addressee to a supper at the Clover Club. The event was a huge success. The celebrities in attendance included Robert Benchley, James Cagney, Charlie Chaplin, Cary Grant, Mark Hellinger, Edward G. Robinson, Randolph Scott, and Jules Stein. Stein donated a full orchestra for entertainment. When a reporter for *Time* asked Romanoff why social queen Elsa Maxwell had not been invited, he explained, "No phonies."

After he combed the confetti out of his hair, Romanoff thought: *Why should such a wonderful thing end? Why not open a restaurant and keep the party going all year round?* Thus, at fifty years old the grifter took on his first steady job and became the most successful restaurateur in Beverly Hills history. The city still had no world-class eateries in 1939. Well, Mike would open the first. He had dined in the best establishments in Europe, and even though he never picked up the check, he had developed a sophisticated palate and discerning eye for presentation. Romanoff had no trouble enlisting investors. They included Robert Benchley, Darryl Zanuck, Joseph Schenck, Charlie Chaplin, James Cagney, and Humphrey Bogart.

He leased a building on North Rodeo Drive, just north of Wilshire in what today is the prime shopping district. Mike hired architect Douglas Honnold to create the interior, but Romanoff oversaw every detail. Honnold later recalled, "Being the royal architect is an education in itself. I learned more about human vanity at the old stand at 326 North Rodeo than I could have from all the philosophers of antiquity." Mike was just as meticulous in the kitchen—where all of the staff were French—and about the dress code. Women could not wear pants, and men—even if they were one of the investors—had to wear jackets and ties. When Humphrey Bogart showed up without a neckpiece, Romanoff sent him home to get one.

Romanoff's opened on December 18, 1939, and became an instant sensation. It wasn't only the great food and Romanoff's personal charisma that drew the town's movers and shakers. Like any good con man, Mike was a shrewd student of psychology. He understood that in the film colony status was everything. So the front room of the restaurant consisted of a curved art deco bar and, facing it along the opposite wall, five booths. The booths became the power stations where only the most formidable figures in the film industry would sit, their rank determined by Romanoff himself. The rest of the clientele were relegated to the rear dining room, which seated 170. The appeal was irresistible. The top names in the industry competed fiercely for a place in those sacred booths. The lesser lights came too because the opportunity to walk past the people in those booths and dine in the same restaurant conveyed the perception that they were in the game. Many stopped for drinks at the bar and stole glances at the coveted tables, hoping that they might one day sit there. This brilliant gestalt made Romanoff more than a prince—he became a kingmaker, and a very rich man.

As Jane Pejsa observed in her excellent biography, *Romanoff—Prince of Rogues*: "the five booths at Romanoff's were society's qualifiers, and the man who controlled the booths its arbiter. Mike Romanoff fulfilled his role with perfection. He could be imperious; he could be gracious; he might be cutting or he might exude warmth. But Prince Michael was always in charge, and he had an uncanny sense of position when it came to the ebb and flow within the film colony. Hollywood knew it was all a game with Mike; yet Hollywood wanted to believe in him, and Mike considered it his royal duty to perform accordingly."

Romanoff's fictional persona and pretensions of grandeur made him the perfect host for the make-believe demigods with their toupees, capped teeth, elevator shoes, padded shoulders and bras, and surgically altered features. On any given night Romanoff's customers might include Errol Flynn, Edward G. Robinson, directors Frank Capra and Howard Hawks, Fred Astaire, Ruby Keeler, Greer Garson, Myrna Loy, and a dozen other celebrities. But Table Number One, the second booth from the left of the entryway, belonged to the undisputed king of Hollywood in the 1940s, Humphrey Bogart. Bogie's entourage usually included his wife, Lauren Bacall; his agent, Irving "Swifty" Lazar; screenwriter Nunnally Johnson; Judy Garland; and Frank Sinatra.

By 1950 Romanoff was prosperous enough to buy a site for a new restaurant on South Rodeo, just a block below Wilshire. In need of a down payment he cabled his old friend Alfred Vanderbilt, who was vacationing in Hawaii: "Send money for a new restaurant—$25,000 will do."

Vanderbilt immediately sent a check and a note: "This is the least I can do for my emperor." Mike hired Honnold again to build a $400,000 neo–art deco palace. "Romanoff's" was spelled on the facade in wrought-iron letters, beginning with an imperial *R* topped by a crown. The new place had a hexagonal dining room with booths along all six walls and two sections of booths in the center of the room—twenty-four booths in all.

Now a respected member of the community, Mike decided the time had come to take a bride. He chose one of his employees, a stunning brunette bookkeeper named Gloria Lister, who was thirty-five years his junior, and bought her a spacious home in the flats at 708 North Beverly Drive.

If Romanoff ever had a close friend, it was Humphrey Bogart. When Bogie wasn't working he often sat at Table Number One all afternoon. Romanoff frequently joined him to either play chess—the games could go on for days; Mike always won—or to entertain the actor with outlandish anecdotes about his aristocratic past. Bogart knew they were tall tales, of course, but he loved to hear the prince spin them. Romanoff would reminisce sonorously about his duel with a German officer in Heidelberg, his defense of the Winter Palace during the revolution, his flight from Moscow, and his ill-fated love affair with the wife of a French general.

Finally, Mike would glance at his watch and murmur that he'd better get back to the kitchen and prepare for the dinner rush. *Just one more story, old man*—Bogie would implore—*tell me about when you first visited Paris.* Romanoff would settle back against the plush leather of the booth, eyes growing misty as he emitted a world-weary sigh. "Ah, my friend, that was a time when you and I were much younger, not long after the Great War. I recall that Paris had come alive with victory, but she was still a bit tattered; I might add that so were we all. I was courting a young Hapsburg princess at the time—God what a beauty she was. And we had much in common, for we were both refugees from fallen empires and desperately poor as well. Somehow I had gotten together a few francs so that we could spend an evening at the Moulin Rouge—a first time for both of us. I had even bought a corsage for the princess, and she wore it with such pleasure. . . ." As he on he went on, Bogie leaned in, eyes bright, hanging on the prince's every word.

When Bogart was stricken with cancer in 1956, Romanoff offered unflagging support. Bogie underwent surgery twice, and during his hospital stays Mike delivered food to his room. When the actor returned home, he often sat alone in his living room during the long quiet afternoons—Bacall was either working on a movie set or with Sinatra, who lent his support by seducing Bogie's wife. Every day between the lunch and dinner rushes, Romanoff arrived with food and to take his friend's mind off the pain.

Old man—Bogart would say in a weak raspy voice—*remind me again about that princess you fell in love with. Remember the time you took her to the Moulin Rouge?*

And Mike would lean back, a misty look overtaking his eyes. *Ah, yes*. "We took a table discreetly removed from the stage, for the front tables were left to the cruder men. Young and old and without inhibition, these men lusted after the girls of the Moulin Rouge. I ordered two glasses and a bottle of decent wine; then we sat back to enjoy the evening—the princess and I. . . ." And on Mike would talk into the fading afternoon light, the two of them bonded not by the truths they shared, but by the beautiful lies.

The next unlikely arbiter of status was a former banquet manager at the Beverly Hilton. He acquired a small clothing boutique at 273 Rodeo Drive in 1962, just a few doors down from Romanoff's first restaurant, and over the next thirty years transformed the street from a string of upscale provincial shops to a world-class retail district.

Fred Hayman was born on May 29, 1925, in the Swiss textile town of Sankt Gallen. Like Romanoff, he never really knew his father, who died of a heart attack when Fred was four. A year later his mother married Julius Hayman, a prosperous silk importer. When World War II erupted, the family moved to New York City. Fred's parents wanted him to go to college, but he had his heart set on becoming a gourmet chef. "They had higher ambitions," Hayman later explained. "I wanted to prove to them that you don't have to go to a lot of schools to be successful. And wherever I went I tried to excel."

One of the first places he went was the Waldorf-Astoria—the scene of Romanoff's great Beaux Arts Ball triumph in 1933. Hayman landed a position as an apprentice cook and quickly rose through the ranks to become banquet manager. It wasn't his dream job, but it was plenty prestigious nonetheless to be booking the best parties in all of Manhattan. "The Waldorf was the ultimate," Hayman recalled, "like Beverly Hills [later became] for me."

The young man proved so adept at providing New York's finest with superb service that he soon caught the eye of Conrad Hilton, who sent him west to become the banquet manager of the newly opened Beverly Hilton. Hayman found Beverly Hills to be exciting but "terribly backward. I brought with me a whole new standard of French service." Under Hayman's supervision, the Hilton hosted post-Oscar parties and equally opulent affairs for such superstars as Elizabeth Taylor, Jerry Lewis, and Sammy Davis Jr.

His private life, unfortunately, did not follow so smooth an upward curve. Fred married twice and had three children. It was during his second marriage that he hired a stunning nineteen-year-old cocktail waitress named Gale Gardner Miller to work the banquets at the Hilton. They soon began a torrid affair. Fred left his second wife and his job, and in 1962 he and Gale took over a Beverly Hills boutique that Hayman owned a part interest in. It was called Giorgio. Some of his friends thought the move ill advised. *What does he know about the retail business?*

They needn't have worried. Fred and Gale turned out to be a great team. They ordered sleek new gowns from New York designers like Halston and Giorgio di Sant'Angelo as well as a lot of unconventional things. "We had chiffon gypsy gowns," Fred recalled, "Eskimo clothes, tie-dyes in psychedelic colors." And more classic fare, such as Dunhill blazers. Hayman was already hardwired into the society circuit, so before long their customers included Natalie Wood, Janet Leigh, and Norma Shearer. Fred knew the level of service his clientele expected and gave it to them. When new merchandise arrived, Fred or Gale would ring up a customer. *Natalie, I just got the most incredible gown in from Halston's this morning. No, of course not, you were the first person I called. You know I always have my eye out for something special for you.* And after a sale, they always sent a personal thank-you note, often with a gift—no mass-market giveaway plastic crap, but a piece of Waterford crystal or a bottle of rare wine, something that personally connected to the customer in some way. "It was all showbiz, style," Hayman later explained. "A new way of marketing entirely."

The 1952 Silver Wraithe Rolls-Royce that he parked outside of his shop was another marketing ploy, a little Old World razzle-dazzle that wowed the West Coast nouveaux riches; they liked it even better when he sent the Rolls around to deliver packages to their homes. *No delivery van for Giorgio.* Once, Gale told a reporter that Fred was the best salesman she'd ever seen. Fred interrupted her and said, "I am not a salesman. I am an impresario."

The Beverlyites loved Fred's pretentious manner, Swiss accent, and regal bearing; from the way he carried himself you would think he was a count or a duke instead of an ex-banquet manager. Romanoff's impersonation of a Russian prince played for his customers as a kind of psychodrama, a gestalt of their own clumsy efforts to acquire a patina of continental polish. But Fred came off as a genuine European aristocrat. "We were the host and hostess," Gale recalled. "It was like an inn. It was like living theater. You never knew who would come in next. One day Imelda Marcos came in and bought a Nehru jacket in every color we had." Another time they had to close Giorgio down for a few days because a Saudi prince and his wives bought all of the evening gowns in the store. The Haymans recalled such incidents with pride. It never seemed to occur to them that they too were profiting off of the millions who lived in abject poverty because Imelda's husband, Ferdinand Marcos, had robbed his country blind.

Fred didn't have time for such bleeding-heart ruminations; he had window displays to orchestrate and a store interior to decorate. He installed a fireplace and a pool table to keep the husbands amused while their wives tried on gown after gown, and a bar that served espresso in ivory cups and just about any fine liquor your palate desired. He hung autographed pictures of their customers on the walls—Frank Sinatra, Barbra Streisand, Elizabeth Taylor, Charlton Heston, Suzanne Pleshette, the Gabor sisters—which of course motivated more famous names to make purchases and join the Giorgio club.

By the early '70's Giorgio was the premier clothing shop on Rodeo, and Fred and Gale were well on their way to being as wealthy as their clients. But Fred had even larger ambitions. He had shopped on not only Fifth Avenue but also London's Bond Street and the Champs-Elysées, and he saw no reason why Rodeo Drive could not compete with those world-class retail districts. With the explosive growth of the Pacific rim, Los Angeles was swiftly overtaking New York as the most prosperous city in America, and with the influx of visiting Asians, Middle Easterners, and the recent wave of Persian immigrants, Beverly Hills was poised to make the transition from a provincial to a truly cosmopolitan city. All that was required was a little vision and a lot of leadership.

So in 1972 Hayman formed the Rodeo Drive Committee. Composed of the street's most prominent retailers, the group hired a publicist to promote Rodeo's image on the international market. By the early 1980s Rodeo had gained a worldwide reputation, thanks to the committee's campaign and the arrival of designers like Bijan and Gucci, and the Rodeo Collection, built on the site of the old Luau Restaurant. The Collection had fifty retail spaces and opened with great fanfare in 1982. It was promoted as the world's most upscale shopping mall on a street known for its freestanding high-profile stores. The media coverage caught the attention of other major international designers. Soon Armani, Ralph Lauren, Valentino, Cartier, and Chanel opened stores on Rodeo. The international designers in turn drew international customers; Saudi Arabians, Japanese, Koreans, and Europeans flocked to Rodeo and completely changed the character of the street. Sidewalk cafés sprung up and more and more five-star restaurants, spas, hairstylists, luxury car dealers, and rare-art purveyors. The provincial characteristics of the old Beverly Hills faded as the commercial district came to resemble a boutique version of Paris or Milan.

Meanwhile, the Haymans had moved on to the next fantasy: creating the first Beverly Hills perfume. Rodeo Drive retailers had been selling the world's finest scents for decades, all of which originated from the great fragrance houses of New York and Paris. The Haymans thought it was time for the city to come up with one of its own. Gale worked with New York perfumers for two years to create a scent. "They'd never had a woman from California come out from a store that they'd never heard of, without any professional plan, and ask for a fragrance," Fred recalled. "Gale wanted florals. They told her florals were out. Women today wanted green fragrances, light, fresh and grassy. No, Gale insisted, the women who shopped at Giorgio would want florals."

After two years of trying sample after sample submitted by various manufacturers, Gale finally discovered the aroma she'd been looking for: a potent blend of jasmine, tuberose, and gardenia. They called it Giorgio and put it on the market at $150 an ounce. It was unheard of for a small boutique—particularly a West Coast boutique—to attempt to break into the international fragrance market, but that didn't daunt the Haymans. They spent $300,000 on the initial publicity campaign. Fred drew upon all of his instincts as a master showman. The perfume's debut party was held under a circus tent that covered an acre of Rodeo Drive. Twelve hundred guests gorged on food from five of the best Beverly Hills restaurants. Merv Griffin served as master of ceremonies. Fred's Rolls-Royce was on display, its trunk and passenger compartment overflowing with bottles of Giorgio, which were given away to every woman who attended.

The Haymans hired a pair of brilliant marketing executives, David Homer and James Roth Jr., and they unleashed a publicity blitzkrieg that redefined how perfumes would be marketed. They placed scented ads in *Vogue* and *Harper's Bazaar;* pumped Giorgio through the air-conditioning system at Robinson's; stationed models wearing white blouses, black bow ties, and sun yellow bomber jackets adorned with the Giorgio crest in department stores to offer free samples. They filled boutiques that carried the fragrance with jonquils imported from Holland, and draped their exteriors with brightly striped promotional banners. Fred launched the perfume in Paris at the American embassy and sprayed Giorgio in the air outside of his Beverly Hills boutique. "Giorgio came out of left field using techniques that nobody was using," Annette Green, vice president of the Fragrance Foundation, observed.

One of those techniques was drawing upon the city of Beverly Hills itself as part of the campaign. The Haymans understood that to millions of people around the world the city was an icon of the infinite possibilities of the American Dream. "It still represents an I-can-have-it-all spirit to the average person," said Annette Green. And now that average person didn't need millions to buy into the dream. For less than $40 they could buy a quarter ounce of Beverly Hills in a bottle. The approach succeeded beyond everyone's wildest expectations. By 1985 Giorgio generated $100 million in sales in more than 300 retail outlets. A year later, it became the number-one-selling perfume in America.

But as soon as the Haymans realized their wildest aspirations everything began to unravel. Fred and Gale got a divorce in 1983 but tried to keep their relationship amicable. They remained business partners—Fred retained 51 percent of Giorgio and Gale 49 percent. But they soon began to bicker publicly about who had been the real mastermind behind Giorgio's success. Gale argued that she had created the fragrance; Fred countered that his marketing savvy was responsible for its phenomenal sales figures. When Gale insisted she be given control of the perfume business, Fred fired her and changed the locks on the building. James Roth Jr. and David Homer quit soon afterward, citing Fred's oppressive micromanagement style as the reason for their departure. The couple continued to battle for control of the company in court, then finally threw in the towel and sold Giorgio to Avon for $165 million in 1987. It was a nice return on their initial $100,000 investment in the boutique, but that failed to wash away the bitterness.

"It was traumatic, painful, expensive," Fred explained afterward. "I'm thrilled it's over. . . . But there may never be another couple as great as we were. Or a store as great as Giorgio was. And there's a lesson in this . . . that power and greed do strange things to people, that too much ego and too little loyalty are disgusting things, and that all this comes out just when you have something very successful. It's really a damn shame, to be honest with you."

Nikki Finke wrote in the *Los Angeles Times* that the Haymans had "cultivated a public image as 'the perfect couple.' And their divorce also brought down more than a marriage; it brought down a marketing phenomenon."

After selling the company to Avon, Fred bought back one of its assets for $6 million: the Giorgio boutique. He renamed the store Fred Hayman. Fred and Gale launched their own perfume lines, which did respectable business, but there would not be another Giorgio in their lives, no second act, just a slowly deflating denouement. Fred's ads said: "The sexiest women in Beverly Hills have Fred Hayman's number." But his core clientele—Elizabeth Taylor, Suzanne Pleshette, the Gabor sisters—had withered into ghoulish caricatures of their formerly glamorous personas. He landed a position as the fashion coordinator for the Academy Awards show, but fewer and fewer of the new stars turned to him as their glamour consigliere. "They're besieged now by designers," Hayman explained. "The interest now in fashion is phenomenal. So I guess we have succeeded."

But Fred vowed he would never retire. "Boring, boring, boring. No, I wouldn't have a grand old time on Frank Sinatra Drive in Palm Springs or at my beach cottage in Malibu. I'd have a grand old time for maybe a week. But then what would I do? I don't have any hobbies. I'd drive everyone around me crazy. I love work. I love the business. I love the enormous opportunity and challenge. . . . Beverly Hills is my country." He had many plans: more fragrances, an expanded line of accessories, an autobiography, and his own department store. "That department store would be the last thing I would do that's grand and special and different and conversational and successful. . . . And more fun than just being all day in that damned beach house!"

Meanwhile, all around him, Rodeo Drive continued to change. In 1989 another massive shopping mall, Two Rodeo Drive, opened at the confluence of Rodeo and Wilshire. Built at the cost of $200 million, it increased the retail square footage on Rodeo by 50 percent. It was a theme park rendition of the shopping districts of Europe, with a cobblestone street, limestone sidewalks, outdoor cafés, two bronze sculptures, and a fountain designed by Italian artists. The complex attracted such tenants as Tiffany & Company, Gianni Versace, and Porsche Design, and quickly became the red-hot center of retail activity.

Next came Barneys. In 1993 the New York retailer opened a five-story, 108,000-square-foot, $30 million outlet on Wilshire Boulevard's department-store row, which included Saks Fifth Avenue, Neiman Marcus, and I. Magnin. By the late '90s there was virtually a 100 percent occupancy rate on Rodeo. The street had more than 300 retailers and there were now more than 640 in the entire Golden Triangle. The unprecedented economic boom of the dot-com era produced a frenzy of expansion. Tommy Hilfiger opened a 20,000-square-foot white-trellised store in November 1997 with a star-studded party hosted by MTV. Ermenegildo Zegna doubled its retail space; Frances Klein Estate Jewels and Guess? also received face-lifts. New stores included Hugo Boss, Lladro, Holland & Holland, Prada, and Lacoste. The new buildings sported a superabundance of verandas, terraces, and atriums. Gucci undertook a $10 million renovation. Hermès expanded to 17,000 square feet from 1,300. Its new building featured a retractable atrium, a garden terrace, and a new limestone facade that cost more than $700,000. Inside, a portrait of Louis XV, by eighteenth-century painters Charles Parrocel and Jean-Baptiste van Loo, hung on the first-floor wall.

The prices of commercial property rose 20 percent. Lladro paid $15 million for its 15,000-square-foot site. Rents had skyrocketed from $1 per square foot in the early 1970s to $20 per square foot by the end of the 1990s, and following a pattern taking place in retail districts throughout America—from giant megalopolises to modest suburban communities—independent entrepreneurs and mom-and-pop stores were forced aside by the big corporate chains. Lowell & Edwards, which had been on Rodeo for seventeen years, had to pull out, as did Mathews, a women's apparel store that had been on the street for thirty-five years.

In 1997 the Rodeo Drive Committee celebrated its twenty-fifth anniversary with a massive street party. The 1,000 guests included entertainment industry heavyweights like Paramount Pictures' head of production, Sherry Lansing, producer Joel Silver, stars like Mimi Rogers, Cindy Crawford, Forest Whitaker, Stacy Keach, Kelsey Grammer, Elizabeth Hurley, Dennis Hopper, Catherine Zeta-Jones, Samuel L. Jackson, and Jennifer Lopez. Fred Hayman was also there. He had a lot to savor—his dream of transforming Rodeo Drive had been realized. The future promised even more explosive growth. Too bad he would not be a part of it.

A year earlier he had announced he would close his boutique in June 1998 and lease his 10,000-square-foot space out to one of the international retailers who now ruled the scene. Louis Vuitton had made him an offer he couldn't refuse. "It was an agonizing decision," Hayman admitted. "But an expanded Vuitton will be good for Rodeo. I'm pleased with my time on Rodeo because it's transformed from a village street to a world-class avenue." But in the deep lines of Fred's face one could read an unspoken realization: the days of the independent entrepreneur were closing fast.

Once, a wildcat operator like Hayman had been able to demand that designers like Halston and Giorgio di Sant'Angelo allow him to exclusively peddle their wares. Now the big designers had their own stores on Rodeo, which were just one of many outlets for their multinational corporations. Hayman told a journalist: "Somebody just at lunch the other day said to me, 'You know, it was so much fun—that little store and all the hot new things that you had. Why can't you have that today?' And I told her nobody can have that today. It just doesn't exist anymore. Times change. That's the reality."

There were still a few independents left: Herb Fink at Theodore Man, Rahim and Ali Soltani at David Orgell, Bijan—but even Bijan was in trouble now. His major push to follow Hayman into the perfume business was petering out at a stiff cost to his bottom line. The designer still put on an upbeat facade for journalists, tossing off references to the hundreds of millions of dollars his fragrances were reaping worldwide. Since his company was privately held, it wasn't possible to verify his claims, but it was suspicious how Bijan's numbers varied widely—anywhere from $100 million to $300 million per year—from interview to interview and sometimes within the space of one interview. In 1987 Bijan told a reporter he'd been offered $600 million to sell his company to a big corporation. When he heard that, Herb Fink, of Theodore Man, laughed. "You couldn't sell this whole street for that." But Fink acknowledged that hyperbole is the common language of Rodeo Drive. "The public loves fantasy, we give it to them."

Former Bijan employees who were recently downsized during a drastic cost-cutting campaign offer a stark picture of the reality behind the hype. They say Bijan has overextended himself by trying to become a major player in the fragrance business. "The original perfumes, Bijan Fragrance for Men and Bijan Perfume for Women, sold well," says a former employee, "but all of the others that came after that didn't do that well. DNA never really took off. He gave that maybe two or three years and then he decided to stop producing it altogether. People just didn't like it, and the market became saturated. It was all over the place. You started to see it in discount stores. That used to make Bijan so mad. He'd scream at the distributors, 'How is my stuff getting in discount stores?' "

Bijan was still averaging $20 million a year on his clothing sales, and for a while his boutique was able to carry the perfume business, but how much longer would Bijan be able to hang on? Only he and Mahboubi knew the answer to that question. Ah well, that was no longer Fred Hayman's concern. He sold off his merchandise and took the yellowed celebrity photos down from the wall at 273 North Rodeo Drive in the spring of 1998. Karen Stabiner wrote in the *Los Angeles Times:* "His departure symbolizes the end of the era when brash, ambitious entrepreneurs muscled onto Rodeo and turned it into a street of dreams. There is no longer room for him in the wonderland he created; Vuitton's move signals the dominance of the international retailer. Success in the 1970s was about designer exclusives and the personal touch; in the 1990s it's about the global luxury broker and a Rodeo Drive Web site. . . . He has everything he ever hoped for, except a place in the future he helped to create."

Fred shipped his pool table and part of the bar to "that damned beach house" in Malibu, and then made the long drive out there himself.

★ 7 ★

Security Chic

Only a few manage to climb the grid from Baja to the flats north of Wilshire, and finally to the hills above Sunset. But after they buy a 20,000-square-foot Mediterranean villa and fill it with antique Persian rugs, Impressionist paintings, Louis Quinze furniture, and glittering baubles from Tiffany and Lalique; pack the closets with Versace gowns and Armani suits, and the garages with Ferraris, Bentleys, and Lamborghinis; after they have at last acquired every material possession their hearts desire, they make an unpleasant discovery. They cannot sit back and savor their triumph but instead must fret and sweat and obsess about a brand-new dilemma: the people who are scheming and plotting to take all those lovely things away from them.

There are the business managers, of course, and the stockbrokers, bankers, lawyers, and real estate promoters, and the less legitimate hustle artists who comb the hills and canyons like coyotes ravenously sniffing out their next kill. But the rich do not worry too much about those characters—they know how to deal with them. It's the other ones: those who favor a more straightforward approach, who show up in the master bedroom suite at three in the morning with a loaded gun in their hand. They're the ones who make the moneyed toss and turn at night, and soak their silk sheets with clammy sweat.

Which is why the security industry is booming in Beverly Hills. On the big estates north of Sunset Boulevard, stars, media moguls, and business tycoons have built electronic moats around their castles; video cameras, motion detectors, night-vision devices, and high-tech alarm systems assure that not so much as a ground squirrel penetrates their "defense perimeters" undetected. And should an intruder cross the line of demarcation, the Beverly Hills warlords are ready to dispatch private armies of security agents and attack dogs to intercept the infiltrator.

The security boom began out of fear and a very real threat of violence. Beyond the heavily patrolled borders of Beverly Hills, the world has become a volatile and savage place. The old-timers shake their heads and bitch and moan about what this country's coming to and how in their day they never even bothered to lock the front door. But the younger residents have discovered that the heightened need for personal protection has an upside because it has created a whole new arena for demonstrating one's wealth and social status. If one landowner employs nine armed bodyguards 24/7, his neighbor hires eighteen. If one fellow has a security team made up of ex-LAPD officers, the next hires ex-FBI agents, or better yet ex-Secret Service. If a rival has a half-dozen trained Rottweilers roaming his grounds, outdo him with pure-bred German shepherds imported from the Fatherland and trained to respond with Prussian precision to Teutonic commands. One of the most coveted status symbols these days is a "command center"—a room lined with banks of television monitors and more complex electronic devices than can be found at the Johnson Space Center. Money is no object, because the number, quality, and complexity of a person's security forces calibrate their social standing just as surely as the car they drive, the square footage of their house, and the artwork hanging on their walls.

The Security Chic phenomenon has spawned a plethora of personal protection companies with James Bondian names: the Omega Group,

Close Range International, Galahad Protective Services, and Talon Executive Services. They specialize in not only protecting the superrich, but also in stroking their egos and providing the sense of theater that is de rigueur in a city that values appearances above all else.

"Marvin Davis [an oil and real estate magnate and former owner of Twentieth Century Fox] has a security staff of eighteen full-time people," says one veteran of the L.A. security industry. "A retired Secret Service agent runs it for him. When he goes to dinner at the Beverly Hills Hotel, it looks like a foreign dignitary arriving. You've got Davis, a follow-up vehicle. He walks in with three or four guys in charcoal suits wearing radios with earpieces and lapel mikes—the whole Secret Service look. David Geffen's got just about as many bodyguards as Davis. He got freaked out when Gianni Versace got killed down in Miami. Because President Clinton has stayed at his house, he put in all kinds of security, armed men patrolling the grounds, video cameras, motion detectors, the works."

When Cybill Shepherd arrives for a personal appearance at the *Los Angeles Times* Festival of Books at UCLA, she pulls up in a black stretch limo. Before she steps out, two charcoal-suited personal protection operatives leap forth and scrutinize the rooftops for snipers. Only when they're satisfied the perimeter is secure does the star emerge and proceed toward her autograph booth, surrounded by a phalanx of Secret Service knockoffs.

"You'll see these guys, the head of a movie studio, out at dinner with a guy in a dark suit and earphone standing beside the table," says the owner of one security company. "I mean, realistically, why does a guy like that need that level of security, other than to say, 'Hey, look at me, I am somebody.' Somebody like Madonna, yes, she needs people like that as a buffer. But a studio executive? And why the earphones and lapel mikes? For what, to call the limo driver to pull up at the front of the restaurant after he's finished eating? It's a little silly."

Some seize the opportunity to make a bold fashion statement by defying the recent Secret Service craze. Elizabeth Taylor favors a team of shaved-headed Israelis with the slit-eyed, cheap-suited Mossad look.

Eddie Murphy wants a more phat, hip-hop image, so when he steps out in public he's escorted by an armada of 300-pound homies from the 'hood. They may not know much about the subtleties of securing a perimeter, but if anyone tries to get close to the main man, then they take care of business with style, baby!

This obsession with security might seem a tad overzealous when one looks at the crime figures. There were only 231 burglaries in Beverly Hills in 1999, 942 thefts, 84 robberies, 77 stolen automobiles, and those figures dropped an average of 13 percent from the previous year. Most of the burglaries were grab-and-runs: someone kicks in a window or door, grabs an item or two, and hauls ass. The vast majority of robberies are purse snatchings or shoplifting incidents; there are only a handful of muggings. The reputation of the Beverly Hills police force keeps most professional criminals at bay. But the glitterati aren't worried about the professionals. They're worried about the ones who would separate them from their possessions by other means, such as killing them. The fans. The ticket buyers. The ones who plaster their bedrooms with photos of their celebrity heartthrobs. The ones on the other side of the moat who want in.

They can be seen at the "Maps to the Stars' Homes!" stands on Sunset Boulevard at the eastern and western borders of Beverly Hills, on the other side of the velvet ropes at premieres, in the little tourist shops on Beverly and Canon Drives, staring at the lush postcards of the Beverly Hills Hotel and Rodeo Drive, and on the tour buses, pressing their faces against the glass as they glide down the palm-lined boulevards. Their features are plain, their stature unassuming, but their eyes burn with a desire to be lifted from their anonymity into the spotlight.

They come from the dreary dust-choked backwaters of South Texas and the rusted-out mill towns of Pennsylvania; from fluorescent-lit warehouses where they spent thousands of hours stocking and sorting parts for machines they never saw; from airplane hangars where every morning they polished the same section of concrete floor, over and over again; and from studio apartments, where they holed up after work, watching television late into the night.

Only then, basking in the blue-green glow of the cathode-ray tube, did they feel truly alive. Inside that television screen there were never moments of tedium, confusion, or aimlessness. The plot always kept things moving, every event propelled you relentlessly forward so that every second burned with excitement: car chases, explosions, gunfights, passionate love scenes; every moment, even those of failure and despair, scored with lush music that elevated even despondency into something grand and noble. Later and later each night, they lingered in that incandescent world until it began to seem more fully dimensional than the somnambulistic shuffling the others called "Real Life." So one day they quit their job, hopped on a bus, and headed west, to Beverly Hills, where the stars lived, to claim that dream life for their very own.

"We are a nation that gives rise to and authenticates virtually unlimited expectations," Dr. Mark J. Mills, a forensic psychiatrist and professor of psychiatry at UCLA, has observed. "We are taught to feel if we work hard enough we can do anything and be anything. And very few people want to be ordinary." In fact in America it's seen as a profound failure, and so some are willing to "do anything to be recognized. It's part of the American myth that anybody can be unique and remarkable and important."

And so you get yourself a Beverly Hills T-shirt with a picture of a Rolls-Royce cruising down Rodeo Drive, a Beverly Hills baseball cap with multicolored palm trees stitched on the crown, and a "Map to Movie Star Homes & Hangouts." And suddenly you are standing in front of her estate. Your favorite star. A concrete wall and a hedge are all that separate your world from hers. You must cross over. You must! The passion's so strong, how could anyone possibly stop you?

You step up to the great iron gate at the mouth of the driveway and press the button under the speaker box. You're expecting her to answer, but instead a metallic male voice barks: "Who are you?"

The question bewilders you. *Nobody yet. But let me in, I'll become somebody all right, the biggest somebody the world's ever seen.* How do you put that into words the little black box will understand? How do you make it see that—

"What do you want?" the box demands, with rising anger.

To live here. To be a part of it.

A man appears on the other side of the gate, peering through bars at you. He wears a charcoal suit, a plastic tube grows out of his ear, and pitch-black glasses hide most of his Jack Webb face. "Get lost, freak." Did Jack Webb say that, or the little black box? Maybe the house said it. "No, you can't come in. Not now, not ever. If you try, if you so much as press that button again, I'll have the cops throw your ass in jail. *Comprende?*"

So you return to the shabby little hotel room you rented in Hollywood, and as you listen to a hooker argue with a john in the other room, you wonder: *If I were to die tonight, right here in this bed, who would care? Who would know? It would be as if I'd never even been here at all.* And you realize you've been cheated by all those candyass lies about how anyone can make it if they have enough passion, perseverance, and pluck. All of those rags-to-riches stories in the pages of *People* and on *Entertainment Tonight, Access Hollywood, The E! True Hollywood Story,* all of them conveying the same subliminal message: it could happen to you, all you really need is heart. Lies! The truth is you're ugly, awkward, and terminally ordinary. The world on the other side of that wall will never be yours. *Never.*

Then it suddenly hits you. This hard knot of anger rising up in your chest can be the instrument of your salvation. Yes, of course! Instead of leaving your footprints in wet cement, you'll make your mark in blood. You'll play the part of the villain, the man they love to hate. They'll hiss and boo, but never forget you, for you'll play a vital role in one of America's most beloved dramatic genres: the celebrity tragedy. The poignant tale of a brilliant talent cut down before her time by a mad-dog assassin. There will be hundreds of TV documentaries, books, magazine and newspaper articles. . . . Your place in history will be secure.

Their ranks have swollen tenfold in the last two decades. Arthur

Jackson, Robert Bardo, Mark Bailey, Robert Dewey Hoskins—an endless procession of them, stepping off of buses in downtown Los Angeles with a dog-eared copy of *Catcher in the Rye* in one pocket and a gun or knife in the other, ready to send celebrities to hell for failing to recognize their inner beauty. The Age of the Stalker—which in turn gave birth to the phenomenon of Security Chic—may have dawned only recently, but these lonely predators are as old as Beverly Hills itself. Since the city's inception they have shadowed the beautiful ones and, from time to time, murdered them.

In the 1920s Edward L. Doheny was the living personification of the Horatio Alger myth. His origins were appropriately humble: born in 1856 in Fond du Lac, Wisconsin, the son of a poor Irish immigrant laborer who barely supported his five children. Determined to carve out a better life for himself, Edward followed Horace Greeley's advice and headed west at age eighteen. In 1893 he struck oil in Los Angeles, and a few years later the advent of gasoline-powered automobiles made him wealthy beyond his wildest expectations. By 1926 Doheny's oil empire—which now stretched across the Los Angeles basin and southward deep into Mexico—was worth a staggering $100 million.

The Irish wildcatter was now seventy years old and ready to turn the reins over to his son, Edward "Ned" Doheny, who had recently married. The old man decided to build a palace for his heir: Greystone mansion, a fifty-five-room, 46,000-square-foot English Tudor manor house on 415 acres high in the hills above Sunset. But shortly after Ned moved into Greystone he and his personal secretary, Theodore "Hugh" Plunkett, were killed in a mysterious double shooting in one of the mansion's guest suites.

Hugh Plunkett was not a stalker. Ned Doheny had been the one to draw Hugh into his inner circle, and the two had known each other for fourteen years by the time of the shooting. And yet the emotional dynamics of their relationship bore many similarities to those of modern stalkers and their targets. Plunkett was infatuated with Doheny's life of fantastic luxury and willing to do almost anything to be part of that world. But when his romantic illusions about Ned crumbled, that infatuation turned to homicidal rage.

Ned Doheny and Hugh Plunkett were introduced in 1914 by Ned's fiancée, Lucy Marceline Smith. Hugh worked as a machinist for Lucy's father, William Henry Smith, the vice president of the Pasadena Rapid Transit District Company. Ned and Hugh seemed unlikely comrades, for they came from vastly different worlds. Hugh spent his days pulling engines apart; Ned's hands had never changed a tire or touched an oilcan. But it was precisely their differences that brought them together. Ned admired Hugh's physical prowess, mechanical aptitude, and street sense. Hugh was dazzled by the glamorous world of high finance that Ned glided through with such apparent ease.

When Ned traveled across the country and abroad on business trips, he frequently took Hugh with him as a companion. Their personal relationship evolved into a professional one when Ned employed Plunkett as his private secretary. It was everything Hugh hoped for and more. He traveled with Ned on luxury liners, in first-class train compartments, stayed in the world's finest hotels, and dined in the most exclusive restaurants.

On one trip, he went with Ned to Washington, D.C., where they called upon none other than the secretary of the interior, Albert Fall, at the prestigious Wardman Park Hotel on Connecticut Avenue. Ned handed Fall a leather satchel filled with $100,000 in cash, and they sat with him as he counted it on the kitchen table. Plunkett had never seen so much money in his life.

But as Greystone neared completion in 1928, Hugh's wondrous existence among the wealthy and powerful came apart at the seams. Albert Fall was being prosecuted by the Justice Department for his part in the Teapot Dome scandal, the most infamous government corruption case in U.S. history. Fall was accused of, among other things, accepting a $100,000 bribe from one E. L. Doheny in exchange for leasing government oil reserves to him for ludicrously low prices. And who had delivered the bribe in question? Ned Doheny and Hugh Plunkett.

The prospect of getting up on a witness stand terrified Plunkett. He was no Einstein, but he was smart enough to know a good attorney could cut him to pieces. With the slightest slip of the tongue he might be prosecuted as an accomplice, or incriminate not only the old man but also Ned. When he voiced these fears, Ned shifted uncomfortably and explained that Hugh needn't worry about implicating him. Ned had been given immunity for his testimony during the prosecution of another oil magnate involved in the scandal, Harry Sinclair, so he was free and clear. Stunned, Hugh asked if he might be able to cut a similar deal. No—Ned replied—it was too late for that. Plunkett would have to take his chances in court, unless. . . . There was one other option open to Hugh—Ned explained. He could commit himself to a state mental hospital and thus avoid having to testify at all. Plunkett almost went along with this scheme, then balked. What if the doctors at the hospital refused to let him out after the trial was over? They could claim he was emotionally unstable and keep him in there for years. He didn't want to live out the rest of his days in a madhouse. But as he thought about it, Ned began to see why the Dohenys might favor this option. They might pull all kinds of strings to keep him in that hospital and thus effectively silenced.

Suddenly he saw with horrible clarity the real difference between himself and Ned, the only difference that really counted: money. Ned had the vast wealth of the Doheny family at his disposal, money to buy all the legal support and political influence he needed to stay out of prison. Hugh had only a meager savings account that couldn't begin to pay for decent legal protection. For fourteen years he'd been allowed to share Ned's world. He had been a confidant and—he thought—Ned's closest friend. But now it became obvious that they had never really been close. A great gulf divided them and always would. He had been little more than a glorified valet and now perhaps a fall guy. He, not Ned, would have his name splashed across headlines from coast to coast as a briber; he, not Ned, would suffer the indignity of being arrested in front of his wife; he, not Ned, would lose years of his life in prison. And what would happen to Ned, Ed Sr., and the rest of the Dohenys? F. Scott Fitzgerald might have been describing them when he wrote in *The Great Gatsby:* "They were careless people . . . they smashed up things and creatures and then retreated back into their money or their vast carelessness . . . and let other people clean up the mess they had made."

In October 1928 Plunkett's wife of eleven years, Harriet Marian Hall, divorced him on the grounds of desertion. She could no longer endure the long hours he worked, and his volatile emotional state frightened her. The divorce accelerated Plunkett's psychological deterioration. On Christmas Eve, 1928, Hugh collapsed. The Dohenys' physician, Dr. Ernest Clyde Fishbaugh, diagnosed a nervous breakdown and prescribed bed rest. Ned offered to let Plunkett recuperate in the guesthouse at Greystone. A generous gesture, or simply a manipulative attempt to keep the lamb fat and happy before the slaughter? Plunkett's doubts and anxieties began to spin out of control. He had to do something; he couldn't just wait for the cops or the men in white coats to come and haul him away. Somehow he had to find a way to take control of his fate.

On February 16, 1929, at 9:30 P.M., Plunkett drove up to the massive iron gates of Greystone in a dark blue Dodge Sport Cabriolet. As remarkable as it may seem, at that time most Beverly Hills estates had no security whatsoever. Greystone was an exception. A guard manned the gate and another patrolled the grounds, but they made no move to detain Plunkett because Hugh was a regular guest.

Ned and Lucy were getting ready for bed when Hugh burst into the master bedroom suite in a highly agitated state. Ned was dressed in his pajamas. He threw on a silk robe and led Plunkett to a downstairs guest suite so they could talk. Ned poured a couple of drinks and the two smoked and drank as Doheny tried to calm Hugh down. But Plunkett soon became hysterical, so Ned called Dr. Fishbaugh and told him to hurry over. Within minutes of Fishbaugh's arrival at 11 P.M., shots rang out from the guest suite. Fishbaugh rushed in to find Hugh lying facedown in the entrance of the suite with blood puddling out of his shattered skull. The doctor hurried on to the bedroom, where he found Ned also on the floor next to an overturned armchair, bleeding from a wound in his head. Doheny was still breathing. Fishbaugh tried to stabilize him, but the oil heir died shortly afterward.

At first glance, it appeared to the authorities that Plunkett shot Doheny and then killed himself. But on closer examination the physical evidence was inconclusive. One detective, Leslie T. White, was troubled by the lack of fingerprints on the murder weapon and the odd angle of Doheny's bullet wound. White theorized that Doheny had actually fired the first shot, then turned the gun on himself, and that the Greystone staff had tampered with the weapon to make it look like it was the other way around.

No one will ever know for certain what happened in that bedroom. Some suspect that Plunkett may have been blackmailing Doheny, either with things he knew about Teapot Dome or over an alleged homosexual relationship between the two, and that this provoked Doheny into firing the first shot. Or perhaps, as the DA concluded, Plunkett fired the first shot to demonstrate to his friend that the very rich are not so different from the rest of us after all—that their blood is just as red and easy to spill.

Female stalkers are far less common than male stalkers, but they can be just as dangerous, as Buster Keaton discovered in 1931. "Somebody brought a girl, a bit player, to my bungalow [at MGM studios] for lunch," Keaton later recalled. "Later that afternoon [my butler] Carruthers had gone, and I was there alone. She came back. 'I've decided,' she announced, 'to let you keep me.' 'Just dandy,' I said, 'and now, kid, I've got news for *you*—I'm not keeping you or anybody. Now flag your ass out of here quick.'

"Good Christ! She starts screaming like Louise Fazenda, whips out a knife, and jumps me. I knocked the knife out of her hand, but she scratched my face and ripped my shirt and undershirt. I finally got her off me and backhanded her with all I had. Her screams brought the studio police."

The woman kicked one of the security guards in the genitals and gave the other a black eye before they managed to remove her from the lot, but that didn't stop her from threatening to sue Keaton and MGM for the injuries she allegedly sustained. Louis B. Mayer forced Buster to pay her $10,000 to avoid damaging publicity. Keaton bitterly resented doing so, but compared with his friend Charlie Chaplin, he got off lightly.

As far back as she could remember, Joan Berry had dreamed of becoming a star. In her cramped apartment in Brooklyn, she whiled away the hours poring over fan magazines. They were packed with stories about beautiful young women plucked from obscure existences in soda shops and diners by sharp-eyed talent agents, casting directors, and big-time producers. Joan was an attractive girl. The boys in the neighborhood told her so as they slipped stealthy fingers up her blouse. So she saw no reason why she shouldn't head west to try and earn a healthy return on her assets.

She came to Hollywood in 1940, changed her last name from Berry to Barry, took a job in a restaurant, and waited for a Hollywood big shot to come along and pluck her from the crowd. A year later she was still waiting, with aching feet and the first smolderings of disillusionment when suddenly, out of nowhere, her big shot arrived in the form of oil tycoon J. Paul Getty, who was living in Beverly Hills at the time. Getty invited Joan on a trip to Mexico and was so pleased with the pretty young woman's bedroom skills that he introduced her to other wealthy men in search of companionship, among them a film executive, A. C. Blumenthal, and Tim Durant, a writer and personal assistant to the biggest star in all of movies, Charlie Chaplin.

Durant knew his employer had a taste for young women and so asked Barry to have dinner with Chaplin and himself. Chaplin liked what he saw and invited Barry to one of his Sunday tennis parties at his Summit Drive mansion in Beverly Hills. So she found herself driving up

Benedict Canyon to Chaplin's Mediterranean manor, which towered on top of a wooded hill, just a stone's throw from Pickfair and Harold Lloyd's Greenacres. Invitations to Chaplin's tennis parties were highly coveted among the elite of the entertainment industry, and now here was Joan, playing doubles with movie producers and stars and tennis legends like Bill Tilden, Don Budge, Fred Perry, Pauline Betz, and Helen Wills. After tennis, there was a high tea with chicken sandwiches and crumpets.

Then Charlie—he insisted she call him that—whisked Joan off in his limousine to Romanoff's for dinner. Romanoff's! It was like a fantastic Fred Astaire and Ginger Rogers musical—in fact, Fred Astaire was right there, at the next booth! Chaplin gave her his undivided attention, listening with total absorption to every silly word that tumbled off her nervous lips.

They continued seeing each other, and one night he asked her to read some lines from a play he'd just bought the rights to, *Shadow and Substance,* by Paul Vincent Carroll. *Marvelous*—Charlie murmured—*you're so spontaneous. Just the quality I'm looking for.* He took her down to his studio on La Brea Avenue in Hollywood, put her in period costume and makeup, and filmed a screen test. *Fantastic!*—he exclaimed—*better than I had hoped for.* He signed her to a contract at $250 a week and during their dinners at Romanoff's talked excitedly about the many facets of their upcoming production. He was sure it would be his greatest film, and she would be his greatest leading lady, he would see to that.

But then, by degrees, his enthusiasm for her abilities seemed to cool. She was talented, he admitted, but undisciplined. She needed to develop her craft, so he sent her to Max Reinhardt's drama school. She was beautiful, but her teeth were too crooked and discolored, so he had them capped. At first, she cheerfully went along with his efforts to transform her, but slowly it began to eat at her. *I thought my spontaneity was my great quality.* At Reinhardt's they drilled every ounce of spontaneity out of her. It wasn't fun or glamorous to work on the same scene over and over again, but tedious—more mundane than waiting tables. At least as a waitress she got to be herself. And what was so bad about her teeth anyway? They didn't seem to bother him the first night he took her to bed.

By the spring of 1942 her anger began to boil to the surface. She'd show up at Chaplin's house unannounced in the early morning hours, drunk and belligerent. Once, coming up the long curved driveway, she lost control of her Cadillac and crashed. Chaplin—whose father had died of alcoholism—was repulsed by her behavior and worried about its affect on his two young sons from a previous marriage. Joan could feel him pulling away. She asked him outright what was wrong. He said he needed time to himself to concentrate on his work. *His work.* Now it was no longer theirs. Infuriated, in one bitter argument she smashed several of the windows in his mansion.

When Charlie discovered Barry had stopped attending Reinhardt's classes without telling him, he canceled her contract, paid off $5,000 of her debts, and bought her a one-way train ticket back to New York.

Just like that, it was over. After all those dinners, all the promises, the hours spent discussing every minute detail of the picture they would make together, he simply moved on as if she had never been a part of his life. As she sat in her airless little flat back in Brooklyn, staring out the window at the soot-blackened brick of another apartment house, the loneliness and loss became unbearable. She couldn't accept it, *would not* accept it. He wasn't going to sweep her under the rug so easily. No, sir!

When Chaplin came to New York for a speaking engagement, she telephoned his hotel. They said he was out, so she left a message. He didn't call back, so she called him again. And again and again. Finally, he took her call and reluctantly agreed to see her—but not alone. Tim Durant was with them the whole time. Charlie's hands trembled, his eyes were wide and a little dazed, his words stilted. *He's afraid of me*—she realized. For the first time she sensed she had the upper hand.

When Charlie returned to Beverly Hills, Barry followed him. Like most of the stars at that time, Chaplin had no security on his estate. So it was easy for Joan to slip onto the grounds on the night of December 23 and climb a ladder to an upstairs window. When she confronted a startled Chaplin in his bedroom, he became angry. So she pulled a gun from her purse and threatened to kill herself. It was a delicious sight: the biggest box office star in the world, the greatest comedian in the history of the cinema, an artistic genius, pleading with her, little Joan Barry from Brooklyn. He wouldn't forget her now, no sir. Chaplin finally talked Joan into putting the gun away. A limousine arrived with his two young sons. They had come from their mother's to visit him for a few days. Charlie told them to go to their rooms. Then, to avoid a scene while they were in the house, he agreed to let her spend the night in a guest room. The next morning Charlie sent Barry away again with another thick roll of greenbacks in her purse.

She came back a week later. This time Chaplin called the Beverly Hills police. A judge gave Barry a ninety-day suspended sentence and ordered her to leave town. An employee of the Chaplin studios gave her another $100 and yet another train ticket. But if Charlie thought he was rid of her at last, he was sadly mistaken. Joan returned in the spring of 1943 and announced to the press that she was pregnant with Charlie Chaplin's child.

Right-wing politicians and journalists who bitterly resented Chaplin for making such "Communist propaganda" as *Modern Times* and the "premature antifascist" satire *The Great Dictator* saw this as a golden opportunity to bruise the comedian's public image. Barry's paternity suit generated three court trials and a maelstrom of negative press. It was the most notorious Hollywood scandal since Fatty Arbuckle had been accused of raping and murdering Virginia Rappe some twenty years earlier. After Barry's baby was born, a blood test proved Chaplin couldn't possibly be the father, but that didn't stop a jury from ordering the comedian to make child support payments and giving Joan's daughter the right to adopt Chaplin's name. Instead of being just another anonymous starlet who drifted in and out of the master bedroom at Chaplin's Summit Drive home, Joan Barry managed to win cover shots on newspapers across the nation and have her name inextricably linked to the comedian's in history books.

Of all the stars that Joan Barry read about in her movie magazines, Lana Turner had the most legendary rags-to-riches story. Turner was discovered in 1936 by W. R. Wilkerson, the publisher of the *Hollywood Reporter,* who noticed her while she was drinking a Coke in a soda shop called the Top Hat Café. In five short years Turner's combination of explosive sexuality and small-town winsomeness propelled her to stardom. In fact, she became the biggest female star in the biggest studio in Hollywood: MGM. But if Barry had been able to talk with Lana about the hidden costs of fame, she might have hesitated before boarding a train for Hollywood, for Turner's personal life was about as glamorous as a fourteen-car pileup. By 1957 Lana had been married and divorced four times. Behind the lustrous mane of blond hair, the dirigible-size breasts, the white fur and diamonds, was a desperately insecure woman who constantly needed to be reassured that she was adored, not only by her fans, but also by her lovers and husbands. She rebounded like a billiard ball from one gorgeous male hunk to the next—Artie Shaw, Tyrone Power, Stephen Crane, Bob Topping, and Lex Barker. Without a handsome man on her arm who professed to revere her, Lana felt lost and toppled into a free fall of despair. Given this, perhaps her actions after her marriage to Barker fell apart in the spring of 1957 are not so hard to understand. Certainly this chapter in Lana's life has to be one of the most bizarre murder stories in the history of Beverly Hills.

In April of '57, a stranger named John Steele began to bombard Turner with flower deliveries, love notes, and phone calls. Steele claimed to be an acquaintance of Ava Gardner, who was living in England at the time and unavailable to confirm his story. His persistence and clever banter intrigued Lana. After all, these were the same qualities that her leading men—Robert Taylor, Clark Gable, John Garfield, and Spencer Tracy—used to win her heart in her movies. John had exquisite taste for a man; the flower arrangements he sent demonstrated a discriminating eye for balancing shape and color. Then he began sending record albums by her favorite musicians. It was almost eerie. Could it be that they had the exact same taste? she wondered. Later Turner learned John had contacted the young production assistant who was in charge of playing music for Lana between camera setups on her movie sets. This made her like him even more, for it showed he was resourceful and had an ability "to get things done." So she finally agreed to have a drink with him after work one night at her house. She gave him her telephone number and asked him to call her one evening so they could set a date.

That night she pulled her long gray Cadillac into the parking spot in front of her apartment building. She got out and opened the passenger door to grab a script from the backseat. As she did so, Lana glanced across the boulevard to where a black Lincoln Continental sat under a streetlight. A man was in the driver's seat, staring intently at her. As Lana walked toward her building, she heard the Continental's door open, then close, and the click of footsteps behind her. She shivered, frightened and strangely excited as she hurried to the elevator and pressed the button. Her Mexican maid, Arminda, greeted her at the door of her apartment. Had anyone called? Turner asked. *No, señora,* Arminda replied. Lana headed down the hall toward her bedroom. A knock sounded on the apartment door. Arminda answered, then appeared in Turner's bedroom moments later to say a Señor Steele was here to see her. The hairs on Lana's neck stood up. She told Arminda to show him into the living room.

Yes, it was a little strange the way he showed up unannounced, but then again it was just the kind of thing her don't-take-no-for-an-answer leading men always did in her movies. She freshened up, then went out to the living room to meet him at last and was pleased and titillated to discover he was tall, husky, dark-haired, and handsome. As they talked he exuded self-assurance and a dangerous sexuality she found quite intoxicating. They started dating. Steele showered her with diamonds and gold jewelry, and they soon became lovers. He bought a horse for Lana's teenage daughter, Cheryl, and named it Rowena after the horse Lana had ridden in her last movie, *Diane*. Again, she was touched by the fact he would remember such an apparently trivial detail. Steele was a tantalizing combination of dichotomies, a mixture of rough masculinity and sensitivity that she found altogether refreshing. Before she knew it, John had insinuated himself into her everyday life. He established a warm rapport with Cheryl, picking her up after school and taking her to the riding academy so she could ride Rowena. But his pillow talk was oddly unsettling. Lana asked him about his background. Steele claimed to be a record producer; when she pressed for specifics he became evasive.

Then one day a friend came to Lana in a highly agitated state and told her that John Steele's real name was Johnny Stompanato. He had no connection to the recording industry but was very connected to the Mafia, as a foot soldier for Mickey Cohen. Cohen owned a floral shop, which was where Stompanato got all the flowers. When Turner confronted John and told him she didn't want to see him anymore, he laughed derisively and said, "Lana darling, just try and get away from me!" She began seeing other men, but Stompanato's perseverance, which had seemed so charming and flattering in the beginning, now took an ominous turn. He telephoned over and over again. She would hang up, but he would call right back, so she let the phone ring and ring and ring.

One evening Stompanato climbed the fire escape of her building and picked the lock on the back door to her apartment. Lana awoke to the sound of her bedroom door opening. A shadow lunged toward her and shoved a pillow over her face. She fought frantically, but he was too big and too strong for her. As she began to slip into unconsciousness, John took away the pillow but kept her pinned to the bed. He leaned forward to kiss her; she tossed her head aside and threatened to call the police if he didn't leave her alone. But she was bluffing, and he knew it. If Turner called the police, the press would get wind of it and the headlines—"Lana Turner Has Spat with Hoodlum Lover!"—would damage if not destroy her career. And besides, in the darkest recesses of her mind, she later admitted, his passion and power excited her. Here was a man who could handle her, who wasn't intimidated by her fame and beauty and power; here was a man who knew how to take control.

And so they became a couple again. Stompanato's obsessive devotion soothed Lana's insecurities and placed her right where she wanted to be: the center of attention. John asked her not to judge him by his past. He was through with the mob. He was going straight; all he wanted was a chance to prove it to her. Stompanato, like so many citizens of Beverly Hills, longed to re-create himself. But when they went to England—where Turner was producing and starring in *Another Time, Another Place*—the relationship quickly deteriorated again. Stompanato was determined to become a player in the movie racket—a producer, like Louis B. Mayer or Harry Cohn. They were the men with the real power, and—like Mickey Cohen and Lucky Luciano—they knew how to use it. John tried to buy the rights to a book. He planned to write the screen adaptation, and produce and star in the picture, just like Lana. He was confident he could put the financing together—hell, he knew plenty of loan sharks with large cash reserves. But his confidence eroded when negotiations with the author broke down.

Stompanato grew sullen and angry. Lana was always busy on the set, and when she came home she never had time for him; wouldn't even take him out to dinner because she was afraid to be seen in public with him. He was a sensitive, creative individual, as creative as any of her high-handed Hollywood friends. He tried to make her understand this, but she refused to listen. Okay, maybe he reacted a tad defensively when he strangled her to the brink of unconsciousness, but she didn't have to turn around and have him deported back to the United States like he was some kind of degenerate, for chrissake. John tried telephoning her to clear the air, but she wouldn't take his calls. He tried wiring her, but the only response he got was a telegram declaring that their relationship was over. John knew she didn't mean it.

All they needed was a little quality time together and they'd be able to straighten things out. Hell, they always had before. So he decided to surprise her.

After wrapping *Another Time, Another Place*, Turner headed for Acapulco for a much-needed vacation. When she stopped to change planes in Copenhagen, Stompanato was waiting at the gate with a boarding pass for her connecting flight. "Lana, you know in your blood that I'm never going to let you go," he said. He could tell by the way her face flushed that she was happy to see him. But the old resentments quickly came to a boil, and the vacation was spoiled when he lost his temper, punched Lana in the stomach, and threatened her with a gun.

John felt bad about that and said so. Back in Beverly Hills he tried to turn things around. When Turner was nominated for an Academy Award for her performance in *Peyton Place*, Stompanato couldn't have been more supportive. He showered her with presents and praise. John imagined himself walking down that red carpet to the Pantages Theater with Lana on his arm, flashbulbs exploding, the crowd clawing to get at them, an interviewer thrusting a microphone toward him. *Say a few words about Lana for the folks at home, won't you, Mr. Stompanato? Do you think she deserves to win tonight? I should say so, Steve.*

His jaw fell open when Lana told him she didn't want him to come with her. After all they'd been through together, she had the nerve to leave him at home to watch on TV as she waltzed up the red carpet with her mother and Cheryl, and then was whisked off in a limo afterward to the ball at the Beverly Hilton. How humiliating! What a ball buster this bitch turned out to be. There wasn't a man in the world who would blame him for waiting in Lana's room at the Bel Air Hotel to give her a little private reception of his own when she returned from the ball. He left her black and blue and unconscious. Lana's daughter, Cheryl, had been in the next room, listening to her mother's cries as he hit her over and over again.

A couple of weeks later, on April 4, 1958, Stompanato lashed out at Turner again in her Bedford Drive home because she refused to go to a movie with him. He shook her by the shoulders, and screamed, "This time you'll get it. No one will ever look at that pretty face of yours again!" He was mistaken. It was John's face that no one would look at again. Cheryl burst into the room with a carving knife and stabbed him to death. A court later ruled that Cheryl had committed justifiable homicide. She had also helped Stompanato realize his dream of becoming a Hollywood legend. Tour guides and history books memorialized him as the victim/villain in one of movie land's most sensational murder cases.

In the 1960s rock and roll spawned a new pantheon of exotic pop icons who came to rival if not surpass movie stars. Bob Dylan, Meat Loaf, Eddie Van Halen, George Michael, Phil Collins, Herbie Hancock, Elton John, Rod Stewart, Bruce Springsteen, Belinda Carlisle, Luther Vandross, and Neil Diamond were among a few of the rock stars who bought or rented homes in Beverly Hills in the '60s, '70s, and '80s. And with the rock stars came a new breed of celebrity jackal.

On March 21, 1967, Charles Manson was released from Terminal Island prison in San Pedro, California. The son of an alcoholic prostitute who did time for burglary, he had spent seventeen of his thirty-two years in prison for charges ranging from grand theft to armed robbery and rape. Now he headed north to San Francisco where the Summer of Love was in full bloom. Haight-Ashbury was crawling with self-proclaimed gurus who ran free-love communes in the district's crumbling Victorians. It was a sweet deal for the pseudo holy men—they wielded almost total power over their followers and got all the sex their considerable libidos could handle. So Manson set up shop and began recruiting teenage runaways, mostly girls, into his "Family of Infinite Soul." He told his disciples that he was the second coming of Christ, a living embodiment of love, who had come to save a chosen few from an apocalyptic race war between blacks and whites that would soon bring an end to a corrupt and evil civilization.

In 1968 Manson and his "family" moved to the L.A. area and settled on a decrepit movie ranch in the far reaches of the San Fernando Valley. They engaged in LSD-fueled orgies while Manson played the Beatle's *White Album* and preached to his followers that the British rockers were sending coded messages to him about the coming revolution, which he claimed they had dubbed Helter Skelter.

But Charlie had set his sights higher than being a mere messiah. The Beatles declared they were now more popular than Christ, so Manson decided to go for the big brass ring and become a rock star. He took up guitar playing and wrote a repertoire of folk songs. All he needed now were the contacts. Then, as if by divine hand, one was delivered to him. Dennis Wilson of the Beach Boys had a voracious appetite for young hippie chicks. One day he stopped to pick up a pair of nubile hitchhikers who belonged to the Manson Family. Before long Charlie and his entire tribe moved into Wilson's estate on Sunset Boulevard, which had once belonged to comedian Will Rogers, the first honorary mayor of Beverly Hills.

Manson badgered Wilson for an opportunity to record his music, so Dennis rented a studio in Santa Monica and taped some of his songs. Wilson then introduced Charlie to a number of people on the fringes of the record industry, including Terry Melcher, Doris Day's son, who had become a record producer and lived at 10050 Cielo Drive in Beverly Hills. Melcher listened to Manson's songs but wasn't impressed. He made a halfhearted attempt to secure him a recording contract, but when no one expressed enthusiasm he dropped the matter. In May 1969 Manson went up to the Cielo Drive house to try and renew Melcher's interest but was shocked and disappointed to discover Melcher had moved to Malibu. The people who now lived in the house were abrupt and rude, or so Manson believed.

Charlie seethed with resentment. He'd been so close, *so close*, to entering a world that most of his life had seemed hopelessly beyond his reach. He knew in his heart that he wrote better songs than the Beatles, Bob Dylan, and certainly Dennis fucking Wilson. All this hippy-dippy bullshit about equality, breaking down class barriers, doing away with materialism and status was a con. He knew why they didn't give him a recording contract, because he came from the wrong side of the tracks and still carried the stench of poverty and prison. They were never going to let a person like him inside their golden kingdom, never had any intention of it. They'd only been playing mind games, having a little fun with the hippie who dared to dream of becoming one of them. All right then, time to get it on, time to show those fuckers that all their money and gates and walls couldn't protect them. Time to bring Charlie's world to them and strike the sparks that would ignite Helter Skelter. And that house full of snotty rich white "piggies" on Cielo Drive would serve as his piece of flint.

On August 9, 1969, he dispatched a group of family members with knives and guns. They climbed the fence at the Cielo Drive house and brutally slaughtered five people: Sharon Tate, an actress and wife of film director Roman Polanski; Abigail Folger, heiress to the Folger coffee fortune; Voytek Frykowski, Abigail's lover; Jay Sebring, a hairstylist and close friend of Tate's; and Steve Parent, a local boy who had been heading down the driveway to leave the estate when Manson's followers shot him. Tate was eight months pregnant. The family members stabbed her sixteen times as she pleaded for her baby's life, then wrote "Helter Skelter" on the living room wall with the actress's blood.

The revolution Manson predicted never materialized. He and four of his family members were eventually arrested and convicted for the murders. But the slaughter on Cielo Drive did provoke a flash flood of adrenaline in the canyons of Beverly Hills. Not since the Lindbergh kidnapping in 1932 had any single event so terrorized the rich and famous. *Did you hear? A bunch of LSD-crazed hippies went in and cut them to pieces!* The longhaired tie-dyed kids that congregated outside of the rock and roll clubs on the Sunset Strip at the eastern border of Beverly Hills were no longer a harmless bunch of eccentric teenagers. In an instant they had become barbarian hordes massing for an invasion. Jerry Lewis fortified his estate with a sophisticated alarm system and the first network of closed-circuit television cameras to monitor the grounds for intruders. Frank Sinatra went into hiding, and Connie

Stevens turned her home into a fortress. The Beverly Hills police became even more draconian than usual, stopping pedestrians who looked even slightly suspicious and subjecting them to intense questioning. Private security firms tripled their business, and the price of guard dogs shot up from $200 to $1,500.

But Manson was only the curtain raiser. In the decades that followed, arbitrary eruptions of violence became a common feature of American life. Terms like "serial killer," "road rage," and "drive-by shooting" entered the vernacular. The evening news became a parade of horrors: dutiful sons who shot the entire family, wives who sexually mutilated their husbands, elderly women who filled their gardens with the corpses of murdered boarders. Something had gone terribly wrong out there in the great unwashed expanse of ordinariness that celebrities called "the public," and they could no longer insulate themselves from it. The first warning signs appeared in their fan mail. Obsessive and overly effusive fans had been around since the beginning of movies. But now instead of writing just one, two, or at the most a half-dozen letters, some of them began to write hundreds, even thousands of letters, five or six letters a day, some as much as twenty pages long, filled with convoluted sentences that vacillated wildly from expressions of love to hostility. Fans had always sent presents: a lock of hair, a photo of themselves, perhaps a piece of clothing or jewelry. But now some began to send bizarre items, like dead fish, vials of blood, teeth, human and animal feces, and . . . bullets.

What was happening here? For one thing, there had been an economic sea change. The shift from the Industrial Age to the Information Age meant slow death by strangulation for many communities that had developed out of the old economy. As Silicon Valley bloomed into a sprawling megalopolis of high-tech plants and palatial homes, small towns in the Midwest withered; family farms failed and were gobbled up by faceless conglomerates. The huge steel mills, textile mills, and auto plants of the Northeast closed their doors and laid off thousands of workers, and the cities that had been dependent on them atrophied as young people moved elsewhere in search of work. But they were untrained for the demands of the high-tech economy and only able to land unskilled labor or service jobs for little more than minimum wage.

Many bachelors in their early twenties found themselves working in unfamiliar towns without the support of family and friends. They took jobs as janitors, warehousemen, fast-food cooks, or construction workers. They rented little studio apartments, didn't go to church or the Elks or the YMCA because the people in these new towns already had lives and their own groups of friends and seemed to regard strangers as vaguely suspicious. They were adrift in the vast and unfamiliar sea of the New America. Some couldn't take the loneliness and monotony and began to have strange thoughts. "It's created a situation where a dog is running without a leash; social and cultural restraints that would be put on if you felt connected to the church and the community are no longer there," says Dr. Michael Zona, a forensic psychiatrist and former member of LAPD's antistalking unit. "In the past, you had a large extended family. Your uncle lived three houses up the street. Four of your eight uncles lived in the same town as you, and so did your cousins. Everybody knew each other and everyone had a reputation to protect. So if you began to act strangely, that support system would help straighten you out and keep you out of trouble."

But now the support system was gone, and the only source of solace was the television set the young men came home to every night. Thus the Age of the Stalker was born. It began on December 8, 1980, not in Beverly Hills, but back east, when Mark David Chapman murdered John Lennon outside the Dakota, an exclusive residential building on Manhattan's Central Park West. Then in March of 1981 John Hinckley shot President Ronald Reagan outside of a Washington, D.C., hotel in a deluded attempt to impress the love of his life, actress Jodie Foster. Both Chapman and Hinckley carried copies of *Catcher in the Rye* with them on their assassination missions.

But it didn't take the stalkers long to make their way west to Celebrity Central. The following year Arthur Jackson journeyed from Scotland to Los Angeles, where he stabbed actress Theresa Saldana ten times. She recovered after undergoing heart and lung surgery.

In 1986 Robert Bardo was a sixteen-year-old high school dropout working as a janitor in a Jack in the Box in Tucson, Arizona. Later, after it all went down, he admitted that leaving school had been a mistake. "I was isolated. I didn't have friends, never had a girlfriend. I felt alienated, but I liked watching movies on TV." Which is where Robert met Rebecca Schaeffer, a fresh-faced curly-headed young star of the television series *My Sister Sam*. "She just came into my life at the right time. . . . She was like a goddess for me, an icon. . . . I worshipped her."

Robert began writing to her, and she—or more likely her publicist—replied with a handwritten postcard that said his first letter was "the nicest and most real." She drew a peace symbol on the card and signed it "Love, Rebecca."

Ecstatic, Bardo wrote in his diary: "When I think about her I feel that I want to become famous and impress her." He traveled to Burbank Studios where Schaeffer's series was filmed, and showed up at the gate with a large teddy bear and another letter for her. The guards turned him away. He returned a month later only to be rebuffed again. His love began to curdle into rage. "I thought she was turning arrogant," he later recalled. Robert found a new pen pal, Mark David Chapman, and he started reading everything he could about Arthur Jackson. When he came across a *People* magazine article that gave a detailed account of Jackson's attack on Theresa Saldana, Robert's course of action became clear. Like Jackson, he paid a private detective to track down Rebecca Schaeffer's address, then he traveled to L.A. with a .357 Magnum and a copy of *Catcher in the Rye*.

Bardo visited Schaeffer's apartment in the Fairfax District of Los Angeles twice on a hot July day in 1989. The security intercom was broken, so the actress had to come to the front door of the building to see who it was. The first time he had a cordial one-minute conversation with her during which he handed her yet another letter. As she closed the security door, Rebecca bid him farewell by saying, "Take care, take care." An hour later, after a lunch of onion rings and cheesecake at a local diner, Bardo returned. This time when Rebecca opened the door, he pulled the Magnum out of a plastic grocery bag and ended her life with a single shot to the chest.

Bardo was sentenced to life imprisonment without parole for his crime. Since then, there have been dozens of magazine, newspaper, and television news stories about him, and he now has his own Web page on E! Online. His life story and dastardly deed are chronicled in full lurid detail under the headline "Features—Special—Stalkers." He has come to know the stresses of the celebrity life himself. "All the fame that I have achieved from this results in me getting death threats and harassment," he complains. "The media says things about me that aren't even true. I have no control over them invading my privacy, bringing up my case over and over again on TV so they can make money off it. They portray me in ways I never saw myself."

Rebecca Schaeffer's murder sent a fresh shock wave through Beverly Hills. The entertainment industry's top personal managers quickly organized a conference to address the stalking "epidemic." At that meeting all eyes turned to one man, an individual who had established himself as show business's foremost authority on celebrity security: Gavin de Becker, CEO of Gavin de Becker Inc., security broker to the stars.

De Becker was in one sense an unlikely security maestro. He had never been in the CIA or the FBI, never served as a police officer, a county sheriff, or even a meter reader. But he did possess some vital qualities for succeeding in Beverly Hills: an uncanny theatrical instinct and a prodigious ability for self-promotion. In a city full of re-created people who preferred legends to facts under any and all circumstances, these qualities far outweighed such mundane trivialities as experience and professional qualifications.

Gavin de Becker's rise from obscurity to High Priest of Celebrity Security was almost as inspiring as Hershel Geguzin's journey from Lithuanian peasant to Russian prince. The product of a broken home that was rife with domestic violence, de Becker in his own words "grew up on welfare and food stamps." When he reached his teens, Gavin moved into a one-bedroom apartment in South Central Beverly Hills so he could attend Beverly Hills High. He struck up a friendship with Dean Martin's daughter, and when he graduated from Beverly High in 1975, Martin's wife, Jeanne, recommended Gavin for a position as a bodyguard for Elizabeth Taylor and Richard Burton. To the nineteen-year-old de Becker, it was a job that, he later admitted, "I was in no way qualified for." But "I had moxie and some ability."

He possessed a natural charisma and air of authority that was quite unusual for a man not yet twenty years old. Taylor took a liking to him and began recommending him to friends. Over the next decade his client list rapidly expanded to include Cher, Robert Redford, Dolly Parton, Jane Fonda, Joan Rivers, Victoria Principal, Brooke Shields, Olivia Newton-John, Tina Turner, Bill Cosby, and John Travolta. By 1989 Gavin had more than a hundred celebrity accounts.

As his client list expanded, so did de Becker's ambitions. He took note of the growing number of demented fan letters that his customers received, and decided to keep files on the individual letter writers. By the time of Rebecca Schaeffer's murder he had more than 200,000 letters and had kept track of the writers who became violent, and those who made threats but never took action. De Becker then joined forces with a forensic psychiatrist, Park Dietz, who had testified at the trials of John Hinckley and other stalkers. It was a mutually advantageous alliance: De Becker gave Dietz an unprecedented mother lode of research data, and Dietz helped de Becker develop a computer program that analyzed the language patterns of demented letters to determine which fans were harmless and which were likely to pose a physical threat to a celebrity.

The psychological profiling angle created a whole new revenue stream for de Becker. He now insisted that his clients turn all of their fan mail over to him so he could identify potential stalkers and neutralize them before they showed up at a celebrity's doorstep with a .357 Magnum. The star of a hit television series received as many as 20,000 letters a week, which translated into thousands of billing hours for de Becker. Celebrities forked over anywhere from $30,000 to six figures a year for Gavin's mail-reading service.

And once he controlled the mail, de Becker controlled the clients. He advised them not to file restraining orders against psychotic fans, or to inform the police that they were being harassed. The police are hamstrung by civil rights laws, Gavin argued. Restraining orders have no teeth and might provoke a violent response from a psychopath. A more prudent course of action was to let Gavin put a surveillance team on a potential troublemaker and discreetly monitor his activities. If a stalker actually tried to make a move, de Becker's operatives would swiftly move in to intercept him. Of course this approach had other benefits. By keeping law enforcement officials out of the loop, Gavin precluded the possibility that they might bring the case to a swift conclusion or question de Becker's judgment when he decided to put a fan under costly twenty-four-hour surveillance.

Identify two or three potentially dangerous stalkers per client and you've boarded an express train to fat city. De Becker charged customers anywhere from $225,000 to $475,000 a year for twenty-four-hour protection. His prices were exorbitant—some law enforcement veterans would say ridiculously exorbitant—but in a city that equates price with quality this only served to prove that de Becker was the best in the business.

So when he spoke for more than two hours at the emergency summit of entertainment managers in the summer of 1989, the showbiz high rollers did not fidget or complain but sat in rapt attention as Gavin assailed the police for treating stalking victims with indifference and hostility. What was needed, de Becker argued, was an elite corps of stalking specialists within the LAPD to deal with the crisis. Also in the audience that afternoon was Robert Martin, a supervising detective with LAPD. Martin was keenly aware of the new antistalking bill that had just been passed by the California legislature, which made it a crime to willfully or maliciously follow, harass, or instill fear in a person. Rebecca Schaeffer's murder had put LAPD under tremendous pressure to take some kind of action, and Martin thought de Becker had just spelled out what that action should be.

So Martin established the LAPD's Threat Management Unit (TMU) to deal with stalking cases, and enlisted de Becker as a special consultant. It was a beautiful maneuver that further solidified Gavin's position as the world's leading expert on stalking. After Martin retired from LAPD he went to work as a vice president for Gavin de Becker Inc.

In 1997 de Becker placed the final capstone on his personal myth by publishing *The Gift of Fear*, a melodramatic chronicle of his career in the personal security industry that became a bestseller. In it he portrayed himself as part spymaster, part psychoanalyst extraordinaire engaged in high-stakes chess games with evil genius stalkers who were out to rob the world of his glamorous clients. The book was plastered with endorsements from celebrities—Theresa Saldana, Victoria Principal, David Mamet, Janet Reno—and in the acknowledgments Gavin expressed gratitude for the encouragement and support he received from his "extraordinary friends" Joan Rivers, Brooke Shields, Jennifer Grey, Michael J. Fox, Tom Hanks, Jeff Goldblum, Laura Dern, Garry Shandling, Oprah Winfrey, Robert Redford, Tina Turner, Michael Eisner, and on and on.

Gavin de Becker, refugee from a broken home in Baja Beverly Hills, had made it to the other side of the rainbow. He joined the beautiful people in their walled-in paradise by helping them to keep others out. "He's more than an employee, he's a member of the family," says the personal assistant for an A-list movie star, who reports that de Becker attends all of the star's parties and invariably shows up each time with a new starlet on his arm. "He's quite the ladies' man. He's even dated some major stars, like Geena Davis and Alanis Morrissette."

But for all of his marketing savvy, de Becker failed to anticipate that in throwing the spotlight on himself and pushing for the formation of the Threat Management Unit he was creating a Frankenstein monster. Before long others began to see that *hey, there's a shitload of money to be made here! If some little Beverly Hills brat with no law enforcement experience can cash in on this stalking bonanza, why not me?* Like the sorcerer's apprentice, Gavin unwittingly created a legion of de Becker clones who stampeded into the marketplace.

After Robert Martin departed from the Threat Management Unit, Lieutenant John Lane took over. During the seven years that Lane ran the TMU he worked a number of celebrity cases and hooked up with a forensic psychiatrist of his own, Michael Zona, who served as an adviser and reserve officer in the LAPD. In 1997 Lane and Zona retired from the force to set up their own private security company, the Omega Group, which followed the de Becker template by offering mail-reading services, psychological profiling, and intensive 24/7 security and surveillance teams. Park Dietz, the forensic psychiatrist who initially served as de Becker's adviser, also started a company of his own—Threat Assessment Group—which advises corporations on how to deal with stalking problems in the workplace. Dietz trademarked the term "Threat Assessment" in an attempt to preserve his identity as one of the pioneers in the field. And two of de Becker's security men, Dennis Bridwell and Dan Palmer, defected to start another knockoff, Galahad Protective Services. Galahad added a brilliant touch of theater by placing their HQ in a nondescript building with blacked-out windows and a sign for a fictitious business on the front door—a James Bondian ploy that provokes laughter from veteran private detectives and police officers, but plays like gangbusters with the customers.

De Becker haughtily denounces all these Johnny-come-latelies as "frauds or wannabes," pretenders to his throne as security guru to the stars. But there's an undercurrent of stridency in his words; the first beads of cold sweat are forming, for his business has suddenly gotten a lot more competitive.

Some of his rivals specialize in undercutting him. Instead of performing a lengthy and expensive background investigation and psychological profile of a stalker, followed up by even more costly surveillance work, one private detective prefers a more confrontational and cost-effective approach. "I had a client who was a television executive. An ex-boyfriend who she hadn't heard from in a year and a half started calling her and getting real weird—sent her some very strange Halloween cards and stuff. So one night he called her at home, and as soon as she hung up she paged me. So I called him up right away. I said, 'Hey listen, you don't know me. Let me tell you my background and how this is gonna work if you call her again. I'm coming down to where you work and I'm gonna tell your boss that I want to talk to you and I'm gonna give your boss my business card, which says private investigator on it, and then I'm gonna come in and talk to you. After I talk to you then I'm gonna start watching everything you do, and if you call her again, I'm going to start keeping track. I'm going to go to the police and we're going to file a civil suit and we're gonna do this and we're gonna do that and at some point in time it's all going to become public record and then I'm going to tell your boss and he's gonna fire you because you're a fucking psycho. So you know what? Don't fucking call again.' He never called her again. End of case."

But the discount operators are the least of de Becker's worries. With celebrity security now generating more than $100 million in revenue each year, this market niche has now become attractive to the big boys. Kroll International, the Microsoft of the private security industry, has thrown its hat into the ring. Kroll's core business is corporate security, but recently it's begun to recruit officers from the TMU. Industry insiders see this as a clear signal of Kroll's intention to invade the celebrity market.

The harsh reality is that the days when a single entrepreneur like de Becker could monopolize celebrity security are over. In the new Darwinian environment, independent operators who carve out even more specialized niches have the best chance of surviving. Some have already done it. Basil Stevens, CEO of Close Range International, provides security to rock and pop stars like Madonna, Celine Dion, Michael Jackson, the Rolling Stones, and Run-D.M.C.

As a Secret Service agent during the Ford administration, Chuck Vance had to stick close to President Gerald Ford's daughter, Susan. So close that he ended up marrying her. Vance retired from the Service in

1979 and opened his own security firm, Vance International. Drawing upon his father-in-law's copious connections, Vance specialized in providing security for visiting foreign dignitaries, especially filthy rich Saudi Arabians.

The Saudis migrate to Beverly Hills in droves in the summer, which retailers refer to as the "Saudi Season." It's as crucial as Christmas to Beverly Hills retailers because a Saudi prince can walk into a store and, in a matter of minutes, buy every suit, pair of shoes, and accessory in stock. "I was working as a security man for a young Saudi guy, he was seventeen," says one American. "He went into Gucci and bought like thirty-five pairs of shoes and ten coats. You're talking twenty-five thousand dollars and it literally took him twenty minutes because he didn't even try the shoes on. He walked around and tried on one pair. They were size nine and then he walked around and said, 'I want these, these, these, and I want this coat and that coat and that coat.' And of course the salespeople were falling all over themselves because they knew this was going to be incredible."

The Saudis are just as free-spending when it comes to security. "Every single Saudi that comes here from the royal family has security," says a member of the personal protection industry. "The money's incredible—huge! I've been trying to get a piece of that for five years. Every time they come in they stay at the Peninsula, or the Beverly Hills Hotel, or the Beverly Wilshire, and they hire ten security guys around the clock. It's all arranged through the Saudi consulate here in L.A. I've tried to get a meeting with the Saudi diplomat that arranges it, but he won't meet with me. They were at the Beverly Wilshire last month—a Saudi princess and her family. They took a whole floor and they had ten security guys around the clock. And when they go anywhere they have chase cars and all of that. Now that's some serious cash, because Vance charges the Saudis sixty to seventy-five dollars an hour per bodyguard. Normally, the going rate is fifty to sixty dollars an hour. But the Saudis don't mind because it's a huge status thing with them, as much as security. They like the whole gofer aspect of it, because they have somebody to get the cars and luggage and call for this and that."

The Saudis aren't alone. The Hollywood honchos also enjoy the gofer aspect of personal security. "Basically, you are a valet with a gun," says a veteran Beverly Hills bodyguard. "If somebody gets out of the car, you open the door. If they've got luggage, you carry it. If they need a cab, you call a cab. That's an awful lot of it. It's not in the strictest sense security because there's nobody in Beverly Hills who would let you work for them like the Secret Service works. The Secret Service doesn't pick up bags or run out for pizza. If you're doing security in Beverly Hills, you walk the dog and give it its pills. You pick up the kids from school and you run downtown to pick up a prescription at ten o'clock at night from the twenty-four-hour pharmacy. Every Christmas Marvin Davis puts his security team to work wrapping Christmas presents. It sounds glamorous to say 'I'm in celebrity security,' but in reality you are a gofer with a gun. It's not what you would call a very exhilarating existence."

While most Beverly Hills security brokers pad their profit margins by selling a wide array of high-tech accessories—microcameras, sound and motion detectors, optoelectric heat sensors, and electrified fences—Howard Rodriguez has carved out a lucrative niche for himself by offering a more traditional approach.

At a seminar entitled "The Dynamics of Stalking: An Extensive Half-Day Workshop Exploring the Dynamics of Stalking and the Stalking Epidemic," sponsored by the American Society of Industrial Security, Rodriguez argues that there's only one way to respond to stalkers: with pure animal aggression. He then launches into a demonstration of the destructive power of his California K-9 Academy "protection" dogs. Rodriguez—a slightly built man with a receding hairline and a goatee, dressed stylishly down in khaki slacks and hiking boots—explains that he has trained dogs for Michael Douglas, Janet Jackson, Bo Derek, Sinbad, Jason Alexander, Shannen Doherty, Shania Twain, and Britney Spears. He then brings a ten-month-old

German shepherd called Puppy out on the stage. Puppy weighs eighty pounds and sits rigid as a soldier at attention; his eyes have crosshairs in them, and his triangular ears are sharp enough to cut steel. And teeth, oh yes, he's got a dozen ivory daggers in that two-foot-long mouth. "This dog was imported from Germany three weeks ago," Rodriguez explains. "He was bred in Germany, trained in Germany to respond to Teutonic commands. The Germans are very passionate about the development of this breed." He allows this thought to float there for a moment, confident of the images it conjures in the minds of his listeners: lines of German shepherds snarling and tearing into naked Jews, herding them into the gas chambers. They get the job done, all right. Their coiled power is as chilling and seductive as a well-oiled .357 Magnum. The crowd is on the edge of their seats now, listening with keen interest.

When you buy a dog from Rodriguez—for a crisp $25,000—the training does not stop there. He likes to keep the animal's instincts sharp by staging mock attacks at your home every few months. For instance he might hide in the bushes beside your driveway and wait for you to come home from a night on the town. As you get out of the car and proceed toward the front door—a window of opportunity that the subhuman stalkers favor—Rodriguez will pounce on you in a padded suit. If the dog fails to respond with adequate blood lust, his aggressive instincts are honed to a finer edge by further training.

Another excellent test of the canine's response skills is to pull a Manson. That is, Rodriguez breaks into the house in the middle of the night to see how quickly the dog nails him. "I like to do a three-o'clock-in-the-morning situation at least once in the first three months that a customer owns the dog. Put the kids to sleep, put the nightgown on, get into bed. I'll be there at three o'clock in the morning, because that's what may happen. And leave this window open and make sure that door is not locked, and if there's any security, let them know this is a simulated situation and we're there to reenact what may possibly happen in your life."

Such exercises assure that if a real intruder tries to pull a Manson, the dog will zero in on him like a heat-seeking missile, and that maw of ivory daggers will shred his flesh faster than an industrial-grade meat slicer. But Rodriguez feels no pity for the cretins his Cujos rip open because "when a stalker decides to interfere with a person's lifestyle because of his own sick mind," he deserves the worst these carnivores can dish out.

Rodriguez's German shepherds are good not only for patrolling the defense perimeter of your estate. They also make great companions when you venture out in public. A shepherd can sense when someone with a malformed psyche is about to launch an aggressive attack. For instance, if you're at an event signing autographs and a stalker posing as a fan approaches with a concealed weapon, the dog will neutralize the miscreant before he can make his move. "There's a certain amount of lactic acid that we produce in fearful, aggressive situations that emits a smell like ammonia," Rodriguez explains. "The dog picks up on that right away because his senses are keener."

Rodriguez decides to demonstrate how the dog will deal with the "asshole" in such a situation. He calls an assistant, Mario—a short, stocky Hispanic in padded overalls and a long-sleeved jacket—onto the stage. As Mario approaches Rodriguez, he reaches into his jacket and yanks out a plastic stick resembling a knife. Like a fur-covered cruise missile, Puppy streaks across the stage and engulfs Mario's forearm in his powerful jaws. Feral growls and snarls rumble forth as Puppy shoves Mario back and tears at the fabric of his padded forearm. Mario cries out in mock agony, but beneath his feigned terror there's more than a grain of genuine fear because the dog isn't acting. His searing-hot eyes are saying: *Come on, motherfucker, make a move, just one little move, and I'll show you how we party in Prussia!*

Rodriguez watches with a paternal smile, and the audience bursts into enthusiastic applause.

Yet despite the clapping, the smiles and nods of approval, the unmistakable odor of barely checked hysteria fills the auditorium. For despite all the theatrics and jockeying for status, the Security Chic phenomenon is at rock bottom propelled by a dark fear—of the have-nots, the armies of the night who might scale the castle walls, sack the palace, and kill the king and queen. For the moment, Rodriguez has enabled them to keep the fear in check and cling with a white-knuckled grip to the conviction that they can spend their way to safety. "These are people," writer Pete Hamill has observed, "who still believe that money can make them perfect, that life can be freed of its inherent tragedy."

★ 8 ★

High Times

Beverly Hills High School first appeared on American movie screens in Frank Capra's Hollywood Christmas carol, *It's a Wonderful Life.* Since its initial release in 1946, the film has played almost constantly in revival houses and can be found on almost every television screen in the country on Christmas Eve. One of the movie's most memorable sequences occurs in Beverly High's famous Swim Gym. Built by the WPA in 1940, the gym has a retractable floor. At the press of a button, powerful motors engage to part it in the center and uncover an Olympic-size swimming pool beneath. In Capra's movie, Jimmy Stewart and Donna Reed share their first dance at a high school prom in the storybook town of Bedford Falls. Miraculously, this small midwestern community has been able to build an exact duplicate of the Beverly Hills Swim Gym. Stewart and Reed are performing a frenzied Charleston together when a jealous rival, Carl "Alfalfa" Switzer, presses the button and slides the floor open behind them. The other dancers emit cries of apprehension, but the couple mistakes them for enthusiastic cheers for their dancing and they execute a deft backward shuffle that topples them into the abyss. A great plume of water rises, then Stewart and Reed gamely resume dancing in the chest-high pool. The other partyers are swept up by the giddiness of the moment and begin leaping into the water in their tuxedos and ball gowns.

The sequence elevates a common middle-class rite of passage—the prom—to something larger than life through the charismatic presence of Stewart and Reed and the magnificent piece of slapstick. Every madcap high school prank we ever committed or heard about, every memory of ecstatic teenage abandon, is expertly distilled by Capra into one archetypal event.

Since that auspicious debut, Beverly Hills High School has been featured in hundreds of movies, books, magazine stories, and television shows. It may not loom as large as John Ford's Monument Valley in our collective imagination, but it has become an integral part of our mythological landscape.

In recent years movies and TV have offered polarized visions of the school, presenting it as a richly upholstered color-coordinated utopia full of supermodel children in *Beverly Hills 90210* and *Clueless*, or as a malevolent breeding ground for rabid materialism and moral depravity in *Menendez: A Killing in Beverly Hills*. Our conflicted feelings about Beverly High and what it represents so fascinate us that sightseeing buses have made it a regular photo-op stop. Television crews periodically lay siege to the place for biographical sketches of infamous former students—the Menendez brothers, Monica Lewinsky—or for "lifestyle" pieces about the nation's most privileged educational institution. "At Beverly Hills High School," E! Entertainment's Julie Brown solemnly intones, "tennis is not just a sport, it's a way of life!"

The media has shaped our image of Beverly Hills High and in turn been shaped by the school's graduates. The list of famous alumni is impressive: Betty White, André Previn, Richard Chamberlain, Rob Reiner, Richard Dreyfuss, Carrie Fisher, Albert Brooks, Nora Ephron, Lenny Kravitz, Jamie Lee Curtis, Gina Gershon, Nicolas Cage, Crispin Glover, David Schwimmer, Angelina Jolie, Antonio Sabato Jr., Guns n' Roses guitarist Slash, producer Gary Foster, writer Michael Tolkin, writer-producer Jon Turtletaub, and media mogul Barry Diller. A 1960 yearbook photo of Diller shows him in front of an adding machine with the caption: "Business Genius Barry Diller figures up his allowance for the week." Today, Diller adds up the hundreds of millions of dollars that he makes off of his 1.5 percent piece of the profits from Universal Studios, of which he is the CEO.

It's not surprising that so many Beverly Hills High students have gone on to make their mark in show business. Many of their parents are well established in the industry, and the school offers a performing arts program that outshines those of many universities. It has a state-of-the-art television station, KBEV, that broadcasts daily to the city's 32,000 residents via the local cable provider. The school offers classes in playwriting, screen acting, filmmaking, stage design and production, and advanced television production. Students learn how to write and produce one-hour television dramas, situation comedies, soap operas, and talk shows. The theater department's productions rival many off-Broadway shows and are closely monitored by Hollywood agents on the lookout for new star material. *The Single Guy*'s Jonathan Silverman was discovered at age sixteen in a production of *A Midsummer's Night Dream*. Less than a year later, Silverman left school to replace Matthew Broderick in *Brighton Beach Memoirs* on Broadway.

90210 and *Clueless* depict Beverly Hills High as a school filled with relentlessly hip fashion mavens who, with unlimited funds at their disposal, treat the world as a vast amusement park constructed for their personal enjoyment. It's not an altogether inaccurate portrait; many students do in fact lead lives of outrageous excess. "When I went there," says David Schwimmer, "I knew kids who had their own apartments. I knew guys who were given allowances of a thousand dollars a week and drove Porsches." The student parking lot is crowded with Mercedeses and BMWs, and the halls are packed with kids wearing the latest designs by Tommy Hilfiger, Fred Segal, Ralph Lauren, and Bebe.

But there are just as many kids driving beat-up Hondas and VWs, and a good number can't even afford a car. Some are being raised by single working mothers who live in the rent-controlled apartments of Baja Beverly Hills and labor long hours as legal secretaries and salesclerks in the posh stores of the commercial district so their children can attend a school that has one of the highest rates of spending per student—more than $7,000 annually—in the state, and that consistently ranks academically in the top 10 percent of all California public high schools. It has become a mecca for families that want their kids to get a first-class education but can't afford to send them to private schools. Some are willing to go to extraordinary lengths to enroll their children there, which is why the district employs a private detective who checks to make sure all of the students actually live within the city limits.

Attend a meeting of the school's Academic Decathlon team and it's readily apparent that scholarship, not fashion, is the number one priority for a large percentage of the student body. The Decathlon team consists of six members—two A students, two B students, and two C students—and three alternates. They will compete in a nationwide contest that will test them on a range of subjects, including language, literature, social science, math, economics, and fine arts. Beverly Hills Decathlon teams have placed second in the nation three times, third in the state three times, and first in Los Angeles County once. But there's another objective besides filling the school's trophy case: the Decathlon brings together diverse students who might never otherwise interact and teaches them to work together and enrich one another's academic experience.

When the nine students gather one afternoon in a library conference room, the conversation quickly turns to popular misconceptions about their school. They dread traveling to other parts of the country because they know they will be inundated with stupid questions the moment someone discovers they go to Beverly Hills High. *Is it true you have valet parking and moving sidewalks in the halls? Evian in the drinking fountains? Caviar in the cafeteria? Leather armchairs in the classrooms? Do you take spa instead of PE?*

"We're just normal kids," Mark Rosenblatt insists. Three of these nine students live in apartments in Baja, five live in houses in the flats, and only one lives north of Sunset in the moderately opulent Trousdale Estates. "My family lives on the southern end of town, right next to Doheny Drive," says Rosenblatt. "They're not large homes in our neighborhood, but they're good size. It's a middle-class neighborhood. Our house is one story and two thousand square feet. It's only worth about a million dollars."

The others erupt with hoots of laughter. "Oh yeah, that's middle class, all right!"

Rosenblatt blushes and shrugs. "Well, it's middle class for this community."

Only one of them has a mother who's a "homemaker"; the rest are professionals, like their husbands—doctors, nurses, attorneys, teachers, economists, television journalists, electrical engineers, insurance brokers, and jewelers. All of the team members are seniors and have already been accepted to universities—Princeton, Yale, Duke, Colorado School of Mines, and University of California, San Diego. They plan on studying architecture, law, business, cinema, computer science, physics, and medicine.

Adam Levyn—son of Beverly Hills city councilman and former mayor Tom Levyn—is the one going to Princeton. He praises his alma mater with the slick phrasemaking of a professional PR man. "Beverly Hills High gives you the private school education but the public school environment. It's not a select group of screened students. Yet the school still performs extremely well and has challenging classes, and also provides the mixture of different groups of people, races, and religions. It's a melting pot of cultures that prepares you for the real world instead of being the programmed environment that many private schools offer."

They're an impressive group of teenagers, no doubt about it. But are they representative of the entire student body? The question provokes an eruption of laughter. When it dies, Levyn answers for the group. "We represent the top half of the school. There are all kinds of subcultures here, and there is definitely a percentage of students who probably wouldn't be willing to sit down for an hour and talk." The others laugh again.

The school's principal, Ben Bushman, who arranged this gathering, speaks up from his seat in the corner. "These are all incredibly top kids. I'm not going to lie to you."

After the meeting breaks up, Bushman conducts a tour of the school's serpentine hallways. About fifty, his brown hair thinning on top, he wears a blue button-down shirt, brown slacks, and the essential accoutrement of high school principals everywhere: a massive collection of keys on an expandable chain hooked to his belt. Bushman wears a perpetual expression of harried preoccupation as he moves swiftly down the corridors, rattling off factoids: the school was built in 1926, a number of new wings were added to the main structure in the 1960s, which is the reason for its convoluted geography; it has two television soundstages, a 1,500-seat state-of-the-art theater, and a planetarium; the student newspaper has won numerous awards, the Madrigals singing group recently performed at Lincoln Center, and so on and so on. And yet the hallways and classrooms are far from opulent, lined not with marble or carpet but with linoleum that's wearing thin on the edges of the steps in the stairwells. A dingy institutional beige is the dominant aesthetic. The teachers Bushman pauses to talk to wear the plaid button-down Kmart shirts, JCPenney slacks, Target dresses and blouses that dominate the wardrobes of high school teachers from coast to coast.

The teenagers who crowd the halls between periods are more diverse than those of *Clueless* and *90210*. Only 52 percent of the students are white these days; 25 percent are Persian, 14 percent Asian, 5 percent black, and 4 percent Latino. Half of those black and Latino kids are bused in from other Los Angeles school districts, but that practice is about to come to an end. California voters recently passed Proposition 209, which called for an end of all school affirmative action programs. Many of the kids wear baggy shorts and T-shirts, but a large number of fashionistas are also in evidence: tanned, blue-eyed muscular boys in Diesel jeans, Fubu sneakers, Gucci leather jackets, and Prada loafers; tall slender, elegantly featured young women in Fred

Segal, BCBG, Ron Herman, and Madison ensembles, carrying their books not in backpacks or unwieldy satchels, but in the sleek black carry-on bags with expandable handles and wheels that are favored by airline flight attendants.

When Bushman heaves open a door and leads the way onto the school's rolling front lawn, another clique reveals itself. They are congregated around front steps that lead down the hill to Moreno Drive. The boys wear frayed and faded jeans, baggy khaki jackets, and sun-faded baseball caps; the girls, bohemian skirts and peasant shirts. Their skin is pale, their hair unkempt, and they reek of tobacco and marijuana. Bushman nods uncomfortably at them as he walks past. The tallest boy in the group swivels a pair of bloodshot irises beneath hooded lids and says with a serrated edge of sarcasm, "Enjoying your little tour of our school?" The others erupt in derisive laughter.

The back of Bushman's neck turns crimson and his pace picks up. "This way," he says. "I want to show you our Alumni Hall of Fame."

We'll call him Jim Forester. Today he is a sober, successful graphic artist who lives with his girlfriend in a fashionable loft in downtown Los Angeles. But a few years ago he stood among the slackers that have traditionally hung out on the front lawn of Beverly Hills High School. Just one of the school's many cliques—such as the jocks, the drama freaks, the brainiacs, and the Persian mafia—the slackers are defined as much by what they don't do—extracurricular activities, community service, homework, attend classes—as by the one thing they love to do above all else: get high. The overriding passion for a righteous buzz led Forester on a Dantesque journey through a Beverly Hills underworld of pushers, dropouts, delinquents, scam artists, and sleazoids, and finally to death's doorstep. But the journey began, he realizes now, not on the front lawn of the high school but all the way back in elementary school, when he first moved to Beverly Hills.

The year was 1980. Jim moved to the city with his mother and stepfather. His mom was an actress, his stepdad a documentary filmmaker. They certainly couldn't afford a house north of Sunset or even one in the flats, so they moved into a weathered two-bedroom apartment in Baja. It was a spacious place, laid out railroad style, starting with the living room, then a dining area, the kitchen, his parents' bedroom, and finally Jim's room. It had been built back in the mid-'20s, the plumbing was ancient, the plaster walls betrayed water damage in places, and the living room fireplace had been sealed with bricks decades before. Still, his mom filled the apartment with a modest collection of antique furniture and exotic but inexpensive art pieces that gave it a warm homey feel.

He saw his real father—a tall, handsome ex-musician who now owned a small business—sporadically. "Because he wasn't around much, Dad would buy stuff for me to make up for it," Forester explains. "Every time he came to see me he brought presents, things like Matchbox cars, remote control cars, or Micronauts, which were these small intricate action figures with futuristic vehicles with missiles and other supercool weapons. It was a big deal to me because my mom didn't have a lot of cash and would rarely buy me stuff just for the hell of it—it would have to be an occasion. And you know what, that works with an eight-year-old kid. I idolized my dad." Meanwhile, his mother and stepfather got stuck with the inglorious task of raising him—enforcing rules, prodding him to work hard in school, and suffering all of the recriminations and resentments an eight-year-old boy flings at authority figures on a daily basis. "My mom got really bummed about it sometimes, but she tried hard, she really did."

On his eighth birthday, Jim's mother got him a bike, a Schwinn Stingray. The frame was painted in a gradient of colors—yellow to green to black—it had a black vinyl Harley-Davidson-style seat and handlebars. Forester's pulse raced as he ran a hand over the slick frame, his nostrils drinking in the odor of new paint, metal, and machine oil. Riding a couple of blocks to Beverly Vista Elementary the next day, he leaned back, slouch-shouldered, imagining himself to be a hairy, leather-bound, bad-ass Hells Angel as the thick tread of the tires hummed on the concrete and the metal frame sent soothing vibrations through his young limbs.

But his love affair with his new bike ended abruptly when he pulled up to the schoolyard bike racks. A group of his new classmates stood beside their aerodynamic, vert-ramp-tested Huffy Pro-Thunder BMX bikes and even more expensive aluminum-framed Diamondbacks and Redlines. They gazed at Jim's Stingray with disdain. "Hey, guys, check out the banana seat and ape hanger handlebars on Forester's new chopper," one of them said. Snickers of derision bubbled through the crowd. The tormentor stared at Jim's bike as if it were a clump of dog shit. "Man"—he shook his head—"that bike sucks beans."

Forester ignored their hoots and catcalls, locked up his bike, and walked toward class, but couldn't resist glancing back at it and, when he did, noticed that the Stingray had changed. The seat had grown longer and thinner and did indeed resemble the comical contours of a banana, and the handlebars, Jesus, they were too long and too high, ridiculously high, ugly, and malformed. It had become a hopelessly dorky cartoon bike to him now, and he knew he would never be able to like, much less love, it again.

It was the same with his clothes. In the early '80s the de rigueur status rags for eight-year-olds were Lacoste shirts, OP shorts, and Vans sneakers. Jim's mom couldn't afford to waste money on designer wear that her son would outgrow in a few months, so she bought knockoffs that were virtually identical to the originals—in fact, they were probably made by the same subcontractors; all they lacked was the label. But in Beverly Hills—Jim's classmates taught him—the label is everything. *Hey, what're you trying to pull, Forester? Did you really think you'd fool anybody with that cheap Korean shit? Where you really from, Forester—East L.A.? No more bullshit, you got beaner blood in your veins, don't ya?*

Like the bike, his clothes grew ugly before his eyes—Third World cheap, ungainly, and fraudulent. He hated them, and himself in them. "I was raised by my mom, mainly, and I was a sensitive kid," he explains, "so I really carried that around with me. I developed a gnarly less-than complex. I didn't feel good enough."

At first he tried to conquer his feelings of inferiority the same way so many Beverlyites before him had: by re-creating himself. Because his dad was rarely around, he became a perfect fantasy figure for Jim to embellish. He told the other kids about how his jet-set father flew in from far-flung locations to whisk him off to amazing adventures. Dad took him to boxing matches in Vegas and let him shoot craps, to safaris in Africa, to the tops of volcanoes, and to tropical islands on his magnificent hundred-foot yacht. It worked beautifully. The other kids' eyes widened in amazement. *No kidding! So what's your dad do for a living?* "He owns . . . a toy store." *A toy store, no shit!* "Yes shit, and he lets me walk down the aisles and pick out anything I want. It's pretty cool, I guess." *I'll say! Take me with you sometime. And me, I want to go!* "And then of course, there's his dolphin ranch." *His what?* "Dolphin ranch. He raises dolphins down by San Diego." *Does he let you swim with them?* "Sure. Course I gotta get up at the crack of dawn to milk 'em, that's kind of a drag, but if you don't, they dry up on you."

"It was beautiful, I had them eating out of my hand," Forester recalls, "until one afternoon when my dad picks me up from day care. All the kids gathered around him in a big circle and yelled out, 'Do you really have a dolphin ranch?' My dad was really pissed. He said no. He didn't lie for me. But I didn't realize until much later that I probably really hurt his feelings, because who he really was wasn't good enough."

By seventh grade Forester had stopped trying to reinvent himself, for he had discovered a new equalizer that wiped the superior smirks off the rich kids' faces but quick: his fists. "I had been held back a year, so I was big," he explains. "I wasn't going to take any bullshit." If someone said something about his bike or his clothes, he pounded them. It was thrilling to see the arrogance melt away as he drew blood from their noses, how the color drained from their faces and the whites of their eyes bulged like panicked animals, how they cowered on the ground as he sank his knuckles into their soft cheeks. *Okay, okay, I'm sorry, okay? Don't hit me, okay, please don't, please don't hit me again!* They didn't say a fucking word now when he pulled into the bike racks.

Dropped their eyes when he looked over at them and whispered in soft cautious tones. Sometimes, for a little added fun, he'd wheel on one of them. "What'd you just say?" They'd hold up trembling hands and back away. *Nothing, Jim, I swear it.* He'd grab their shirtfront, buttons popping and bouncing on the asphalt, their heart pounding against his clenched fist as he smiled and purred: "Just tell me what you said, man. I heard you whisper something, let me in on your little joke." Tears welled in their eyes. *Jim, I swear to God, nothing, I didn't say anything!* Then he'd let go of the crumpled shirt and turn away, feeling their fear-knotted bodies behind him as he walked off. They weren't laughing now. Not a titter.

"I had one kid," he recalls, "I used to make him call me 'My Lord.' I'd literally storm toward him and he would drop to his knees and say, 'I'm sorry, My Lord.' "

The other kids laughed nervously and joined in the taunting. They hoped that by keeping the focus on the kneeling boy they could prevent Jim from turning on them. But even as Forester basked in his newfound power, something else writhed in his gut as he looked down at the kneeling boy's dry trembling lips and terrified eyes—a sickening worm of shame. "Even as I was laughing at him, I felt really shitty," Forester says softly, shaking his head. "I sold that kid out, humiliated him so I could look cool, so no one would humiliate me. I still think about that. I remember every detail of it. That kid's probably cleaning a shotgun right now, thinking about me."

He didn't try to keep up with the clothing trends anymore; instead he dressed in opposition to them. "I started wearing weird clothes. My mom loved it. She bought me some fucked-up clothes because my mom's wild, and I was cool with that. I wore polka-dot shirts. This is the '80s—you don't wear polka dots. I started growing my hair out. It was like I was saying 'fuck you!' to all of them.

"Then one day we have this substitute teacher. We were really bad to subs, and the class is running amok. She can't control us. She gets pissed and decides to call the principal's office. Well, I knew a way to disconnect the phone line without her realizing it. She's yelling into the receiver, 'Hello? Hello, can you hear me?' Everybody thought it was really funny and I thought it was really funny . . . until the entire class narced on me through anonymous letters. It was a drag. They were scared of me. The notes said things like, 'Jim did it, but please, please, please don't tell him I told you!' And that really bummed my mom out—to find out that I was so feared.

"So then the teachers gave me an IQ test. They were hoping I'd do really poorly because if I got below a certain mark they could say I needed to go to a special school. But when they gave me the test, I blasted. I have a nearly photographic memory, and they had this memory portion where you had to memorize this complex series of colored boxes and I nailed it. The woman's jaw dropped. She said, 'No one ever gets this.' Of course my teachers were really disappointed because they wanted me out of there. They thought I was a bad kid. And I wasn't a bad kid, I really wasn't that bad. Beating a couple kids up and disconnecting a phone doesn't, is not, I mean I knew kids that would throw a Molotov cocktail at a brand-new Mercedes. You know what I mean? That's a bad kid."

He had hooked up with some new friends and hung with them every day after school. "Obviously they were also very angry. One of them was an upper-crusty kid. He lived in this bad-ass house north of Sunset. They had a pool, a pool table, and a big-screen TV when you didn't see many of those in people's homes. He would shoot slingshots at people's windows and things like that. Another good friend of mine Krazy-Glued every lock in the school. Nobody could get in. He got caught for that and went to military school for a year. His family didn't have any money either.

"One night my friends bought this thing of butane and were squirting it right in the middle of the street, playing with fire. And I'm like, 'Okay, I'm starting to get weirded.' I said, 'Fine. Fuck you guys, I'm leaving.' I start to walk away, I get about a half a block and this cop car comes screeching up. They made us sit in front of the squad car for an hour and a half while they went through all the case files and then they arrested all three of us on suspicion of arson. Took us to jail. Thirteen-year-old kids. Beverly Hills has these big green trash cans that all of the residents use. They cost thousands of dollars apiece, and it turned out these kids I was with had burned about twenty of them. At the jail the cops strip-searched us. . . . It was a drag . . . a real drag. They put us in a holding cell and our parents came and my parents were upset. I explained that I had been walking away when the cops pulled up, and I convinced the cops I had nothing to do with the trash cans, but my parents grounded me. You get grounded whether you're guilty or not.

"That's when I realized that vandalism is lame. It's useless. Drugs, on the other hand, kick ass. Drugs give you power; they give you pussy; they give you money. And you know what? All these things I like. So I started partying."

He had been exposed to drugs years earlier. "When I was eight. I was in third grade, and my friend was in fifth grade. His father used to get him high, so he got me high. This kid was ten years old and his dad used to smoke pot with him. Wouldn't do hard drugs with him, but did hard drugs openly around him. His dad was a real '70s-type guy, with the beard and long hair. I don't know what he did for a living, but he had cash—lots of money.

"I'll tell you one thing about growing up in Beverly Hills. Rich people are fucking weird. Money makes you weird. What I finally realized was these people worked their whole lives, a lot of times—it's not old money, it's tons of new money—worked their whole lives to get this stuff that's gonna fix 'em, that's gonna make everything okay, you know, the wife and the car and the house . . . and it doesn't work. So they get really pissed off and start acting out in really strange ways, like doing large amounts of cocaine and sleeping with prostitutes. People's fathers were doing things like that. My friend Enrique was from South America. He was staying with a relative. She was this full-on nightlife beautiful exotic chick who would bring these strange guys home and smoke opium in the house all the time. It was really a trip growing up in this environment. Huge amounts of corruption and drugs and sex. I remember kids in fifth grade that were already in recovery. They had AA chips, but I didn't know what they were at the time. The moms are constantly on antidepressants—these are soccer moms. There are huge things of pills in everyone's house. They would take their kids to the doctor if they had a bad haircut. Everybody I knew was on some sort of allergy medicine, Ritalin or Valium or Percodan, *something*—everybody was being treated."

Jim took a few puffs off of joints in grammar school, but he didn't really start inhaling until seventh grade. "There were these eighth graders in the neighborhood, they were longhaired guys that listened to Led Zeppelin and one was a drummer. They all smoked weed." Jim started smoking with them, inhaling now, and suddenly he was *baked*. What an incredible toasty warm deep-fried feeling! He started going to school stoned. The designer clothes of his classmates, their obsequious efforts to please the teachers and get good grades, their relentless quest to win approval from their peers by dressing the right way, talking the right way, no longer seemed intimidating but absurd, as silly as a Warner Brothers cartoon. For the first time he could laugh at it all, for the first time he didn't care. When his eyes met those of his fellow stoners, a secret twinkle of understanding passed between them. *Check this out, man!*—the twinkle said—*you see how crazy all these assholes are, how silly?*

Of course the spiritual tranquillity faded with the high. And the next time it took more dope to get back in the zone. Forester realizes now that the zone was an illusion, and weed was no magic potion but an anesthetic. "I was not comfortable in my own skin," he explains. "I had a gnarly less-than complex. When I got high, I didn't have to worry about that shit. The goal was to get it so the heart and the lungs were doing their thing and everything else was just *off*. What I didn't realize until much later is that your problems get worse and worse and worse while things are off.

"One day after getting high with these guys I was walking home—I'll never forget this—I was on the corner of Charleville and Rexford and it hit me, it was a moment of clarity: *You know what, I like getting high. I like this. I'm going to go this way.*

"After eighth grade I had to attend summer school at Beverly High for algebra, and I met a girl there. I started hanging out with her and smoking a lot of weed and met a couple of other people that were really into that lifestyle and I started really getting into it. This girl would steal lots of money from her dad and keep us in supply of weed—good shit, in Beverly Hills there is some good shit. Her dad was into charity fund-raising, so there was a lot of Hollywood money rolling through his house. When you start dealing with dollars at that level there's a lot of runoff."

When Forester entered Beverly High as a full-time student in his freshman year, he had no more anxieties about fitting in or being accepted because he went to school every day with an ounce of marijuana in his backpack. It won him an instant circle of admirers. "I didn't sell it, I wasn't interested in making money. I was much more interested in the weed, in having it to pass around, in being the guy who had the group following him to get high in the secret place across the street. If possible, we would get high before school started, but definitely at lunch and always after school. There were two lunch periods, and you had either the first or the second one depending on your class schedule, but I always took both. We had a lot of secret smoking spots. There are a bunch of apartment buildings and houses across from the high school with alleys running behind them. They had really cool attics or basements that we found."

Leaving school was risky. Technically it was a closed campus and security guards patrolled the perimeter to keep students from leaving, but their effectiveness was at best sporadic. "I left all the time," says Forester, "and I was constantly being busted for being off campus. One of the security guards was nicknamed Speedy. Every time he caught you smoking he'd pick up his walkie-talkie, call the command post, and say 'Biiiingoooo!' He was a funny guy."

Forester quickly discovered he could avoid paying a price for his truancy by pulling the rich-kid bluff. "There were a lot of kids from wealthy families in the school and the administrators coddled them with kid gloves. They were afraid if they came down too hard the kid's family would get some thousand-dollar-an-hour lawyer to come fuck with them. So I found out I could get away with murder even though I wasn't a rich kid. I didn't have to imply I was rich. I just made sure they got that 'don't fuck with me' vibe. And they thought: 'This kid must be rich, he doesn't give a fuck.' They would say to me, 'Tell you what, just go to PE, okay?' In other words, everything would be cool, no matter how many absences I had in any class, as long as I went to PE. I liked playing sports, so I was perfectly happy with that arrangement."

Jim spent lunch on the front steps of the school "where all the stoner chicks and all the cool people were. I started dressing in all-black and I had my hair dyed jet-black, and I had a pager that didn't work that I wore because it looked cool on my belt. I was a freak."

He was aware that there were other cliques besides the fashionistas who had tormented him in his early years. There were the offspring of the entertainment industry's elite, including the children of movie stars, and kids who were already stars themselves—like Christina Applegate, a regular on the hit television series *Married . . . with Children*—and those who would later become celebrities, like Pauly Shore. Then there were the brainiacs—the straight-arrow kids who were intensely focused on getting into a good college and didn't seem to care about being popular or accepted. "They really had it together. They knew the game way before they arrived and they came prepared. They were serious about school—their parents had given that to them. And there were some middle-of-the-road people who would hang out and get high with us but then go home and do their schoolwork. I always respected those guys: the dudes who liked to party but still handled their shit, because I always felt I couldn't do that. I mean, I didn't see the point of memorizing the names of Roman emperors who'd been dead for two thousand years, or learning the gross national product of Sudan, or how to say 'Excuse me, could you direct me to the library?' in freaking French. What the fuck did that have to do with me?"

His parents sensed something was wrong; so did some of his teachers and they tried to talk to him. "But unfortunately I was way too good a bullshit artist. I could bullshit myself and I could bullshit any counselor. My whole thing was to bullshit enough so that I could do whatever the fuck I pleased whenever I wanted to. I wouldn't have been able to hear good advice. I'm sure I got some, but I was so manipulative and so good at that game that I didn't see a point at playing the other one where you tried to get straight As. Why go through all that turmoil? *I got this game handled.*"

Pot was easier to come by now. Kids either got it from their siblings in college, stole it from their parents, or grew their own. "But Beverly Hills would get dry sometimes and you couldn't get anything. So as a last resort we could always drive to Pico and Hoover in downtown L.A. and buy some dirtweed from the Mexicans. They hang out on the streets and run up to your car when you drive up and say, 'What do you need, *homes*?' The interesting thing about Mexican culture is they are businessmen. They want you to come back and be their customer, so they treat you right."

For two long languid years life was sweet. "I got plenty of pussy. Girls liked me. I was a bad kid in Beverly Hills with all these good Jewish girls around. It was lucrative in that department. I had fan clubs and shit. It was a trip."

One of his favorite places to hang was Saul's house. "Saul lived with his mom in this house on the east side of Beverly Hills. His mother ran a telemarketing scam. They sold vitamins, and if you bought so many they sent you a free grandfather clock. Only the grandfather clock was about six inches tall! They actually told people, 'When you get your clock, please take a picture of yourself standing beside it and send it to us.' And they actually got pictures of these people standing next to these little clocks. Dude, it was hard-core. Saul had a big bong collection and bags and bags of really expensive weed, the kind of shit you see in *High Times*. He got it through these older Israeli dudes in BMWs with big gold chains and shit. There's this whole underworld in Beverly Hills. It's bigger than most people would think, and if you choose to, you can get knee-deep in it easy."

Forester even had rich kids for friends now. And with rich friends came the toys—the cars, the stereos, big-screen TVs, swimming pools, and hot tubs. "One kid had a Lamborghini. His parents were oil tycoons and they had died. He bought his best friend a Mercedes for his sixteenth birthday. My friend Joe, his dad owned a motorcycle company, and he gave Joe a Toyota Supra. I really dug that stuff, rolling around in their rich cars, smoking their rich weed. You know what I mean? I learned how to do that. I was manipulative enough to make friends with them, become good friends with them, their confidant, their right-hand man, their road dog, whatever. It wasn't a conscious thing. I would just find out what it is they liked most and be their best friend. Most of the time it coincided with what I liked anyway."

Now that he'd been accepted by rich kids, he felt a resurging desire to dress like them. "People started to get into hip-hop, so you started to see baggy jeans a lot and Nike Air Jordan shoes. Baseball caps, expensive thirty-dollar baseball caps, were really big. Guess? stuff was in; those big Guess? jackets that took a whole wash load were huge, and all the kids had them; lots of really expensive Guess? denim and stuff like that."

But Jim wasn't about to wear knockoffs again. This time he wanted the real stuff and hit upon a great way to get it. "I'd go to the lost and found in school and I would clean house, man. They had a little display case with all the stuff in it. I'd walk by, check it out, then go in and say, 'That's mine.' They never asked any questions. I'd get rad sweaters and shirts and all kinds of shit. I got a *Space Invaders* watch. Interestingly enough, I never felt good about that stuff, so I'd always break it or give it away."

By the middle of his freshman year, Forester's mother had had enough. She realized she couldn't control Jim anymore, so she sent him off to live with his father, who had moved to Las Vegas. The high school there gave Forester a rude awakening. "At that time Las Vegas was basically a blue-collar town. The people who lived there were mostly cocktail waitresses and poker dealers, or they owned small businesses. My high school was now a two-story cement slab with no windows. It was like a prison, and they had a 'we don't fuck around' mentality. If you missed one class, they marked you absent for the entire day. If you got more than eighteen absences in a semester, they gave you das boot. If you gave them any trouble whatsoever, they suspended you. They weren't catering to a bunch of rich kids who they had to handle with kid gloves. That was a big shock for me, because I was used to getting away with murder at Beverly Hills High."

Call her Lexie Byrne. She also hung around the front steps of the school, but in the late 1990s, ten years after Jim Forester was a fixture there. She transferred to Beverly Hills High from a private school and, like Forester, was at first tormented by the fashionistas.

"If you don't care what they think, then it's no big deal," Lexie explains. "And a lot of kids didn't—the ones who were really into school and focused on going to college. But if looks are important to you and you try to keep up but can't, it's devastating. Because those girls can be very exclusive, and you have to have something to be accepted. It's not necessarily a big house because a lot of these people don't have a lot of money. When it comes down to it, the real rich kids are for the most part in private school. These aren't the ones living in the mansions north of Sunset. They may have a nice house in the flats, but they aren't the superrich. They're the wanna-be-superrich. They're the ones who have to show off their stuff and have numerous Prada bags and a different outfit for every day of the week.

"One girl asked if I wanted to go to Fred Segal to buy outfits for the next week. This girl came out with five different outfits, spending thousands of dollars. Girls would call their closet their 'sanctuary' and talk about how they'd sit underneath all their clothes and meditate. I wasn't used to that. I came from a small private school where there were sixty kids in my class and there was a dress code and everybody wore clothes from the Gap. Suddenly I was in this competitive dressing society. At first I tried to keep up. I bought six pairs of pants in different colors for a hundred and twenty dollars each. I used to shop at Bloomingdale's, now I shopped at Barneys."

Clothing was only one arena of competition. There was also jewelry. "A girl came into class one day and announced that gold was passé. Platinum was now the thing. She said all of her jewelry had been updated. She now had platinum earrings, platinum necklaces." And by their junior year there were cars. "You were known by your car. A BMW was a cool car to have. A lot of people had Mustangs. One guy had an old Rolls-Royce, another had a 280-SL convertible Mercedes. This girl was driving her Ford Explorer down to Palm Springs with some friends for spring break and she flipped it, so she got a BMW instead. No big deal."

Lexie finally cracked under the stress. "My mom used to drive me to school, and I would put my makeup on in the car. One morning I forgot my makeup, and I refused to go to school. I made my mom drive me home. She said, 'If I drive you home, you're grounded for a month.' I said, 'That's fine. I don't care. I'm not going to school without my makeup on!' And I didn't go to school that day."

Mom put her foot down. "She was not going to throw her money around on five-hundred-dollar pairs of pants for a kid that doesn't take very good care of her clothes anyway," Lexie explains. "So I started trading clothes with my friends, then it just got old and I stopped caring. It was too hard for me; I couldn't compete with them, so my group of friends changed."

Like Forester, Lexie gravitated to the slackers, who positioned themselves as the polar opposite of the fashionistas. "I hung with the trashier girls—the girls who wore the little miniskirts and vampy makeup, not like the gothic stuff, but real dark; the kids who ditched, the kids who smoked pot and did not have a lot of money."

She began ditching too. "On a typical day I would either go to my second-period class or go to the Coffee Bean and get a coffee and come into class in the last ten minutes so I could erase my absence mark. The teacher left his attendance book on a chair, so I would just erase it. I had no problem cutting classes. I really worked the system there and never got busted or into any trouble. You're only allowed to have five unexcused absences, after that you're dropped from a class.

By the second semester of my senior year I had twenty-five unexcused absences in one class, but the teacher never dropped me. None of my teachers dropped me because I was never disruptive in class. I was just rarely there. All my teachers really liked me because when I was there I talked a lot in class discussions. If you have something to say, say it. If you yap away, the teacher thinks you've been doing your reading and are involved. And I always made a point of establishing a personal relationship with the teacher. I don't want to say that I flirted with my male teachers, but my male teachers certainly took more of a liking to me than to most of the other girls in the class.

"I never had any trouble with the security guards. I would drive my car off campus and they never bothered me. A lot of people would befriend them and buy them lunch and do things so they would let them off, and sometimes that worked and sometimes that didn't. I just stayed away and didn't really let them know who I was and kind of just slid by, because if you're not getting in trouble smoking in the bathroom or whatever, you're not on their radar screen.

"When I was doing a lot of speed, I would just go home and sleep the rest of the day. Speed was a really big thing at the time. All of the popular guys were doing it. But you needed to recuperate. It takes a toll on your body."

God, how Lexie loved it—that lockjawed, mind-humming rush, like plunging down a ninety-degree hill on a roller coaster, but the hill just keeps going and going and doesn't level out for hours. Way better than sex, better than a Super Mocha Latte with whipped cream and chocolate sprinkles, better than "I Get Around" by Tupac Shakur cranked up to ten on the stereo, better than just about anything Lexie could think of.

Lauren was her speed buddy. The two of them would hole up at Lexie's house if her parents were away, or if they were home, at Lexie's condo in Malibu where they would speed the night away. Lauren was a tall, slender girl with high cheekbones, hot as a *Cosmopolitan* cover girl, and adept at snowing mothers with kiss-ass superlatives: "Oh, I love what you've done with your hair, Mrs. Byrne, it makes you look younger, it really does, and where did you get those shoes, they're outrageous!" *I really like that Lauren*—mothers would say after she departed. *She's got a good head on her shoulders.*

Lauren loved speed even more than Lexie did. They would stay up all weekend listening to Tupac, the Outcasts, Wu-Tang Clan, and Notorious B.I.G.; talking on the phone, doing their nails, and putting together picture albums filled with snapshots of their friends. Or they would go out to Barnes and Noble and read books on astrology and the Kama Sutra for hours on end.

Most of the time they bought the speed from other kids. Everybody seemed to be doing it, except for the brainiacs, of course, and some of the jocks. "The guys tended to do it together in groups and the girls paired off." But occasionally, when nobody was holding, Lexie and Lauren would have to drive all the way to Eagle Rock, a decaying crime-plagued suburb northeast of downtown L.A., to buy from a dealer. "He was a friend of a friend. I don't even know how we hooked up with him. We met him on a corner where there was a Blockbuster Video and a gas station and bought it in the parking lot. I always felt uncomfortable. I was really paranoid about the situation, and he had such a drug-dealer car—an old Honda Accord, completely souped up, totally loaded with the big shiny wheels and stickers all over it."

Their parents were either too preoccupied with their own lives and oblivious to their children's drug use, or in some cases all too aware. "Some kids thought it was so cool that their parents bought them cigarettes, smoked pot with them, and talked about the hot sex that they had had the night before," says Lexie. "I didn't think it was cool. I found it appalling. This one girl would throw parties and her mom would come into the bedroom and smoke bongloads with everybody. That was not the kind of house that I felt comfortable in."

When asked why she thinks she drifted into the slacker lifestyle, Lexie falls silent for a moment, then shrugs. "It was the only one that I could keep up with. I wasn't the student. I wasn't the rich girl from Beverly Hills who was perfect. It was a lifestyle that didn't demand anything from you. It's really easy to slip into it."

But it became more demanding in her senior year as the giddy speed trips began to careen out of control. Something, Lexie slowly began to realize, was wrong with Lauren. "If she couldn't get any speed she would throw temper tantrums, rolling around on the floor, kicking and screaming, the whole bit."

Lauren lived in a two-bedroom apartment in Baja with her mother, who was divorced and had moved to Beverly Hills so her daughter could get a good education. Her father lived overseas and didn't contribute much financial or emotional support. Mom was in retail sales and did well enough to keep Lauren outfitted in stunning Neiman Marcus ensembles so she would fit in with the other students. But now Lauren's mother also began to realize something was wrong. When Lauren was caught off campus by the school's security officers, her mom grounded her and cut all of the phone lines in the house. "Then her mom started snooping around in Lauren's room," Lexie explains. "She opened a drawer and found pictures of Lauren naked with three guys. That's when she started going in for the kill and planning the intervention. She planned it for five-thirty on a Tuesday morning. All of Lauren's friends came over and woke her up and convinced her to go into rehab.

"I didn't want to be there, being that I had partaken in the activities with her; I didn't feel like I should be there. But I did go at seven in the morning, just before she was to leave, to say bye. She came out to my car as I was getting ready to pull away and tried to climb through the window. She asked me to take her away. When I said I couldn't, she handed me a bag of coke. . . . That was the last time I saw her.

"Her mother borrowed ten thousand dollars from one of her wealthy male friends to send Lauren out of state to this rehab center, but it didn't work. She left the center and got right back into drugs and never came home again. She called a girl we used to hang out with not long ago and told her she's living in the Midwest. She is a lesbian exotic dancer and does ecstasy on the weekends. She says she's had a couple of suicide attempts. They took her to the emergency room to pump her stomach and she says she has liver damage. Who even knows if this is all true? She's clearly out of touch with reality."

Lexie falls silent again. She adjusts her latte in its saucer and fiddles with the napkin in her lap, then shrugs. "I don't know why Lauren went off the deep end . . . I'm sure that it has something to do with her father. She said at one point that he was a heroin addict. She hated her mom and thought she was nuts, but other than that she didn't seem all that unhappy until the end." The napkin twists in her hands until it's a tightly wound coil of damp cloth. Despite all of those long amphetamine-fueled weekends together, Lexie now realizes she never really knew Lauren. The girl was a phantom, a ghost who drifted into her life, then swirled away into thin air.

Did Lauren's breakdown give Lexie second thoughts about the slacker life? She shrugs, holding tightly to the napkin. "Not really. I don't think that I looked at Lauren and said: 'Oh, she's losing her shit, I may too, I'd better quit.' It wasn't like that. It was like: 'Well, I've got my shit more together than she does and that's too bad that she can't handle it, but I can, so I'll keep doing it."

Jim Forester also felt he could handle his drugs. By 1991 he had dropped out of high school in Las Vegas and returned to Beverly Hills to live with his mother and stepfather. He was working in a bookstore in the retail district and had enrolled in Santa Monica Junior College. Jim was a talented artist and thought he might like to study architecture. But those plans went out the window when Forester discovered he could beat the bookstore's register. "I'd ring up sales without entering them into the day's total, so by the end of my shift I'd pocket three to four hundred dollars. I'd lost all my weed connections because everyone had gone off to college, so I would drive down to Pico and Hoover to buy from the Mexicans. Like I say, they were good businessmen, so they started throwing a couple of rocks of cocaine in with the deal. I've got all this extra money, so before I know it I develop this really bad habit. Really bad habit. I'm smoking three to four hundred dollars' worth of crack a day and more than that, as much as I could get my hands on.

"Then I lose my job and I've got this habit and no money. That's when things started to get ugly. Things in my parents' house started disappearing. It's a really weird thing, because those Mexicans down on Pico will take anything—jewelry, camera equipment, old Beatles albums, work boots, watches, rings, silverware, remote controls, CDs—*anything*. Of course my parents finally noticed the stuff was gone and I had to come clean. They put me in a recovery program and they went to Alanon, where they learned all about tough love. They became black belts, and when I got kicked out of the recovery program, they wouldn't let me come home. So all of a sudden, I'm out on the street.

"The only friend I had was this guy who used to live in the neighborhood. He had moved away with his parents and right in the middle of my downward spiral he came back and we hooked up and started partying together. I feel bad I got him into the coke scene. He had lost his leg in a drunk-driving motorcycle accident and he had a prosthetic leg. There were two friends of his and they had a beater muscle car but no place to stay either. Then I remembered Saul's house. Saul and his mom had left the country. The feds were investigating them for telemarketing fraud, so they took off. So we went over there and sure enough it was empty. We managed to squeeze through the doggie door. One of those guys had a phone in his car. He plugged it in a jack and said, 'Dude, this shit works. This is so cool, we stole a house!' "

They lived there for about six weeks, but it seemed like six years, or six hundred, for time barely seemed to pass in the huge quiet hollowed-out rooms. "We hardly slept, just little catnaps here and there. Twenty-four/seven, it was always, always, always about getting loaded or getting your next stash or getting your next hit. You'd get loaded and it lasted about thirty seconds and you'd think about getting loaded again. It was lame. Because I was so good at shoplifting, I would go to the grocery store and steal food. There was no stove or refrigerator, so I would start a fire in the fireplace and cook hot dogs and shit like that. It was bad.

"It finally ended when the owner of the house came in one day. We were like: 'Hey man, what's up?' He wasn't happy. He kicked us out and said if he ever found us there again, he would call the cops. So my friend and the other two guys went their way and I went mine and I never saw them again. I don't know what happened to them."

He had nowhere else to go now, but down to Pico and Hoover, where he begged the Mexicans to let him sell crack alongside them. "One guy gave me four rocks for the price of one. So if I sold one I'd get three and that's the way it works so you can stay in supply all day. And then I just stayed down there, twenty-four hours a day. I didn't sleep much; when I did, it would be in an abandoned house and there'd be four other people in there. All of the dealers on the tier that I was on were addicts, but the business guys weren't. None of them would touch it. They knew better. Can't last very long, you just can't, it's vicious.

"It was lame. Incredibly lame. There's a really interesting thing about the Mexican community. Whites cry to each other when they want to get something. The Mexicans call it 'the red eyes.' That's not the way Mexicans get what they want in their culture. It's also a gang mentality—you're never supposed to show emotion; that's the hardened street mentality. Emotion is your downfall. But when I was down there on Thanksgiving night, I didn't care. I got really sad and cried, thinking how fucked up everything was and how other people were with their families.

"You don't have any real friends when you're out there, just temporary alliances. And you needed those 'cause it was a competitive business and a highly gang-oriented neighborhood, so there were shootings all over the place. The first time I heard gunshots, I ran and dove in the bed of a truck. The second time, I ran onto a porch. After a while I stopped running. You get desensitized to it.

"But I never had any trouble. The Mexicans loved me. It was a prestigious thing to have me there. *Here's this guy from Beverly Hills, a white guy right here, hanging out with us!* They loved me."

It was as if he had finally gotten that BMX bike and a house north of Sunset. Jim Forester was an upper crusty at last.

★ 9 ★

The Maginot Line

The citizens of Beverly Hills are extremely proud of their police force. Many have moved there not only for the great public schools, but also for the sense of security that the Blue Knights provide. Indeed, most residents fire off pro-police statistics with the polished élan of professional press agents. *One police officer for every 250 citizens. Compare that to L.A., which has a ratio of one officer per 1,000 people. That's four times the protection that our neighbors to the east have!*

With an annual budget of $26 million, the Beverly Hills Police Department is the single most expensive and powerful public institution in the community. The city spends $571 in police protection per citizen every year, more than any other community in California. Its two neighbors, Santa Monica and Los Angeles, respectively spend only $158 and $278 per resident. The BHPD is headquartered in a six-story complex, which includes a high-tech jail, a state-of-the-art forensics lab; numerous command and communications centers; traffic, narcotics, and vice divisions; an Emergency Operations Center; and a firing range—all connected by an intricate web of intercoms, closed-circuit cameras, sensors, electronic doors, locks, and alarm systems. Its state-of-the-art communications network facilitates an average response time to emergency calls of just 2.8 minutes. Granted, Beverly Hills isn't that big, a little over five and a half square miles, but as Lieutenant Edward T. Kreins, head of the department's Internal Affairs Division, explains, "Response time is a reflection of not only the size of the city, but also the attitude and leadership of the force."

And the response time is only one of many impressive statistics. Compare the 2000 crime stats of Beverly Hills with those of its neighbor Santa Monica:

	Beverly Hills	Santa Monica
Homicide	1	2
Rape	7	31
Aggravated assault	46	343
Robbery	66	266
Burglary	302	603

Enter most police stations and you will be greeted by a battleship gray, Formica-topped counter manned by a doughnut-bloated sergeant equipped with little more than a notepad, a chewed-up Bic pen, and an ancient beige telephone with only a half-dozen lines on it. The Beverly Hills desk sergeant is thin, tanned, and toned, and doesn't even have a desk. He's encased in a massive chamber of bulletproof glass known as "the aquarium." His lipless mouth barely parts when he asks if he can help you, and his eyes have no time to make contact, they're too busy darting from a communications console to a computer screen then to a monitor that offers a view of the street entrance you just stepped through. His fingers dance across the machinery that ensnares him, and he seems like a machine himself, like *Star Trek*'s Data, preparing to fire phasers at an incoming Romulan Warbird.

But Lieutenant Kreins—who doubles as the department's press liaison officer—seems human enough. As he conducts a tour of the facility, he resembles a French general doing his best to convince a politician that the millions of francs poured into the Maginot Line were well spent. The first stop is the watch commander's room. The watch commander supervises all of the officers on duty during his shift. He sits amid an even larger array of communications consoles and monitors, including one that offers a view of the aquarium sergeant watching his monitors. It's a bizarre hall-of-mirrors image, an endless chain of police officers watching one another through an infinite network of surveillance screens.

Kreins heaves a heavy metal door open and leads the way into a set of concrete and steel chambers. The jail. The odor of cement and machine oil hangs in the air; it's cool as a wine cellar and quiet as an empty church. Business is slow today; all twenty-eight jail cells lie empty. There are no mints on the pillows or fresh flowers, but the accommodations look a tad more comfortable than your average Motel 6: crisp clean well-ironed sheets, thick blankets, gleaming stainless-steel toilets, sinks with mirrors for prisoners to primp before, and intercoms should they want to call for cell service. Kreins notes that every accoutrement is "top of the line." The locks on the doors weigh 1,500 pounds and cost $1,000. The plumbing for each cell costs $5,000, and the city spends more than $1 million a year to maintain this single cell block. Kreins's voice rings with pride as he rattles off the exorbitant cost of each feature, because even here, at the very bottom rung of the Beverly Hills status grid, money calibrates quality and prestige.

The jailer monitors every square inch of the facility from yet another elaborate communications console. Without leaving his chair, he can speak to all of the prisoners in their cells and control all points of entry through a network of electronic locks. Surveillance monitors line his console, and the camera that covers the service entrance can be moved via an electronic toggle to follow anyone leaving along the sidewalk and out to the curb. When the jailer receives a call that a squad car is approaching with a prisoner in its backseat, he flips a switch that slides a steel door open in the station's underground garage complex. One or two squad cars can then drive through the door into a concrete chamber. When the door slides shut behind them, the officers remove the prisoner from the backseat of the car and escort him or her to an elevator that takes them up three floors to yet another chamber of bulletproof glass. The suspects remain there, under the watchful eye of the all-powerful jailer, until officers are ready to take them to the digital biometrics booking area, where their picture is taken by a digital camera and their fingerprints electronically scanned and fed into a database. No more messy ink pads or laborious scrutinizing of epidermal ridge patterns. Fingerprints gathered at crime scenes can now be matched to suspects with just a few keystrokes!

Surveillance doesn't end on the day prisoners make bail. The complex's intricate network of cameras follows them all the way out to the street. In fact, Kreins brags that one released prisoner was spotted scrawling graffiti on the elevator on his way down to the street and rearrested before he could leave the building.

Even after they escape the confines of the complex, criminals are not free of the long eye of the law. Beverly Hills was one of the first cities in the country to install a camera at one of its busiest intersections—Wilshire and La Cienega Boulevards—to catch motorists running red lights. The electronic eye proved so successful at reading the license plates of violators, the city added cameras at many other busy intersections. They quickly proved to have additional law enforcement applications when LAPD called to inform Beverly Hills police that a murder suspect may have passed through their community. The BHPD checked the surveillance cameras, spotted the suspect's car, reported the location and direction he was headed, and LAPD was able to apprehend the man. In addition to the stoplight cameras, there are electronic eyes in virtually every bank, office building, clothing, jewelry, and convenience store, and on every sizeable estate in the city. Almost every move an individual makes in Beverly Hills is recorded; the day is swiftly approaching when there will be no place left for criminals to hide.

Beverly Hills is the most secure city in Los Angeles County, if not the state, but security comes at a stiff price, as Robert K. Tanenbaum learned when he befriended a family with a pigmentation that the community has deemed aesthetically undesirable.

Moacir Jones developed an aptitude for athletics at an early age. At five he began playing soccer. Baseball and basketball soon followed, and he proved superb in all three sports. "Moacir was always competitive," says his mother, Cheryl. "He was always very disciplined about sports. He just had that intensity, a maturity that most other kids didn't have." Cheryl worked as a private chef for a number of wealthy clients in Beverly Hills. Her husband, Ralph, was a professional musician who played the saxophone and flute with a Los Angeles–based band. Together they earned a decent living, but raising a child proved more expensive than they had anticipated, so Ralph enrolled in UCLA to get a degree in ethnomusicology, which would enable him to supplement his sporadic income with a steady paycheck as a schoolteacher. They had fourteen years to save up enough money to send Moacir to college. Suddenly that didn't seem like very much time. But if Mo continued to be an outstanding athlete, he might be able to win a scholarship and pay his own way, so Ralph devoted himself to his son's athletic development.

Because they lived and worked on the west side, Ralph enrolled Mo in sports programs at a number of Beverly Hills recreation centers, including the YMCA. The Y had a basketball league. Ralph signed Mo up for one of the two teams in his age group. At eight years old, he already stood five feet three inches and outplayed everyone else on the team, but the coach and his fellow players seemed far from grateful for his contributions. No one was outright hostile, but Ralph got the feeling they weren't wild about a black kid invading their lily-white turf. Then one day, the tall barrel-chested coach of the other team in Mo's age group approached Ralph. "I've been watching your son," he said. "He's got a lot of potential. I'd like to have him on my team." He handed Ralph his card. "Think it over and give me a call." As the big man walked away Ralph looked down at the card. His mouth fell open when he saw that the man, Robert K. Tanenbaum, was a member of the Beverly Hills city council. Ralph had been getting the cold shoulder for months and suddenly one of the city's leaders was inviting his son to join a team.

Mo played on Bob Tanenbaum's team for the next five years. "Bob was one of the best coaches Mo ever had," says Ralph. "He taught Mo not only the fundamentals of the sport, but why they were important. Instead of directing him to do this or that, he explained the reasons why he wanted him to do things." And he was more than a coach. He took the team out for pizza after the games. Bob's son, Roger, became a close friend of Mo's because they were both very serious about sports and basketball in particular. "Bob really extended himself to us," says Ralph. "When he was going to be appointed mayor, he invited us to the inauguration."

Mo had been attending Carthay Elementary School on Olympic Boulevard, just east of Beverly Hills. But as he was getting ready to enter fourth grade in 1988, the Joneses began to worry. The average class size at Carthay was increasing, and textbooks, computers, science, music, and art equipment were in short supply. The wealthy sent their children to private schools that cost as much as, or more than, most universities, but middle-class people like the Joneses didn't have that option. They talked to Tanenbaum about the problem, and he suggested they enroll Mo in a Beverly Hills school. Mo qualified for enrollment under a special child-care permit because Cheryl worked in the city. From the beginning, Cheryl had reservations. She worried about the enormous economic and cultural disparities that would yawn between her son and most of the other students—and of course about the most crucial disparity of all: skin color.

It was common knowledge among African Americans that Beverly Hills did not throw out the welcome mat for people of their pigmentation. In fact, most blacks avoided visiting or even driving through the city because of the BHPD's reputation for pulling African American motorists over for bogus reasons. "Your taillight is out," the cops would claim. Or: "You didn't come to a full stop at that stop sign back there." Or: "You fit the description of someone who's been committing robberies in this neighborhood." Then the cops would subject them to intensive searches and hostile questions, not because they actually suspected the blacks of committing a crime, but simply to convey a message: *You're not wanted here*.

They had, in fact, never been wanted. When Burton Green laid out the blueprints for his city of the future with his architect, Wilbur Cook, shortly after the turn of the century, a key element of the design had been the exclusion of African Americans. The first generation of Beverly Hills homes had covenants attached to their deeds that specifically forbid the owners to sell their property to blacks, and all other people of color. These racist covenants were routinely passed on from owner to owner throughout the 1920s, '30s, '40s, and '50s. When future president Ronald Reagan and his wife, Jane Wyman, bought a parcel of Beverly Hills land in 1941, it carried a standard covenant that stated: "No part of said property shall at any time be sold, conveyed, leased or rented to or inherited by or otherwise acquired by or become the property of any person whose blood is not entirely that of the Caucasian race."

Yet, ironically, one of the most talented young architects who worked in Wilbur Cook's office while he was putting the final polish on his blueprints for Beverly Hills was a black man—a black man who would later have a major influence on the city's residential and commercial architecture—Paul R. Williams.

Williams would design more than 3,000 residential and commercial projects over his nearly sixty-year career. Approximately 300 of them were located in Beverly Hills, including: the Music Corporation of America (MCA) building (1937), a stunning white Colonial Revival complex that he developed for Lew Wasserman and Jules Stein; the Saks Fifth Avenue (1939) and the W & J Sloane (1948) department stores; and homes for such stars as Frank Sinatra, Cary Grant, Bing Crosby, Tyrone Power, Fanny Brice, Humphrey Bogart, William Holden, Lucille Ball and Desi Arnaz. His style varied from English tudor to American Colonial to art deco to contemporary, but all of the projects shared a sense of restraint and proportion that made them elegant yet not pretentious, impressive but not overblown.

By 1947 Williams's star had risen so high in the architectural firmament that Hernando Courtright hired him to renovate and add a new wing to the city's oldest and most venerable institution, the Beverly Hills Hotel. Williams designed an entirely new complex on the eastern end of the hotel. Known as the Crescent Wing, it included the legendary Polo Lounge and a curvaceous stairway that led to a small but elegant art deco coffee shop just below the Polo Lounge.

The Crescent Wing—with its eye-popping banana leaf wallpaper, overstuffed art deco furnishings, proliferation of aerodynamic curves, and ultramodern cutout ceilings that heaved and rolled like froth in a blender—was the apogee of luxury and glamour in the swinging, swanky jet-set era of post–World War II America. Yet it has also stood the test of time. More than fifty years later, if you mention the words "Beverly Hills Hotel" most people think of the Polo Lounge, the coffee shop, and the cream white letters that spell out the hotel's name on the exterior of the Crescent Wing. Williams's work overshadows both the original Spanish mission–style exterior, and the Gensler & Associates 1994 remodel that turned the west wing of the hotel into Persian kitsch.

Fierce ambition, quiet tenacity, and remarkable talent had enabled Williams to thrive professionally in a hostile environment, but he never completely overcame the racism that crouched in the shadows of those palm-lined boulevards. Williams redefined the Beverly Hills Hotel, and in doing so extended its commercial life for another half-century. But when construction was completed on the Polo Lounge in 1947, he was forbidden to dine in his own creation.

Overt racism soon withered under the force of the civil rights movement. By 1945 African Americans had filed more than twenty lawsuits against racial covenants, and in 1948 the United States Supreme Court ruled, in the case of *Shelley v. Kraemer,* that racial covenants violated the Fourteenth Amendment. By the 1960s black celebrities such as Sidney Poitier, Sammy Davis Jr., and Ella Fitzgerald broke the color barrier in Beverly Hills by moving into some of the largest estates north of Sunset.

But a handful of wealthy black landowners did not bring an end to discrimination in the city. More subtle forms lingered as Cheryl Jones discovered during the first years she worked there. Whenever she shopped in the department stores on Wilshire—Neiman Marcus or Saks, which Paul Williams designed—the salespeople would follow her. "I was in the costume jewelry section of Saks once, trying on earrings, bracelets," Jones recalls. "I must have had every saleswoman in Saks come over and ask if they could help me." The look in their eyes made it clear they weren't interested in assisting her. They wanted to make sure she knew she was being watched.

But in the summer of 1988 Cheryl wondered if such minor humiliations were serious enough to deny Mo a Beverly Hills education. Bob Tanenbaum argued that, while not completely free of prejudice, Beverly Hills had changed in recent years and was actually much more tolerant than many other cities, including Los Angeles. Beverly Hills schools were no longer lily-white. The Persians had taken care of that. And besides, what were the other options? Catholic school? Better than public school, but still expensive and nowhere nearly as well equipped as the Beverly Hills schools, with their vast computer rooms, state-of-the-art libraries, science labs, athletic departments, and performing arts facilities—and all of it *absolutely free*.

"Why don't we try it for a year?" Ralph said. "If we don't like it, if Mo doesn't like it, he doesn't have to stay there."

Mo loved the idea. He already had a lot of friends there from all of the sports teams he'd played on, and didn't seem to have any fears about fitting in. So Cheryl relented. "All right, we'll give it a try."

Tanenbaum suggested they enroll him in El Rodeo with his son, Roger. Mo had no trouble acclimating. He liked his teacher, made more friends, and was invited to many birthday parties and sleepovers. Like Bruce Nelson a half-century before him, Mo felt as if he'd been swept away to a never-never land filled with azure swimming pools, game rooms that rivaled the best amusement parks, and "home theaters" that put most multiplexes to shame.

But then there were the other moments. Fleeting, true enough, momentary anomalies in an otherwise tranquil continuum. But their shadows lingered long after they passed. The first time was at recess. Mo was playing basketball with a couple of friends. Suddenly, another kid from another class, someone he barely knew, dashed between them, stole the ball, and brought the game to a halt. Mo asked for the ball back. The kid refused. The exchange grew heated and the kid spit the word out like a white-hot gob: "Nigger!" It took six boys to hold Mo back. The strange kid laughed, delighted at the power that one little word had given him, dropped the ball, and danced away in triumph.

"Look," Cheryl said, "you don't have to stay there. You don't have to go to that school."

Mo shrugged. He liked El Rodeo. All his friends were there, and they were nothing like that kid. So he stayed through fifth and sixth grades. He had dropped soccer and basketball by this time to focus exclusively on football and had already earned a shelf full of trophies. "He really showed promise, very early," says Cheryl.

Seventh grade loomed. Junior high and high school were combined at Beverly Hills High, but Mo wouldn't be able to enroll on a child-care permit. If he really wanted to go to Beverly High, his parents would have to move to an apartment within the city limits. Mo had set his sights on a college football scholarship, so the Beverly Hills team would be the deciding factor. Ralph took him to watch a couple of practices. The coach, Carter Paysinger, was a black man and an alumnus of the school. "Mo liked Carter because he played the best player for a particular position," Cheryl explains. "There was no favoritism or playing a kid because his parents were putting on pressure, or because his dad was rich. It was based on performance. Which is not something that all coaches do."

That settled it. They moved into a two-bedroom apartment on Reeves Drive, in Baja Beverly Hills. There were a handful of other black families living in Baja, and Mo quickly gravitated to them. Brandon Nash—who lived around the corner on Olympic Boulevard in a two-bedroom apartment with his mother, Yolanda, and brothers, Brent and Billy—soon became Mo's best friend. "Mo never had brothers," Cheryl explains, "but the Nashes just looked at him like he was an extension of the family. He and Brandon were always together. And then there was Jomo Kenyatta, who lived on Wilshire and Gale near the Big Five sporting goods store. They all played football together."

By his sophomore year Mo stood five feet eleven and weighed 165 pounds. He played quarterback on the sophomore team; Brandon played wide receiver and Jomo running back. They were all headed for athletic scholarships. All in all, the Joneses had to admit things had gone quite smoothly. Mo had encountered very little bigotry from teachers or classmates, or the police. Cheryl finally began to relax a bit.

She got the phone call in January 1995, at ten thirty on a Thursday night. Mo was in his room listening to music. Cheryl and Ralph were in their room watching TV when the phone rang. Cheryl felt a twinge of anxiety as she picked it up. They didn't usually get calls this late. Both of their parents were getting up there and ripe for a fall, a stroke, or a heart attack. She was relieved to hear Yolanda's voice, but noticed it was high and tight with anxiety. "Cheryl, I'm sick of this mess. I'm on my way to the police station."

"Wait a minute, Yolanda, hold on. What are you talking about?"

Yolanda paused in surprise. "You don't know?"

"Know what?"

"The boys were stopped by the cops today. They handcuffed them in the middle of Olympic Boulevard. . . . Didn't Mo tell you?"

Now Cheryl's voice was high and tight. "No, no he didn't. Let me call you back."

Cheryl slammed the phone down. Ralph lowered the remote, his brow rumpling. "What's up?"

"That's what I'd like to know. MOACIR! GET IN HERE!"

Her son dropped his eyes as she repeated what Yolanda had told her, and demanded an explanation. Was it true they'd been stopped by the cops? It was, Mo murmured. Why on earth didn't he tell them about this? He shifted his big shoulders, as if his shirt had suddenly grown too tight, and said he thought he'd get in trouble and didn't want them to worry. "Well, you'd better tell us now," Cheryl said, "from the beginning, exactly what happened."

And so he did.

It was around 7:30 P.M. You could see the tiny square lights of offices in the glass and steel towers of Century City from Brandon's apartment, which is where Mo, Brandon, and Jomo had been hanging out when they decided to walk to Movies 'n More on Olympic to check out the new video games. As they strolled past the Cadillac dealership, Mo grew irritated with his two friends, who kept falling behind as they goofed with each other. He turned to see what they were up to. Jomo had planted his hands in the pockets of his loose-fitting athletic jacket and was swatting at Brandon with his elbows. The two of them were laughing so hard they could hardly stand up. Mo let out an exasperated sigh. "Come on, guys. We ain't got all night."

A siren yelped. Mo wheeled around as a Beverly Hills cruiser screeched up, its cherry lights whipping. It seemed to have popped up from the asphalt. The door flew open and a cop rose from behind it with a gun. *Whoa.* Mo barely heard the barked orders. *Freeze! . . . Hands in the air! . . .* He was too busy looking down that blue-black barrel. No one had ever pointed a gun at him before. His mind tried to grasp the reality of the moment. His forehead grew hot and prickly. His thighs began to tremble, like someone was running an electric current through them. Then he remembered Jomo's hands. *In his jacket pockets. Pull your hands out slowly, Jomo. Don't give them an excuse . . .*

"Turn around, slowly, and put your hands up against the window," the cop said.

They did as they were told, even Jomo, Mo surmised, because no one started shooting. The glass was cold against his damp palms; an icy trickling of sweat ran from his armpits down his rib cage as he tried to remain absolutely still. There were more cops now, motorcycles and cars wailing in from all directions. *What the hell do they think this is, another Rodney King riot?* Someone frisked him, then grabbed his hands and cuffed them tight, the metal biting into his wrists.

A policeman ordered them to sit down on a narrow ledge that bordered the plate glass window of the Cadillac dealership. The half-dozen BHPD vehicles took up an entire lane on Olympic. Traffic crept by in the free lane, motorists and passengers staring with fascination at the handcuffed boys, their eyes all filled with the same thoughts: *Ah, caught three of them. Wonder what those little bastards were doing.* Mo's face burned like it had been in the hot sun for hours. He wanted to run, wanted these cuffs off his hands, to get away from that procession of accusing gazes. *This is fucked up. This is fucked up big-time.*

The cops milled about, almost aimlessly. Some talked to one another in relaxed tones, others consulted radios or waved traffic through. None of them looked or spoke to the three boys on the window ledge. Finally Mo asked the cop standing nearest to them why they were being held. "Be quiet," the cop said.

Jomo and Brandon glanced apprehensively at him and remained grimly silent. But Mo couldn't help himself. He was beginning to get angry. "What's going on?" he asked another cop. "We didn't do anything wrong. We were just walking to the video store."

"Someone in the Cadillac dealership called us," the cop replied. "They said they heard someone banging on the door, trying to break in."

"We didn't bang on any door. We were just going to the video store like I told you." The cop seemed not to hear. He stared off at the slow-snaking traffic. Mo sighed. *What a bunch of bullshit.*

Over the next forty-five minutes he asked several other cops why they were being held, and got a different answer every time.

"We got a report of someone who looked like you guys trying to break into a car on Olympic Boulevard."

"Someone saw you guys trying to steal a Cadillac off of the lot."

Mo and his friends knew the score; it was the same lame-ass we-got-an-anonymous-tip excuse cops all over L.A. used when they wanted to mess with you.

Finally, one of the cops strolled over from his squad car where he'd been on the radio, and asked the boys why they were in this area to begin with. When Mo told him they lived here, that they were students at Beverly Hills High School, the cop gave him a shocked look and asked to see their student IDs.

At this point, Brandon's little brother, Brent, came out of his apartment house. He'd heard the sirens and wanted to see what was going on. When he spotted his brother and friends handcuffed and surrounded by a platoon of blue uniforms, his eyes widened and he ran back inside to fetch his mother. Yolanda came barreling across the street just as the cops were taking the cuffs off the boys. "What's going on here? Why did you stop them?" Yolanda demanded. The cops muttered something about a misunderstanding and the boys being free to go, then sped off in their various vehicles as quickly as they had arrived.

When Mo finished his story, Cheryl shook her head and Ralph said he couldn't believe it. Mo showed them the red marks on his wrists. It was real all right. Too real, for him. Then he revealed this wasn't the first incident. In the last year and a half the police had stopped him a half-dozen times. He never told them because he thought he might get in trouble. But this was the first time the cops slapped the cuffs on him. Inwardly, Cheryl cringed. The police had been able to make her son feel guilty, that somehow this was his fault. She picked up the phone, called Yolanda back, and told her they'd meet her at the station.

They arrived to find Yolanda already tearing into the aquarium sergeant. "I want something to be done about this! They handcuffed these boys, treated them like criminals, and they'd done nothing, absolutely nothing wrong. Now what are you going to do?"

The sergeant stared back from the glassy depths of his fluorescent-lit chamber, like an overfed blowfish barely able to keep his eyes open. "We can't do anything right now, ma'am. Like I say, you need to fill out a complaint form. We'll look into it and get back to you."

Cheryl felt her own blood coming to a rapid boil. She introduced herself as Moacir's mother and explained her son had also been handcuffed, searched, and questioned for no valid reason. The sergeant gazed back at her from beneath his heavy eyelids with a somnambulistic expression that seemed to say: *so what?* "Look," she said, "can we see your report on the incident?"

"My report?" the aquarium sergeant asked with a mixture of puzzlement and disdain.

"The department's report," she explained, "the report filed by the officers. They must have filed a report."

The aquarium sergeant shifted uncomfortably, his chair emitting a metallic squeak. "Well, I don't know what kind of report it's going to be, because I was there."

"You were there?"

"That's what I just said, ma'am."

"Then maybe you can tell me why my son was put in handcuffs."

The aquarium sergeant shifted about in his groaning seat, unable to find a comfortable position. He glanced at his communications console, wishing an important message would extricate him from this. "We got a call that someone was breaking into the dealership."

"It was seven thirty. How do you break into a dealership that's already open for business? All they had to do was walk in the door; it wasn't locked. The place was full of salespeople."

The aquarium sergeant looked as if he'd been stricken with a severe gas pain. "I don't know, look we got a call, they thought the kids were trying to steal one of the cars."

"Well, if they did something wrong, why weren't they arrested?"

As the aquarium sergeant stumbled through another haphazard rationalization, Ralph shook his head in disgust.

Cheryl and Ralph returned home that night frightened for their son's life. They knew young black men were the prime target in racial profiling and feared the harassment of Mo might escalate. Not knowing where else to turn, they called Bob Tanenbaum.

Tanenbaum was no longer mayor or even a member of the city council. While still in office in 1992, he had made a grave political miscalculation. Tanenbaum insisted on a thorough audit and strategic study of the police department's $18.9 million budget. The other members of the council smiled. Tanenbaum had made the fatal mistake of assuming that the seat of power resided in the council chamber. BHPD Chief Marvin Iannone took it upon himself to educate the would-be reformer. In the 1994 election the powerful Beverly Hills Police Officer Association refused to endorse Tanenbaum and instead threw its support to rival candidates. The association mailed letters to Beverly Hills residents that claimed Tanenbaum had "voted against providing the Beverly Hills police officers with adequate facilities and claimed all we needed was a locker and a desk. He constantly has attacked and berated and belittled the police department, even suggesting that we are nothing more than 'desk jockeys in suits.' " Tanenbaum suffered an overwhelming defeat.

Now a member of a private law firm, Tanenbaum was appalled when he heard what had happened to Moacir Jones. Despite his own bitter experience with the BHPD, he never dreamed they could be capable of such a blatant act of harassment. He still believed Beverly Hills was run by decent people who would be as shocked as he was when they learned of this incident. So he advised the Joneses to go through the formal complaint process with the city. Eventually, justice would be done.

The police did finally launch an investigation. Mo, Brandon, and Jomo were called into the station for a series of meetings with a community affairs officer, then were split up for individual interviews with investigators. The parents were also called in, and at one meeting, according to the Joneses, an officer suddenly assumed a confidential and conciliatory tone. "Listen, we have an unwritten rule that minority males between eighteen and thirty-five are stopped. The community expects us to take a very aggressive approach to keep out the criminal element, and that's a key part of the approach. I'll tell you what you should do. Bring Moacir back down to the station and we'll introduce him to all of the patrol officers. That way, when they see him on the street they'll know who he is and he won't have a problem."

Cheryl was reminded of her husband's friend who lived in South Africa years ago under the apartheid system. His employers arranged for him to have the words "Honorary White" stamped on his passport so he could travel through exclusive Caucasian enclaves without fear of being attacked by the authorities. Cheryl glared at the BHPD officer, who smiled back warmly, hoping he had offered a compromise that would bring an end to a thorny public relations issue. "Why," Cheryl asked, "do I have to bring my son in and justify his right to live here without being harassed?"

Beads of sweat broke out on the officer's broad forehead. His big hands groped each other. "It was just a suggestion."

Meanwhile, at school, Mo had to endure humiliating fallout from the incident. A couple of days after it occurred a girl approached him in computer class and asked, "Was that you I saw getting arrested on Olympic Boulevard the other day?" She had been in one of the hundreds of cars that drove past while it was going down. Mo admitted it was, then hurried on to explain how he'd done nothing wrong, didn't get arrested or even a ticket. It had all been a misunderstanding. "That's good to hear." The girl nodded. He looked into her eyes, trying to gauge if she believed him, but couldn't tell. He wanted to explain more, about how there was going to be an investigation and eventually he'd be completely cleared, but someone called the girl's name and she moved off.

In English class the teacher, Ms. Goeler, decided to make the incident a topic for class discussion. Mo felt the trickle of icy sweat down his rib cage as his classmates raised their hands to weigh in. Most expressed shock, thought Mo had been treated unfairly, and hoped he would eventually be exonerated by the internal investigation. But a few said things like, "The police were only doing their job." And: "I don't know, I think he and his friends must have been doing something. The police don't just come down on you for no reason. They have better things to do than arbitrarily hassle people." These were kids Mo had always thought of as friends. It wasn't only their words that bothered him, it was the way they talked about him in the third person and never once looked over at him, the way the corners of their mouths turned up ever so slightly to hint at a taunting smile.

He responded of course. Explained in detail what had happened and again asserted that the investigation would prove everything he was saying was true, but those kids never looked at him, the corners of their mouths remained upturned. He became painfully aware of the ineffectiveness of his words and a tremor of emotion at the back of his throat.

"I remember coming home and telling my mom that this happened," he recalls some six years later. After a long pause, he sighs. "I was hurt because those were my friends, you know? And then for them to think . . . Shoot, it was a messed-up situation."

Cheryl tried to bolster his spirits. "You know, Mo," she said to him, "you kids are really too young to form your own opinions on issues like this. It takes a while to develop your own sense of morality and social conscience. Whatever these kids are saying, it's what they heard at home. Unfortunately, they have very bigoted parents, so the kids can't help it." That made it more understandable, but no easier to live with. If that was true, then it was more than just a couple of snotty kids; it was their parents, their brothers and sisters, and the friends of those parents, maybe. Something sinister hunched behind those manicured shrubs, stately oak trees, and the grand facades of the Beverly Hills homes. The veil had been lifted from Mo's eyes; the threat was no longer a handful of overzealous cops but something much uglier and far more virulent and covert. For Mo, Beverly Hills fell from grace that day, but little did he know it had much further yet to fall.

After the initial round of interviews the Joneses waited to hear from the police department. Cheryl called repeatedly to check the status of the investigation and was told each time that it was still ongoing and that she would be notified of the results when it was finished. After six months passed, in June 1995, they received a letter stating that the investigation had been concluded and that it had uncovered no evidence of wrongdoing by the officers involved. The Joneses were shocked and outraged. "How could they come to that conclusion?" Cheryl asks. "Those police officers treated my son like a common criminal. If somebody from the city had just come forward and apologized, we might have been able to let it go. But nobody did. Nobody came to us and said, 'We're so sorry about what happened to your kids. It was terrible, it'll never happen again, please accept our apologies.' The police refused to accept that they had done anything wrong. The arrogance was reeking."

So they called Bob Tanenbaum again, told him what had happened, and asked if he'd be willing to serve as their lawyer. Tanenbaum couldn't believe what he was hearing. "I thought that the city would handle it properly. I was flabbergasted." Then his bewilderment gave way to outrage. He had encouraged the Joneses to move to this city, thinking he was doing them a favor. Sure, Beverly Hills had its shortcomings—no one knew that better than he—but Bob never dreamed it would treat his friends so shabbily. Yes, he told the Joneses, of course he would represent their son, and his two friends, in a class-action civil rights suit against the city.

As Tanenbaum and the Joneses prepared their case in the fall of 1995, more racial profiling victims came to their attention and joined the suit. Mo got to talking with the cocaptain of the football team, another African American, Jerry Lafayette. Jerry lived with his parents in an apartment in the flats, near Doheny and Burton Way, and drove to school and back every day. In the last eighteen months, Jerry admitted, the police had pulled him over more than twenty times, once in his own driveway. They always had a reason, of course. Yet they never once arrested him or issued a ticket. The situation got so bad that his grandmother, Audrey Bowen, who had lived in Beverly Hills for twenty years, followed a police officer's advice, took Jerry down to the station, and introduced him to all of the patrol officers. It didn't help. The cops continued to pull him over. He was so humiliated in front of his white friends in a 1994 incident that he almost stopped driving his car. "I don't want to become the next Rodney King," he told his parents. After talking to Mo, Jerry decided to join Tanenbaum's class-action suit.

Then Tanenbaum learned about Pat Earthly, a twenty-nine-year-old African American janitor who worked for the All Saints Episcopal Church in Beverly Hills. When Earthly pulled into the church parking lot at 7 A.M. on Mother's Day in 1995 to report for work, a BHPD squad car squealed in behind him. An officer leaped out. "Get back in the car!" he ordered. But Earthly had swallowed a bellyful of abuse from the Beverly Hills men in blue. He'd already been pulled over on seven other occasions. Once, an officer pointed a gun at his head and demanded to know where he was going. *To a doctor's appointment*—Earthly had responded on that occasion. But this time he didn't feel particularly cooperative. Instead of getting back into his car, Earthly demanded to know what he'd done wrong. The policeman dropped a hand to the butt of his revolver and ordered Pat to lie down on the ground. Earthly refused.

Fortunately for the janitor, members of the congregation spilled out of the church at that moment along with the minister, the Reverend Carol Anderson, to see what the ruckus was. "The police quickly resolved it when they saw people coming around," says Anderson. Earthly was cited for a burned-out taillight and the cops beat a hasty retreat.

But for Earthly the bitter aftertaste of this and past encounters lingered long after the cruiser's exhaust fumes dissipated. "It made me feel belittled and humiliated and terrible," he later said.

Many members of the congregation—including Sharon Davis, wife of future California governor Gray Davis—wrote letters to the police department and city officials. They protested the mistreatment of Earthly and demanded that officials review police procedures that might have led to such an incident. The police never responded, but, says Reverend Anderson, "the city manager [Mark Scott] actually came over to apologize to Earthly. It was sort of an embarrassment to the city. He even offered for the chief of police and for himself to come and apologize to the congregation, and then of course as time moved on and the lawsuits started, it was all never brought up again."

Earthly joined Tanenbaum's suit, as did Richard Hill, an Antelope Valley landscaper, who'd been ordered out of his car at gunpoint by BHPD officers when he was on his way to meet his wife, who worked for a Beverly Hills neurosurgeon, for lunch. And Tanenbaum filed another suit on behalf of Democratic State Assemblyman Kevin Murray, who'd been pulled over by Beverly Hills police while driving down La Cienega Boulevard with his fiancée. A female officer told Murray she stopped him because she had run a computer check on his license plate but couldn't retrieve information on it. Murray explained that legislators have special plates on state-leased cars; the registration information is not readily available to protect the privacy of assembly members. He gave the officer his state assembly ID, registration, and his license. Then he asked why she ran the plates. The officer said, "We don't have to have a reason."

Tanenbaum filed his class-action suit on November 21, 1995. He named the city of Beverly Hills, two city council members, Vicky Reynolds and Allan Alexander, and Police Chief Marvin Iannone and Captain Robert P. Curtis of the BHPD as the defendants for fostering racial bias. Tanenbaum asked for monetary damages for his clients and for an injunction against the city to prohibit racial profiling. It looked as if he had a strong case, but he was up against a formidable opponent. The city of Beverly Hills had millions of dollars at its disposal and was determined to prevail in court by whatever means necessary. Individual employees like city manager Mark Scott may have expressed regret for the overzealous activities of some policemen, but every city official understood that they could not afford to admit to a systematized pattern of harassment. That would expose the city to countless lawsuits and millions of dollars in liability, enough to drain even Beverly Hills's enormous resources. No, better to spend a million or two now to nip this thing in the bud.

So they went to one of the best bud-nippers in the business, a Century City legal eagle by the name of Louis "Skip" Miller. Miller specialized in scuttling civil rights lawsuits against police departments. He had helped the city of Los Angeles develop its key legal strategies to deal with Rodney King's multimillion-dollar civil rights lawsuit. "I've never lost a defense case," Miller boasted with characteristic modesty. "I know how to win." In April 2001, Miller would be publicly reproved by the California state bar and ordered to undergo ethics training after he met with the foreman of a jury for a trial in which he was defending the LAPD. The jury foreman had been dismissed from the case. Miller discussed the jury's conduct with him, then petitioned for a mistrial, based on information he obtained in the meeting. Afterward Miller told the press, "I acknowledged I broke the rules. I didn't do it intentionally."

Miller's modus operandi was to wage the battle not only in court but also in the press. If Miller could use the media to win over public opinion, it would exert tremendous pressure on both Tanenbaum and his clients. Beverly Hills was a small town where everybody knew their neighbors, and if your neighbors turn against you, most people lose their stomach for a prolonged fight.

Miller began his public campaign by categorically dismissing the plaintiffs' allegations. "Beverly Hills has absolutely no policy of discriminating against anybody, period," he told the press. "The City of Beverly Hills is absolutely and unequivocally dedicated to equal treatment and protection of all people. If Mr. Tanenbaum felt there were any problems he certainly knows where City Hall is located; he certainly could have picked up the phone and called his former colleagues on the council at any time. The first we heard about this from Mr. Tanenbaum was when his seventy-five-page [an exaggeration by three pages] lawsuit arrived on our doorstep last week."

Miller ignored the fact that the Joneses had struggled for more than six months to get the city to react, to no avail; and that numerous parishioners of All Saints Church had written to city council members to complain of Patrick Earthly's mistreatment and received no response. Miller pointed out that the BHPD's Internal Affairs Department had probed each complaint and found that the officers had "reasonable suspicion" to stop each of the members of the suit. And, Miller went on, "we can say that Beverly Hills is no different today than it was when the plaintiffs' lawyer, Robert Tanenbaum, was mayor and a member of the city council from 1986 to 1994." How come Tanenbaum never raised any concerns about police conduct toward African Americans, then?—Miller wondered, implying that Tanenbaum's present concern was motivated not by altruism but by greed. This last point was the most important. Because the linchpin of Miller's press strategy was to divert attention from the merits of the plaintiffs' allegations and make Tanenbaum the issue instead.

Miller reminded reporters that Tanenbaum had clashed with the police department in the past. Tanenbaum didn't take this case out of a noble concern for civil liberties, Miller told reporters, he took it to wreak vengeance against an old and hated enemy. Miller even went so far as to imply Tanenbaum may have sought out the plaintiffs, like a sleazy ambulance chaser, and talked them into filing the suit with promises that they would all get rich from the damage awards. Miller neglected to tell reporters that he, in the meantime, would collect more than $1 million for defending the city.

It was a cunning strategy that appealed to the public's greatest fears and delivered a powerful subliminal message: *If Tanenbaum and his get-rich-quick clients succeed, it could damage our police department's effectiveness. The 2.8-minute response time, the low crime statistics, and sense of security we've all come to enjoy may begin to erode. Is that in our best interests?*

Local reporters followed Miller's lead and wrote blistering condemnations of Tanenbaum in the *Beverly Hills Courier*. Staff writer Scott Huver quoted "sources" who claimed Tanenbaum had "been lying in wait for a case to come along that he could use to even the score" with the BHPD.

Tanenbaum tried to redirect the discourse to the issues raised by the lawsuit. "This [case] has nothing to do with the lawyers," he told the press. "This has everything to do with the victims which have suffered as a result. If I didn't have this case, some other lawyer would have it. Johnnie Cochran would have this case."

But Tanenbaum's arguments fell on deaf ears. You could feel it in the air—public opinion had turned on him. Most residents now saw their former mayor as an insincere fast-buck artist, and his plaintiffs as, at best, his dupes, or at worst, his accomplices. As the personal attacks intensified, Tanenbaum went to his clients and said, "Listen, if you guys think I'm weakening your case, if you feel you'd have a better chance with another attorney, I'll step down. I'll hand over all of my files and my notes and won't ask for any money." But they refused to take him up on the offer.

"I got very disgusted by the way they painted him in the press," says Ralph Jones.

Dozens of citizens charged into the city council meetings to defend their police department. Ken Goldman, a prominent community activist with close ties to some influential homeowners associations, accused Tanenbaum of seeking "cheap publicity" and proclaimed that "we [homeowners] are shocked and outraged by this alleged civil rights lawsuit. We believe in our police, we as a community support our police and the city is behind you one hundred percent and we will be."

Other white citizens declared that they had been pulled over by the police on occasions but never complained because they wanted the BHPD to take a "proactive" approach. Former mayor Chuck Aronberg said, "I see white people stopped all the time and they're not complaining about racism. Blacks have a chip on their shoulder; [they] think bad things happen to them because they're black."

Like-minded Caucasian activists formed a new lobbying group called Police and Community Together (PACT). As depositions were taken from the Joneses, Pat Earthly, and the other parties of Tanenbaum's lawsuit, PACT members decided to show their support for the BHPD by tying blue ribbons around the trees in their front yards. The Reverend Carol Anderson came out of her house one morning and noticed there were blue ribbons in front of every house on the street but hers. The sight shocked and saddened her. It was, she thought, a stark illustration of a community in denial, a community that was unwilling to accept the fact that something was terribly wrong with its police department . . . and the people it served. Members of Anderson's congregation had continued to write to members of the city council to persuade them that the BHPD needed to be reformed, but had still received no responses. And Anderson had tried to mobilize other churches and synagogues to speak out on behalf of civil rights and to counteract the reactionary activities of PACT, but no other Beverly Hills religious institution wanted to take a stand. When Cheryl Jones saw the blue ribbons lining her street, she was infuriated. To her they delivered a harsh message: *Go back where you belong. You're not wanted here.* Cheryl grabbed a pair of scissors, headed for the door, and told her husband, "I'm going to cut down every damn ribbon I see."

Ralph grabbed her and said, "Cheryl, you can't do that."

Meanwhile the lawsuit dragged on, in and out of court, for months, and then years. Moacir graduated from Beverly Hills High School in June 1997. Bob Tanenbaum attended the ceremony. Mo won a four-year football scholarship to the University of Nevada at Reno. Tanenbaum could take pride in the fact that he'd played a pivotal role in the young man's athletic and scholastic development. On the legal front, his efforts to help the Joneses proved frustrating. In October of that same year, the U.S. Ninth Circuit Court of Appeals dismissed Tanenbaum's suit against individual members of the Beverly Hills city government and police force. Miller had mounted a persuasive argument that in each instance the detention of the plaintiffs by the BHPD had been motivated by probable cause. Most of his evidence was the testimony of the police themselves, but in some instances there were third-party witnesses. Tanenbaum continued to press on with his suit against the city itself. There were more motions, more maneuvering, more delays. In 1998 the Joneses moved out of Beverly Hills and attempted to go on with their lives, despite the lack of resolution.

Richard Hill's case was dismissed in the spring of 1999, and Kevin Murray's in February 2000. The court again cited a lack of compelling evidence that the police's actions had been motivated by racial prejudice.

Murray's defeat was particularly stinging because he was ordered to pay for the city's court costs. But Murray, who was now a state senator, managed to score a victory in another venue: the state capital. Just days before his suit was struck down, the state legislature passed a bill authored by Senator Murray that outlawed the practice of racial profiling and required every law enforcement officer in California to receive expanded diversity training. Governor Davis must have taken particular pleasure in signing it, because his wife, Sharon, had witnessed the altercation with Pat Earthly in the parking lot of her church and been one of the congregation members who wrote protest letters to city officials. "In the end, all the police officers of Beverly Hills are going to have to get training and refresher courses," Murray told the press. "We did declare that it's against the law. Hopefully that makes a statement."

Eight months later, Robert Tanenbaum agreed to an out-of-court settlement to his lawsuit against Beverly Hills. The city paid his clients no monetary damages, but it did agree to form a Human Relations Commission that would hear citizen complaints about police misconduct and promote tolerance and ethnic diversity. It was, at best, a marginal victory. Tanenbaum had advised his clients to settle in part because of a recent federal appeals court ruling in a case that accused the U.S. border guards of practicing racial profiling. The Latino plaintiffs had lost that case, which made the outcome of Tanenbaum's case look very doubtful. And if his clients lost, the court might order them to pay the city's legal costs, as had happened to Murray.

"Bob said, 'Listen, if we lose this case, these kids will come out of college with eighty to ninety thousand dollars in debts from the court costs,' " Ralph Jones recalls. But even more disturbing than the potential financial liability was the change Ralph saw in Tanenbaum. The fiery idealist who had first befriended him some ten years before had vanished and in his place stood a stranger. "He didn't have the fight in his eyes. It was gone, and I saw them drag it out of him. . . . He couldn't take it. I never saw him back down from anybody when he was in the right. But they beat the fight out of Bob, and that scared me when I saw that."

Meanwhile, the very rich and very white citizens of Beverly Hills find that the justice system is more responsive to their needs. Witness the case of Scott Sterling, son of real estate billionaire and L.A. Clippers owner Donald T. Sterling. Scott was a hard-partying nineteen-year-old with a hearty appetite for booze, drugs, and group sex. But the good times stopped rolling shortly after midnight, September 11, 1999, on the front lawn of his father's American Colonial mansion on North Crescent Drive. Scott quarreled bitterly with his best friend, Phillip Scheid, and decided to end the discussion with a shotgun blast that sent Scheid to the emergency ward with a load of buckshot in his legs. Sterling told police he'd fired on Scheid in self-defense. Only one problem: ballistics experts confirmed that Scheid had been shot from behind and was undoubtedly fleeing from Sterling at the time.

The BHPD officers working the case believed there was strong evidence for initiating a criminal prosecution against Scott. When Detective Mike Hopkins telephoned the Sterling household to set up a time for the teenager to come into the station for questioning, Donald Sterling got on the line. Sterling senior said it was unfair for his son to be subjected to more interviews and mentioned his close relationship with BHPD Chief Marvin Iannone. He did not realize that Hopkins was recording the call. "I, you know, am very close to the police department," said Sterling, "and I want to cooperate as much as possible." Then he went on to say, "One day in life you're gonna be passing through and you may need a lawyer to give you good, honest advice. . . . And I'm that lawyer. Donald Sterling, on the corner of Wilshire and Beverly Drive. . . . Please put my name somewhere in your wallet. Sometime in the course of your career you will want to call me. You know what I'm saying? And your name again is spelled? . . . May I put your name down?"

Hopkins passed a transcript of the conversation over to his supervisor, Detective Sergeant Jack Douglas, who swiftly sent a memo to the office of L.A. District Attorney Gil Garcetti. Douglas called Donald Sterling's comments "an outrageous attempt at intimidation and influence peddling." The district attorney declined to prosecute either

Donald, or his shotgun-toting son, Scott. Less than three weeks after the DA decided not to press charges, Donald Sterling cosponsored a $500-per-plate fund-raiser for Garcetti, who was running for reelection. The event grossed $100,000.

Pat Earthly no longer works in Beverly Hills. Yolanda Nash and her sons have moved out of the city, as have the Joneses. When Moacir Jones comes back to Southern California during college breaks he, like most blacks, avoids even driving through the city. "I was so happy when we got out of there," he says. "I'll never live in that town again."

★ 10 ★

Death of a Salesman

The play grew from simple images. From a little frame house on a street of little frame houses, which had once been loud with the noise of growing boys and then was empty and silent and finally occupied by strangers. Strangers who could not know with what conquistadorial joy Willie and his boys had once reshingled the roof. Now it was quiet in the house, and the wrong people were in the beds. It grew from images of futility: the cavernous Sunday afternoons polishing the car. Where is that car now? And the shammy cloths carefully washed and put up to dry. Where are the shammy cloths? . . . Above all, perhaps, the image of a need greater than hunger or sex or thirst, a need to leave a thumbprint somewhere on the world; a need for immortality, and by admitting it, the knowing that one has carefully inscribed one's name on a cake of ice on a hot July day. And always throughout, the image of private man in a world full of strangers. A world that is not home nor even an open battleground, but only galaxies of high promise over a fear of falling.

—ARTHUR MILLER

It is not on a street of little frame houses. It is an 18,000-square-foot English mansion, just off Summit Drive, on a knoll that overlooks what remains of Pickfair, Charlie Chaplin's Renaissance manor, and Buster Keaton's Italian villa. Its name, Grayhall, and its massive quarry stone exterior convey a sense of solidity and permanence, as if it has loomed there since the dawn of time, and in Beverly Hills terms, it has. One of the few existing structures that date back to the city's inception, it has become part of the community's mythos, as close to a sacred institution as one can find in this city of the eternal now.

The first edifice to occupy the knoll was a hunting lodge, erected in 1909 by H. D. Robinson. The hills above Sunset were still undeveloped then, except for a few widely scattered cabins and ranch houses. The next owner was a Boston banker, Harry D. Lombard—godfather to a five-year-old girl named Jane Alice Peters who would later take his name when she became the actress Carole Lombard. Lombard tore down the hunting lodge and built a 14,000-square-foot quarry stone mansion in its place. Silsby Spalding—the golf ball king, an early Beverly Hills booster, and the city's first mayor—purchased Grayhall, as it was now called, in 1919. Eager to compete with the other fantastic palaces pushing out of the hills and canyons around him, Spalding bought adjoining lots until he amassed fifty-four acres. Then he hired architects Sumner Hunt and Silas Burns to add another 4,000 square feet, including a grand ballroom half a football field long with a wood-beamed ceiling imported from a Spanish castle, frescoed walls, and a massive hand-chiseled limestone fireplace.

Grayhall's "high-class" aura was the chief attraction for many of its later owners—men who hoped that, like a Brooks Brothers suit, Grayhall would cloak them in respectability; men like George Hamilton, who specialized in cultivating his tan, courting rich older women, and giving Imelda Marcos dance lessons to make ends meet; men like Bernie Cornfeld, the mutual fund king accused of defrauding hundreds of thousands of investors out of hundreds of millions of dollars;

and finally, Grayhall's last master, Mark Hughes, the health supplement wunderkind who parlayed a trunkful of vitamin pills into a billion-dollar empire known as Herbalife.

Grayhall was a far cry indeed from the little tract house in Camarillo where Hughes began his long and winding journey to become the most successful salesman in American history. Like the little frame house in Brooklyn that Willy Loman labored over with his boys, it became a repository for the wreckage of his misplaced aspirations. But of course that wasn't what he had intended. The mansion was supposed to be the linchpin of a real estate empire, which included a 7.5-acre beachfront estate in Malibu with a brand-new 18,000-square-foot home, and a 157-acre parcel at the very top of Beverly Hills, where Hughes was going to build his own San Simeon, a 70,000-square-foot Italian palazzo with a bell tower that would have been taller than the Hollywood sign.

Hughes's grandiose plans were interrupted by a death in the family. His own. On the night of May 20, 2000, Mark, his family, and friends celebrated the eighty-seventh birthday of his grandmother, Hazel, at the Malibu estate. Hughes partied late into the night and, after the guests departed, fell asleep on the living room couch. His fourth wife, Darcy LaPier Hughes, attempted to get him to bed at around midnight, but couldn't rouse him. Darcy later claimed she tried again an hour later, then gave up and went to sleep on a sofa in a room adjacent to the master bedroom. At ten thirty the next morning she entered the master bedroom and found Mark sprawled on their bed in his black T-shirt and bikini briefs. He didn't look right. Instead of rushing to her husband's side, she called the estate's security personnel. They called in the paramedics, who tried but failed to resuscitate him.

The coroner determined that Hughes's blood-alcohol level was .21 percent—nearly three times the legally defined level of intoxication. Members of his staff reported that he had been on a four-day drinking binge. The coroner concluded that his death was due to an accidental combination of alcohol and the antidepressant Doxepin, which had been prescribed by his Beverly Hills psychiatrist, Dr. Stephen Scappa, who was treating Hughes for alcohol abuse.

After a monthlong legal battle with the trustees of the Mark Hughes estate, Darcy LaPier Hughes abandoned her fight for more money, took the $34 million guaranteed to her by her prenuptial agreement, and split for Portland, Oregon, where she'd grown up. She left behind many of Mark's personal effects, and nobody else must have been interested in them because when Realtors held an open house at Grayhall—which the estate's trustees had put on the market for $29 million—the items were still on display.

It was an eerie afternoon. Platoons of Armani- and Christian Dior–clad real estate agents filed through the rooms, past the personal debris of a man's life, their eyes blind to the family pictures, the books and collectibles he'd so carefully accumulated; uninterested—as they discussed square footage, plumbing, and room capacity—in the clues these scattered jigsaw pieces offered about the enigma of Mark Hughes.

When Hughes bought Grayhall in 1992, he spent millions remodeling it. The result can best be described as schizophrenic. It is a house with an identity crisis, the product of a half-formed personality that groped for an ensemble of stylistic flourishes that would add up to something of substance, authority, and grandeur. But instead the look is, as John Bercsi might say, "Liberace meets Camelot."

The Arthurian elements are evident in the Silsby Spalding ballroom, just off the marble-lined foyer, with its orchestra platform framed by four spectacularly carved wood pillars, and French doors embossed with the Grayhall insignia. And in the octagonal dining room, with its oak paneling and ornate coffered ceiling, and in the European oil paintings and tapestries that grace many of the walls.

But mixed indiscriminately with these classic elements are expanses of tiger-striped carpet and leopard-skin chairs and couches; hideously ornate gold-framed mirrors, bronze buffalo tub spouts, brass cupids, stationery and towels emblazoned with rococo monograms of

Hughes's initials, marble chess sets, gold cupid lamps, and massive bronze Egyptian sphinxes.

Books on coffee tables and shelves throughout the house testify to the fact that the former juvenile delinquent from La Mirada with only a ninth-grade education, who earned hundreds of millions of dollars in just a few short years, took the responsibility of joining the ranks of the Beverly Hills elite very seriously. He studied diligently so that he might assimilate with the superrich. There are books on how to collect Fabergé eggs and fine art; books on Harry Winston jewelry, Roman gardens, and the design principles of Italian villas; volumes entitled *The Cigar Connoisseur Book* and *The Best the World Has to Offer in Everything from Martinis to Lawyers to Watches and Jeans*; another called *Europe's Elite 1000 Ultimate List: Interior Decorators, Grand Hotels, Specialist Stores, Restaurants, Yacht Clubs, Art Galleries, Private Banks, Gold Clubs, Jewelers, Schools, Private Villas, Palazzos, Castles, Ski Lodges, Sporting Estates, Florists, Gentlemen's Clubs, Travel Consultants, Wine Merchants, Health Spas, Music Festivals, Property Consultants.*

But of all the personal effects Hughes left behind, the pictures are the most haunting. On tables, on dressers, and hanging from walls are shots of Hughes on European ski slopes, on a yacht in the Mediterranean, on the beach in Hawaii; his skin a tanning booth shade of walnut, hair as sleek and expertly woven as an Armani suit, his clothes *GQ*-immaculate. There are photos of him with Darcy, a three-layered diamond necklace dangling in her awesome cleavage, her skin as brown and supple as an expensive leather sofa, her smile as bright as a crescent moon, but her eyes as dead as those painted on a cheap doll. Outnumbering all the others are pictures of Mark with his son, Alexander, on boating and skiing trips in Colorado, Maui, the French Riviera, the Swiss Alps, and at a birthday party thrown on Grayhall's back patio. Hughes clearly loved his son, or wanted to. There is a disturbing undercurrent in the pictures. They look too perfect, the colors too vibrant, the wardrobe too well pressed, the smiles and embraces too perfectly posed. Beneath Mark's tan you detect a bloodless pallor, and above the Colgate smile the eyes appear to be seized with panic, like those of a small animal caught in a trap, regarding an approaching hunter with a club in his hand.

He was born in 1956 as Mark Stuard Hartman and grew up with his two brothers, Guy and Kirk, in a spacious custom-built ranch-style home in Camarillo, California, a small town about thirty miles north of Los Angeles. His father, Stuard Hartman, owned a company that supplied aircraft parts to the U.S. government. In the golden age of the military-industrial complex, the Hartmans did very well, and on the surface, Mark's childhood was *Leave It to Beaver* idyllic. His mother, Jo Ann, dressed in fashionable outfits and drove a gold Cadillac. They had a housekeeper and a Chris-Craft powerboat that they took on fishing trips to the Channel Islands. Mark was the least outgoing of the three boys, but those who knew him well noticed a quiet intensity. He rode a Schwinn, played softball, and had his mother's dark hair and olive skin.

But behind the closed doors of the Hartman home, life was anything but ideal. Mark's mother had become hooked on a pair of highly addictive and destructive pain pills that doctors prescribed with abandon during the 1960s: Percodan and Darvon. By the time Mark entered the third grade she had a $2,000-a-year habit—an astronomical figure at the time. Slowly at first, then with accelerating momentum, Jo Ann spiraled into an opiate-soaked stupor. She stopped buying groceries and cleaning, and provided her sons with little or no supervision. When Stuard, a strict disciplinarian, came home to an empty dinner table, a grime-coated house, and the boys running wild, he exploded. The inconsistency of the two parents had to be confusing to the Hartman brothers, and it certainly fed Mark's growing resentment toward his father.

Stuard and Jo Ann's bitter arguments grew more and more frequent. When she suffered a seizure in 1969, it proved to be the breaking point. Jo Ann and the boys moved in with her parents in a small tract house in La Mirada, a working-class community just south of L.A. Mark's alienation from his father was complete. "He blamed me for breaking up the family," Stuard Hartman later explained. Seventeen years later, Mark's maternal grandparents would introduce him to another man, Jack Reynolds, who they said was his real biological father. It must have been yet another shattering moment in his tumultuous life. Further confusing the issue was Hartman's vigorous insistence that he, not Reynolds, was Mark's real father. Whether it was true or false, the Reynolds revelation provided Mark with the perfect rationalization for turning his back on the man who had raised him and never facing their many unresolved conflicts.

In La Mirada, Mark was free of all restraining influences and quickly followed his mother's self-destructive path. At thirteen years old he was guzzling wine by the gallon and swallowing pills by the handful. "He was out of control, completely out of control," one childhood friend later recalled. After several drug busts he ended up at CEDU, a rehabilitation facility for troubled teens in Running Springs, a dusty desert town in the foothills of the San Bernardino Mountains. "We were building character by instilling a strong work ethic," a CEDU staff member, Michael Rosen, later recalled. "You would see what you were like through the eyes of other people. You really got strong feedback on how the world perceived you." Looking for self-esteem in the eyes of others, relying on them to provide you with a sense of identity, was a precarious path to self-actualization, especially if your parents had presented you with radically divergent role models and values. But starved for a sense of stability and guidance, Mark applied himself to the new program with a zeal that soon won the hearts of his counselors.

CEDU received a number of public subsidies, but that didn't generate enough income to keep the program in the black, so it also relied upon a door-to-door fund-raising operation that used the teenagers themselves to appeal for money. Mark joined the sales force and found himself on a bus with other kids, riding down the wide palm-lined streets of Beverly Hills, where the really fat scores could be made. He pressed up against the breath-fogged glass, taking in the huge homes. No litter on the streets, no graffiti, no one loitering on the corners; huge carpets of emerald lawn, stately oaks, pines, and massive Mediterranean, English tudor, and American Colonial façades. It was a long way from La Mirada—a whole universe apart.

The bus stopped. They piled onto the ice-cream-white sidewalk, then fanned out to take different streets. He approached a massive black iron gate, looked for a latch, but found none. Then noticed the small squawk box on the left side of the brick driveway and pressed the white plastic button. Waited. Pressed again. No answer. Suddenly he was straddling the top of the gate, legs swinging over, then airborne sailing through space into the garden on the other side. Pulse pounding in his ears, blood racing as he strode up the great arc of driveway. The air thick and sweet with the smell of grass, roses, carnations, and massive pine trees. The house looming up before him now, *like Buckingham fucking palace. My god, people live here, people actually live in these places!*

When he pressed the doorbell, it resonated through the chambers of the vast interior. The deep ferocious bark of a dog, far away, drawing closer, claws clicking on marble, then the voice of a woman. "Sit, King. Sit!" The great slab of door parted, and the woman stood there, blond, a handsome face that had once been beautiful, richly curved but thickening body in a blouse and jeans, the material expensive, the best that money could buy. A gold chain studded with diamonds around her tanned wrist, another about her neck dangling a tear-shaped gemstone of some kind, and on her wedding finger a diamond big enough to choke a python. A gleaming sheet of marble trailed into the depths behind her, the glowing green eyes of a large chocolate Lab sitting there, panting like an idling locomotive. Overhead dangled a great gold and crystal chandelier, like something D'Artagnan might swing on in *The Three Musketeers*. "May I help you?" She frowned. He could see by the tightening of her eyes that she was about to ask how he got past the gate.

But he didn't give her time; launched right into his pitch the way the counselors had told him to. He described his mother's drug addiction and his own substance abuse and delinquency, and how the CEDU counselors saved him from a life of prison and destitution. He was so moved by his own suffering and life-affirming redemption that tears rolled hotly down his cheeks.

The woman's lower lip trembled as she fumbled for her checkbook.

Mark quickly became CEDU's leading salesperson. "He could project his energy and feelings tremendously," said Rosen. "He was a star at it." Such a star that after he turned eighteen years old, he remained with CEDU as a staff member, earning a 5 percent commission on all of his sales, and they were considerable in those years before the estates were patrolled by private armies to keep the commoners out. He even knocked on the door of Ronald Reagan—former governor of California, soon to be president of the United States, and himself a master of the sentimental anecdote. It only took a few minutes for Mark to manipulate the great communicator into writing a $500 check.

Nothing could stop him now, it seemed, not even the death of his mother. She succumbed to acute drug intoxication in 1975. Mark's grandfather found her in her apartment with several empty vials for prescription drugs beside her bed. Mark seemed to take it in stride. He smoothly incorporated her death into his hard-luck tale of delinquency and redemption. CEDU had taught him that every setback was an opportunity, if you knew how to use it; every loss, no matter how staggering, could be overcome by a positive attitude. His colleagues saw him as a tremendously focused and resilient young man. If a few noticed that he threw himself into his work with an almost maniacal fury now, they reacted with admiration rather than alarm. Instead of falling back on his old crutches of booze and pills, he had channeled his grief in a positive direction and made productive use of it.

A year later Mark left CEDU to go to work for Seyforth Laboratories, a "multilevel sales" organization that peddled a liquid protein formula called Slender Now as a miracle weight-loss product.

A miracle in a bottle—the concept was as old as the Constitution. Since the earliest days of the frontier, snake oil salesmen had traveled from town to town in luridly painted wagons, putting on shows with dancing girls, minstrels, or even a Shakespearian scene or two to draw a crowd. At the conclusion of the performance a "professor" or "doctor" would hold up a gleaming bottle of exotically colored "tonic" composed of a secret combination of Indian and Far Eastern herbs that cured everything from whooping cough to syphilis, lumbago, gout, tuberculosis, cancer of the colon, lung, and big toe; it also helped you lose weight and regain a youthful appearance via its "blood-cleansing agents," and if used topically it removed warts and excess facial hair. Snake oil salesmen often employed shills to burst forth from the crowd and "spontaneously" testify to the tonic's miraculous powers. The labels on the bottles rarely revealed the true source of the compound's euphoric effects: alcohol, laudanum, and heroin.

In 1906 the American people spent $80 million on patent medicines, but they were buying more than tonic. The medicine shows brought excitement and adventure to small towns across the continent, momentary relief from the dust-choked monotony of everyday life. The snake oil salesman became an icon, as potent as the cowboy—a beloved rogue who could transform a worthless object into a valuable commodity through the sheer force of his personality, wit, and eloquence. A nation of hucksters, drummers, and traveling salesmen revered the con artist, for he understood that successful people make their own rules. They don't let legal technicalities and moral soul-searching impede their quest for material rewards.

Sales became a quasi religion in America. Alfred C. Fuller, founder of the Fuller Brush Company, considered his salesmen to be "missionaries of new ideas" who spread the gospel of spiritual development through material enterprise. And if salesmen seemed like preachers, tent show revivalists took on many of the characteristics of snake oil salesmen, staging transcendent extravaganzas for the quietly desperate masses and raking in greenbacks as their divine reward.

By the 1970s snake oil salesmen and preachers had discarded their wagons and canvas tents and now peddled their wares on television and in vast convention halls. Miracle diet potions such as Slender Now were the latest rage, and thanks to "multilevel marketing," they were capable of generating hundreds of millions of dollars in profits. Larry Stephen Huff is considered the father of multilevel marketing. He concocted a cosmetics line called Holiday Magic in 1973. Instead of paying salespeople salaries or commissions, Huff recruited "distributors" who bought the product from him at a discount, then resold it at the retail price to their relatives and friends. If they sold enough product, distributors earned a larger discount on their purchases and a percentage of all the sales made by the new distributors whom they recruited.

It was, in effect, a pyramid scheme, in which those at the top of the organization earned fantastic sums. The revenues of multilevel marketers can accelerate at a breathtaking rate. If each distributor recruits three more people, the sales force grows to 2,000 after just six layers of distributors have been enlisted. If it continued to grow at that rate, the company could enlist every man, woman, and child on the planet in just thirteen months. It never does, of course, because the flow of new recruits inevitably slows as the market reaches the saturation point. And when the pyramid ceases to grow, it quickly collapses. Which is why the authorities take a dim view of multilevel marketers. Larry Stephen Huff was eventually charged with defrauding his distributors after the Holiday Magic pyramid collapsed in 1973. (Huff later became a high-ranking distributor for Herbalife.)

But hucksters recognize a good scheme when they see one, and after Huff's pyramid caved in, dozens of others rose to take its place. Thus, a few years later, Mark Hartman became a distributor for Slender Now. Drawing upon the same charisma and tenacity that had made him a star at CEDU, he quickly became one of the company's top one hundred earners. He was making $80,000 a year, a fortune for a former juvenile delinquent with a ninth-grade education, but it was only the beginning. When the Slender Now pyramid collapsed in 1979, Mark hooked up with another multilevel marketer of health supplements and exercise equipment, Golden Youth, led by none other than Larry

Stephen Huff. When it folded a year later, Mark had a sudden inspiration. *The man at the top of the pyramid makes the really big bucks. Why settle for $80,000 a year when it could be $80 million?* The time had come to take control of his destiny.

Mark approached Richard Marconi, a street-savvy native of Gary, Indiana, who had made his way to California, picked up a mail-order doctorate in nutrition from a nonaccredited "university" in Huntington Beach, and set up a factory in Orange County to produce miracle protein, vitamin, and herb potions for Slender Now and other companies of its ilk. "You've got the infrastructure to pump out the product," Mark said. "I have a team of distributors ready to go and the sales ability and the marketing concept. Let's go into business together." Marconi eyed the lean twenty-four-year-old standing before him, wearing shoulder-length hair and a cheap neon blue Zachary All suit. He frowned doubtfully and asked what the concept was.

"A whole new product line," Mark announced, as if he had unveiled the Rosetta Stone. "It'll combine Eastern herbalogical secrets with the latest Western scientific advances in vitamin and mineral compounds! You put up the money. I'll be the first distributor, and we'll go out and build a company called Herbalife that you'll never forget as long as you live."

Marconi emitted a small laugh. He couldn't help but admire the kid's moxie, it reminded him of himself when he was young. Sure, he looked like a pot dealer dressed up for a court appearance, but the boy had a diamond-in-the-rough charisma and that all-important fire in the belly. And his customer base would be people who also bought suits from Zachary All; this boy spoke their language, shared their dreams of transcending middle-class life. With a little guidance and polishing he could become a big producer. *What the hell*—Marconi concluded—*every once in a while you gotta roll the hard six.*

So they went to work developing a product line. First they needed a launch vehicle—Marconi explained—a core product to win new customers who could then be sold a variety of ancillary products. Vitamins wouldn't work because they produced no tangible results. The results had to be immediate and visible. Vanity was the key. Appeal to the customer's vanity and you're through the door. Convince somebody they'll look better by using your product, and they'll reach for their wallet. After some spitballing, they came up with the Herbalife weight-loss program. It called for dieters to eat only one meal a day of no more than 1,000 calories, to drink two glasses of skim milk spiked with Herbalife's specially formulated "protein powder," and to gulp down twelve vitamin and herbal tablets that would help "cleanse the system so that you can more easily absorb nutrients" on a reduced diet. It would be the magic formula—*take it and you will be transformed into one of the beautiful people!* Then, like a thunderclap, Mark hit upon the slogan: "Lose Weight Now, Ask Me How!"

Marconi nodded and smiled. That said it all in six simple words. *Brilliant, absolutely fucking brilliant!* They would hang it on banners in convention halls, plaster it on every flyer and brochure, wear it on buttons fastened to their lapels. It would be their mantra, their creed, their open-sesame incantation that would slide back the door to the sacred treasure chamber.

Then around the weight-loss program they built an elaborate menu of other miracle cures, such as Cell-U-Loss, which eliminated cellulite; and Herbalife N.R.G., which provided a "natural lift" (thanks to a generous dose of caffeine) to those who felt tired or depressed; and Herbalife Formula #2, which helped cure seventy-five different maladies, such as age spots, herpes, jaundice, cancer, bursitis, lumbago, and impotence. The list grew longer and longer as they pored over the catalogs and brochures of other multilevel marketers such as Slender Now, Golden Youth, and Shaklee.

"Now," Marconi said, "all we need is a guru." A charismatic figurehead who would pitch their products to the multitudes with evangelical zeal.

Mark sat up in his chair and proclaimed, "I'll be the guru."

Marconi looked at the kid, dressed in shorts and tennis shoes, and said, "Mark, you're competing against Forrest Shaklee and Rich DeVos of Amway. You look like a kid."

Mark's face hardened with determination. "I can do it. I'm gonna be the guru."

All right—Marconi relented—then the first thing they had to do was work on his appearance. The neon blue Zachary All suits were given to the Salvation Army. Marconi took Mark to a tailor and dressed him in navy blues and blacks to make him look older and more serious. Then to a hairdresser who shaped his wild mane of surfer hair into a blow-dried and sprayed Prince Valiant cut.

Next they worked on his pitch. "He practiced with us a hundred times before he went on the road," Marconi recalls. "And that was the exciting thing, to watch him fine-tune things that you gave him. It was like the birthing of a child to watch him grow. You knew this guy was gonna be a success very quickly because he could metamorphose into this giant when he spoke to an audience. And he was a quick study. If he got a question he couldn't answer, he'd listen to me answer it and the next time he'd give the same answer, letter perfect. After a while he could talk like an MD." And he also was adept with the snake oil salesman's most essential tool: hyperbole. Anytime he mentioned a product, Mark slathered on time-honored superlatives—*fantastic, unbelievable, revolutionary, stupendous*—and a few new ones of his own—*monstramental, fabulistic, superextraordinary, marvelutionary!* "He was great at combining words like that," says Marconi.

Even more remarkable and key to the extraordinary success that followed was his ability to project emotion into his soliloquies. "He could cry on command," says Marconi. "I watched him do it in a thousand performances, in the exact same part of the presentation, every time. He would well up with tears whenever he talked about his mom."

No doubt the emotion was real, but like his hair the story of his mother's death had been teased and shaped to make it more appealing to an audience and to fit the new product line. His mother no longer OD'd on painkillers. Now it was deadly diet pills that had done her in. Mark would tell audiences that she had a weight problem. "My mom was always going out and trying some kind of funny fad diet as I was growing up," he would recall again and again at Herbalife rallies.

"Eventually she went to a doctor to get some help, and he prescribed to her Dexamyl, kind of a fad diet then. For those of you who don't know about it, it's a drug, a narcotic. It's a form of speed, or amphetamine. You're not able to eat or sleep. [In fact, it's a combination of an amphetamine and a barbiturate to offset the effects of the speed.]

"After several years of using it, she ended up having to eat sleeping pills for her to sleep at night. And after several years of doing that, her body basically started to deteriorate. She started seeing four or five doctors to keep her habit up."

Mark claimed the tragedy of his mother's death had propelled him on a life mission to develop safe and effective weight-loss products for the American public. In the three-page bio that he cooked up, Mark said that he'd learned about herbs "while attending a major symposium . . . by a trade delegation from China."

The last but far from least important alteration made to his identity was his name. He discarded Hartman, the last name of the father who had raised him but to whom he no longer spoke, and took his mother's maiden name, Hughes, which reverberated with the memory of an American icon of fabulous wealth and power. Like so many who came to Beverly Hills before him, he had re-created himself, fashioned his own myth. It would make him wealthy beyond his wildest dreams and would eventually devour him.

His first "international headquarters" was in an old wig factory on Robertson Boulevard in Baja Beverly Hills—no more than a tiny storefront office with secondhand furniture and a cramped storeroom. "He couldn't stand the fact that it was south of Pico," says Marconi. "It really ate at him." But that only fed his competitive fever. Seyforth's Slender Now had grown from zero to $300 million in sales in three years; Mark vowed to Marconi that he would beat that record. But in the first lean months, his prospects didn't look promising. Once a week, Hughes would drive up to Marconi's plant in a 1970s model Fleetwood Cadillac, load the trunk up with pills and potions, and take off again. "The only distributor he had at that point was Paco Perez," says Marconi. "Paco had been a bellman at one of the hotels in L.A.

The two of them started selling the stuff to their relatives and friends, and they were hustling people right there on Robertson in Beverly Hills." Hughes finagled a few interviews with cable TV stations and did them in the tiny storefront. Little by little, the business grew. He began loading the Cadillac's trunk up every other day, then every day, then he was piling cases of product into the backseat, all the way to the ceiling. When Mark pulled out of the drive, the rear bumper screeched against the concrete. Finally, Marconi said it was time to ship via truck.

Suddenly, the multilevel mathematics kicked in and the business doubled and redoubled in size, like an algae bloom. In its first five years the company's annual sales grew from $386,000 to $423 million, a 100,000 percent increase. Hughes had started with one distributor, now there were more than 700,000, and the international headquarters had moved out of the wig factory into an industrial park, and finally to a fourteen-story high-rise just off the 405 freeway, emblazoned with the Herbalife logo for millions of motorists to see every day. It was, in short, the greatest multilevel marketing company of all time. And Mark Hughes, the man at the top, became a multimillionaire before his thirtieth birthday.

A key element of this phenomenal success was the slick infomercials that Hughes ran on USA Cable Network and TV stations across the country. They ran two and three hours long and were packed with inspiring testimonials from common folk whose lives had been transformed by Herbalife. They described how these miracle products cured their eczema, diabetes, varicose veins, and lupus. And here was the sweet part: these products not only made you beautiful, they also made you rich when you became a distributor and sold them to your friends and neighbors. The TV shows and the Herbalife brochures and magazines were jam-packed with real-life stories of housewives, truck drivers, construction workers, secretaries, and welfare mothers who were now earning $25,000, $40,000, even as much as $100,000 *a week*.

Hughes threw incredible extravaganzas for his top distributors in theaters and arenas across the country and hired entertainers such as Donny and Marie Osmond, Rod Stewart, and Elton John to pump up their adrenaline. In 1985 Uncle Miltie himself made an appearance at a Herbalife gathering at the Aquarius Theater in Hollywood. Berle laid a lame one-liner on the crowd. "I am thrilled to be here on behalf of Herbalife. And I'd like to be half of Herbalife." Then he segued into some of his old reliable routines. Miltie was happy to have the gig; after all, there weren't many venues left for him to command a spotlight in, besides the Friars Club. But the old vaudevillian seemed a little befuddled by this latest permutation in live entertainment. Displays of Herbalife pills and potions—soups, shampoos, conditioners, diet pills, protein powders, vitamins, herbal supplements, energy enhancers, nerve tonics, and skin lotions—lined the stage, towering all the way up to the lights. The audience—dressed in tuxedos and billowing chiffon evening dresses, all with "Lose Weight Now, Ask Me How!" buttons on their lapels—roared ecstatically when Hughes appeared in a pin-striped midnight black tuxedo and made his way to the stage. They reached out to shake his hand or just to touch the hem of his garment, faces red with excitement, eyes gleaming with tears. Berle had never seen such adulation for a performer, not even for the great Jolson himself.

And Hughes lived like a star now. Zachary All was a dim memory. He now shopped at Battaglia on Rodeo Drive, where they fit him for Brioni suits and $2,500 sports coats. He got $300 haircuts at one of the style emporiums on Beverly Drive, sported custom-made gold cuff links in the shape of the Herbalife three-leaf logo on his sleeves, a diamond Cartier watch on his tanned wrist, and tooled around town in one of his two Rolls-Royces, or if he was slumming, in his Mercedes. Excessive? Not in the slightest. Because, as Willy Loman advised his sons, "the man who makes an appearance in the business world, the man who creates personal interest, is the man who gets ahead. Be liked and you will never want."

Hughes shelled out $7.3 million for Liongate, a 15,000-square-foot mansion that was designed by Paul Williams in 1938. Mark added a disco, a game room, a gazebo with an elevator, and a heated marble floor in one of the two master bathrooms. He traded his first wife—a former Miss Santa Monica, Kathryn Whiting—for a sleek new foreign model—Swedish beauty queen Angela Mack. Wayne Newton entertained 300 of the groom's closest friends at the wedding.

And yet, if anybody had bothered to look closely enough, they might have noticed that something was wrong. There was, for instance, his frantic workaholic pace: on the road twenty to twenty-five days each month, jetting across the continent, making one- and two-day stops for meetings, rallies, and teleconferences in Dallas, Houston, Orlando, San Diego, Phoenix, Chicago, Minneapolis, Detroit, Toronto, Boston, Atlanta, and Valley Forge. Not even pausing to rest on the plane. The flight attendant would ask about the "Lose Weight Now, Ask Me How!" button on his lapel, and he would launch into a sales pitch. By the time they touched down, he'd signed her up as a distributor.

Even during the five or ten days he was home each month, he rarely rested. His first wife, Kathryn Whiting, later said he was so obsessed with money that he would sit up in bed at night going over spreadsheets. He seemed to have the American Dream in the palm of his hand, but Whiting noted, "The sad thing is, it didn't seem to make him happy."

He had climbed into a Halloween costume called Mark Hughes to win fame and fortune, but when did he get to take it off? He had thousands of fawning acquaintances, but they were all strangers who knew the mask, not the man behind it; who loved the celebrity, the myth, but not him. If he peeled off the mask, the whole pyramid might tumble to the ground. Besides, whom could he reach out to? Angela? She was more a fashion accessory than a wife. When he looked into her eyes, really looked into them, he realized he had no idea who she was—no idea at all.

The marriage to Angela Mack lasted only a year. "I remember when he first met Angela," Richard Marconi recalls. "He was so proud. He says, 'And she doesn't need my money, Dick.' Then after he married her he found out that she did like and need his money. She was more focused on that rather than on being what Mark needed: a family to love him. For contrast, I had a tough life growing up with no money, but I knew my mom loved me and I knew Father loved me, and I had two neat brothers and a sister and I knew they loved me. He didn't have that; he never had it. He had no money growing up and no family and no set of standards by which to judge, so he fell in love quickly and easily and they were always trophy people, and he didn't know how to build it into a real relationship. He didn't have the emotional underpinnings to do that."

The prospects for success seemed better with his next wife, Suzan Schroder, a former Miss Hawaiian Tropics and Miss Petite USA. Suzan gave him a son, Alexander. She wanted a family as much as Mark did and was willing to work on the relationship and stand up to him instead of catering to his every whim as almost everyone else in his life did.

A year after Alexander was born, Mark sold Liongate and bought Grayhall for $20 million. The previous owner, Bernie Cornfeld, didn't have the money to maintain the place, and the herds of partyers, courtesans, and hangers-on had taken their toll—the venerable mansion looked pretty threadbare. Hughes poured millions into a remodeling effort that included new air-conditioning and heating systems, furniture, and a restoration of the ceiling beams and hardwood floors. Grayhall's once vast land holdings had been whittled down over the decades to just one acre, but in keeping with the estate mergers of 1990s, Hughes bought three adjoining properties to expand the estate again to 2.5 acres.

For Hughes, Grayhall had become a much-needed distraction. By immersing himself in the restoration he escaped to a fantasyland of inexhaustible luxury and tranquillity, a world he'd dreamed of ever since he scaled that first wall of a Beverly Hills estate to collect contributions for CEDU some twenty years earlier. He needed to escape, because the last six years had been rocky for Herbalife.

The trouble began in 1985 when six governmental bodies descended on the company with allegations that it had committed fraud and marketed unsafe products. The California attorney general and Department of Health, and the district attorney of Santa Cruz County filed a lawsuit alleging Herbalife made false medical claims and operated an illegal pyramid scheme. Canada's Ministry of Health and

Welfare cited the company for twenty-four violations of its Food and Drug Act. The U.S. Senate Committee on Governmental Affairs launched an investigation of Herbalife and called for subcommittee hearings on ninety complaints of illnesses and four deaths allegedly caused by Herbalife products, and another thirty-two reports of fraud. An FDA spokesman announced that the agency had been investigating the company for three years and had cited it for six violations of the Food and Cosmetic Act.

The tsunami of bad press took its toll. Sales went into a 60 percent nosedive. Almost half a million distributors quit. Many of the 260,000 who remained were stuck with up to $20,000 worth of products that they couldn't unload. At the company's headquarters, Herbalife laid off 573 employees. Hughes finally realized he had to do something to stop the hemorrhaging. In October of 1986 Herbalife agreed to pay $850,000 in investigative costs, attorneys' fees, and penalties to the state of California. It was the largest out-of-court settlement ever made by a health products company. Herbalife admitted no wrongdoing but agreed to take a number of questionable claims out of its sales presentations and literature, and to stop selling two of its most dubious products.

By the early 1990s Herbalife seemed to have pulled out of its slump. Gross sales in 1992 were a whopping $405 million, and the company's net profit was $20 million. Herbalife had issued public stock, and Hughes owned 74 percent of it. His cash compensation in salary and dividends in 1992 was close to $10 million. And as the economic boom of the 1990s progressed, revenues continued to climb. Sales had more than tripled by 1997 to $1.49 billion.

But the picture was not quite as rosy as it might appear. Profit margins hovered at around 5 percent because of bloated bureaucracy, and 80 percent of the new sales were in overseas markets. Herbalife had opened offices in England, France, Germany, New Zealand, Israel, and Mexico. In each of these countries sales figures followed a similar pattern: phenomenal growth for a few years followed by an equally rapid drop-off. And in each of these countries, as complaints about the products rolled in, authorities launched investigations that soiled Herbalife's reputation.

By the end of the decade Hughes was pressing into the last frontiers: Asia and Russia. He was running out of fresh countries, and the writing on the wall was unmistakable. Perhaps the knowledge that the gravy train was about to run off the rails explains his own downward spiral, or perhaps it was simply the ghosts of the past catching up with him.

By this time Mark had accepted Jack Reynolds as his real father and made the former plumber the chairman of Herbalife's board of directors. It may have been as much an act of vengeance against Stuard Hartman, the man who raised him and still claimed to be his father, as it was a sincere bonding with Reynolds. Mark harbored a wasps' nest of unresolved feelings for the man he used to call Dad. At one Thanksgiving dinner Suzan made the mistake of mentioning Hartman. Mark flew into a rage. She never dared to repeat that transgression. "When we got together," Mark's brother Kirk later observed, "the past wasn't talked about."

But it was always there, looming over him, no matter how many cities he fled to on his whirlwind schedule. He was forced to face this fact when his younger brother, Guy, died from alcoholism in 1994. He was thirty-seven years old. Their mother, Jo Ann, had been thirty-eight when she killed herself with pills. It was like a sick recurring dream. After the funeral Mark hosted a gathering at Grayhall and, in an apparent moment of magnanimity, invited Stuard Hartman. Mark took the old man on a tour of the forty rooms and 2.5 acres of grounds, smiling warmly as he pointed out every luxurious detail. But after they said good-bye and the old man's car pulled away, a layer of frost settled over Mark's face and he hissed to his brother Kirk, "I showed him. I showed that bastard what I could do." For years his mouth had watered in anticipation of that moment, but now that it had come and gone it left a strange metallic aftertaste.

Of all his wives, Suzan offered him the best chance to transcend the past and become part of a real family. She gave him Alexander, and

Mark seemed to adore the boy. He built a magnificent suite of rooms for him at Grayhall with castle-shaped bunk beds and a mad mosaic of cartoon characters all over the walls and ceiling. He threw spectacular birthday parties on Grayhall's back patio. Hughes and his friends showered the boy with extravagant gifts, such as a miniature electric Ferrari that Alexander could race around the estate. But he saw his son only ten days out of every month and, even when he was in town, spent only a few minutes with him when he got home just before Alex's bedtime, or an hour or two with him on the weekends.

"Where the hell have you been?" Suzan would demand when he finally showed up at Grayhall. "Your plane landed at seven o'clock and it's past midnight." He'd mutter something about stopping by the office for a meeting. "Then why didn't you call?" *I forgot. I was busy, okay? Jesus! How do you think I pay all the bills to keep this place afloat?* He'd start toward Alex's bedroom. She'd stop him. "He's been asleep for hours. He has school tomorrow." And the whole thing would conflagrate into a vicious shouting match.

On November 30, 1996, Suzan found out where he'd been. At 11 P.M. Mark Hughes was pulled over by a Hawthorne police officer for driving his Jeep Cherokee on the wrong side of the road. He was on his way to Bare Elegance, a strip club near LAX. He claimed that he'd had only two glasses of wine, but a Breathalyzer test gauged his blood alcohol level at .22, almost three times the legal limit. The fact that he was still conscious and able to drive a car, however erratically, indicated a high tolerance for alcohol that had been developed over an extended period of time.

Hughes's alcohol "problem" had been a dirty secret whispered about in the top-floor offices of the Herbalife building for some time. He had missed a number of rallies and meetings in recent years because of a sudden "cold" or "flu." But no one dared talk about it in the open, for everyone understood it would be a disaster if the press found out the owner of a health supplement company had a major substance abuse problem. In April of 1997 Hughes pled no contest to driving under the influence. He agreed to pay a fine and serve three years' probation with a suspended license, and to attend an alcohol education program. Mark made a token effort to deal with the problem. He went to see a Beverly Hills psychiatrist, Dr. Stephen Scappa, who prescribed a drug called Antabuse to inhibit Mark's craving for alcohol. Unfortunately, the drug is worthless unless the patient is involved in a recovery program, and Hughes stopped seeing Scappa after only a few sessions.

By September 1997 Suzan had finally had enough. She filed for divorce. They'd been married ten years.

It was a blow, no denying that. But Mark always bounced back. He'd survived the death of his mother when he was nineteen, and then his brother—he could survive this. Not such a terrible thing, he decided, once the dust settled. No one to browbeat him when he came home at night, no more ugly arguments, and he got to see Alex almost as often as when he and Suzan were married. Besides, a bachelor worth $450 million is never lonely for long. Lose one former beauty queen, acquire another.

He met Darcy LaPier six months later, on a blind date. She was a voluptuous, auburn-haired, bronze-skinned former Miss Hawaiian Tropics—as Suzan had been—who had a history of marrying rich men and collecting fat divorce settlements. The only child of Native Americans, Darcy grew up in Molalla, Oregon, just outside of Portland. She dropped out of high school and worked a series of minimum-wage jobs, including catching chickens for a slaughterhouse. One day she had an epiphany. "My girlfriends soon discovered the power of using the right lipstick," LaPier later recalled, "and when I looked in the mirror one day, I thought, 'Hey, I'm pretty good looking!' " So she entered the Oregon Miss Hawaiian Tropics contest, won it, and caught the eye of the owner of Hawaiian Tropics, Ron Rice. The Suntan Lotion King was known as the Hugh Hefner of Daytona Beach, where his company was headquartered. Rice handpicked the models for the Hawaiian Tropics ads and made many of his most exciting discoveries in strip clubs. What drew Darcy to this man twenty-four years her senior? Perhaps it was his exciting lifestyle and passionate temperament, or maybe it was his net worth of $15 million. In any case the couple wed and had a daughter; then Darcy moved on to lusher pastures. Rice divorced her when he suspected that his young wife was having an affair with action star Jean-Claude Van Damme. Then Darcy and Jean-Claude married, partied around the world together, and produced a son, Nicholas, before their marriage flamed out from too much cocaine and, according to court documents filed by Darcy, physical abuse. (Van Damme vehemently denied striking his wife.)

Now Mark Hughes rolled up to Darcy's front door. Her pulse must have quickened when she saw the Rolls-Royce, the $6,000 suit, the Cartier watch, gold rings and cuff links—it was love at first sight.

They married a year later, on Valentine's Day, 1999, in a rose-filled church in Beverly Hills. "The entire church was covered with rose petals," says Jerry Jolton, a Beverly Hills Realtor who attended the ceremony. "Thousands of roses everywhere." After the couple exchanged vows, five hundred of Mark and Darcy's closest friends adjourned to Grayhall for the reception. They dined and danced to a live orchestra in the wide circular driveway, which had been tented for the occasion. The pool had been covered with a wood floor and tented also so it could be converted to an "ice room."

"The bar and barstools were made out of ice," says Jolton, "and there were harpists sitting on these platforms of ice as they played. There was a humongous seafood bar and every kind of vodka you can imagine. It was a million-dollar wedding."

In the first year of their marriage, Hughes showered Darcy with gifts—everything from a single rose each morning to a limited-edition Bentley, a $4 million personal helicopter, and an 18,000-square-foot oceanfront mansion in Malibu. During the twenty days each month that Mark was on the road, she busied herself by spending $1 million redecorating Grayhall and "the beach house" with nineteenth-century French tapestries, gilded Italian lamps, monogrammed towels for herself, Mark, and their three kids, and a $38,000 antique commode. Hughes plugged her—like a spare part—into the role that Suzan used to play as the First Lady of Herbalife. Darcy appeared at rallies and on infomercials and "developed" her own line of Herbalife skin-care products.

The phoniness of it all—of his professed love for Darcy, the grand external gestures that failed to mask the utter lack of real emotion—ate away at him. No matter how hard he strived to fill it with rallies, houses, cars, helicopters, pills, and booze, the great hollow inside him yawned ever wider in the wee hours of the ink black morning, threatening to swallow him whole. Most of the time in the daylight, he was able to keep the growing hysteria at bay with booze and antidepressants and fixes of adulation from his followers. But once—when he whisked Alex and Marconi off for a men-only outing in Portofino, Italy—it burst into the open. They backed Hughes's yacht into the harbor and anchored it next to another that belonged to one of the world's richest men and the owner of the Beverly Hills Hotel: the sultan of Brunei. Mark had fallen into a sullen mood that morning, and a perplexed Marconi tried to lift his spirits by noting that Mark's boat was a few feet longer than the sultan's. Without warning, Hughes burst into tears, bawling uncontrollably, like a traumatized child. Alex froze in terror. Shocked and frightened himself by the intensity of the outburst, Marconi took the younger man, whom he'd come to regard as a son, in his arms. "What's wrong?" he asked repeatedly, but Mark couldn't get words through the convulsive sobs. Marconi felt hot wet tears on his neck, then snot from Mark's nose, then sweat soaking through the back of his own shirt as he repeated ineffectually, "Mark, what is it? What's wrong?"

Finally, strangled staccato words came out between the sobs: "This lifestyle . . . going . . . always going . . . I can't take Alexander with me . . ." He felt like a failure, he explained—as a father, as a husband. He felt trapped by Herbalife, by his role as its leader, by the more than one million distributors who depended on him to keep playing that role for their livelihood. "He wanted a family life, he never had one, and he wanted it," says Marconi. "But he didn't know how to get there. I told him that if you want to make a marriage work you have to put one hundred percent of yourself into it. He couldn't do that, and as he got older he started to realize it." Perhaps he realized too—though he never admitted it to Marconi—that he'd taken the wrong path that fateful day when he came to the older man with an idea of starting his own company, that moment he'd sat up in his chair and said "I'll be the guru." He now lived in an Alice in Wonderland world where he had no real identity, no real friends, no real intimacy. But how could he extricate himself? No way. No way at all.

When Hughes had made a tentative move in that direction in early 1997, it set off an earthquake. He registered to sell one-quarter of his shares of Herbalife, and the stock slid from $37 a share to $6, and Mark's net worth slid with it. Enraged investors complained about the way he had discounted options for corporate insiders by about 50 percent, and Hughes felt compelled to hang on to his stock. Whatever thoughts he had about leaving the company ended then.

In the last years of his life he turned away from a world that had so disappointed him and concentrated on building one of his own: a fantastic palazzo that he intended to place on a 157-acre parcel on the last undeveloped ridgeline in Beverly Hills. It would be taller than the Hollywood sign, as big as the main structure of Hearst Castle, his very own Xanadu! It didn't matter that the cash flow might no longer be there to complete it—like Hitler during his final days building scale models of a fantastic postwar Berlin as his underground bunker shook beneath Allied bombs—Mark Hughes retreated into the realm of make-believe.

He bought the mountaintop from Merv Griffin, who had bought it from the Shah of Iran's sister. Mark paid $8.5 million for it—a bargain when you consider that that same year Paul Allen paid $20 million for 120 acres, only 6 of them on level land. Hughes had 15 level acres.

Mark hired two architects to build his sixteenth-century Renaissance palazzo: Charles Young of New York and William Hablinski, the leading architect in Beverly Hills. Hablinski specialized in authentic Mediterranean villas and had built homes for Arnold Schwarzenegger, Realtor Fred Sands, Keenen Ivory Wayans, Vanna White, Jim Carrey, and gubernatorial candidate Al Checchi. Hughes's 70,000-square-foot structure would stand forty-five feet tall, with a sixty-five-foot cupola and four fifty-foot corner pavilions. There would be a fifteen-door garage, an underground parking area for forty vehicles, a tennis pavilion and a million-gallon lake. But as the estimated construction cost shot up to $80 million, the shadow of reality finally fell over the enterprise. Would he be able to get the money?

Herbalife's fortunes had continued to erode, and his with them. The stock was trading for $12 a share, a far cry from its high of $37, three years earlier. Mark came up with a simple, if dubious, way to stop the decline. He would buy back all of the stock and make Herbalife a private company again! Without a bunch of shareholders peering over his shoulder analyzing his every move, he could make the necessary changes to turn the company around. Then he would take it public again and reap huge rewards. Hughes initially offered to purchase all of the outstanding stock at $17 a share, for a total cost of $486 million. In January 2000 he upped the bid to $17.81 a share, for a total cost of $510 million.

But in April 2000 the hammer fell. Hughes couldn't put together the financing for the deal. Herbalife's stock, which had been bolstered by the prospect of his buyback, plummeted once again. Hughes's personal net worth, which had once been $450 million, shrank to $100 million. The dream of building a palazzo at the top of Beverly Hills died with the deal. Mark fell into a deep depression. His psychiatrist prescribed antidepressants. He began eating them like candy and binging on alcohol, and his forty-four-year-old body could no longer tolerate the abuse.

"I knew he was going to die," Janet Levine, an Herbalife executive who worked closely with Hughes, later said.

A worried Marconi approached Christopher Pair and Michael Rosen—both top Herbalife executives and part of Mark's trusted inner circle. They had been with him since the CEDU days. "I said, 'We got to help Mark,' " Marconi recalls. "Everybody who was close to him knew he had a problem. I said, 'We can't put him in Betty Ford because the press would get hold of it. But I've found a clinic in Switzerland that's completely discreet. Kings and queens have gone there. It's a six-week program so we can trade off—each of us will go there for two weeks to be with him and make sure he finishes it.' "

But to Marconi's dismay, Pair and Rosen reacted with suspicion. They didn't trust Dick or each other to be alone with Hughes for that amount of time, fearing someone would seize the opportunity to orchestrate a power play. "So they went to Mark." Marconi shakes his head sadly, "And they said, 'Hey, be careful. Dick's gonna put you in an institution.' A guy with an alcohol problem is really paranoid anyway, so then Mark didn't trust me."

On the morning of May 20, 2000, Mark Hughes lay dead in the master bedroom of his Malibu mansion in a black T-shirt and bikini briefs.

The funeral was held in the very same house, its every detail stage-managed by Darcy LaPier. When Mark died, she confided to a reporter, "I bought all the roses in Los Angeles—one point four million of them. I covered the swimming pool and the gardens with petals. I loved that man deeply and passionately. Nothing will ever be the same."

A member of the catering staff that worked the funeral had mixed feelings about the affair. Like Hughes's life, it was full of spectacle but disturbingly bereft of genuine emotions. "It was interesting, beautiful, and eerie at the same time. When you drove off of Pacific Coast Highway onto the estate, there were rolling sloping hills and they were all completely dressed in red rose petals. Imagine a field a hundred yards long and four hundred yards wide entirely blanketed in red petals so there's not a stitch of green. There was no extravagance not met."

The house sat on a bluff overlooking the beach and offered a 180-degree view of the shimmering Pacific. "Nicolas Cage lives next door," says the caterer. "And there's a gazebo right at the edge of the cliff. It's amazingly beautiful. The funny part is the wife never really came outside; she stayed inside the whole time. She looked absolutely beautiful and yet seemed relatively composed. The thing is they expected about six hundred people and only about three hundred showed up. There seemed to be a great awkwardness in the air. People were not really sure what to make of it or what to do. A lot of people were associated with Herbalife, but there wasn't a great sense of compassion at all. It was very sterile, dispassionate, certainly no weeping, nothing of that nature. There was an inordinate amount of silence. I don't know much about the gentleman who died, but maybe he led a very closed-off life. Maybe there was some sense of sterilization in his pathology and that was reflected in his memorial service.

"What I thought was absolutely strange and what I found so terribly gauche was that more than one person was taking pictures of the backyard. My God, you would have thought we had tourists from Hollywood Boulevard, snapping pictures of the view like they're on vacation."

No expense was spared, but it didn't come out of Darcy LaPier's pocketbook. She billed Mark Hughes's estate for $100,000 in funeral expenses, including $32,000 for her personal costs, such as $750 paid to celebrity hairstylist Jose Eber for creating her glamorously grief-stricken do.

Darcy's prenup agreement guaranteed her another $34 million; the balance of Hughes's $100 million estate went into a trust for Alexander. But after fifteen months of marriage Darcy felt she was entitled to at least another $30 million. For a month she refused to move out of Grayhall while she waged a legal battle for the lion's share of the spoils. But when hopes of a courtroom victory faded, she took her thirty-four big ones and returned to Oregon and her chicken-catching roots.

Vicious dogfights over the remains of the carcass continued. In May 2001 Suzan Hughes filed suit in Los Angeles Superior Court on behalf of her son, Alex. She accused the estate's three trustees—Christopher Pair, Herbalife's CEO; Conrad Klein, an Herbalife executive vice president; and Jack Reynolds, the company's chairman of the board—of conflict of interest and "an outrageous and brazen display of self-dealing" in their handling of the trust. She claimed that the estate had dwindled drastically through mismanagement and that the trustees had violated their duty through "their animosity to Alex and his mother." Conrad Klein countered that this was a "thinly veiled attempt" by Suzan Hughes to attain assets that she couldn't get in her prenuptial agreement.

The only assets that weren't fought over were the dozens of pictures of Mark and his son, and the other personal effects that had been left behind in Grayhall. Nobody seemed interested in those.

Jerry Jolton, the affable, gray-haired Coldwell Banker Realtor who is holding the open house at the Grayhall estate, takes two other Realtors through the 4,000-square-foot guesthouse that sits on the opposite side of the circular driveway from the quarry stone mansion. In most other neighborhoods in most other cities, the house would seem quite opulent, but in the shadow of Grayhall it seems like a quaint if elegant cottage. The group does not even glance at the framed picture of Mark and Alex on the beach in Hawaii that sits on a table by the front door. Instead, Jerry is eager to direct their attention to the rectangular swimming pool just off the living room. A waterfall empties into it from an attached Jacuzzi. He also points out the gold-plated chandelier, the marble counters in the kitchen, the Lalique crystal sink in the bathroom, and the view from the front porch, which looks down on Pickfair and Charlie Chaplin's old house.

As they pass back through the living room on their way out the front door, one of the Realtors pauses to look at a scale model of a sixteenth-century Italian palazzo, encased in Plexiglas and sitting on a low table against the far wall. "What's that?"

Jolton pauses and looks down at the toy palace. "This was a project that Mark Hughes was going to build on the mountaintop at the end of Tower Grove."

"Holy mackerel!" the Realtor exclaims as he bends over to examine the sprawling complex, which includes a massive fountain before a grand staircase that leads up to the columned entrance; and at the rear of the house, arched doorways leading to a vast patio and another grand staircase that descends to cardboard and papier-mâché replicas of rolling lawns, lakes, and groves of trees.

"They were interviewing architects from around the world for this," says Jolton. "It would have been the likes of a Hearst Castle . . . Well!" He rubs the smooth white palms of his hands together and smiles. "Now let me show you our legendary Grayhall."

They move out the door, talking of square footage and egress, and leave the scale model behind in darkness to await the day when a pair of disinterested hands will toss it in a Dumpster that will carry it out to a vast morass of rotting orange rinds and plastics, to be crushed and buried beneath an avalanche of refuse until it is indistinguishable from the soggy cereal boxes and milk cartons that share its grave.

★ 11 ★

The Last Mountaintop

Jerry Jolton pulls his immaculate four-door black Mercedes to a stop before the gate of a chain-link fence at the very end of Tower Grove Drive. Beyond the fence, a naked ridgeline rises, twisting and turning into the sky. There are no other hillsides beyond it, no more palatial homes nestled into the nooks of canyon walls. Nothing, except a dirty thumbprint of a cloud, high up in the vacuum of space.

"The end of the road," Jolton's passenger, Rodrigo Iglesias, observes.

Jerry nods. "The last frontier."

They stare at the ridgeline with a mixture of lust and wonder. Like Jerry, Rodrigo is a Realtor for Coldwell Banker. His territory is Bel Air, a few miles to the west, but his pocket organizer is crammed with A-list buyers, so Jerry has brought him here to see the 157-acre parcel that the Mark Hughes Trust has just put on the market.

"Stay here," Jerry says as he opens the door, "I'm gonna unlock the gate." His polished loafers crunch softly on the new white concrete. He thunks the door closed and starts toward the gate, pushing his designer sunglasses up the bridge of his long nose. Inside the car, the air conditioner has only been off for a minute or so, but already the atmosphere grows thick and warm. Rodrigo pulls back the lapels of his green cashmere jacket to expose the brown sweater beneath it, but this offers little relief. He's a handsome man with a broad, tanned forehead, an impressive pompadour of coffee-colored hair, and an aristocratic Spanish accent. Jerry fiddles with a key in the gate's padlock but can't get it open. He whips out a cell phone, speaks into it, then returns to the car. "Somebody changed the lock," he explains. "I just called Jean-Paul, the estate manager; he's on his way up to open it for us."

Jolton slips a key into the ignition. The Mercedes's engine sends a barely perceptible vibration through the black leather seats, and cool air streams through the vents again. Jerry produces a bag of trail mix and offers some to Rodrigo. Iglesias declines and breaks out his latest toy, a Casio multimedia player. He's been dying to show it to Jerry and now is the perfect opportunity. "This is my CD-ROM business card," he explains, holding up a small disc. He slips it into the handheld device and presses some buttons. "If I am at a dinner party and I meet a potential client who might be interested in one of my properties, I lay this on him."

Jerry crunches trail mix as the small screen sputters to life, illuminating the image of a lush Southern California canyon, seen through the windshield of a speeding car. Over a tiny speaker comes the voice of Sting singing "Desert Rose."

"This is to give you the feel of the canyon," Rodrigo says, "leading up to the house."

"Now, are you filming this as you drive your car?" Jolton asks. "Or did you hire a crew?"

"I hire a crew," Iglesias says, offhandedly.

"You're kidding."

"No, I hire a crew that does the whole rigmarole and we cut and edit it and put in the music—not that I got the rights for the song."

"Well, as long as Sting isn't at the dinner party."

They share a conspiratorial laugh, then Rodrigo waves Jerry quiet.

"Okay now, I have some eye candy coming up. It's a lady who works as my right hand. She just came here from Hawaii. I said, 'Put on a bathing suit, we're going to film a shot.' "

Jerry chuckles appreciatively. "You really want to sell this house, don't you?"

"Yeah." Rodrigo nods eagerly. "Wait till you see her, she's quite a woman."

The image on the screen dissolves from the home's exterior to its lavishly appointed interior, and true to his promise, Rodrigo's right hand appears, her minimalist white bikini filled with curves worthy of Anita Ekberg.

"Is that her?" Jolton asks breathlessly, his bag of trail mix forgotten. Rodrigo nods as the woman moves through the house, pointing out marble floors and wood-beamed ceilings in the stilted manner of a *Price Is Right* merchandise model. Jerry rubs the side of his nose, its reddened skin stitched with an intricate pattern of tiny blue veins. "Is this your girlfriend?"

"No. I am happily married for ten years. It is a bachelor-type house, so we wanted to give it that feel."

"If Bernie Cornfeld were alive, you'd have closed the sale by now."

As their raucous laughter dies, the girl on the screen wraps up her tour with a purring, Barbara Feldon voice, "On Stone Canyon Road in Bel Air. Five bedrooms and five baths for just $2,790,000."

The image fades out as Jean-Paul arrives with a pair of bolt cutters. A few minutes later he swings the gate open and Jolton's Mercedes glides up the naked ridgeline toward the sky. It passes two bulldozed indentations on the left and right. Those were the spots—Jolton explains—where Mark Hughes was going to place a pair of man-made lakes. Rodrigo nods thoughtfully. "And for this you are asking what, Jerry?"

"Thirty-five million. It's subdivided for six lots, approximately two acres each. Or it can be sold as one large parcel. It has approximately fifteen acres flat at the top, but all of this land that you're looking at on the left"—he gestures to a vast expanse sloping down to lower ridgelines and small canyons—"is part of the property. So depending on what style somebody wants to build up here, they could leave the surrounding hills as indigenous brush, or they could go all out and . . ."

Iglesias nods and smiles. "Make it a party."

". . . spend a hundred million dollars and landscape it beautifully."

Jolton pulls to a stop on a flat graded area just below the ridgeline's summit. One last bulge of land rises another twenty feet above them; at its base, another huge indentation has been gouged by a bulldozer. "That's where Hughes was going to put his parking garage," Jolton explains. They step out of the car. "Now up there"—Jerry gestures to the summit—"you get a three-hundred-and-sixty-degree view of the Los Angeles basin and the San Fernando Valley. You can see all the way to the Burbank Airport. But standing here you can still get a pretty good sense of it."

They walk over shards of pulverized rock to the edge of the slope and gaze down at Benedict Canyon. From this distance the great houses of the Billionaires' Horseshoe, including Bruce Nelson's pseudo Beaux Arts château, look like tiny Lego blocks. Rodrigo shakes his head, grinning like a hungry hyena. "What a spot! The top of Beverly Hills."

Jolton nods. "The last mountain. You're looking down on the Billionaires' Horseshoe. You're looking down on Paul Allen, on—"

"All of them. This has got to be twelve hundred feet above sea level."

"Thirteen hundred. You're up here with the hawks."

He nods at a red-tailed raptor turning lazy circles above Benedict, like a leaf floating on the wind. Beyond it, in a crinkle of hills, a silver-blue sliver of the Stone Canyon Reservoir glimmers, and beyond that, the high-rises of Santa Monica push up from a sea of orange-brown smog, and beyond that, not visible today, lost behind the dense particulates, the Pacific looms, a presence felt rather than seen. As their talk fades, the men become aware of the silence. Only the whisper of a thin wind rushing up through the dry grass. The vast panorama of city eerily mute. And for a moment in this quietude, looking upon distance falling into distance, it's possible to sense what it once was, in the beginning, before a single castle lined the canyons.

When he was building Pickfair in 1919, Douglas Fairbanks rented Grayhall from Silsby Spalding so he could monitor the construction on a daily basis. On the weekends, Doug would invite a bunch of cowboys who worked on westerns at Universal and other studios out to his wilderness retreat. They would saddle up horses and ride into the hills at night to camp out. Fairbanks's best friend, Charlie Chaplin, was a reluctant participant on many of these expeditions. Far from a dedicated outdoorsman, Chaplin complained that the alkaline in the sagebrush made his throat sore and his nostrils sting; he detested the "sow belly" breakfasts and couldn't sleep at night because the weird, exultant cries of coyotes echoed through the canyons like the spirits of the dead.

One night, on a ridgeline much like the one Jolton and Iglesias now stand on—who knows, perhaps this very same one—Fairbanks and Chaplin gazed up at thousands upon thousands of stars, for the night sky was clear as polished glass then. Even Charlie had to admit it was an awesome sight. He mused philosophically about the ironic contrast between those luminescent heavenly bodies and man's sordid existence on this weary, dust-choked hunk of rock so far below.

Fairbanks, ever the ebullient optimist, chastised his friend. "Look! The moon! And those myriads of stars! Surely there must be a reason for all this beauty? It must be fulfilling some destiny! It must be for some good that you and I are all a part of it! Why are you given this talent, this wonderful medium of motion pictures that reaches millions of people throughout the world?"

Unmoved, Chaplin smiled thinly. "Why is it given to Louis B. Mayer and the Warner Brothers?"

Eighty-two years later, the iridescent moon has grown fuzzy and indistinct in the same carbon-choked sky, and many of those stars have disappeared altogether. But here on the last open mountaintop in Beverly Hills it's possible to catch a whiff of the air Fairbanks and Chaplin once breathed.

Jolton and Iglesias climb back into the black Mercedes and start down the ridge. Rodrigo's thoughts whirr like the wheels of a slot machine, then click to a stop on a realization: "You can't subdivide this property," he declares. "It would be a crime to put six houses in here. This is meant for a *king*!"

Jerry chortles giddily. "It is! It's a compound that would be the likes of San Simeon. I mean, why not?"

The number of potential buyers would discourage lesser men. There are maybe two thousand people in the world rich enough to plunk down thirty-five big ones for this patch of dirt. But to Jolton and Iglesias the glass is more than half full. "In the United States alone," says Rodrigo, "there are two hundred and fifty people who are gonna write a check for this."

Jerry giggles, inebriated by the possibility. "All we need is one. Come on, baby!"

"I'm racking my brain, believe me."

"I know you are, Rodrigo! I know you are. Nothing would make me happier than to do a deal with you."

Rodrigo rubs his palms against his lightly starched slacks, mouth moist with anticipation. "I get all these people who come to me and say, 'I want total privacy. I don't want anybody next to me.' " He gestures to the hills around them. "Fine. Here ya go. Show me your wallet."

"Show me the money, baby!" Jerry crows. "Show me the money!"

Their triumphant laughter fills the car. Sure, another recession may lurk out there, just beyond the smog-choked horizon. But that doesn't worry them. The money doesn't diminish in a recession, it just changes hands; though many will lose their shirts, that critical couple of thousand will get richer. And one thing is as certain as the rising sun: many of them will come here to the Hills of Beverly to build their monuments. And sure, those monuments will be bulldozed one day and the people who build them—like Mary Pickford, Douglas Fairbanks, Buster Keaton, Milton Berle, Norm Zadeh, Bijan Pakzad, Michael

Romanoff, Marvin Davis—will be nothing more than yellowed names in dusty history books. But while the rich may come and go, the common dirt peddlers—Burton Green, Mike Silverman, Bruce Nelson, John Bercsi, Saeed Nourmand, Jerry and Rodrigo—will remain. They were here first and will endure as long as there's a shred of blue sky left to weave into the dream. They build no monuments of their own; there are no Maps to the Beverly Hills Realtors' Homes. This—the entire city sprawled out below them—is their bid for immortality. A smoke-and-mirrors trick that has an everlasting hold on the American imagination.

★ NOTES ★

1 The Billionaires' Horseshoe

Sources for the description of Bruce Nelson's practice, the mansion at 1400 Tower Grove, and the open house held there include: David Weddle's observations of the event; David Weddle's interviews with Bruce Nelson, Raymond Bekeris, Suzanne Marx, and Mike Steere; "Southland Real Estate Giants to Merge" by Jennifer Oldham and Diane Wedner, *Los Angeles Times,* December 2, 2000. Sources on the background of Iris Cantor include the "Hot Property" column of the *Los Angeles Times,* April 27, 2000. Sources for the statistics on the Saperstein house include author's interviews with architect Richardson Robertson III and the "Hot Property" column from the July 23, 2000, edition of the *Los Angeles Times.* Sources on the Beverly Park development include David Weddle's interview with Brian Adler.

Sources for background on the Beverly Hills Hotel's Polo Lounge include David Weddle's interviews with Bruce Nelson; Lisa Marriotte, director of public relations for the Beverly Hills Hotel; Marc Wanamaker, archivist for the Beverly Hills Historical Society; and members of the entertainment industry; *The Pink Palace* by Sandra Lee Stuart; "And the Best Look Is" by Barbara Thomas, *Los Angeles Times,* March 21, 2000; "The Fairy Tale's Over for the Kingdom of Brunei" by Richard Behar, *Fortune,* February 1, 1999; "That Pink Hotel" by Hilary de Vries, *New York Times,* August 13, 1995; "Real Hollywood Never Died: It Was Just Being Renovated" by Rene Chun, *New York*

Times, July 16, 1995; "The Beverly Hills Hotel Reopens; Will Stars Return?" by Pauline Yoshihashi, *Wall Street Journal,* June 2, 1995; "A Grand Hotel, Still Pink, Still Posh" by Bernard Weintraub, *New York Times,* June 1, 1995; "Hotel California" by Barbara Grizzuti Harrison, *Harper's,* February 1981; "Love Letter from Beverly Hills" by Betty Rollin, *Look,* August 12, 1969; "California Dream Hotel," *Holiday,* May 1957.

The sources for Bruce Nelson's lunch at the Beverly Hills Hotel are David Weddle's observations and interviews with Bruce Nelson.

Sources for the development of Beverly Hills and the Beverly Hills Hotel include promotional materials provided by the Beverly Hills Hotel; David Weddle and Howard Libes's interviews with Robert Anderson and archival materials provided by Robert Anderson; David Weddle's interviews with Marc Wanamaker, archivist for the Beverly Hills Historical Society; *American City Planning*, by Mel Scott; Beverly Hills City Council Minutes 1914–1924; *Beverly Hills Historic Resources Survey* by the Office of Historic Preservation for the state of California; *Americans and the California Dream* by Kevin Starr; *Inventing the Dream: California Through the Progressive Era* by Kevin Starr; *Beverly Hills* by Genevieve Davis; *Dream Palaces* by Charles Lockwood; *Daily Variety,* March 28, 2000; "Where the Elite Keep an Eye on the Prize" by Kathleen Craughwell, *Los Angeles Times,* March 28, 2000; "Gleam Team Parties" by Bill Higgins, *Daily Variety,* March 27, 2000; "Nominees' Day Out," *Los Angeles Times,* March 14, 2000; "They're Feeding on Excitement at the Oscar Luncheon" by Lorenza Munoz, *Los Angeles Times,* March 14, 2000; "Davis' Record Turnout" by Don Waller, *Daily Variety,* February 24, 2000; "Golden Evening" by Bill Higgins, *Variety*, January 31–February 6, 2000; "Sultan of Brunei to Pay $200 Million for Beverly Hills Hotel, Sources Say" by Kathleen A. Hughes, *Wall Street Journal,* October 1, 1987; "For Sale: The Beverly Hills Hotel" by Gene G. Marcial, *Business Week,* October 20, 1986; "Down and Out in Beverly Hills" by Dan Dorfman, *New York,* September 15, 1986; "The Grand Hotelier" by Michael Kolhenschlag, *Forbes,* May 11, 1981; "California Dream Hotel," *Holiday,* May 1957; "Coast Host" by Pete Martin, *Saturday Evening Post,* April 15, 1944; "Annual Civic Banquet Set for Jan. 22," *Los Angeles Times,* December 22, 1939; "Mrs. Anderson Sells Property," *Beverly Hills Citizen,* November 1928; "Beverly Hotel to Be Wonder of Southland," *Los Angeles Sunday Times,* May 14, 1911. Sources on the background of Burton Green include *The National Cyclopaedia of American Biography.* Sources on the background of Wilbur Cook Jr. include *The Los Angeles Architectural Guide*.

Sources for the description of the Beverly Hills Hotel during the 1940s,

1950s, and 1960s include David Weddle's interviews with Bruce Nelson, Svend Peterson, Mike Silverman, Marc Wanamaker, and members of the entertainment industry; promotional materials provided by the Beverly Hills Hotel; *Beverly Hills* by Genevieve Davis; *The Kid Stays in the Picture* by Robert Evans; "Beverly Hotel to Be Wonder of Southland," *Los Angeles Sunday Times,* May 14, 1911; "Annual Civic Banquet Set for Jan. 22," *Los Angeles Times*, December 22, 1939; "Coast Host" by Pete Martin, *Saturday Evening Post,* April 15, 1944; "California Dream Hotel," *Holiday,* May 1957; "The Grand Hotelier" by Michael Kolhenschlag, *Forbes,* May 11, 1981; "The Poolside Prince of the Pink Palace" by Steve Root, *Los Angeles* magazine, June 1990.

Sources for the description of Mike Silverman's meeting with Bruce Nelson include David Weddle's interviews with Mike Silverman, Bruce Nelson, and Svend Peterson.

The source for the description of the conclusion of Bruce Nelson's lunch and his encounter with Svend Peterson was David Weddle's observations.

2 HIGH COTTON

Sources for the contemporary description of the Italian villa and the process of selling and restoring it include David Weddle's observations and interviews with Steven Sherman, Marc Wanamaker, archivist for the Beverly Hills Historical Society, and John Bercsi.

Sources for the overview of Buster Keaton's career include David Weddle's observations; *My Wonderful World of Slapstick* by Buster Keaton and Charles Samuels; *Keaton* by Rudi Blesh; *Keaton—The Man Who Wouldn't Lie Down* by Tom Dardis; *Harold Lloyd—The Shape of Laughter* by Richard Schickel; *Harold Lloyd—The Man on the Clock* by Tom Dardis.

Sources for the development of movie star mansions in Beverly Hills include David Weddle's interview with Marc Wanamaker; *Beverly Hills Historic Resources Survey* by the Office of Historic Preservation for the state of California; *Americans and the California Dream* by Kevin Starr; *Inventing the Dream: California Through the Progressive Era* by Kevin Starr; *Beverly Hills* by Genevieve Davis; *Dream Palaces* by Charles Lockwood; *My Wonderful World of Slapstick* by Buster Keaton and Charles Samuels; *Keaton* by Rudi Blesh; *Keaton—The Man Who Wouldn't Lie Down* by Tom Dardis; *Harold Lloyd—The Shape of Laughter* by Richard Schickel; *Harold Lloyd—The Man on the Clock* by Tom Dardis; *Pickford: The Woman Who Made Hollywood* by Eileen Witfield; *Salad Days* by Douglas Fairbanks Jr.; *Doug & Mary* by Gary

Carey; *Mary Pickford and Douglas Fairbanks* by Booton Herndon; *Mary Pickford—America's Sweetheart* by Scott Eyman; *His Picture in the Papers* by Richard Schickel; *Douglas Fairbanks—The Fourth Musketeer* by Ralph Hancock and Letitia Fairbanks; *The Fabulous Tom Mix* by Oliver Stokes Mix with Eric Heath; *Tom Mix* by Paul E. Mix; *The Life and Legend of Tom Mix* by Paul E. Mix; *The House of Barrymore* by Margot Peters; *The Barrymores* by Hollis Alpert; *Valentino* by Irving Shulman; *Rudolph Valentino—The Man Behind the Myth* by Robert Oberfirst; *Valentino the Unforgotten* by Roger C. Peterson; *Chaplin—His Life and Art* by David Robinson.

Sources for the description of John Bercsi's tour of the Italian villa include David Weddle's observations and interviews with John Bercsi. The sources for the description of the unraveling of Keaton's personal life include *My Wonderful World of Slapstick* by Buster Keaton and Charles Samuels; *Keaton* by Rudi Blesh; *Keaton—The Man Who Wouldn't Lie Down* by Tom Dardis; *Buster Keaton—Cut to the Chase* by Marion Meade.

Sources for the description of John Bercsi's travels through Beverly Hills are David Weddle's observations and interviews with John Bercsi and John Levin. Sources for the description of Tom Mix's, Charlie Chaplin's, Mary Pickford's, and Harold Lloyd's final days include: *Chaplin—His Life and Art* by David Robinson; *Harold Lloyd—The Shape of Laughter* by Richard Schickel; *Harold Lloyd—The Man on the Clock* by Tom Dardis; *Pickford: The Woman Who Made Hollywood* by Eileen Witfield; *Salad Days* by Douglas Fairbanks Jr.; *Doug & Mary* by Gary Carey; *Mary Pickford and Douglas Fairbanks* by Booton Herndon; *Mary Pickford—America's Sweetheart* by Scott Eyman; *His Picture in the Papers* by Richard Schickel; *Douglas Fairbanks—The Fourth Musketeer* by Ralph Hancock and Letitia Fairbanks; *The Fabulous Tom Mix* by Oliver Stokes Mix with Eric Heath; *Tom Mix* by Paul E. Mix; *The Life and Legend of Tom Mix* by Paul E. Mix.

Sources for the description of the storage shed at the Italian villa include David Weddle's observations and interviews with John Bercsi. Sources for the description of Keaton's final years include *My Wonderful World of Slapstick* by Buster Keaton and Charles Samuels; *Keaton* by Rudi Blesh; *Keaton—The Man Who Wouldn't Lie Down* by Tom Dardis; "How Keaton Commanded His Last Stage" by Caryn James, *New York Times,* October 6, 1996; "Agent Debunks 'Poverty' Myth; Keaton Earnings Remained Big" by Ben Pearson, *Daily Variety*, January 4, 1978; "Gloomy Buster Is Back Again," *Life,* March 13, 1950; "Keaton, Ex-Slapstick King, Now Has Pauper's Pittance" by Harold Heffernan, *New York Daily News,* November 18, 1941; "Alimony Battle Won by Keaton," *New York Herald Tribune,* January 1,

1937; "Buster 'Busted' Begs for 'Break' " by Joseph Cowan, *New York Herald Tribune,* December 28, 1936; "Buster Keaton Fights to Save His Salary, *New York Herald Tribune,* November 9, 1936; "Buster Keaton? Who Is He? Justice Asks," *New York Herald Tribune,* November 2, 1936; "Keaton Income Down $135,000," *New York Herald Tribune,* November 17, 1936; "Buster Keaton's Wife Files Suit for Alimony," *New York Times,* September 18, 1936; "You Can't Judge by Appearances," *Vanity Fair,* October 1935; "Norma Talmadge, Ex-Wife's Sister, Always Disliked Him, Comedian Says," *New York Herald Tribune,* October 29, 1936; "Keaton in Asylum," Associated Press, October 21, 1935; "Nerves Gone, Keaton Put in Strait-Jacket," Associated Press, October 21, 1935; "Buster Keaton Is Gravely Ill in Hollywood," Associated Press, October 21, 1935; "Keaton Collapses—Condition Serious," Associated Press, October 21, 1935; "Buster Keaton Denies Wife's Charges," *New York Times,* October 5, 1935; "Keaton Out Gunning for Enemy Cupid," Associated Press, July 28, 1935; "Buster Keaton Signs Five-Year Contract to Appear in Comedies for Educational Films," *New York Times,* January 3, 1934; "Buster Says He's Broke," *New York Daily News,* July 14, 1933; "Health Makes Keaton Quit Films," *New York Herald Tribune,* February 4, 1933; "Buster Keaton Quits the Screen," *New York Times*, February 4, 1933; "Buster Keaton's Wife Brings Suit for Divorce," *New York Times,* August 9, 1932.

3 BACHELOR IN PARADISE

Sources for the opening description of the cocktail lounge of the Four Seasons Hotel and the Beverly Hills bimbo vortex include David Weddle's and Howard Libes's observations; *High Concept* by Charles Fleming; *MADAM 90210: My Life as Madam to the Rich and Famous* by Alex Adams and William Stadiem; *You'll Never Make Love in This Town Again* by Robin, Liza, Linda, and Tiffany as told to Jennie Maxine Frankel, Terrie Maxine Frankel, and Joanne Parent; *Once More with Feeling (or You'll Never Make Love in This Town Again Again)* by Michelle, Sophie, Jewel, Tatiana, and Jennifer as told to Joanne Parent; *Heidi Fleiss—Hollywood Madam,* produced and directed by Nick Broomfield; "Hooking Up" by Dave Gardetta, *Los Angeles,* October 2001; "Grasping for a Star" by Mimi Avins, *Los Angeles Times,* May 21, 2001; " 'Hollywood Madam' Faces Parole Charge," *Los Angeles Times,* March 31, 2001; "Adieu to L.A.'s Gazillionaire-Widow Tax Base" by Gina Piccalo, *Los Angeles Times,* February 13, 2001; " 'Babydol' Gets 3-Year Prison Term" by Karima Haynes, *Los Angeles Times,* May 16, 2000; " 'Babydol' Convicted on Three Counts Involving International Call Girl Ring" by Caitlin Liu,

Los Angeles Times, April 8, 2000; "Fleiss Convicted on 3 Pandering Charges" by Shawn Hubler and Nora Zamichow, *Los Angeles Times,* December 3, 1994; "Modern Madams," *Los Angeles Times,* December 3, 1994; Classified Ads in *Beverly Hills Weekly, L.A. Weekly, Los Angeles New Times,* and on www.la-exotics.com.

Sources for the section on Norm Zadeh at the Four Seasons include David Weddle's and Howard Libes's observations and interviews with Eileen Koch, Norm Zadeh, Ashley Degenford, Jennifer Snow; and back issues of *Perfect 10* magazine.

The sources for the description of Norm Zadeh's childhood include David Weddle's and Howard Libes's interviews with Norm Zadeh; "Bull Market Lothario" by Bill Alpert, *Barron's,* February 19, 2001; the University of California at Berkeley Web site's biography of Lofti Zadeh; the author's review of back issues of *Playboy* magazine from the 1960s and 1970s.

Sources for the passage on Howard Hughes include *Howard Hughes: The Untold Story* by Peter Harry Brown and Pat H. Broeske; *Empire—The Life, Legend and Madness of Howard Hughes* by Donald Bartlett and James B. Steele.

Sources for the passage on Hugh Hefner include David Weddle's interview with Richard Rosenzweig, president of Playboy Enterprises, Inc.; David Weddle's tour of the *Playboy* mansion; promotion material provided by Playboy Enterprises; back issues of *Playboy* from the 1960s and 1970s; *The Pump House Gang* by Tom Wolfe; "City of Angles" by Gina Piccalo and Louise Roug, *Los Angeles Times,* December 12, 2001; *A & E Biography: Hugh Hefner;* "Hugh Hefner" by Chris Colin, *Salon.com;* "A Conversation with Hugh Hefner" by Chris Colin, *Salon.com;* "Playboy Sheds 'Gentleman's' Cloak, Buys 'XX' TV Channels" by Sallie Hofmeister and Ralph Frammolino, *Los Angeles Times,* July 3, 2001.

Sources for Playboy Enterprises' civic contributions to Beverly Hills include David Weddle's interview with Richard Rosenzweig; "Free Playboy Jazz Concert" by Norma Zager, *Beverly Hills Courier,* May 6, 2001.

Sources for the passage on Bernie Cornfeld include David Weddle's interview with Marc Wanamaker and tour of Grayhall; "Died, Bernie Cornfeld," *Time,* March 13, 1995; "The Real Financial Dream: Take the Money and Run" by Bryan Burrough, *Los Angeles Times,* March 5, 1995; "Bernie Cornfeld—Ran Ill-Fated IOS Fund," *Los Angeles Times,* March 1, 1995; "Bernie Goes Bananas" by John R. Hayes, *Forbes,* December 21, 1992; "Ranking Milken Among the Rogues" by Paul Richter, *Los Angeles Times,* April 29, 1990; "The Return of Bernie Cornfeld" by Ruthanne Sutor, *Financial World,*

August 23, 1988; "Cornfeld Home Listed—Ownership Disputed" by Ruth Ryon, *Los Angeles Times,* November 8, 1987; "Developer Buys Grayhall—Once Home of Stars" by Ruth Ryon, *Los Angeles Times,* May 2, 1987; "Cornfeld Home in Beverly Hills Is Being Sold" by Bill Sing, *Los Angeles Times,* October 1, 1986; "Do You Sincerely Want to Make Out?" by Richard L. Stern, *Forbes,* January 16, 1984.

Sources for the passage on Robert Evans include David Weddle's observations; *The Kid Stays in the Picture* by Robert Evans; *High Concept* by Charles Fleming; *MADAM 90210: My Life as Madam to the Rich and Famous* by Alex Adams and William Stadiem; *You'll Never Make Love in This Town Again* by Robin, Liza, Linda, and Tiffany as told to Jennie Maxine Frankel, Terrie Maxine Frankel, and Joanne Parent; *Once More With Feeling (or You'll Never Make Love in This Town Again Again)* by Michelle, Sophie, Jewel, Tatiana, and Jennifer as told to Joanne Parent; "Man of a Thousand Lives" by John Connolly, *Premiere,* April 2001; "Modern Madams," *Los Angeles Times,* December 3, 1994.

Sources for the passage on how Norm Zadeh became wealthy and founded *Perfect 10* include David Weddle's and Howard Libes's interviews with Norm Zadeh; back issues of *Perfect 10;* "See No Evil" by Seth Lubove, *Forbes,* September 17, 2001; "Bull Market Lothario" by Bill Alpert, *Barron's,* February 19, 2001; "Are They for Real?" by Deanna Kizis, *Buzz,* December 1997; "A Gloom with a View" by Gregory Rodriguez, Laura Mecoy, Christopher Noxon, Joshua Tompkins, James Rubin, *Los Angeles,* December 1997; "All Natural au Naturel" by Betsy Streisand, *U.S. News & World Report,* December 15, 1997; "Investment Champ Makes Big-Money Comeback" by John O'Dell, *Los Angeles Times,* February 6, 1990; "Trading Champs Steer Clear of Inside Scoops" by Susan Antilla, *USA Today,* July 13, 1987; "Champion Market Investors" by Carrie Brown, *Los Angeles Times,* March 1, 1987; "Investments Bring Big Prize as Well as Profit" by Jeff Rowe, *Los Angeles Times,* June 29, 1986.

Sources for the description of the photo shoot at the *Perfect 10* mansion are Howard Libes's observations and interviews with Norm Zadeh and Amber Rangel; "See No Evil" by Seth Lubove, *Forbes,* September 17, 2001; "Bull Market Lothario" by Bill Alpert, *Barron's,* February 19, 2001.

4 The East Side Kids

Sources for the description of Milton Berle's funeral include David Weddle's observations; "Los Angeles Send-Off Filled with Laughter," *Los Angeles*

Times, April 2, 2002; "A Special Farewell to 'Uncle Miltie,' " *USA Today,* April 2, 2002; "Obituaries," *Variety,* April 1, 2002.

Sources for the description of the Friars Club new membership event include the observations of David Weddle and Howard Libes; promotional materials provided by the Friars Club; Howard Libes's interview with Michele Horner; David Weddle's interview with Frank More.

Sources for the description of the present-day Friars Club include David Weddle's observations; Howard Libes's interviews with Michele Horner, Larry King, Steve Allen, Rudy Cole, Ted Shaffrey, and Dick Van Patten.

Sources for the description of Milton Berle's last days at the Friars Club include David Weddle's and Howard Libes's observations; David Weddle's interviews with Milton Berle; Howard Libes's interviews with Larry King, Steve Allen, Rudy Cole, Ted Shaffrey, and Dick Van Patten.

Sources for the passage on the origins of the East Side Kids and the development of Milton Berle's career include David Weddle's interviews with Milton Berle; Howard Libes's interviews with Steve Allen, Dick Van Patten, and Bruce Charet; *Here's to the Friars* by Joey Adams; *B.S. I Love You* by Milton Berle; *Milton Berle: An Autobiography* by Milton Berle with Haskel Frankel; *George Burns: The Hundred-Year Dash* by Martin Gottfried; *Sundays at Seven: The Jack Benny Story* by Jack Benny and Joan Benny; *King of Comedy* by Shawn Levy; *Groucho: The Life and Times of Julius Henry Marx* by Stefan Kanfer; *Joys of Yiddish* by Leo Rosten; *My Wonderful World of Slapstick* by Buster Keaton and Charles Samuels; *Keaton* by Rudi Blesh; *Man on the Flying Trapeze* by Simon Louvish; *W. C. Fields by Himself* by W. C. Fields and Ronald J. Fields; *The Vaudevillians* by Anthony Slide; *Inside Beverly Hills,* produced by NBC Television.

Sources for the description of the gradual deflation of Milton Berle's career and the decline of the Friars Club include David Weddle's observations and interviews with Milton Berle; Howard Libes's interviews with Steve Allen, Dick Van Patten, Rudy Cole, Ted Shaffrey, and Bruce Charet; "Friars Club Will Honor Comedienne," *Westside Weekly,* January 7, 2001; "NBC Finds Milton Berle's Historical Kinescopes" by Steve Gorman, *Yahoo! News,* July 21, 2000; "Take My Aging Friars Club—Please" by Ted Shaffrey, *Westside Weekly,* June 4, 2000; "First Woman Heads Friars Club" by Norma Zager, *Beverly Hills Courier,* June 2, 2000; "Who Killed Chasen's" by Shirin Danielpour, *Beverly Hills Weekly,* May 18–24, 2000; "Uncle Miltie Sues NBC for His Old Kinescopes" by Ann O'Neill, *Los Angeles Times,* May 21, 2000; "Uncle Miltie's Comedy Class" by Paul Brownfeld, *Los Angeles Times,* July 24, 1999; "Only in L.A." by Steve Harvey, *Los Angeles Times,* January 22, 1999;

"Ancient Friars Opens Its Doors to Young Comics" by Paula Span, *Washington Post*, July 14, 1998; "All the Young Dudes" by R. J. Smith, *Los Angeles Times*, March 22, 1998; "Enter Laughing, Again" by Claudia Puig, *Los Angeles Times*, September 22, 1996; "Letters in View: On Danson," *Los Angeles Times*, October 24, 1993; "Commentary: Ted and Whoopi's Outrageous Adventure" by Michelle Williams, *Los Angeles Times*, October 24, 1993; "Roasts Come Under Fire" by Greg Braxton, *Los Angeles Times*, October 21, 1993; "Whoopi's Shock Roast" by Jeannie Williams, *USA Today*, October 11, 1993; "No Holds Barred at Roast" by Greg Braxton, *Los Angeles Times*, September 23, 1993; "Rosie Sees Red, Jokes Are Blue" by Frank Swertlow, *Daily News*, September 23, 1993; "Take Our Club Please" by Billy Frolick, *Los Angeles Times*, August 9, 1992; "Friarsgate" by Frank Feldinger, *Spy*, April 1989; "Drag Vet: Does Uncle Miltie Ru the Day He Went on MTV?" by George Wayne, *Vanity Fair*, February 1994; "Hot Property" by Ruth Ryon, *Los Angeles Times*, May 9, 1993; *Hollywood Reporter*, July 19, 1991; "Milton Berle Salute: Mister Television Talks" by David Hajdu, *Hollywood Reporter*, July 1990; "Age Can't Slow 'Uncle Miltie' " by Steve Brennan, *Hollywood Reporter*, May 16, 1990; "Auction," *Los Angeles Times*, April 22, 1990; "Hot Property" by Ruth Ryon, *Los Angeles Times*, April 1, 1990; "Hot Property: Penthouse Catches Uncle Miltie's Eye" by Ruth Ryon, *Los Angeles Times*, February 4, 1990; "Hot Property" by Ruth Ryon, *Los Angeles Times*, October 1, 1989; "Milton Berle" by Ken Gross, *People Weekly*, January 25, 1988; "Milton Berle: Three Generations of Laughs" by Alan Bunce, *Christian Science Monitor*, January 21, 1988; "First Lucy and Now . . . Miltie's Back!" by Maurice Zolotow, *Los Angeles* magazine, November 1986; "Milton Berle Looks to Feature Prod'n," *Hollywood Reporter*, January 10, 1967; "So He Mounted His Shining Plane and Flew Off to Show Them He Was King" by Dick Hobson, *TV Guide*, December 10, 1966; *Mirror News*, September 22, 1958.

5 THE PERSIAN FRANK SINATRA

Sources include David Weddle's and Howard Libes's observations; Howard Libes's interviews with Hamid Gabbay, Nejat Gabbay, Dariush Fakheri, Gina Nahai, Shirin Danielpour, Nanaz Pirnia, Saeed Nourmand, Rahim Soltani, Ali Soltani, Behrouz Mahboubi; *Irangeles: Iranians in Los Angeles*, edited by Ron Kelley, coedited by Jonathan Friedlander, associate editor Anita Colby; *Teenage Refugees from Iran Speak Out*, edited by Gina Strazzabosco; *Cultural Learning and Cultural Adaptations Among Iranians in California*, a dissertation by Diane Hoffman, Stanford University; "Iranians in Southland Flex Political Muscle" by

Soraya Sarhaddi Nelson, *Los Angeles Times,* July 17, 2000; "Bringing the Music to Iranian People" by Dana Calvo, *Los Angeles Times,* March 29, 2000; "Light Over Darkness: A Nowruz Celebration" by Shirin Danielpour, *Beverly Hills Weekly,* March 16–20, 2000; "Tehran Nights" by Shirin Danielpour and Josh Gross, *Beverly Hills Weekly,* November 25–December 1, 1999; "Revolution in Iran Revolutionizes Beverly Hills" by Shirin Danielpour, *Beverly Hills Weekly,* November 4–10, 1999; "Iranians Bridging Cultural Gaps in Beverly Hills" by John L. Mitchell, *Los Angeles Times,* July 6, 1999; "When Truth Is Given the Wings to Fly" by Charlotte Innes, *Los Angeles Times,* June 7, 1999; "A Story of Layered Oppression" by Michael Harris, *Los Angeles Times,* April 20, 1999; "Faces of Exile" by Mathis Chazanov, *Los Angeles Times,* May 12, 1994; "A New Persian Empire" by John L. Mitchell, *Los Angeles Times,* December 31, 1989; "Post-Revolution Boom for Iranian Yellow Pages" by James Bates, *Los Angeles Times,* June 18, 1989; "Lifting the Veil" by Karen Newell Young, *Los Angeles Times* (Orange County Edition), October 1, 1988; "Iranian Sense of Justice Demands Family Payments" by William Beeman, *Los Angeles Times,* July 6, 1988; *LA Weekly,* October 12–18, 1979; "Beverly Hills Approves Industrial Zone Land Trade" by Richard C. Paddock, *Los Angeles Times,* November 30, 1978; "Beverly Hills Moves to Get More Land for Parks," *Los Angeles Times,* May 11, 1978; "Councilman Declared to Have No Conflict" by Richard C. Paddock, *Los Angeles Times,* May 7, 1978.

6 "BEVERLY HILLS IS MY COUNTRY"

Sources for the passage on Bijan Pakzad include David Weddle's interviews with Bijan Pakzad, Jayne Brandonisio, and former Bijan employees; David Weddle's tour of Bijan's Beverly Hills boutique; promotional materials provided by Bijan Pakzad; *Brand Slam* by Frank Delano; "What Recession?" *Advertising Age,* January 15, 2001; "Bijan's Bijoux" by Holly Peterson, *Talk,* December 2000/January 2001; "Bijan Dresses the Wealthy for Success" by Andrea Bermudez, *California Apparel News*, December 1–7, 2000; "Bijan Is Back with a New Women's Scent" by Katherine Bowers, *Women's Wear Daily,* October 27, 2000; "The Sultan of Sartor" by Frank Swertlow, *Los Angeles Business Journal,* May 15–21, 2000; "Bijan—A Designer's Success" by Roberta Naas, *Millionaire,* May 2000; "Above and Bijan" by Romy de Courtay, *DNR,* March 22, 2000; "Shockvertising Jolts Ad Viewers" by Michael McCarthy, *USA Today,* February 23, 2000; "Designer's Ad Campaign Says Bit Is Beautiful," *Los Angeles Times,* January 21, 2000; "Bijan Stands for Luxury—But Luxury What?" by Jennifer Steinhauer, *Dallas Morning News,* January 6,

1999; "Elusive and Exclusive Clothier to the Rich" by Jennifer Steinhauer, *New York Times,* December 29, 1998; "What Drives Bijan?" by Roberta Naas, *Robb Report,* September 1996; "Bijan—Living in the Lap of Luxury" by Stephen O'Shea, *Vogue,* 1993.

The sources for the description of Rodeo Drive today are David Weddle's observations. The sources for the description of the early development of the commercial district include *Beverly Hills Historic Resources Survey* by the Office of Historic Preservation for the state of California; *Beverly Hills* by Genevieve Davis; *Dream Palaces* by Charles Lockwood.

Sources for the Michael Romanoff story include *Romanoff—Prince of Rogues* by Jane Pejsa; "The Education of a Prince" by Alva Johnston, *Life Stories—Profiles from the New Yorker;* "Snobs of Yesteryear," *Newsweek,* December 24, 1962; *Los Angeles Herald Examiner,* December 12, 1962; *Los Angeles Herald Examiner,* June 28, 1958; *New York Times,* March 17, 1958; "Prince Mike's Place" by Lucius Beebe, *Holiday,* March 1954; *Los Angeles Times,* January 21, 1951; *Los Angeles Herald Examiner,* July 5, 1948; *Los Angeles Times,* July 5, 1948; *Time,* February 23, 1948; *Los Angeles Times,* September 15, 1946; "Life Goes to Romanoff's Restaurant," *Life,* October 29, 1945; "Knight of the Corner Table," *New York Times Magazine,* September 2, 1945; "Harry Gerguson [Mike Romanoff] Discards Self-Bestowed Title," *New York Times,* July 4, 1933; *Time,* June 19, 1939; "Harry Gerguson Gets 90-Day Sentence," *New York Times,* April 6, 1933; "Character Witnesses Testify for Harry Gerguson," *New York Times,* February 7, 1933; "Court Defers Sentence of Harry Gerguson," *New York Times,* January 31, 1933; "Harry Gerguson Indicted on Charges of Perjury," *New York Times,* January 17, 1933; "P Arno Denies Aiding Harry Gerguson's Entry into U.S.," *New York Times,* January 15, 1933; "Harry Gerguson Will Be Released from Ellis Island," *New York Times,* January 7, 1933; "M. W. Garsson Assigned to Investigate Harry Gerguson's Entry into U.S.," *New York Times,* January 5, 1933; "Harry Gerguson Found to Have Arrived on S.S. *Europa,*" *New York Times,* January 4, 1933; "Harry Gerguson Held at Ellis Island," *New York Times,* December 30, 1932; "Harry Gerguson Arrives in U.S.," *New York Times,* December 24, 1932; "Harry Gerguson Deported to France," *New York Times,* May 11, 1932; "Harry Gerguson Awaits Deportation at Ellis Island," *New York Times,* May 10, 1932; "Harry Gerguson Escapes from Ellis Island," *New York Times,* May 7, 1932; "Harry Gerguson Detained at Ellis Island," *New York Times,* April 26, 1932; *New York Times,* November 29, 1922.

Sources for the section on Fred Hayman and the development of Rodeo Drive in the 1970s, 1980s, and 1990s include "Jaguar's Tribute to Style," *Los*

Angeles Times Magazine, March 4, 2001; "Hilfiger to Close Flagship Rodeo Drive Store" by Willoughby Mariano, *Los Angeles Times,* February 4, 2000; "Designer's Ad Campaign Says Big Is Beautiful" by Barbara Thomas, *Los Angeles Times,* January 21, 2000; "King of the Hills" by Karen Stabiner, *Los Angeles Times,* February 15, 1998; "Fred Hayman to Vacate Rodeo, Lease to Vuitton" by George White, *Los Angeles Times,* November 20, 1997; "Revival on Rodeo" by George White, *Los Angeles Times,* November 16, 1997; "What $20 Million Smells Like" by Beverly Beyette, *Los Angeles Times,* November 14, 1996; "A Pearl of Beverly Hills Loses Some of Its Luster" by George White, *Los Angeles Times,* March 15, 1996; "A Tale of Two Beverlys" by Maureen Sajbel, *Los Angeles Times,* July 20, 1995; "Dollars and Sense" by G. Jeanette Avent, *Los Angeles Times,* December 13, 1992; "Two Rodeo Drive—A Collage of What Beverly Hills Is All About" by Aaron Betsky, *Los Angeles Times,* December 5, 1991; "Some Bumps in the Road for Rodeo Drive" by Kenneth J. Garcia, *Los Angeles Times,* June 27, 1991; "The Pricey but Potent Romantic Fragrance" by Martha Groves, *Los Angeles Times,* May 10, 1991; "Highfalutin' Fantasy Trip" by Libby Slate, *Los Angeles Times,* January 10, 1991; "A Street Named Desire" by Garry Abrams, *Los Angeles Times,* November 30, 1990; "This Is a Mini-Mall?" by Kenneth J. Garcia, *Los Angeles Times,* September 16, 1990; "Japanese to Buy Stake in Mall on Rodeo Drive" by Tom Furlong, *Los Angeles Times,* June 5, 1990; "Fred Hayman, Late of Giorgio, Hopes America's Got His Number" by Jamie Diamond, *People Weekly,* May 7, 1990; "Can He Do It Again?" by Nikki Finke, *Los Angeles Times,* March 7, 1990; "Town That Tells Time on a Rolex" by David Ferrell, *Los Angeles Times,* January 28, 1990; "Ex-Giorgio Owner Ordered to Change Ads" by Kathryn Harris, *Los Angeles Times,* March 18, 1989; "Eau de L.A." by Paddy Calistro, *Los Angeles Times,* November 13, 1988; "The Perfume Wars: Giorgio Saga Continues" by Mary Rourke, *Los Angeles Times,* April 1, 1988; "The Romance Turns Gothic at Giorgio" by Faye Rice, *Fortune,* June 9, 1986; "Rodeo Retailers: Life, Death in the Flash Lane" by Diane Reischel, *Los Angeles Times,* February 7, 1986; "Rodeo Drive Opts for Old, Pricey Image" by John L. Mitchell, *Los Angeles Times,* February 3, 1985.

7 SECURITY CHIC

Sources for the passage on the booming security business in Beverly Hills include David Weddle's and Howard Libes's observations; Howard Libes's interviews with Dr. Michael Zona, John Lane, Michael Eubanks, Heidi Prince, general manager of the Counter Spy Shop; David Weddle's interviews with members of the personal security industry, Beverly Hills residents, and personal assistants to feature-film stars; Howard Libes's correspondence with Gavin de Becker; *The Gift of Fear* by Gavin de Becker; promotional materials provided by the Omega Group and the Officers Group; promotional materials provided by the Counter Spy Shop; "I'll Be Watching You" by Lisa Leff, *Los Angeles*, March 2000; "The Follower" by Bill Hewitt, *People,* February 28, 2000; "Wilson Signs Tough Anti-Stalking Bill" by Lisa Fernandez, *Los Angeles Times,* August 6, 1997; "New D.A. Unit to Stake Out Stalking Cases" by Jose Cardenas, *Los Angeles Times,* July 23, 1997; "Stalking in L.A." by Jeffrey Toobin, *The New Yorker,* February 24 & March 3, 1997; "When the Law Can't Protect" by Miles Corwin, *Los Angeles Times,* May 8, 1993; "Inside Celebrity Obsessions" by Scott Hays, *Los Angeles Times,* October 17, 1990.

The source for current crime statistics in Beverly Hills is *Beverly Hills Economic Profile—2001–2000,* published by the Beverly Hills Chamber of Commerce.

Sources for the overview of the stalking phenomenon include Howard Libes's interviews with Dr. Michael Zona, John Lane, Michael Eubanks; David Weddle's interviews with members of the personal security industry; *Obsessed: The Stalking of Theresa Saldana* by Ronald M. D. Markman and Ron Labrecque; "Kidman Wins Restraining Order," *Los Angeles Times,* May 31, 2001; "Long, Strange Trip," *Los Angeles Times,* May 29, 2001; "City of Angles" by Ann O'Neill, *Los Angeles Times,* May 15, 2001; "She's Not Interested," *Los Angeles Times,* May 11, 2001; "Stun Gun Justice," *Los Angeles Times,* April 20, 2001; "Quick Takes," *Los Angeles Times,* March 29, 2001; "Actor Spade Attacked by Intruder in Beverly Hills Home," *Los Angeles Times,* November 30, 2000; "Key Advice on Stalkers: Don't Underestimate Their Tenacity" by Gina Piccalo, *Los Angeles Times,* October 15, 2000; "I'll Be Watching You" by Lisa Leff, *Los Angeles,* March 2000; "The Follower" by Bill Hewitt, *People,* February 28, 2000; "Wilson Signs Tough Anti-Stalking Bill" by Lisa Fernandez, *Los Angeles Times,* August 6, 1997; "New D.A. Unit to Stake Out Stalking Cases" by Jose Cardenas, *Los Angeles Times,* July 23, 1997; "Stalking in L.A." by Jeffrey Toobin, *The New Yorker,* February 24 & March 3, 1997; "Madonna Bodyguard Describes Intrusion" by Andrea Ford, *Los Angeles Times,* January 5, 1996; "When the Law Can't Protect" by Miles Corwin, *Los Angeles Times,* May 8, 1993; "In the Mind of a Stalker" by Mike Tharp, *U.S. News & World Report,* February 17, 1992; "Inside Celebrity Obsessions" by Scott Hays, *Los Angeles Times,* October 17, 1990.

The source for the passage on the murder of Ned Doheny is *Dark Side of*

Fortune: Triumph and Scandal in the Life of Oil Tycoon Edward L. Doheny by Margaret Leslie Lewis.

The sources for the description of Buster Keaton's encounter with a stalker include *Keaton* by Rudi Blesh and *Keaton—The Man Who Wouldn't Lie Down* by Tom Dardis.

The source for the passage on Joan Berry and Charlie Chaplin is *Chaplin: His Life and Art* by David Robinson.

The source for the passage on Lana Turner is *Lana* by Lana Turner.

Sources for the passage on Charles Manson include *Helter Skelter* by Vincent Bugliosi and Curt Gentry; "The Long Chilling Shadow of Manson" by Richard C. Paddock, *Los Angeles Times,* August 6, 1994.

Sources for the widening gap between America's rich and poor include "A Nation Divided" by Mortimer B. Zuckerman, *U.S. News & World Report,* October 18, 1999; David Green, *U.S News & World Report,* July 26, 1999.

Sources for the passage on the development of the stalking phenomenon include Howard Libes's interviews with Dr. Michael Zona, John Lane, Michael Eubanks; David Weddle's interviews with members of the personal security industry; *Obsessed: The Stalking of Theresa Saldana* by Ronald M. D. Markman and Ron Labrecque; "Kidman Wins Restraining Order," *Los Angeles Times,* May 31, 2001; "Long, Strange Trip," *Los Angeles Times,* May 29, 2001; "Quick Takes," *Los Angeles Times,* March 29, 2001; "City of Angles" by Ann O'Neill, *Los Angeles Times,* May 15, 2001; "She's Not Interested," *Los Angeles Times,* May 11, 2001; "Stun Gun Justice," *Los Angeles Times,* April 20, 2001; "Actor Spade Attacked by Intruder in Beverly Hills Home," *Los Angeles Times,* November 30, 2000; "Key Advice on Stalkers: Don't Underestimate Their Tenacity" by Gina Piccalo, *Los Angeles Times,* October 15, 2000; "I'll Be Watching You" by Lisa Leff, *Los Angeles,* March 2000; "The Follower" by Bill Hewitt, *People,* February 28, 2000; "Wilson Signs Tough Anti-Stalking Bill" by Lisa Fernandez, *Los Angeles Times,* August 6, 1997; "New D.A. Unit to Stake Out Stalking Cases" by Jose Cardenas, *Los Angeles Times,* July 23, 1997; "Stalking in L.A." by Jeffrey Toobin, *The New Yorker,* February 24 & March 3, 1997; "Madonna Bodyguard Describes Intrusion" by Andrea Ford, *Los Angeles Times,* January 5, 1996; "When the Law Can't Protect" by Miles Corwin, *Los Angeles Times,* May 8, 1993; "In the Mind of a Stalker" by Mike Tharp, *U.S. News & World Report,* February 17, 1992; "Inside Celebrity Obsessions" by Scott Hays, *Los Angeles Times,* October 17, 1990.

Sources for the development of Gavin de Becker's career and the growth of the stalking industry in Los Angeles include David Weddle's observations and interviews with members of the personal security industry, Beverly Hills residents and personal assistants to feature-film stars; Howard Libes's interviews with Dr. Michael Zona, John Lane, Michael Eubanks, Heidi Prince, general manager of the Counter Spy Shop, and correspondence with Gavin de Becker; *The Gift of Fear* by Gavin de Becker; promotional materials provided by the Omega Group and the Officers Group; promotional materials provided by the Counter Spy Shop; "I'll Be Watching You" by Lisa Leff, *Los Angeles*, March 2000; "The Follower" by Bill Hewitt, *People*, February 28, 2000; "Wilson Signs Tough Anti-Stalking Bill" by Lisa Fernandez, *Los Angeles Times*, August 6, 1997; "New D.A. Unit to Stake Out Stalking Cases" by Jose Cardenas, *Los Angeles Times*, July 23, 1997; "Stalking in L.A." by Jeffrey Toobin, *The New Yorker*, February 24 & March 3, 1997; "Mister Know-It-All" by Steve Daly, *Entertainment Weekly*, August 23, 1996; "When the Law Can't Protect" by Miles Corwin, *Los Angeles Times*, May 8, 1993; "Inside Celebrity Obsessions" by Scott Hays, *Los Angeles Times*, October 17, 1990; "High-Tech Methods—He Stars as Protector of Celebrities" by Beverly Beyette, *Los Angeles Times*, March 10, 1989.

Sources for the description of "The Dynamics of Stalking" seminar include Howard Libes's observations and promotional materials provided by California K-9 Academy and Picore & Associates.

8 High Times

Sources for this chapter include David Weddle's observations and interviews with Ben Bushman, Mark Rosenblatt, Adam Levyn, Zach Safired, Shelley Sorger, Jenny Platt, Nathan Sengz, Yoav Lurie, Matt Karns, Michael Tang, and former students of Beverly Hills High School; documents provided by Beverly Hills High School; "Beverly Hills Seeks to Keep School Diversity Program" by Bob Pool, *Los Angeles Times*, April 26, 2000; "Beverly Hills High May Scrap Diversity Effort" by Bob Pool, *Los Angeles Times*, April 22, 2000; "Fast Times at Beverly High" by Deanna Kizis, *Harper's Bazaar*, April 1999.

9 The Maginot Line

Sources include Howard Libes's and David Weddle's observations and interviews with Cheryl, Ralph, and Moacir Jones; Howard Libes's interviews with Robert Tanenbaum, Louis "Skip" Miller, Billie Green, the Reverend Carol Anderson, Diop Kamau, Lieutenant Edward Kreins, Mark Scott, Rabbi Laura Geller, Karen Hudson; *The Will and the Way: Paul Williams, Architect* by Karen E. Hudson; *Paul Williams, Architect: A Legacy of Style* by Karen E.

Hudson; "Justice, Beverly Hills Style" by P. R. McDonald, *Los Angeles New Times,* May 31–June 6, 2001; "Sheriff to Study Racial Data on People Deputies Stop" by Beth Shuster, *Los Angeles Times,* January 1, 2001; "Beverly Hills Law & Order" by Fred Dickey, *Los Angeles Times Magazine,* December 17, 2000; "Civil Rights Case Reaches Settlement" by Michelle Omura, *Beverly Hills Weekly,* October 19–25, 2000; "Beverly Hills Off the Hook in Racial Profile Suit" by Gina Piccalo, *Los Angeles Times,* October 12, 2000; "City Settles Five-Year Discrimination Suit" by Norma Zager, *Beverly Hills Courier,* October 6, 2000; "Controversial Racial Profiling Bill Ok'd" by Miguel Bustillo, *Los Angeles Times,* August 8, 2000; "Racial Profiling: Are We All Equal in the Eyes of the Law?" by Debra Dickerson, *Los Angeles Times,* July 16, 2000; "Davis Backs Bill Banning Profiling" by Miguel Bustillo, *Los Angeles Times,* April 28, 2000; "City's Lawyer in Civil Rights Case Punished by the State Bar" by Josh Gross, *Beverly Hills Weekly,* April 20–26, 2000; "Lawsuit Against City and Police Dept Dismissed" by Norma Weitz Zager, *Beverly Hills Courier,* February 4, 2000; "Senator's Claim of Race-Based Traffic Stop Is Rejected," *Los Angeles Times,* October 6, 1999; "A Legacy Restored" by Bettijane Levine, *Los Angeles Times,* August 8, 1999; "Black Legislator Sues Police Over 'Targeting Stops' " *Los Angeles Times,* October 11, 1998; "Murray's Victory Marred by Traffic Stop" by Dan Morain, *Los Angeles Times,* June 4, 1998; "Court Rejects Blacks' Harassment Suit Against Beverly Hills" by Eric Malnic, *Los Angeles Times,* October 16, 1997; "Black & White in 90210" by Gail Schiller, *People,* January 15, 1996; "Charges of Racism Tear at Beverly Hills Image" by Duke Helfand and Susan Steinberg, *Los Angeles Times,* December 27, 1995; "City's Lawyer Answers Charges in Lawsuit Filed by Former Mayor" by Scott Huver, *Beverly Hills Courier,* December 1, 1995; "Beverly Hills Cop IV—The Lawsuit" by Tom Plate, *Los Angeles Times,* November 21, 1995; "Stops Prompt Suit" by Sally Ann Stewart, *USA Today,* November 21, 1995; "Suit Accuses Beverly Hills of Racism" by Duke Helfand and Susan Steinberg, *Los Angeles Times,* November 22, 1995; "Former Mayor Files Racial Suit Against City" by Scott Huver, *Beverly Hills Courier,* 1995; "O Tanenbaum, O Tanenbaum, The Holiday Season Is a Sad Time" by Rudy Cole, *Beverly Hills Courier,* 1995; "City's Lawyer Calls for Dismissal of Charges Against Individual Defendants" by Scott Huver, *Beverly Hills Courier,* 1995; "A Tenacious Bulldog Who Hates to Lose" by Krysten Crawford, *California Law Business,* August 8, 1994; "Traffic Stop Focus of Probe by Police" by Catheryn Franklin, G. Jeanette Avent, *Los Angeles Times,* April 17, 1994; "Few Local Police Chiefs See Need for Reform" by James Rainey, *Los Angeles Times,* August 1, 1991; "Changing of the Guard" by Mathis Chazanov, *Los Angeles Times,* April 27, 1989; "Councilman Accused of 'Grab for Power' " by John L. Mitchell, *Los Angeles Times,* November 8, 1987; "Beverly Hills OKs Civic Center Plans" by Mathis Chazanov, *Los Angeles Times,* November 6, 1986; "Reagan's Racial Covenant" by Richard Ryan and Elsa Dixler, *The Nation,* October 13, 1984.

10 DEATH OF A SALESMAN

The opening passage was written by Arthur Miller for an audio production of *Death of a Salesman* by the Theatre Recording Society, directed by Ulu Grosbard in 1965.

Sources for the passage on the open house held at Grayhall include David Weddle's and Howard Libes's observations and interviews with Jerry Jolton, and promotional materials provided by Jolton.

Sources for the passage on Mark Hughes's final days include David Weddle's and Howard Libes's interviews with Jerry Jolton, Marc Wanamaker, and William Hablinski; Howard Libes's interview with Richard Marconi; "Under Investor Pressure, Herbalife's CEO Resigns" by Melinda Fulmer, *Los Angeles Times,* October 19, 2001; "Herbalife After Death" by Ann O'Neill, *Los Angeles Times,* May 30, 2001; "Shades of Grayhall" by Scott Huver, *Beverly Hills Weekly,* February 22–27, 2001; "Death and Denial at Herbalife" by Matthew Heller, *Los Angeles Times Magazine,* February 18, 2001; "Adieu to L.A.'s Gazillionaire-Widow Tax Base" by Gina Piccalo, *Los Angeles Times,* February 13, 2001; "Widow of Herbalife Founder Awarded $20 Million," *Los Angeles Times,* January 19, 2001; "Death Be Not a Punch Line" by David Rakoff, *New York Times Magazine,* January 7, 2001; "Herbalife Exec's Death Prompts Bizarre Fallout" by Jerry Hirsch, *Los Angeles Times,* December 20, 2000; "Neighbors Defeat Plans for Mansion Atop Peak" by Gina Piccalo, *Los Angeles Times,* November 30, 2000; "Herbalife Founder Was on 4-Day Binge, Coroner Says" by Bob Pool, *Los Angeles Times,* August 12, 2000; "The Big, the Bad, the Lovely" by Ruth Ryon, *Los Angeles Times,* August 13, 2000; "Hot Property" by Ruth Ryon, *Los Angeles Times,* August 6, 2000; "A View to Die For" by Ann Marsh, *Forbes,* July 24, 2000; "Hot Property: Yes, He Showed Them the Money" by Ruth Ryon, *Los Angeles Times,* June 11, 2000; "Autopsy Showed Them the Money" by Ruth Ryon, *Los Angeles Times,* June 11, 2000; "Autopsy on Herbalife's Hughes Finds No Trauma," *Los Angeles Times,* May 24, 2000; "Herbalife COO Is Named Firm's Acting President" by Jerry Hirsch, *Los Angeles Times,* May 23, 2000; "Mark Hughes, Founder of Herbalife, Dies at 44" by Douglas P. Shuit, *Los Angeles Times,* May 22, 2000; "Lack of Cash Forces Herbalife Exec to Scrap Plan to Go Private" by James F. Peltz-times, *Los Angeles Times,* April 11, 2000; "Darcy LaPier," *Hello! Magazine,* 2000.

Sources for the section that describes Mark Hughes's childhood and early years as a salesman include Howard Libes's interview with Richard Marconi; "Death and Denial at Herbalife" by Matthew Heller, *Los Angeles Times Magazine,* February 18, 2001; "But Where Are the Distributors' Yachts?" by Seth Lubove, *Forbes,* October 1997; "Hot Property: Mogul Moves Mountaintop" by Ruth Ryon, *Los Angeles Times,* June 1, 1997; "Betcherlife Herbalife" by Dana Wechsler Linden and William Stern, *Forbes,* March 15, 1993; "Unbridled Growth" by Curtis Hartman, *Inc.,* December 1985; "Self-healing" by E. Paris, *Forbes,* November 17, 1985; "Herbalife Settles Suit Filed on Medical Claims" by Jube Shiver, *Los Angeles Times,* October 16, 1985; "Herbalife Lays Off 573, Blames Slowing Sales" by Kathleen Day, *Los Angeles Times,* May 29, 1985; "Testifies at Stormy Senate Hearing, Herbalife President Calls Diet Powders, Pills Safe" by Robert L. Jackson, *Los Angeles Times,* May 16, 1985; "Herbalife Diet Plans Questioned" by Robert L. Jackson, *Los Angeles Times,* May 15, 1985; "Report Criticizes Weight-Loss Products" by Robert L. Jackson, *Los Angeles Times,* May 14, 1985; "Selling Health and Money" by Ian Austen, *MacLean's,* May 13, 1985; "Selling Herbalife's Way" by John Carey with Pamela Abramson and William J. Cook, *Newsweek,* April 8, 1985; "Herbalife Suit Against FDA Is Withdrawn" by Heidi Evans, *Los Angeles Times,* April 5, 1985; "The Questions of Herbalife" by Pauline Yoshihashi, *New York Times,* April 5, 1985; "Safety, Methods Questioned, Herbalife: Weighty Profits and Government Probes" by Heidi Evans, *Los Angeles Times,* April 4, 1985; "Herbalife . . . False Claims for Its Products" by Roy J. Harris Jr., *Wall Street Journal,* March 8, 1985; "Agencies Sue Herbalife, Alleging False Claims" by Heidi Evans, *Los Angeles Times,* March 7, 1985; "Herbalife, Anyone?" by Ellen Paris, *Forbes,* February 25, 1985; "Herbalife Claims FDA Statements Defamed It" by Louis Sahagun, *Los Angeles Times,* December 4, 1984; "A Face in the Sun" *Money,* June 1983.

Sources for the passage about snake oil salesmen and the development of sales as a quasi religion in America include *Step Right Up: An Illustrated History of the American Medicine Show* by Brooks McNamara; *Medicine Show: Conning People and Making Them Like It* by Mary Calhoun; *The Great American Medicine Show* by David Armstrong and Elizabeth Metzger Armstrong; "Top U.S. Direct-Sales Companies Are Quasi-Religion, Study Finds" by Russell Chandler, *Los Angeles Times,* November 22, 1986.

Sources for the section that describes Mark Hughes's rise to wealth as the head of Herbalife and his decline and death include Howard Libes's interviews with Richard Marconi and Sandy Margolis; David Weddle's interviews with Marc Wanamaker, William Hablinski, Jerry Jolton, Michelle Peter, and a member of the catering staff at Hughes's memorial; "Under Investor Pressure, Herbalife's CEO Resigns" by Melinda Fulmer, *Los Angeles Times,* October 19, 2001; "Herbalife After Death" by Ann O'Neill, *Los Angeles Times,* May 30, 2001; "Death and Denial at Herbalife" by Matthew Heller, *Los Angeles Times Magazine,* February 18, 2001; "Adieu to L.A.'s Gazillionaire-Widow Tax Base" by Gina Piccalo, *Los Angeles Times,* February 13, 2001; "Widow of Herbalife Founder Awarded $20 Million," *Los Angeles Times,* January 19, 2001; "Death Be Not a Punch Line" by David Rakoff, *New York Times Magazine,* January 7, 2001; "Herbalife Exec's Death Prompts Bizarre Fallout" by Jerry Hirsch, *Los Angeles Times,* December 20, 2000; "Neighbors Defeat Plans for Mansion Atop Peak" by Gina Piccalo, *Los Angeles Times,* November 30, 2000; "Herbalife Founder Was on 4-Day Binge, Coroner Says" by Bob Pool, *Los Angeles Times,* August 12, 2000; "The Big, the Bad, the Lovely" by Ruth Ryon, *Los Angeles Times,* August 13, 2000; "Hot Property" by Ruth Ryon, *Los Angeles Times,* August 6, 2000; "A View to Die For" by Ann Marsh, *Forbes,* July 24, 2000; "Hot Property: Yes, He Showed Them the Money" by Ruth Ryon, *Los Angeles Times,* June 11, 2000; "Autopsy on Herbalife's Hughes Finds No Trauma," *Los Angeles Times,* May 24, 2000; "Herbalife COO Is Named Firm's Acting President" by Jerry Hirsch, *Los Angeles Times,* May 23, 2000; "Mark Hughes, Founder of Herbalife, Dies at 44" by Douglas P. Shuit, *Los Angeles Times,* May 22, 2000; "Lack of Cash Forces Herbalife Exec to Scrap Plan to Go Private" by James F. Peltztimes, *Los Angeles Times,* April 11, 2000; "Darcy LaPier," *Hello! Magazine,* 2000; "Herbalife Chief Ups Bid to Settle," *Los Angeles Times,* January 11, 2000; "Privatization Bid by Founder of Herbalife Draws Fire" by Jeff Leeds, *Los Angeles Times,* September 16, 1999; "Neighbors Aghast at Diet Guru's Mansion Plan" by Monte Morin, *Los Angeles Times,* July 18, 1999; "Van Damme's Wife Alleges Drug Abuse," *USA Today,* December 2, 1997; "But Where Are the Distributors' Yachts?" by Seth Lubove, *Forbes,* October 1997; "Hot Property: Mogul Moves Mountaintop" by Ruth Ryon, *Los Angeles Times,* June 1, 1997; "Betcherlife Herbalife" by Dana Wechsler Linden and William Stern, *Forbes,* March 15, 1993; "Romancing Van Damme," *USA Today,* January 18, 1993; "California's Highest-Paid Executives" by Kathy M. Kristof, *Los Angeles Times,* May 28, 1991; "Executive Pay & Perks" by Kathy M. Kristof, *Los Angeles Times,* May 26, 1991; "Hot Property" by Ruth Ryon, *Los Angeles Times,* July 16, 1989; "Where Are They Now?" *Inc.,* December 1987; "Hot

Property: Herbalife's Hughes to Build Mansion" by Ruth Ryon, *Los Angeles Times,* May 24, 1987; "Herbalife Goes Public, Plans $14 Million Stock Offering," *Los Angeles Times,* December 4, 1986; "Top U.S. Direct-Sales Companies Are Quasi-Religion, Study Finds" by Russell Chandler, *Los Angeles Times,* November 22, 1986; "Herbalife Says All Queries into Tactics Now Resolved" by Jube Shiver, *Los Angeles Times,* October 17, 1986; "Unbridled Growth" by Curtis Hartman, *Inc.*, December 1985; "Self-healing" by E. Paris, *Forbes,* November 17, 1985; "Herbalife Settles Suit Filed on Medical Claims" by Jube Shiver, *Los Angeles Times,* October 16, 1985; "Herbalife Lays Off 573, Blames Slowing Sales" by Kathleen Day, *Los Angeles Times,* May 29, 1985; "Testifies at Stormy Senate Hearing, Herbalife President Calls Diet Powders, Pills Safe" by Robert L. Jackson, *Los Angeles Times,* May 16, 1985; "Herbalife Diet Plans Questioned" by Robert L. Jackson, *Los Angeles Times,* May 15, 1985; "Report Criticizes Weight-Loss Products" by Robert L. Jackson, *Los Angeles Times,* May 14, 1985; "Selling Health and Money" by Ian Austen, *MacLean's,* May 13, 1985; "Selling Herbalife's Way" by John Carey with Pamela Abramson and William J. Cook, *Newsweek,* April 8, 1985; "Herbalife Suit Against FDA Is Withdrawn" by Heidi Evans, *Los Angeles Times,* April 5, 1985; "The Questions of Herbalife" by Pauline Yoshihashi, *New York Times,* April 5, 1985; "Safety, Methods Questioned, Herbalife: Weighty Profits and Government Probes" by Heidi Evans, *Los Angeles Times,* April 4, 1985; "Herbalife . . . False Claims for Its Products" by Roy J. Harris Jr., *Wall Street Journal,* March 8, 1985; "Agencies Sue Herbalife, Alleging False Claims" by Heidi Evans, *Los Angeles Times,* March 7, 1985; "Herbalife, Anyone?" by Ellen Paris, *Forbes,* February 25, 1985; "Herbalife Claims FDA Statements Defamed It" by Louis Sahagun, *Los Angeles Times,* December 4, 1984; "A Face in the Sun," *Money,* June 1983.

Sources for the tour of the Grayhall guesthouse include David Weddle's and Howard Libes's observations and interviews with Jerry Jolton.

11 THE LAST MOUNTAINTOP

The sources for the description of Jerry Jolton and Rodrigo Iglesias's journey to the last undeveloped mountaintop in Beverly Hills were David Weddle's and Howard Libes's observations and interviews with Jerry Jolton and Rodrigo Iglesias. The source for the flashback to the camping expeditions by Douglas Fairbanks and Charlie Chaplin was *My Autobiography* by Charles Chaplin.

★ ACKNOWLEDGMENTS ★

Howard Libes was my collaborator, in the fullest sense of the word. This book would not have been possible without his tireless efforts. Howard conducted many of the interviews and transcribed most of them. He spent hundreds of hours in the library digging up newspaper clippings, documents, and books, and hundreds more on the telephone scheduling interviews. He also helped lay out the book's structure, wrote rough drafts of several chapters, and had an incalculable influence on my thoughts as I sat down to write the final manuscript. Howard also contributed to the editorial process by carefully reading my material, offering encouragement and, more importantly, criticism. He suggested many of the cuts that brought the text down to a publishable length, encouraged my best impulses, and defended me from my worst. This is as much Howard's book as it is mine.

I also received assistance from hundreds of people who generously donated their time, enthusiasm, and expertise to this project. Unfortunately, space permits me to express my gratitude to only a few key individuals. First, I would like to thank my agent, Kristine Dahl, who contributed key insights and suggestions from this project's inception to its completion. She intuitively grasped the style, form, and substance of this book from our earliest conversations and passionately committed herself to getting it published. Kris is, quite simply, the best agent a writer could hope to have. Her assistants, Jud

Laghi and Sean Desmond, also provided important assistance on numerous occasions.

I also owe a great debt to my editor, Henry Ferris, who believed in this project, provided important insights, guidance, and exercised extraordinary patience while waiting for the completed manuscript to finally arrive on his desk. When it did, Henry empowered me to be ruthless with my own material, helped to shape and refine the text and make this a much better book. Copy editor Shelly Perron made a significant contribution with her sharp eye for detail. Shelly corrected misspellings and made hundreds of suggestions that strengthened, tightened, and sharpened the clarity of the text. And my good friend Jesse Graham, as always, offered constructive criticism and helped me make a number of important improvements to the prose.

I would also like to thank: Marc Wanamaker, archivist for the Beverly Hills Historical Society, for his truly breathtaking knowledge of the city's history, which he lent to me on a number of occasions; Robert Anderson, for providing key insights and archival material on the city's formative years; John Bercsi, for his unceasing generosity and honesty, and for providing the inspiration from which this book sprang; Bruce Nelson, for his time and for digging deep into his memories of Beverly Hills's golden era; Leonard Maltin, for obtaining a rare videotape of Beverly Hills's fiftieth anniversary; Joe Hecht and Dick Van Patten, for their help and support; Michael Moldofsky and Amy Archibald, for their adventurous spirit and unconventional insights; Cheryl, Ralph, and Moacir Jones, for courageously unearthing painful memories; Richard Marconi, for his remarkable candor; Richardson Robertson III, for all his time, patience, and expertise; Dennis Kightley, who was there at the beginning and contributed important photographs; Bradley Thompson, who also donated his photographic expertise.

I would also like to thank the staff of the Beverly Hills Planning Department, the city clerk's office, and numerous other city employees who never failed to go the extra mile to produce hard-to-locate facts and documentation, and who always did so with boundless enthusiasm. The same can be said for the staffs of the Beverly Hills Public Library, the Los Angeles Public Library, the Payson Library at Pepperdine University, the Malibu Public Library, and the Margaret Herrick Library at the Academy of Motion Picture Arts and Sciences in Los Angeles. And a special thanks to Val Almendarez at the latter institution, who never fails to guide me in the right direction and put forth a special effort when I call upon him for assistance.

★ INDEX ★